Praise for *Clearance and Copyright*

"Your film can win many festival prizes, but you still have to obtain the proper clearances or your film is undistributable, and sometimes even unshowable at some festivals. Too often the independent filmmaker does not realize how important the issues of clearance, copyright, insurance, and licensing are in the arena of selling your film. This book guides you through all of these areas."
—Geoffrey Gilmore, Director of Film Festival, Sundance Institute

"Donaldson provides an indispensable guided tour of an area of law- filled with landmines- that filmmakers cannot afford to ignore. A wealth of information is presented in a clear, accessible, and even friendly manner. Read it once for background, then keep it for reference."
—Marcie Bloom, Co-President and Co-Founder, Sony Pictures Classic

"We could not have made *This Film Is Not Yet Rated* without Michael Donaldson's shrewd guidance through the minefields of fair use (134 film clips from major motion pictures), right of privacy, when location releases are and are not needed, and much more. *Clearance and Copyright* contains the legal information a documentary filmmaker needs in one indispensable book."
—Kirby Dick, Director, *This Film Is Not Yet Rated*

"Everything you need to know about clearance and copyright is in Michael Donaldson's book, a must for everyone in the film business."
—Barbara Boyle, Chair, UCLA Department of
Film, Television, and Digital Media

"'Let's make a movie.' It's never that simple. Michael Donaldson has written an invaluable book on the A to Z of pitfalls that all independent filmmakers should be aware of before they start to shoot one frame of film. Essential reading."
—Piers Handling, Director and CEO, Toronto
International Film Festival Group

"Anything that can make an independent filmmaker's life easier is much appreciated by this community, and Michael Donaldson's book does just that. He makes complex issues understandable and even interesting."
—Dawn Hudson, Executive Director, Film Independent

CLEARANCE & COPYRIGHT

CLEARANCE & COPYRIGHT

Everything You Need to Know for Film and Television

3rd Edition ■ Revised, Updated & Expanded

BY MICHAEL C. DONALDSON

SILMAN-JAMES PRESS ■ LOS ANGELES

Third Edition
10 9 8 7 6 5 4 3 2 1

Library of Congress Cataloging-in-Publication Data

Donaldson, Michael C.
Clearance and copyright : eveything you need to know for
film and television / by Michael Donaldson. -- 3rd ed., rev.,
updated, and expanded.
  p. cm.
Includes index.
ISBN 978-1-879505-98-8 (alk. paper)
  1. Copyright--Motion pictures--United States--Popular works.
  2. Copyright--United States--Popular works. 3. Copyright
clearinghouses--United States--Popular works. I. Title.
KF3070.D66 2008
346.7304'82--dc22
2008029936

This book is sold with the understanding that neither the author
nor the publisher is rendering legal advice with regard to any
specific situation or problem. This book is for your general education on the subject of clearance and copyright. If you need legal
advice, seek the services of an attorney. The publisher and the
author cannot in any way guarantee that the forms in this book
are being used for the purposes intended, and, therefore, assume
no responsibility for their proper and correct use.

Cover design by Heidi Frieder

Printed and bound in the United States of America

Silman-James Press
1181 Angelo Drive
Beverly Hills, CA 90210

To inquiring clients to whom I have said,
"Buy a book". . . and there was none.

CONTENTS

INTRODUCTION   *xvii*

ACKNOWLEDGMENTS   *xix*

PART I
A STROLL THROUGH COPYRIGHT LAW   *1*

1. **COPYRIGHT AND IDEAS: THE BIG PICTURE**   *1*
   A LITTLE BACKGROUND   *1*
   COPYRIGHT COVERAGE TODAY   *6*
   WHEN DOES A WORK QUALIFY FOR COPRIGHT PROTECTION?   *7*
   WHAT ACTIVITIES ARE COVERED BY COPYRIGHT LAW?   *7*
   HOW LONG DOES PROTECTION LAST?   *9*
   WHO OWNS THE COPYRIGHT?   *10*
   WHAT ABOUT IDEAS   *11*
      The Good News   *12*
      Submission Agreements   *17*
      Non-Disclosure Agreements   *18*
   PROTECT YOURSELF   *19*
      Writers Guild Registration   *20*
      Self-Mailing   *21*
      The Ultimate Idea Protection: Hide Your Candle Under a Bush   *21*
   1.01 Non-Disclosure/Non-Circumvention Agreement   *23*

2. **FAIR USE**   *25*
   SOME BACKGROUND   *25*
      Fair Use—A shield, not a sword   *27*
   FAIR USE AND FILM CLIPS   *29*
      One Plaintiff, Three Cases, Same Results—The AIP Cases   *30*
      One Plaintiff, Two Cases, Testing Fair Use for News—
         The Bob Tur Cases   *32*
      Get to the Heart of It   *33*
      Enter Transformation   *34*
   THE GRATEFUL DEAD CAN STILL BREAK NEW GROUND   *35*
   DOCUMENTARY FILMMAKERS TO THE RESCUE   *36*

DONALDSON'S SAFE HARBOR FOR FAIR USE   *41*

TO ASK OR NOT TO ASK? THAT IS THE QUESTION   *42*

TO PAY OR NOT TO PAY ACTORS, DIRECTOR, AND WRITER? THAT IS THE BIGGER QUESTION   *43*

AND WHAT ABOUT CREDIT???   *44*

FAIR USE IN THE FILM DOES NOT NECESSARILY MEAN FAIR USE IN ADVERTISING   *45*

ADVERTISING THAT SELLS YOUR FILM CAN KILL YOUR FILM   *49*

DOES FAIR USE AVOID THE NEED TO CLEAR MUSIC?   *50*

2.01 Template Clearance Log   *55*

3. **PARODY, SATIRE, AND JOKES**   *56*

DEFINITION OF PARODY   *56*

A TRUE PARODY DOES NOT HAVE TO BE CLEARED   *58*

   Humorous Book but Not a Parody   *60*

   Ridicule Is Not Always a Parody   *61*

   Serious Book Was a Parody   *62*

   Parody and Personal Rights   *63*

TRADEMARK PARODY   *65*

WHAT PARODY IS NOT   *66*

PARODY IN A FILM SCORE   *67*

SATIRE   *67*

THE CASE OF THE JOKE   *71*

   Foxworthy's Redneck Humor—A Case of Its Own   *72*

4. **PUBLIC DOMAIN**   *74*

WHAT IS PUBLIC DOMAIN   *74*

FACTS AND EVENTS   *77*

   The Amy Fisher Story   *78*

   Sensational Criminal Stories   *79*

   Facts—An Exception   *82*

OLD PROPERTIES   *82*

TECHNICAL FLAWS   *84*

GOVERNMENT PROPERTIES   *86*

CREATIVE COMMONS   *86*

ORPHAN WORKS   *89*

RECAPTURE   *91*

BEWARE OF SHORTCUTS   *93*

4.01 Annotation Guide for Scripts Based on Facts   *94*

5. **CHARACTERS AND COSTUMES**   *95*

TWO TYPES OF CHARACTERS   *95*

VISUAL CHARACTERS   *96*

   A Nightmare of a Case   *97*

   Rocky Prevails   *98*

   Now You See It, Now You Don't   *99*

STORY CHARACTERS   *101*
    James Bond Always Wins   *101*
    Character Doesn't Have to be Visually Depicted to Get
        Copyright   *102*
    Tips for Dealing With Story Characters   *103*
TWO WAYS OF LOOKING AT THINGS   *105*
COSTUMES   *106*

PART II

GETTING A COMPLETED SCRIPT   *109*

6. **ACQUIRING THE RIGHTS TO SOMEONE ELSE'S
    PROPERTY**   *111*

    WHAT RIGHTS TO ACQUIRE   *111*
    CHARACTER(S)   *116*
    WHOM TO CONTACT   *116*
        Fictional Books and Stories   *117*
        Comic Books   *120*
        Non-Fiction Books, Magazine Articles, and Newspaper
            Stories   *120*
        Songs   *121*
        Plays   *122*
        Old Movies   *124*
        6.01 Option and Purchase Agreement (for Underlying Rights)   *126*

7. **HIRING A SCRIPTWRITER—WORK FOR HIRE**   *135*

    CHOOSING A WRITER   *135*
    WHAT IS WORK FOR HIRE?   *136*
    INDEPENDENT CONTRACTOR   *139*
    WRITERS GUILD OF AMERICA (WGA)   *140*
    THE WORK-FOR-HIRE AGREEMENT   *141*
    7.01 Writer Agreement – Work for Hire   *143*
        Exhibit A—Credit Determination   *151*
        Exhibit B—Certificate of Authorship   *154*

8. **WRITING WITH A PARTNER**   *155*

    A SPECIAL KIND OF PARTNERSHIP   *155*
    JOINT WORK   *158*
    SILENCE IS GOLDEN   *161*
    HIRING COLLABORATORS   *162*
    8.01 Collaboration Agreement   *164*

9. **BUYING SOMEONE ELSE'S COMPLETED SCRIPT**   *168*

    SPEC SCRIPTS   *168*
    PROTECTING YOURSELF AGAINST UNSOLICITED SCRIPTS   *171*

9.01 *Option and Purchase Agreement*   *173*
9.02 *Submission Agreement*   *180*

10. **PROVISIONS COMMON TO MOST AGREEMENTS**   *182*

CONTRACTS AND NEGOTIATION   *182*
Offers and Counteroffers   *183*
Written vs. Oral   *184*
The Structure of a Contract   *184*
International   *186*
BOILERPLATE   *186*
10.01 *Boilerplate Provisions*   *188*

11. **REGISTERING COPYRIGHT OF THE SCRIPT**   *194*

WHEN TO REGISTER   *194*
LEGAL BENEFITS FROM REGISTERING YOUR SCRIPT   *195*
IN WHOSE NAME DO YOU REGISTER THE SCRIPT?   *198*
INSTRUCTIONS TO FILL OUT COPYRIGHT FORMS   *199*
Overview   *199*
Step-by-Step Guide   *201*
Fees   *208*
The Deposit Requirement   *208*
Registering the Book, Article, or Story That Your Film Is
Based On   *208*
SO WHAT IF I MAKE A MISTAKE?   *209*
11.01 *Form PA for a Script*   *210*
11.02 *Form RE/CON—Continuation Sheet*   *212*
11.03 *Script Registration Cover Letter*   *213*
11.04 *Script Registration Postcard*   *214*
11.05 *Form TX*   *215*
11.06 *Form CA*   *217*

PART III
PRINCIPAL PHOTOGRAPHY   *219*

12. **OTHERS WHO MAY HAVE RIGHTS IN YOUR FILM**   *221*

WRITERS   *221*
THE DIRECTOR   *222*
ACTORS   *224*
COMPOSER   *224*
CREW   *224*
NAME AND LIKENESS   *226*
INVESTORS   *227*
BANKERS   *229*

13. **ALL THOSE PESKY PEOPLE WHO SHOW UP IN**
YOUR FILM   *231*

RIGHTS OF PEOPLE   *231*

Right of Privacy   *232*

When Do You Need a Release for People in
    Public Places?   *235*

Right of Publicity   *239*

SOUNDALIKES AND LOOKALIKES   *243*

DEFAMATION: LIBEL AND SLANDER   *244*

False Light   *245*

Defenses to Defamation and False Light   *246*

THE ON-CAMERA VERBAL RELEASE   *247*

THE WRITTEN RELEASE   *248*

13.01 Life-Story Rights Agreement   250

13.02 Individual Release   257

14. TRADEMARKS, LOGOS, AND BUSINESS SIGNAGE   *258*

THE BIG PICTURE   *258*

BUT CAN I USE SOMEONE ELSE'S TRADEMARK IN MY FILM?   *259*

IS IT THE PRODUCT OR THE USER?   *261*

PRODUCT PLACEMENT   *264*

SO WHY DO I HAVE TO CLEAR ALL THOSE LABELS AND LOGOS
    AND TRADEMARKS?   *266*

15. SETS AND SET DRESSING   *268*

CLEARANCE   *268*

Who to Call When You Need Help   *269*

SETS   *271*

Shooting on a Stage   *271*

Shooting on Location—Exteriors   *272*

Buildings and Their Architectural Appointments   *272*

Signs and Logos   *273*

Shooting on Location—Interiors   *274*

LOCATION AGREEMENTS   *274*

SET DRESSING   *276*

A QUILT, A MOBILE, A POSTER, A PAINTING   *277*

State Law protection—Moral Rights for Artists   *282*

MAGAZINES, NEWSPAPERS, BOOKS, AND OTHER WORKS THAT ARE
    NOT DECORATIVE   *283*

PROPS   *283*

WHO TO TALK TO   *284*

KNOCK-OFFS   *285*

SCRIPT CLEARANCE   *286*

15.01 Excerpts From A Script Clearance Report   290

15.02 Location Agreement   292

16. CLEARING ALL MUSIC IN YOUR FILM   *294*

CLEARING PRE-EXISTING MUSIC   *294*

Public Performance Rights   *300*

Reproduction Rights   *300*

Out-of-Context Rights   *301*

Adaptation Rights   *302*

Other Deal Points   *302*

CLEARING THE USE OF A SPECIFIC RECORDING   *304*

MUSIC CLEARANCE HELP   *307*

THE MUSIC SUPERVISOR   *309*

16.01 *Synchronization and Performance Rights Agreement*   *310*

16.02 *Motion Picture Master-Use License*   *314*

17. HIRING A COMPOSER TO WRITE ORIGINAL MUSIC   *317*

WHEN TO START   *317*

A WORTHWILE SEARCH   *318*

NEGOTIATING THE DEAL   *319*

THE PACKAGE DEAL   *321*

17.01 *Composer Agreement*   *323*

17.02 *Music Package Agreement*   *325*

18. CLEARING FILM CLIPS   *327*

CLEARING CLIPS WITHOUT ACTORS OR MUSIC—STOCK
FOOTAGE   *327*

WRITERS AND DIRECTORS   *332*

CLIPS WITH ACTORS   *333*

WHEN THERE IS NO UNION AGREEMENT   *333*

CLIPS WITH MUSIC   *335*

How to Find the Copyright Owner of a Film   *336*

18.01 *Film Clip Release*   *340*

18.02 *Actor's Release for Film Clip Use*   *342*

PART IV

POST PRODUCTION   *343*

19. TITLE CLEARANCE   *345*

HOW TITLES ARE PROTECTED   *345*

Amityville: One Small Town, Six Horror Movies, Three
Production Companies   *347*

Why Copyright Doesn't Help Here   *349*

TITLE PROTECTION   *351*

MPAA TITLE REGISTRATION   *352*

TITLE REPORT   *354*

NAMING PEOPLE AND PRODUCTS IN YOUR TITLE   *355*

19.01 *Opinion Letter*   *359*

19.02 *Title Report*   *360*

20. E&O INSURANCE   *363*

WHEN TO BUY E&O INSURANCE   *363*

WHERE TO BUY E&O INSURANCE   *364*
INSURANCE AND FAIR USE   *365*
HOW TO BUY E&O INSURANCE   *367*
TIPS ON FILLING OUT YOUR E&O APPLICATION   *369*
CONSEQUENCES OF A FAILURE TO DISCLOSE   *371*
WHEN FULL DISCLOSURE REVEALS A POTENTIAL CLAIM   *373*
20.01 E&O Insurance Application   *377*

21. **CHAIN OF TITLE**   *386*

WHAT IS CHAIN OF TITLE?   *386*
RECORDING CHAIN OF TITLE DOCUMENTS   *392*
DOCUMENT COVER SHEET   *393*
21.01 Document Cover Sheet   *396*
21.02 Cover Letter to Record Agreements   *397*
21.03 Return Postcard for Recording Documents   *398*

22. **REGISTERING COPYRIGHT FOR YOUR COMPLETED FILM**   *399*

WHEN TO REGISTER COPYRIGHT IN YOUR FILM   *399*
IN WHOSE NAME DO YOU REGISTER THE FILM?   *400*
FORM OF NOTICE FOR MOTION PICTURES   *400*
APPLYING FOR REGISTRATION OF YOUR COMPLETED FILM   *401*
FILLING OUT FORM PA FOR YOUR COMPLETED FILM   *402*
DEPOSITING ONE COMPLETED COPY OF YOUR FILM WITH THE
    COPYRIGHT OFFICE   *405*
    Exceptions to the Normal Deposit Requirement for Film   *406*
    Mailing   *407*
SPEEDING THINGS UP AT THE COPYRIGHT OFFICE   *408*
22.01 Sample Cover Letter for Motion Picture Registration   *410*
22.02 Return Postcard for Motion Picture Registration   *411*

23. **COPYRIGHT INFRINGEMENT**   *412*

WHAT IS INFRINGEMENT?   *412*
WHAT IF THE COPYRIGHT TO YOUR FILM IS INFRINGED?   *419*

24. **COPYRIGHT ON THE INTERNET**   *421*

THE INTERNET: THE STRONG, NEW FORCE IN THE
    ENTERTAINMENT INDUSTRY   *421*
THE INTERNET IS FREE, NOT THE STUFF THAT IS ON IT   *423*
    Napster, eBay, TiVo, YouTube, and Others That Provide Cool Things
        Through The Internet   *425*
WHEN YOUR FILM SLIPS INTO INTERNET LAND   *426*
INTERNET RESOURCES FOR THE FILMMAKER   *428*
    Research on Your Film's Subject and Potential Cast and Cre   *428*
    Licensing Artwork and Film Clips   *429*
    Interfacing with the Copyright Office   *429*

Advertising and Marketing Your Film Project   *430*
BE CAREFUL ABOUT GRANTING INTERNET DISTRIBUTION RIGHTS   *431*
USING THE INTERNET TO SELL YOUR DVDS   *432*
USING THE INTERNET TO SELL DOWNLOADS OF YOUR FILM   *434*
THE NEW COPYRIGHT LAWS RESPONSIVE TO THE INTERNET   *435*
FUTURE TRENDS IN COPYRIGHT LAW FOR THE INTERNET   *438*
24.01 Copyright Infringement Notification   *441*

25. INTERNATIONAL COPYRIGHT   *443*

THE BIG PICTURE   *443*
START WITH WHAT YOU KNOW   *445*
VIVE LES DIFFERENCES   *447*
MORAL RIGHTS   *450*
IS FAIR USE "FAIR" AROUND THE WORLD?   *453*
RESOLUTION ON FREEDOM OF EXPRESSION AND INFORMATION IN
    DOCUMENTARIES   *455*

26. LEGAL REFERRAL SERVICES   *457*

Appendix A: GLOSSARY   *465*

Appendix B: TABLE OF FORMS   *476*

Appendix C: TABLE OF CASES   *478*

Appendix D: FILMS AND TELEVISION SHOWS MENTIONED IN
        THIS BOOK   *484*

INDEX   *495*

ABOUT THE AUTHOR   *507*

INTRODUCTION
TO THE THIRD EDITION

This third edition brings the book up to date with the many changes in statutory law, case law, and some administrative procedures that have occurred over the past several years. It is a page-one rewrite that includes an entirely new way of looking at fair use, along with many new stories, new forms, and three entirely new chapters: The first is an expansion of the sections on trademark, the second expands my discussion of characters and costume, and the third new chapter addresses international copyright law.

The book's first edition was written for independent film makers who constantly face copyright and clearance questions as their projects progress. I added many examples and cases from the publishing industry since many publishers face issues that are parallel to the ones filmmakers encounter. I have also found that *Clearance and Copyright* shows up on the desks of people clearing content for large film studios, television networks, cable channels, and the countless lawyers who advise them. It is used in more than 50 film schools in the United States and Europe and a few law schools throughout the nation. Its wide acceptance has brought me personal joy and professional satisfaction.

Clearance and Copyright is organized in the chronological order in which you normally meet various real-world legal issues that come up in the film and publishing industry. It begins with an overview of copyright, fair use, parody, and public domain. The next part covers the problems you face in acquiring material. It takes you through development and pre-production. The third part of this edition covers common problems you will face in production, the registration of the completed work, and the release of your project. The final part includes chapters that discuss copyright infringement, the Internet, and international law.

Nothing is overly esoteric here. This is not a legal treatise. It's a book filled with timesaving forms, quick answers, and reminders that certain areas are the domain of experienced legal counsel. This book does not take the place of an attorney's advice. For specific advice, be sure to seek out a knowledgeable attorney.

Use this book to save thousands of dollars by gaining a working knowledge of the issues you need to discuss before you employ an attorney. The more you know, the more efficient your conversation will be with your lawyer. Lawyers bill by the hour, so a one-on-one, personal seminar on copyright basics, copyright infringement, or filling out a copyright form can be a very expensive proposition. The more knowledgeable and organized you are, the more productive your time is spent with your attorney, and the more your attorney will enjoy working with you.

Good luck!

For free downloads of forms in this book, go to www.clearanceandcopyright.com. Use the code: ibotCC3

ACKNOWLEDGMENTS

This book is dedicated to the legion of users and questioners: students, filmmakers, professionals involved with clearing films and television programs, and members of the publishing industry who helped to mold and shape the present edition's contents.

The third edition could not have happened without the support and hard work of my law office staff. My partner, Lisa A. Callif, who led the team. Our associates, Marja M. Lopees and Gregory Bonzer, whose sharp eyes made a huge difference in the accuracy and completeness of the book. Katheleen A. Ebora, Ryan Gooden, Adrian Ricarte, and interns Jeremy Moehlmann, Brandon Dorsky, and Jessica Priel.

Thank you to the professionals who reviewed individual chapters of the third edition of *Clearance and Copyright*: Peter Jaszi, Russell Hickey, Pat Aufderhide, Anthony Falzone, and David Powell, and E. Burak Can.

Let's not forget the people who helped with the previous editions of *Clearance and Copyright*. Ram Bergman and his then producing partner Dana Lustig provided the original inspiration for the book. Thanks to those who reviewed the first edition: Vince Ravine, Ed Blau, Mitch Block, Eric Feig, Craig Gates, Ron Gertz, Betsy McLane, Lou Petrich, Jerry Philips, Lon Sobel, Larry Sugar, and Tom White. These people gave their valuable time to check the accuracy of the book, plus their experience added great value. The second edition was reviewed in whole or in part by Joseph F. Hart, J. Stephan Sheppard, Dixon Q. Dern, Frank Lunn, Doug Irvine, Bruce Polichar, and David Powell.

My editor, Jim Fox, took on a large role in this edition. Many thanks to him and to his business partner, Gwen Feldman, who had the wisdom and flexibility to make our relationship work so well.

Because my work on this book was extensive, there were moments at home that required enormous understanding and support. Special thanks go to my partner, Tim Kittleson. He read the manuscript from cover to cover for architectural integrity, flow, and common-sense. Last but not least, a big thanks and hugs galore to my three daughters, Michelle, Amy, and Wendy and their husbands (who are like sons to me) Ray and John for being cheerleaders in all my endeavors and to Soul and Caden—two grandsons who provide joyful breaks from writing chores.

PART I

A STROLL THROUGH THE COPYRIGHT LAW

This part of the book is for anyone who has anything to do with the rights in anything which could be protected by copyright and that makes up a pretty long list of things. It discusses what copyright covers and what it doesn't cover and what may have fallen into the public domain. It might open a window on some rights that you didn't even know you had to use copyright-protected material.

CHAPTER 1 — **COPYRIGHT AND IDEAS: THE BIG PICTURE**

CHAPTER 2 — **FAIR USE**

CHAPTER 3 — **PARODY, SATIRE, AND JOKES**

CHAPTER 4 — **PUBLIC DOMAIN**

CHAPTER 5 — **CHARACTERS AND COSTUMES**

CHAPTER 1

COPYRIGHT AND IDEAS:
The Big Picture

Before jumping into the fun stuff like fair use and public domain, it would be nice to know about copyright in general. In fact, you should have a general knowledge of copyright before you license footage, make a deal with a writer, or register your work with the Copyright Office. This chapter introduces you to the wonderfully textured landscape of copyright law. After reading it you will be better prepared to talk to an expert about copyright.

A LITTLE BACKGROUND

Let's start with where the word "copyright" came from. When the word was first coined, it meant the right to copy. Nothing more. The world had worked just fine—for thousands of years—on an oral tradition. Commerce, news, entertainment—everything used by the vast majority of people relied on the spoken word. Sure, there had been scrolls and books and written accounts for thousands of years, but to create them was way beyond the ken of ordinary folk. Reading and writing were special skills—not for the masses.

Then along came Johannes Gutenberg with his movable-type printing press, which made the printing of books and pamphlets fast and efficient and would eventually bring the printed word to the masses.

This new invention made its way to England toward the end of the 15th Century (the age of Leonardo da Vinci, Christopher Columbus, and the Spanish Inquisition). Imagine, soon everybody and anybody could have access to the written word. And what did Kings Henry VII and VIII do? They made two demands:

1. Pay some gold to the crown.

2. Let the King (or one of the King's men) read whatever it was you were going to print in order to gain the King's approval BEFORE you could print your copies (yes, official censorship).

Hmmm. I guess the world has always worked in a certain way. Nobody thought of copying as a right. The first edicts handed down about copying had nothing to do with author's rights. The word was nowhere to be found. The practice of printing and copying was granted by the King solely to the Stationers' Company, a guild of printers, bookbinders, and booksellers that was controlled by the King. It was all about the business of printing and how to control it.

Over the next 150 years, more and more people were writing things down—things like stories and poems and plays. And printing presses were multiplying like rabbits. Stationers were getting rich. Authors were not. Slowly attitudes were changing.

So at the dawn of the 18th century, good Queen Anne issued a law—the Statute of Anne—"An act for the encouragement of learning, by vesting the copies of printed books in the Authors. . . ." That is to say that the authors got to decide who could and who could not copy their work. That meant that the authors could demand some money in trade for the permission to print their stories and poems and plays. This was revolutionary! Let's hear it for Queen Anne. And Viva La France, which was a bit ahead of England in terms of authors' rights.

Meanwhile, the Brits had established some colonies across the ocean, and the British law applied in this cluster of communities clinging to the other shore of the Atlantic. That included this new-fangled idea called "copy-right." Yes, it was hyphenated at first. Copy-right was a right held by authors. And it only covered copying. You could make a play from someone's story without asking permission. But you could not make one copy of the story without their permission.

As many of you will recall, the colonies broke away from England, formed a new nation, and wrote a new constitution. But it was loaded with the ideas they brought from Britannia. So in 1776, without controversy, the following clause was written into the United States Constitution:

> "The Congress shall have power … to promote the progress of science and useful arts, by securing for limited times to authors and inventors the exclusive right to their respective writings and discoveries; …"

Stunning. A monopoly had been authorized by the U.S. Constitution. An "exclusive right" is a monopoly. A monopoly stands in stark contrast to the freewheeling entrepreneurship that is the hallmark of the American economy. No wonder it needed a separate provision in the Constitution.

It wasn't long before Congress passed the first copyright law. Like Queen Anne's statute, it gave authors an absolute monopoly over who could make a copy of their creations in order to encourage the creation of new works. Copyright only lasted for a period of 14 years with an option to extend the right for another 14 years. You had to jump through some hoops like sending a copy to the Copyright Office and putting a notice on whatever it was that you wanted to protect, but if you wrote or drew an original work and followed all the rules, you had an absolute monopoly over the business of making copies of your creation. The shift of those rights from printers to authors was an enormous change. And it only took 300 years.

COPYRIGHT COVERAGE TODAY

Today the copyright law covers a wide range of creations. It gives authors a monopoly over a lot more activities than just copying. And you don't have to do a thing to own the copyright. No registration. No notice. The copyright law attaches to every new, original creation the moment it is reduced to a tangible form. But the threshold for originality is pretty low.

Here is a partial list of the creations protected by copyright as long as they are in some tangible form:

Books

Plays

Comic books

Songs

Musical compositions

Recordings of music, even if the music itself is in the public domain

Photographs

Quilts

Choreography

Paintings

Drawings

Sculptures

Jewelry

Fabric designs

Architectural drawings, but not the buildings created from them

Maps, but only the newly created elements, not the location of things on the map

Computer programs

And, of course, movies and scripts for movies and treatments for scripts for movies

And translations of any of the above from one language into another.

WHEN DOES A WORK QUALIFY
FOR COPYRIGHT PROTECTION?

Immediately. The moment that a creation takes on a tangible form, copyright attaches. You don't have to do a thing. You don't even have to know it is happening. In fact, most people don't realize that they own the copyright to every photo they take, every doodle they draw on a napkin, every letter they write. This is an incredible shift in how a work obtains copyright protection under U.S. Copyright Law. It happened in 1978 and it is the law that exists in the U.S. today. Prior to 1978 you had to register your work in Washington and put notices on every copy released to the public in order to achieve copyright protection.

Today, when you write a script or a treatment or a book or you make a video or still photograph or piece of sculpture, it's automatically protected. Without doing anything more, you have a monopoly over a wide variety of uses of the work you created.

WHAT ACTIVITIES ARE COVERED
BY COPYRIGHT LAW?

So let's get to the point. What exactly is it that the copyright owner gets to control?

For the filmmaker, there are four that are of particular interest. They are the following:

1. Making a Copy—that is still the core of the copyright law. The Motion Picture Association of America (MPAA) and Recording Industry Association of America (RIAA) have mounted a multi-million dollar campaign (including lots of lawsuits) to educate people that making a single copy of a protected work is a serious violation of copyright law. Although there are exceptions to be sure, the core of the copyright law still prohibits the making of so much as one

copy, no matter what the reason. In order to make a copy, permission from the copyright owner is needed.

2. Preparing a Derivative Work. A **derivative work** is a modification or alteration of a pre-existing work. You make a derivative work when you make a movie from a script, a book from a movie, or knock-off a famous painting because you can't afford to decorate the set of your motion picture with the original. A lot of filmmakers think that making a few changes to the original will save the day when it comes to clearance. Often, that just means another violation of copyright law—specifically, a violation of the right to make changes in a work, which is a right held by the copyright owner. In order to modify a work, permission from the copyright owner is needed.

3. Distribution. Basically, **distribution** is making a copyrighted work available to the public through sale, transfer of ownership, rental, lease, or lending. In order to distribute a work, permission from the copyright owner is needed.

4. Public Performance. Every time a movie plays to an audience or a song is sung in concert or a poem is read at a gathering of fans, there is a public performance. The defining aspect is whether the public is invited to attend. It doesn't matter if admission was charged, whether there was a profit, or if it was all for a good cause. If the public can attend, the performance was public. In order to publicly perform a work, permission from the copyright owner is needed.

Congress recently added two more activities that are included in the limited monopoly which result from copyright laws. They don't really apply to filmmakers and don't amount to much, but here they are just so you know:

1. Public Display. This applies to the individual images of a motion picture, literary, musical, dramatic, choreographic, pictorial, graphic, or sculptural works. In order to display

one of these works publicly, permission from the copyright holder is needed. Except (and this exception pretty well wipes this right off the books), when folks own a lawful copy of a work (or the original), they have the privilege of displaying it publicly.

2. Digital Audio Transmission of a sound recording. The purpose is to ensure that performing artists, record companies, and others will be protected as new technologies affect the ways in which their creative works are used. This is a very narrow, difficult-to-understand right in sound recordings only. It is in the nature of a public performance right for recordings. Don't worry about it. This doesn't affect filmmakers or authors or publishers.

As I'm writing this, musical performers are asking Congress to add their performance to the protection of the copyright law. Recording artists have descended on Washington once again to achieve their own version of copyright justice.

HOW LONG DOES PROTECTION LAST?

When the United States passed the first copyright law, the answer was—not long. Today copyright lasts for the life of the author plus 70 years. That is a long, long time. If you own the copyright in your film, your children, your grandchildren, and their children could be earning money from exploiting it.

However, if a corporation is the author, because the work was created by an employee within the course and scope of her employment or because it is a work for hire, then the copyright lasts 95 years from the day that work was published, or 120 years from the day it was created (whichever is shorter). That is still a lot of time.

The U.S. Copyright Law provides the longest protection in the world. It was just a few years ago that 20 years were added to the length of copyright. You can expect that there will be some effort to extend the length of copyright protection again when some valuable properties are about to lose that protection. Specifically, Mickey Mouse, which was about to fall into the public domain when the extension was pushed through Congress. Surely, his owners will try for one more extension, regardless of the embarrassment over the tag "Mickey Mouse Extension" that was put on the last one.

WHO OWNS THE COPYRIGHT?

The Constitution says that the copyright law exists to encourage authors to create works. The law says that the author is the creator of the work. This is true, EXCEPT if the creator happens to be an employee working within the course and scope of his employment. Then the employer is the author. It is as though the employer were at the keyboard entering the text. That makes some sense.

But read on for a clever bit of copyright law that applies only to a narrow list of works. It is called **work for hire**. It is unique to the U.S. Copyright Law. It says that if you have a written agreement declaring a commissioned work to be a work for hire, then the author is not the person toiling away to make the creation. It is the person or company who is designated as the author in the work for hire agreement, usually the person or company who paid for the work to be done.

This provision applies to the following and to no others:

1. a contribution to a collective work,

2. part of a motion picture or other audio-visual work,

3. a translation,

4. a compilation,

5. an instructional text,

6. a test,

7. answer material for a test,

8. an atlas, or

9. a supplementary work.

This sea change in the copyright law was triggered by a huge technological innovation—motion pictures. The year was 1905. The early entrepreneurs who made movies realized they had to do something, because so many creative types have a hand in putting a movie together. They needed some legal help to wrangle all these creative folk. They petitioned Congress to add an idea they called "work made for hire" to the copyright law. And it has remained there ever since as an American anomaly on the worldwide copyright stage.

WHAT ABOUT IDEAS?

Copyright law does not protect ideas. Copyright law only protects the "expression of an idea that is fixed in a tangible form." This means that written words are protectable; the ideas behind them aren't. You can't own an idea that's in the air.

You can write up your ideas for movies to your heart's content. The written words can be registered with the Copyright Office. The copyright law protects you from someone copying those words, but your ideas are fair game. You obtain protection for your idea in direct proportion to how much of your idea that you write down.

The more you write, the more protection you have. One or two sentences may express your idea, but if someone steals it, you will never be able to identify your one or two sentences in a feature-length motion picture. As a matter of protecting your idea in the marketplace, the more you write down, the better, because copyright law only protects the written word, not ideas—no matter how original. Many courts have said, "Ideas are as free as the air."

The Good News

More than a mere glimmer of hope shines on you if your idea gets ripped off. Consider the true (and now very famous) case of Victor Desny. Desny was a professional writer with a great idea. The year was 1949, more than two decades after a boy named Floyd Collins was trapped in a cave, a story that the newspapers of the time covered with a vengeance. The Collins story had always fascinated Desny. He wrote a treatment on the incident and included a wholly fictional event as part of his story. He thought that the story was perfect for the famous director Billy Wilder, who was working at Paramount at the time, and asked for a meeting to pitch his idea. Wilder's secretary said that the story was too long for Wilder to read, so Desny condensed his 60-page draft down to three pages and called back two days later. The protective secretary, Rosella Stewart, made him read it over the phone while she took it down in shorthand (secretaries could do that in 1949). He mentioned in that conversation that he wanted to sell the story to Wilder and write the script. Rosella told him that "naturally we will pay for it." His story is used.

Wilder liked the story. He liked it so much that he hired someone else to write the script. Paramount made the movie, *Ace in the Hole* starring Kirk Douglas. The film included the totally fictionalized portion created by Desny.

Not nice. Desny sued. Desny won . . . as well he should have.

The court ruled that Desny had an implied oral contract. An **oral contract** is any non-written contract. An **implied contract** is an agreement that arises without any party specifically stating the terms. One of the parties indicates by their conduct rather than by their words that there is an agreement. In contrast to an implied contract, an **express contract** is one in which the parties have agreed to the terms in specific words, either orally or in writing.

The court said, "Generally speaking, ideas are as free as the air." However, the court found that Desny would not have offered the idea to Wilder except for the prospect that Desny would write it. The court said that a professional writer only pitches ideas for the purpose of employment. Note that Desny had credits but also acted professionally because he kept good records. He had his 65-page, dated story. He had his three-page, dated outline. He recorded his calls to Wilder's office in his writer's diary. The court also said that "the law of implied contracts assumes particular importance in literary idea and property controversies."

What a mouthful! What a case! The courts recognize that writers are not truffle pigs, sniffing out good stories and bringing them to the attention of others only to have the stories snatched from them by those who would use them and grow rich. Courts have little trouble with that concept. The issues today are whether the parties sufficiently establish their relationship to require the idea recipient to pay, whether the idea is the kind of idea that has to be paid for, and whether the material is really used in a way that requires payment.

On the first point, the courts require that both parties be professionals, active in the entertainment business. If your plumber shouts from beneath the sink whilst fixing your drainpipe, "Hey you oughta make a movie about lesbian paraplegics invading Detroit" and you like the idea, you would not be expected to hire him or her to write the script for the film. Therefore, you do not owe him or her any money. The courts have not yet extended idea protection to folks outside the business. Folks outside the business don't like that and often write claim letters. There is no indication right now that the courts have any interest in throwing the net any wider to include more people in the class of protected submitters. In fact, even if you are an active producer, there has to be something more than the mere submission. There has to be some action or event, such as a meeting or other interaction, that creates a contract.

The court in the Desny case made specific mention of the fact that Desny was a professional writer and stated explicitly that he was trying to sell his idea to Wilder. Wilder's secretary said words to the effect that if the idea were used, "Naturally we will pay you for it."

On the second point, the idea must be specific enough to convince a jury that it was your idea that was ripped off. The more general the idea, the harder it is to demonstrate that it was your idea. Also, the idea must have been first conveyed by you and not have come from someone else. If the person receiving the idea already had received it from someone else, they would not owe you, but rather would owe someone else. Originality, of course, is an aspect of this issue, but different states have different requirements on this point. Courts in most states require that the idea be novel. California courts have said that novelty is not an issue, but note that Desny did create one original scene in an otherwise factual story.

Finally, not every idea's use triggers a payment. Even if your idea becomes a line or scene that is used by someone else, it would not be enough to trigger payment. The use of the idea has to be such that it would deny the person who submitted the idea the ability to make money from their own, separate use of the idea. If you unsuccessfully try to develop a project based on a submitted idea, the person who submitted the idea could still write a script and sell it, so it is a "no harm, no foul" situation. Remember, Desny is not a copyright case. It is a contract case. The courts have not yet given money for a use of an idea that did not produce money to the defendant and deny money to the plaintiff. The ultimate use must also be substantially similar to the submitted idea. In the Desny case, the movie followed the three-page treatment faithfully.

Desny's victory inspired others. Julian Blaustein was an experienced producer of 30 years with major credits such as *Broken Arrow* (1950), the landmark sci-fi film *The Day the Earth Stood Still* (1951), and *Bell, Book and Candle* (1958). He had supervised more than 20 films a year at 20th Century Fox. In the mid-'60s, he had a great idea: Let's have Richard Burton and Elizabeth Taylor do a film based on Shakespeare's *Taming of the Shrew*. Some people who observed that couple in public would not think that the idea was particularly original. Nevertheless, Blaustein contacted the then relatively unknown stage director Franco Zeffirelli, who was interested in directing the film. When Blaustein approached the actors' agent about the availability of the world's most famous duo, the agent insisted on hearing the idea. Blaustein disclosed his idea, which included substantial detail of what to cut and what to retain and how to expand Shakespeare's classic.

The agent liked what he heard and pitched the idea to the Burtons, who liked the idea so much that they made a film— with Zeffirelli directing— that incorporated many of Blaustein's ideas. But they made it without Blaustein.

Not nice.

Blaustein sued.

Blaustein won.

The court said that Blaustein should have a chance to prove that he had an implied oral contract to produce the picture with reasonable compensation and appropriate credit. Note that Blaustein was an experienced producer. He had only somewhat developed his film idea, but he would not have revealed any of the above details to the parties without the expectation of producing the picture. If you are not a legitimate producer with something of a track record, be aware of that factor as you evaluate your situation. Think of the world of producers as a spectrum between the likes of Blaustein on one hand and a wannabe producer who, during a meeting, makes the simple, naked suggestion that the Burtons should film *Taming of the Shrew*. In the Blaustein case, every element of Blaustein's idea was used. If this is not the case, then an idea is not stolen, it is an inspiration. Inspiration is good. Theft is bad. Only the taking of someone else's idea is punished. If someone inspires you to create something terrific, good for you and good for them—even if they don't see it that way.

Today, these so-called Desny cases are not uncommon, but they are still tough to win. Here are the exact instructions that the judge gave to the jury when Warren Beatty, Columbia

Pictures, and Robert Towne were sued by a certain Ms. Mann under the Desny theory for their film *Shampoo*:

Mann has the burden of establishing, by a preponderance of the evidence, all of the facts necessary to prove each of the following issues:

1. That plaintiff submitted her ideas to the defendants and that the defendants received them.

2. That before plaintiff submitted her ideas to the defendants, she clearly conditioned her disclosure upon defendants' agreement to pay for those ideas of plaintiff's that the defendants used, if any.

3. That defendants knew, or should have known, the condition upon which the disclosure was being made before the disclosure was made.

4. That the defendants voluntarily accepted the submission on plaintiff's terms and thereby implicitly agreed to pay plaintiff for any of her ideas that they might use.

In order to find for the plaintiff, you must find that she has established, by a preponderance of the evidence, each and every one of the foregoing described issues; otherwise, you must find for the defendants. In this case, the court found for the defendants because Mann, the plaintiff, did not meet the burden of establishing the facts necessary to prove each of the issues above. The court held that the evidence Mann put forward was insufficient to show that she submitted her ideas to the defendants, and that Mann never conditioned the disclosure of her ideas on defendants' agreement to pay for them, as required by the instructions listed above. The rulings in the Desny case are still alive and well.

For years, it was not clear if you could sue a studio for idea theft when the ideas are lifted from spec scripts that were submitted to the studios. A lot of lawyers thought that once a script was completed, the writer could only sue for copyright infringement. Well, Jeff Grosso proved them wrong. He wrote a script set in the then little-known world of high-stakes poker called *The Shell Game*. He submitted the script to The Gotham Group. They had a first-look deal with Miramax. He thought it was a perfect fit.

Nothing happened.

When Miramax released *Rounders*, set in the now better-known world of high-stakes poker, he sued. The court threw out the copyright infringement part of his case because the similarities were not great enough to support such a claim, but allowed the trial to go forward on the Desny theory of an implied contract.

Studio lawyers went nuts. They gave endless interviews about how this was going to make life very difficult for studios. They said that this ruling would spawn a lot of frivolous suits from writers who didn't have a good copyright claim, but might be able to spot a few stolen ideas. Indeed, there was a spike in the filing of this kind of lawsuit, but victories for writers in this situation are hard to come by. Jeff Grosso found that out when he lost his trial. The court said that his case was based on speculation about the evolution of an idea (for the movie *Rounders)*. Even though Grosso ultimately lost his case, the studios were still unhappy because of the principle that had been established.

Submission Agreements

As a result of all the litigation over copyright infringement and idea theft, every studio has devised a submission agreement. Such agreements might better be called waiver-of-all-rights-just-to-get-a-chance-to-pitch agreements. Although many of these agreements have been softened somewhat by smart studio lawyers who don't want them so overbearing that they will be found to be unenforceable as against public policy, the courts have thrown out a lot of submission agreements in other industries for just that reason.

The bottom line is that these agreements are non-negotiable. If you are required to sign one, your choices are clear: Pitch your idea after signing the agreement or don't pitch your idea at all, at least not at the studio that is insisting on a submission agreement.

Just so you can see one before you are presented with one, a typical submission agreement is included at the end of the chapter. If you are an independent producer, you may want to use this form yourself.

Non-Disclosure Agreements

Sometimes writers present independent producers with non-disclosure agreements before writers will pitch their ideas. A **non-disclosure agreement** says that producers will not disclose to others the idea being pitched to them unless they buy the idea. There really is no reason for a producer to sign such an agreement. In Desny's case, Desny could not even get a face-to-face meeting with Wilder. Wilder surely would not have signed an agreement saying that he would not disclose any of the material in order to hear the pitch. He would not want the bother of reading the agreement or the hint of liability that it suggests. Such a thing would have ended the Desny vs. Wilder story before it began.

As you may notice, I am not a big fan of these documents. In my view, such agreements are off-putting at best. At worst, they stop the meeting. The relationship is stillborn, killed by the writer's fear that you will try to steal his idea. The writer's paranoid desire to contractually protect against theft (justified as it may be) results in no pitch, no deal, no movie. A writer who never shops an idea ends up in the same place as the writer who shops an idea and has it stolen: nowhere.

Nevertheless, the submission agreement at the end of the chapter includes non-disclosure provisions with a few notes and observations. Use it in good health. Don't forget that you can download this and all forms from my website (www.clearanceandcopyright.com)

PROTECT YOURSELF

Some writers verbalize the agreement that the court in the Desny case implied. They say, "If you don't want to use this idea, please don't pass it on. I understand that if you like it, I get to write it." As an honest producer, you should already possess this point of view.

After a pitch, some writers send a thank-you letter, not unlike the one your mother taught you to write. It might read: "I enjoyed meeting you last Wednesday and discussing my idea for a folk-dance film set in New York in the not-too-distant future. I'm so glad that you liked the characters Monsoon and Dry Season and the way they interacted with their racially mixed Martian parents. Your sympathy with the dog that caught Lyme disease from biting the masochistic postal worker was truly encouraging. I hope you want to go forward with this project."

If you receive such a letter, keep it. It is part of a paper trail. If you already were working with any of these ideas that the author discussed, write back, "Yes, but don't forget that we have a script in development with that same great Lyme-disease twist, so we won't be able to work on this project together." Or whatever applies. Create your own paper trail at the critical junctures of any idea exchanges.

It is much better for writers to do the work of writing and polishing than to rely on paper agreements for protection. In fact, writers who are too lazy to write down ideas and keep diaries and do the other things necessary to protect themselves probably deserve what they get.

To protect ideas, create a "paper trail" by doing the following:

1. Write down your ideas, the more detailed the better. Save all your drafts.

2. Register whatever you write with the Writers Guild of America (WGA). This registration has no legal effect, but it helps establish the history of the creation of your script.

3. Keep a detailed diary of all your meetings, even telephone meetings.

4. Follow up your meetings with written thank-you notes. This confirms your meeting in a pleasant way, while it creates a paper trail.

Always make sure that the cover of your treatment or script contains a WGA registration number and the maximum amount of information about you: your name, your address, your agent, your lawyer. If a major agency represents you, their distinctive covers tell it all. The fire-engine red cover of CAA or the classic silver cover of ICM directs everyone's attention to a phone number that is already in many of our automatic dialing systems.

Whether you take your idea to treatment or script stage, by writing it down and maintaining a paper trail, you are more protected than if it is purely an idea in your head. Most people do not register the copyright of their works at this stage. It is simply too early. Still, you may feel a need to keep a record. That is a correct feeling. Keep a detailed record in a bound book of every draft, every meeting, every significant event in the life of your project.

Writers Guild Registration

Once you have written out your idea, call it a treatment and register it with the Writers Guild of America. The cost is very low ($30 at this writing). A **treatment** tells the story of the script in abbreviated form. It can be a few paragraphs, a few pages, or more than 20 pages. For purposes of protection of your ideas, the more detailed it is, the better. WGA registration is available to everybody, whether or not you are a member of the Writers Guild. As part of the registration process, the WGA gives the treatment or script a number, puts it in a sealed envelope, and stores it in a vault for five years. You may extend the registration for another five years. No one can withdraw your script without a court order except you. Today, the entire process can be handled online. Just go to www.wgawregistry.org.

Self-Mailing

People might have told you to mail your treatment or script in an envelope addressed to yourself as a substitute for copyright registration or registration with the WGA. You write. You mail. You receive back your postmarked envelope. You do not open it. You save. Does this work? It has always been a mystery why anybody would want to bother with all of this. Yes, this procedure might very well work if such an envelope were dramatically opened at a trial. It would show with some precision what was written on a certain day. However, if there were a lot of money riding on the outcome, you'd better believe that forensic scientists would testify that the envelope was opened and resealed, had been tampered with, was somehow unreliable, or in some other way was not valid. You know how lawyers are. For the low-cost simplicity and absolute reliability of registering your treatment with the Copyright Office or the Writers Guild, why bother with self-mailing?

The folks in Holland have figured this out, however. In Holland, you can take your script to the customs bureau. They will date-stamp each page for you with an official government stamp. You can then mail that script to yourself (after you copy it so that you know exactly what is in the envelope and can show it to your lawyer if you need to). That mailed script will offer a double proof of the date of authorship: the envelope's mailing information and the stamps on each script page. The stamps on each page appeal to me as a form of proof.

The Ultimate Idea Protection: Hide Your Candle Under a Bush

That's right. Share your great ideas with no one. Don't let anybody read it. Don't let anybody look at it. It won't be stolen. It won't be ripped off.

Amazingly, some writers and producers are so paranoid that they prevent anybody from seeing their material rather than run the risk of someone stealing it. Most successful writers and producers are less concerned about idea theft. They take the view that ideas are a dime a dozen; what is valuable is how you execute them.

Sure, creative works are stolen all the time. Not nearly as frequently as amateurs believe to be true, but it does happen. The mechanisms discussed in this chapter protect your rights should such a thing happen. Hopefully, you will enjoy your life without having to face off against a word thief.

1.01 NON-DISCLOSURE/NON-CIRCUMVENTION AGREEMENT

THIS AGREEMENT is made as of _____, 20__, between _____ located at _____ and _____ located at _____.

_____, or its representative and/or assigns (hereinafter referred to simply as I or me), has agreed and intends to from time to time disclose to _____ (hereinafter referred to simply as you), certain client contacts, technical, conceptual, financial, and other proprietary information that it (individually and collectively) considers to be confidential information relating to proposed motion picture and television program opportunities and/or materials, contacts, and concepts relating directly or indirectly thereto (hereinafter referred to as "INFORMATION"), for the sole purpose of allowing you to evaluate such INFORMATION. You and I have agreed to execute and deliver this Non-Circumvention and Non-Disclosure Agreement.

I have indicated that it would like to safeguard such INFORMATION. Accordingly, you agree to maintain such INFORMATION in confidence according to the terms set forth hereinafter:

1. As used in this agreement, INFORMATION shall mean all data, documents, proposals, outlines, technical, conceptual, financial and client contacts, names, addresses, telephone/fax/telex numbers, e-mail addresses economic and loan or investor information, commercialization and research strategies, vendors, trade secrets and know-how disclosed by me to you, directly or indirectly, either in writing or orally, relating to the proposed projects entitled _____, except such information and know-how that (a) can be shown by you to have been in your possession prior to the disclosure to you by me; or (b) at the time of disclosure hereunder is, or hereafter becomes, through no fault of you, part of the public domain by publication or otherwise.

2. This Agreement is a perpetuating agreement for five (5) years from the date above, and is to be applied to any and all transactions entertained by you during the period of this Agreement. This Agreement is also effective upon your heirs, assignees, and designees.

3. You, individually, and any associates, hereby agree that their corporation, divisions, subsidiaries, employees, agents, or consultants will neither intentionally disclose the INFORMATION to any third party, company, and/or individual; nor intentionally use the INFORMATION in competition with my business, for any purpose other than that contemplated under this agreement. In the event you use the INFORMATION, intentionally or otherwise, and are informed of such use in writing, you agree to fully compensate me for such use to date of notice and will cease to use INFORMATION unless mutually agreed upon in writing to do otherwise.

4. In consideration of the foregoing, you hereby covenants and agrees, individually, for yourself and any respective affiliates, partners, officers, directors, corporations, divisions, subsidiaries, employees, agents, and/or consultants, to not communicate with (in writing or verbally), make any contact with, deal with, or otherwise enter into any agreement and/or understanding with any corporation, partnership, person, or other entity introduced by me (and/or my officers, directors, shareholders, partners, and/or agents thereof) relating to or arising out of the INFORMATION or in the areas of funding and financing, without my prior written consent, you hereby further agree to keep completely confidential the names of any corporations, organizations, individuals or group of individuals, buyers or sellers, introduced by me, in connection with the INFORMATION, as well as all non-public documentation, materials, or information supplied to you relating to such INFORMATION.

5. You agree not to make any copies of the INFORMATION, whole or in part, for the purpose other than the purposes contemplated and this Agreement and will, upon my request, return all written materials furnished hereunder and any notes or memoranda of conversations relating thereto, including any copies thereof.

6. Neither this Agreement or disclosure of the INFORMATION by me shall be deemed by implication or otherwise to vest in you any rights in any concepts, trademarks, patents or other properties of mine, and/or my assigns relating directly or indirectly to the television program project and related projects.

7. The parties hereto recognize and agree the remedies at law for breach of the provisions of this Agreement will be inadequate and that I and/or assigns, shall, in addition to any other rights that it might have, be entitled to injunctive relief in the event that such a breach of the Agreement occurs. You further acknowledge and agree that the INFORMATION is unique to me and that your breach of the terms of this agreement will result in material damages to me. Any claim arising out of a breach of this agreement shall be settled by order of the law of the State of California by binding arbitration in accordance with the rules of the American Arbitration Association in Los Angeles, California. The prevailing party in such proceeding may recover attorney fees and costs incurred in connection with such proceeding.

THIS AGREEMENT sets forth the entire agreement between the parties, and supersedes all other oral or written provisions. This agreement may be modified or terminated only in a writing signed by all parties hereto.

<u>**AGREED TO AND ACCEPTED:**</u>

_____   _____

CHAPTER 2

FAIR USE

This chapter deals with those circumstances in which you don't need the copyright owner's permission to use a bit of his or her or its material in your book or film. It is called fair use and it is one of the most interesting and quickly changing areas of copyright law.

SOME BACKGROUND

The concept of fair use was first introduced into the U.S. law of copyright by a court in Massachusetts in 1841. Rev. Charles W. Upham wrote an 866-page, two volume book about George Washington. Three hundred and fifty-three of the 866 pages were letters written by George Washington. The letters were part of a collection owned by a Mr. Sparks, who had purchased them, archived them, published them, and—most importantly—owned the copyright to them.

Rev. Upham's book was based almost entirely on these letters and, without them, the book would have been quite insignificant. What's more, it was the most interesting and valuable letters that Rev. Upham took from Mr. Sparks' collection.

Mr. Sparks sued the good Rev. Upham for copyright infringement. Rev. Upham said, "It is only fair that I be able to use these letters in my book."

Mr. Sparks won.

There were no fair use cases at that time, so the judge had to create the logic for his conclusion. The judge said that when deciding issues of this sort, one must "look to the nature and objects of the selections made, the quantity and value of the materials used, and the degree in which the use may prejudice the sale, or diminish the profits, or supersede the objects, of the original work."

These factors all weighed in favor of Mr. Sparks. In fact, these original factors are the core of the four factors that the courts still use to decide fair use cases today.

While the court didn't use the words "fair use," it obviously didn't think Rev. Upham had been fair in his taking, and this case is where the fair use concept was born. Since then the courts have been developing and refining the concept for more than 160 years. Congress wrote the same basic approach of the courts into Section 107 of the Copyright Law when they overhauled the Copyright Law in 1976. But Congress still left it up to the courts to decide fair use on a case-by-case basis and to make their decisions considering *all of the facts*, not just the answers to the four questions that are set out in the statute.

The language of Section 107 seems simple enough:

The fair use of a copyrighted work, including such use by reproduction in copies or phonorecords or by any other means specified by that section, for purposes such as criticism, comment, news reporting, teaching (including multiple copies for classroom use), scholarship, or research, is not an infringement of copyright. In determining whether the use made of a work in any particular case is a fair use, the factors to be considered shall include:

1. the purpose and character of the use, including whether such use is of a commercial nature or is for nonprofit educational purposes;

2. the nature of the copyrighted work;

3. the amount and substantiality of the portion used in relation to the copyrighted work as a whole; and

4. the effect of the use upon the potential market for, or value of, the copyrighted work.

You can see from the language of the statute that there is no list of uses that are always and under all circumstances permitted under the doctrine of fair use. The language does not give definitive guidance even to the courts, let alone the layperson. Congress merely listed some of the areas in which fair use is possible and some of the questions the courts must ask.

To make matters worse, the appellate courts are not consistent in their opinions about which one of the four factors is most important. In a trilogy of cases decided in 2001, the federal trial courts in New York City took the position that the first factor is the most important. Most of the trial and appellate courts in the rest of the country had been taking the position that the fourth factor is the most important factor. The Supreme Court corrected the matter by stating that all factors were to be explored, and the results weighed together.

Fair Use—A shield, not a sword

Fair use is not an invitation to poach the intellectual property of others instead of creating your own work. Rather, fair use is simply an exception to the monopolistic rights that the law grants the owner of a copyright. Fair use allows you to create something new and different using someone else's creation as an ingredient, a single element in a new mix. Fair use is most often seen as a defense you can use when you are sued for copyright infringement and a defense that can be used against you, if you go after somebody for using for example, a clip from one of your films. This is the most important exception to the rights of copyright owners. It is also the area of copyright law that is changing the most rapidly. If you have not used someone else's copyrighted material, there is no need to address the question of fair use. Fair use is the lubricant between copyright law and your First Amendment right to express yourself for good or bad about this book or anything else.

When you think about fair use, think good manners. They are both rooted in the same basic tenet of consideration for your fellow humankind. There are only a few rules that apply always in all situations. The overriding rule is that there are no rules that apply in every situation. Courts recognized that it simply was not fair to say that every copying of a copyrighted work was a violation of the law. Some copying was necessary to promote the very creativity that the copyright law was designed to promote. For instance, if you are critiquing this book, a quote or two from the book might be helpful. But if I didn't like you or what you had to say about my book, I could stifle your commentary except for the fact that your use would be protected by the concept of fair use.

Since it has been imbedded in Section 107 of the Copyright Law, fair use has only been the subject of a very few cases that have gone all the way to the Supreme Court. Each of the cases was reversed at each level of review. Two of the cases were split decisions at the Supreme Court level (even learned justices do not agree). It is hard to articulate what is fair use in abstract, objective terms. It always requires an examination of the specific facts of the case.

If you are faced with fair use questions, you really need a good lawyer and a solid internal compass to mark the path between the fair use of that which was created by others and the use of someone else's creation that will require that person's permission (which almost always means a payment to that person). As a personal rule of thumb, you should always err in favor of asking for permission and paying a reasonable fee, unless you are absolutely sure it simply will not do any good to ask. Even then it is probably better to ask and get a refusal on record just in case they come after you later. It shows good faith on your part. Sometimes, the message that conveys the refusal to give permission will also express a distaste for your point of view, which bolsters your First Amendment argument in favor of fair use.

When we were clearing clips for the Oscar-nominated film *Smoke and Mirrors*, we faced just such a situation. The film was

about the tobacco industry's use of advertising and product placement in feature films to entice the nation into an acceptance of
smoking by others and the habit of smoking on an individual
basis. The story could not be told effectively without the use of
television commercials for tobacco. But the television commercials
were bought and paid for and owned by the tobacco companies
or their advertising agencies. What were the odds that permission
would be given to make an anti-smoking documentary?

But, how about the clips of feature films showing major
movie stars puffing away? Again, no studio would cooperate in
showing how they were pulled into the campaign to turn on
an entire nation to a deadly habit like smoking. They might be
proud of the film, but they certainly would not be proud of the
hand they had in promoting an often-fatal addiction. Here the
trick was to find particularly clear and fine examples and then
only use a bare minimum in order to get the idea across. Unlike
the commercials, which were generously used, the feature film
clips were used very sparingly in *Smoke and Mirrors* and only
to the extent necessary to get the point across.

FAIR USE AND FILM CLIPS

Fair use does not automatically allow you to take a portion
of another person's copyrighted film and edit it into your
film without specific written permission. Even documentaries,
which are usually in the public interest, should not cavalierly
incorporate uncleared footage from the films of others. Clear
your film clips with a license or solid fair-use opinion from an
attorney approved by the E&O insurance companies in advance
because lawsuits are expensive. It can be even more expensive
to remove a section of your film at some point in the future if
a court rules against you.

The use of film clips is most commonly associated with
documentaries, but many makers of feature-length fiction films
use clips for dramatic effect to recreate historical scenes. *Forrest*

Gump used a variety of film footage. *Apollo 13* masterfully integrated both historical footage with specially prepared live-action sequences to create an amazingly realistic film. Much of it was researched by Take Aim Research (888-TAKEAIM). Film clips are also commonly used in connection with blue-screen projections in front of which actors can perform as though they were halfway around the world.

Now that you have been introduced to the analytical framework and some possible situations in which fair use might arise, let's look at actual court cases to see how it works out in the real world.

One Plaintiff, Three Cases, Same Result—The AIP cases

The New York courts seem to be much more sympathetic to a fair use argument than most courts, largely based on a trio of cases in which the holder of the underlying rights behaved so badly that the courts would have done just about anything to be sure that she did not win. They chose to hand her not one but three defeats—all served up on the platter of fair use.

Two of the great horror-meisters of all time were Sam Arkoff and James Nicholson, who had a company called American International Pictures (AIP) that literally churned these pictures out. Nicholson retained ownership of the copyright for many of the films he made. On his death, the ownership of those copyrights passed to his widow, Susan Nicholson Hofheinz. She administered the distribution rights and the occasional licensing of clips for a hefty slate of horror films.

So it was that she licensed a number of clips to AMC for use on the American Movie Classics channel for a documentary called *It Conquered Hollywood! The Story of American International Pictures*. During post-production, the producers decided they needed one more clip to round out their narrative. They obtained the clip and sent over a clip license agreement containing the same basic terms on which they obtained all the other clips from Ms. Hofheinz. She prepared an amendment to the previous agreement, which AMC signed and returned. Nobody was in a rush for the paperwork. They had a good working relationship, and everybody knew exactly what was going on.

Oops!

After the film was locked, Hofheinz viewed the film and said, "No deal." The filmmakers cried foul and went ahead and released the film. She sued.

She lost.

The court said that one could not make a documentary about the grand masters of horror films without showing a few clips, AMC didn't take more than they needed to take in order to make their point, AMC was making a documentary, not another horror film, and they didn't adversely impact the market for the underlying film. Voilà! That sounds like fair use to me. And it sounded like fair use to the court.

Note that Hofheinz's behavior hurt her when she went to court. Fair use is an equitable relief. An equitable relief is when the court is trying to do what is fair as between the parties, often where there are no strict statutory guidelines. When a plaintiff is asking the court for equitable relief, it is important that the plaintiff has used good faith and fair dealing throughout the transaction.

So you would think that Ms. Hofheinz would have learned her lesson from the last case. She didn't. She sued A&E over a documentary called *Peter Graves: Mission Accomplished*. Early in his career, Graves appeared in several AIP films. A short clip from *It Conquered the World* was included without obtaining permission.

She lost . . . again.

The court said that you could not make a documentary about the career of Peter Graves without showing an early clip. A&E didn't take more than they needed to take in order to make their point, they were making a documentary, not another science-fiction film, and they didn't adversely impact the market for the underlying films. Sound familiar?

As though the third time might be a charm, she came before the same court with the same kind of lawsuit against The

Learning Channel, which made a documentary called *Aliens Invade Hollywood.* They used a variety of clips from various producers. They didn't seek permission from any of them, believing that if they used small snippets of various alien-visitation films to demonstrate the themes and political context of the alien-visitation film genre, it would be fair use. Hofheinz was the only one who sued.

She lost . . . yet again.

The court said that you could not make a documentary about alien-visitation films without showing a few clips featuring aliens. The Learning Channel didn't take more than they needed to take in order to make their point, they were making a documentary, not another alien film, and they didn't adversely impact the market for the underlying films. Do you think she got the message? The court is nothing if not consistent when it comes to Ms. Hofheinz's assaults on documentary filmmakers.

One Plaintiff, Two Cases, Testing Fair Use for News—The Bob Tur Cases

On the West Coast, we learn a lot about fair use from Bob and Marika Tur. They own their own helicopter and use it to gather news footage, which they then sell to various outlets. Because they do not have anyone to answer to except themselves, they are able to make decisions on their own based on when and where they think news might break. That is how they ended up being the only newscopter hovering over South Central Los Angeles when the Rodney King verdict was announced. They were the only team to capture the now infamous footage of the Reginald Denny beating that mushroomed into the L.A. Riots of 1992.

Most news outlets licensed this copyright-protected footage. Those that did not were sued with various results. KCAL-TV (Channel 9 in Los Angeles) asked for a license and was refused, so it obtained a copy of the tape from another station, slapped their logo on it, and broadcast it a number of times, without giving credit to the Turs. Not fair. And not fair use. Actually,

KCAL won at trial, but the appellate court reversed the decision and sent the case back for trial.

When Reuters News Service sent the Turs' footage out over the wires to their subscribers, it was not fair use, even though the footage related to the hottest (excuse the pun) story of the day. Reuters made no changes, just sent out the footage for their own gain and in direct competition to the Bob and Marika Tur. In that case, the court noted that 30 seconds of the four-minute forty-second tape constituted the "heart" of the footage, so the inclusion of the forty-five seconds was more important than the inclusion of other segments.

Get to the Heart of It

The same "heart" idea helped the owners of the character Godzilla protect their property against the use of photographs that "captured the central expressive core" of the Godzilla character. It also helped the owners of the copyright to the Laurel and Hardy films win their lawsuit against the trade paper *The Hollywood Reporter*, which used a single still from one of their pictures on their inside cover in order to announce a new section for placement of advertisements. You probably know the picture and would agree—it is the scene where Laurel and Hardy are balanced on the precipice of a building. The court called it the "high point" of the film and readily identifiable as being from the film. Now get this: The photo had MGM's copyright notice on the back and stated that it could only be used to promote *Laurel & Hardy's Laughing 20's*. Those from *The Hollywood Reporter* surely read that notice. They shoulda known better.

When CNN, ABC, and CBS were sued in New York for using a few seconds from *The Story of G.I. Joe* in Robert Mitchum's obituary, it was held to be fair use. But when CBS was sued for using one minute and fifteen seconds from a Charlie Chaplin film in a news report on his death, CBS lost. No fair use. The court found that amount was substantial and—you guessed it—it was part of the "heart" of the film.

Enter Transformation

Today, the notion of whether the defendant's use of the plaintiff's copyright-protected work is **transformative** seems to be the key to the analysis. A work is considered **transformative** when something new and different is added to the underlying work, when the underlying work is used for a new and different purpose, or when the underlying work is an ingredient in a new and different work. I like to use the example of flour in the cake-making process. The flour spread on the table to keep the dough from sticking has not been transformed. It is unchanged. The flour in the dough has been totally transformed. It has become a cake never to be identified separately again. In the world of fair use, the transformation need not be so drastic to enjoy protection as fair use, but I don't know of a case where fair use was found and transformation was not found. It has to be there somewhere.

Courts spend a lot of time determining whether a work is transformative, even though this word does not show up anywhere in the copyright law! The transformative concept was created in a law review article by a judge trying to make sense out of all the fair use cases. You can see the notion in the three Hofheinz cases. In each one of those cases, the fact that the film using the clips was a documentary, not another horror film, was an important factor for the court. In the two Tur cases, discussed just above, the results were based primarily on the fact that the new use was pretty much the same as the original. Worse yet, it was directly competitive with the Turs' use. Later, you'll read about a different result for Mr. Tur in another case involving the exact same footage. In that case, the footage was transformed.

THE GRATEFUL DEAD CAN STILL
BREAK NEW GROUND

In 2003, Dorling Kindersley published a 480-page coffee table book outlining the history and culture of the Grateful Dead. The book included stories about the band's concerts and images, such as pictures, tickets, and promotional materials that were related to each concert. Material was placed in chronological order. Some of the images were posters promoting the band's concerts, seven of which became the subject of a lawsuit. The publisher of the book had previously sought permission to use these items from Bill Graham Archives, but they couldn't agree on a price. The publisher decided to use the images anyway.

Bill Graham Archives sued.

They lost.

The court sided with the publisher, holding that it used the images pursuant to fair use. The court noted that the publisher's use of the images were plainly different from the original purpose for which they were created. In other words, the publisher's use was transformative. In their original form, the images were works of artistic expression used to promote the band's upcoming concerts. In the book, the images were highly reduced and used as historical artifacts to document and represent the band's concerts and events. Even more interesting, the court said that even though in some instances the link between the image and the story was less obvious and did not enhance the reader's understanding of the text, the images still served as historical artifacts of the band's events. The court reasoned that these images were transformative in that they were significantly reduced in size and enhanced the biographical information in the book. The court also gave us a great summary of fair use:

"The ultimate test of fair use, therefore, is whether the copyright law's goal of promoting the Progress of Science and useful Arts, would be better served by allowing the use than by preventing it."

Case solved. Publisher won.

DOCUMENTARY FILMMAKERS TO THE RESCUE

Of course, filmmakers became frustrated with the uncertainty of fair use. The beginning of the 21st Century seemed to be a good time to do something about it. Under the leadership of Professors Pat Aufderheide and Peter Jaszi of American University financed by grants from the Rockefeller and MacArthur Foundations, documentary filmmakers were brought together to discuss fair use. In meetings across the country, filmmakers discussed the burdens of clearing film clips, music, photos, and other items for their documentaries. They talked about how their creativity was crimped, how their energy and their pocketbooks were drained, and how certain points could not be properly demonstrated cinematically. Aufderheide and Jaszi even documented how some films were not being made and expression was being squelched.

By 2004, Pat and Peter had uncovered many instances of films not made, compromises that had to be made, and widespread instances of filmmakers using fair use while hiding the fact from gatekeepers and insurance companies. Their study was aptly entitled *Untold Stories*.

Pat and Peter went back to the Foundations and received additional money to create a consensus among these same documentary filmmakers that came to be expressed in a booklet entitled *Documentary Filmmakers' Statement of Best Practices in Fair Use*. I should disclose that I and my New York associate Steve Sheppard were the two attorneys in private practice who were invited to join the academic legal scholars on the legal advisory board to this project.

The Statement describes "the actual practice of many documentarians, joined with the views of others about what would be appropriate if they were free to follow their own understanding of good practice . . .Unfortunately, until now the documentarians who depend on fair use generally have done so quietly, in order to avoid undesired attention. In this statement, documentarians are exercising their free speech rights—and their rights under copyright—in the open." This statement is organized around four classes of situations that documentary filmmakers regularly confront in making their films. These four classes do not exhaust all the likely situations where fair use might apply; they reflect the most common kinds of situations that documentarians identified at this point. The document is fairly long, so we have seriously abbreviated it for your convenience.

Summary of Documentary Filmmakers' Statement of Best Practices in Fair Use

Class	Employing copyrighted material as the object of social, political, or cultural critique	Quoting copyrighted works of popular culture to illustrate an argument or point.	Capturing copyrighted media content in the process of filming something else.	Using copyrighted material in a historical sequence.
Use	Specific copyrighted work is held up for critical analysis in the same way that a newspaper might review a new book and quote from it by way of illustration. This activity is at the very core of the fair use doctrine as a safeguard for freedom of expression. So long as the filmmaker analyzes or comments on the work itself, the means may vary, the use may be as extensive as is necessary to make the point, permitting the viewer to fully grasp the criticism or analysis.	Here material of whatever kind is quoted not because it is, in itself, the object of critique but because it aptly illustrates some argument or point that a filmmaker is developing—as clips from fiction films might be used (for example) to demonstrate changing Americana attitudes toward race. The possibility that the quotes might entertain an audience as well as illustrate a filmmaker's argument takes nothing away from the fair use claim. The filmmaker is not presenting the quoted material for its original purpose but harnessing it for a new one.	Documentarians often record copyrighted sounds and images when they are filming sequences in real-life settings. Common examples are the text of a poster on a wall, music playing on the radio, and television programming heard (perhaps seen) in the background. In a documentary, the incidentally captured material is an integral part of the ordinary reality being documented. Where a sound or image has been captured incidentally and without prevision, as part of an unstaged scene, it should be permissible to use it, to a reasonable extent, as part of the final version of the film.	In many cases the best (or even the only) effective way to tell a particular historical story or make a historical point is to make selective use of words that were spoken during the events in questions, music that was associated with the events, or photographs and films that were taken at the time. In many cases, such material is available, on reasonable terms, under license. On occasion, however, the licensing system breaks down.
Limit	The use should not be so extensive or pervasive that it ceases to function as critique and become, instead, a way of satisfying the audience's taste for the thing (or the kind of thing) critiqued. In other words, the critical use should not become a market substitute for the work (or other works like it).	Documentarians should assure that the material is properly attributed, to the extent possible quotations are drawn from a range of different sources, each quotation is no longer than is necessary to achieve the intended effect, the quoted material is not employed merely in order to avoid the cost or inconvenience of shooting equivalent footage.	Documentarians should take care that particular content played or displayed in a scene being filmed was not requested or directed, incidentally captured media content included in the final version of the film is integral to the scene/action, content is properly attributed, the scene has not been included primarily to exploit the incidentally captured content in its own right, and the captured content does not constitute the scene's primary focus on interest, in the case of music, the content does not function as a substitute for a synch track (as it might, for example, if the sequence containing the captured music were cut on its beat, or if the music were used after the filmmaker has cut away to another sequence).	Documentarians show that: the film project was not specifically designed around the material in question; the material serves a critical illustrative function, and substitute exists with the same general characteristics; the material cannot be licensed, or the material can be licensed only on excessive terms that relative to the reasonable budget for the film; the use is no more extensive than is necessary to make the point in question; the film does not rely predominantly or disproportionately on any single source for illustrative clips; the copyright owner of the material used is properly identified.

Fair Use in other situations	Some common misunderstandings about Fair Use
The four principles just stated do not exhaust the scope of fair use for documentary filmmakers. Inevitably, actual filmmaking practice will give rise to situations that are hybrids of those described above or that simply have not been anticipated. In considering such situations, however, filmmakers should be guided by the same basic values of fairness, proportionality, and reasonableness that inform this statement. Where they are confident that a contemplated quotation of copyrighted material falls within fair use, they should claim fair use.	Fair use need not be exclusively high-minded or "educational" in nature. A new work can be "commercial"—even highly commercial—in intent and effect and still invoke fair use. Most of the cases in which courts have found unlicensed uses of copyrighted works to be fair have involved projects designed to make money. Fair use doesn't have to be boring. If a use otherwise satisfied the principles and limitations described in the Statement of Best Practices in Fair Use, the fact that it is entertaining is irrelevant. A documentarian's failed effort to license rights doesn't hurt a claim for fair use. Often, there will be good reasons to seek permissions in situations where they may not be required. It never hurts to try, and it actually can help demonstrate the filmmaker's good faith. And sometimes (as in connection with Principle Four) it can be critically important.

Visit www.centerforsocialmedia.org/resources/fair_use for more information

The upshot of the publication of that little booklet was enormous. The Ford Foundation funded the distribution of the booklet through a number of avenues, including a meeting in New York City attended by many producers and executives. Wheels began to spin in the heads of some of the **gatekeepers**. **Gatekeepers** are those folks who you initially have to deal with, who stand between you and those in real authority and who find it much easier to say "No" than to say "Yes." The Independent Film Channel (IFC) under the leadership of Evan Shapiro approved the use of fair use in Kirby Dick's documentary *This Film Is Not Yet Rated* and invited me to help guide the project.

It would not and could not have been made without fair use. The film was highly critical of the MPAA's film rating system. No studio would license clips from its films for such a use. The film had over 100 clips. Every one was used without a license pursuant to the fair use doctrine. *This Film Is Not Yet Rated* went to Sundance and was the buzz of the festival because of its subject matter and because the filmmakers relied on the fair use provisions of the copyright law. Since then, it has been released theatrically, aired on IFC, and set a Netflix record.

IFC then decided to rely on fair use on a film about the history of road films called *Wanderlust*. Without fair use, this film would never have seen the light of day. The filmmakers had budgeted a substantial amount for film clip licenses, but the film was still way over budget due to the high cost of the clips they used. Even after a bit of begging, the prices were out of reach for the filmmakers.

IFC asked me to see what I could do. With a little tweaking, all the clips fell within fair use, so I called each owner and offered $1,000 per title and let them know the alternative was that we would use the clips pursuant to fair use and they would receive nothing. It took a lot of educating in the form of long letters, a free copy of this book, and the *Statement of Best Practices*. Out of 18 copyright owners, 14 agreed to the new terms and four declined. Those four received nothing. The cost of clips dropped from more than $450,000 to $47,000. *The New York Times* ran a long story detailing the negotiations. The film aired without incident and is still available on DVD through Netflix.

Both of these films were examples of the second class of works that the *Statement of Best Practices* set forth as fair use. Both of these hued carefully—even conservatively—to the limitations set forth for this class.

Let me give you a bird's eye view of fair use that might make a little more sense out of all of this. Think of fair use as a spectrum of possibilities, rather than a bright line that provides a definitive "yes" or "no" in all cases. In fact, the courts have specifically said, in case after case, that there is no bright line, that they have to consider all relevant factors in each case. In this way, fair use is like good manners. There are situations in which a use is clearly not fair and situations in which a use is clearly fair and then there are a number of situations where reasonably well-informed practitioners in the field might differ.

To help you with this concept we have taken some of the cases we have discussed in the book and spread them out along a spectrum from definitely not fair use to safely fair use. When you read the cases and hear the stories, they always turn out as one or the other because at the end of the day, the judge has to make a decision. And after a decision is made, an opinion has to be written that explains and supports that opinion and its either thumbs up or thumbs down. In fact, when you're struggling with these issues during production, it would be nice to know what is safe, what is definitely not, and what is in the gray zone. Stay away from the gray zone unless you like litigation.

I will spread some of the cases we have discussed along the spectrum to show where each lands up.

Fair Use Spectrum

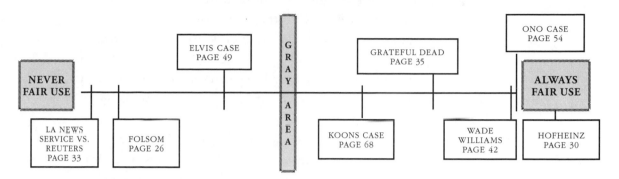

DONALDSON'S SAFE HARBOR FOR FAIR USE

Still confused? You want more certainty? I have defined a **safe harbor** for fair use that we use with our clients. A **safe harbor** is a term borrowed from maritime law. If there is a storm, a boat can go into any harbor in order to safely ride out the storm, and the skipper does not have to ask permission or pay a fee to the owner. It is a place you can always go and be safe from the storm. In the federal income tax code, safe harbor is the provision that allows you to pay estimated taxes based on the previous year and be safe from penalties, even if you earn a lot more money; it's a sort of penalty-free zone. The phrase fits aptly into this discussion

Here is one situation that will provide a safe harbor. If you can honestly answer the following three questions with an objective "yes," your use will definitely, always be a fair use.

1. Do you need to use this item to make the point being discussed at that time, cinematically?

2. Did you only use as much as needed to make the point?

3. Would the connection between the item you are using and the point you are making be clear to the average viewer without any further explanation?

On the last point, I ask clients if the connection would be clear to a sleepy judge, which might be a better way to state the question. If you answer "yes" to the above questions, you are in a safe harbor. I am using the word "need" in a strict sense, as in "necessary" as opposed to "really cool to have." The latter is the way we so often use the word in our consumerism society: "I need a new pair of shoes." That is not what I mean by the word "need."

When talking to clients, I like to start with the above three questions because if the answer to each is a "yes," we don't have to go through the four-prong test set out in copyright law. And there is a lot of fair use room left over. Refer to the chart above. Note that the safe harbor is on the far right of the chart. Review the cases listed on the right-hand end and you will see exactly what we are talking about. And there are a lot of situations that are comfortably fair use between the safe harbor and the gray area.

TO ASK OR NOT TO ASK? THAT IS THE QUESTION

When I went to law school, the rule was to make up your mind in advance. We were taught that you shouldn't ask for permission to use something protected by copyright if you think you are going to get a "no." That is NOT the court's thinking today. The courts have said that a failure to ask for permission does not equate with bad faith.

A good statement of the general attitude of the courts came in a case that Wade Williams filed against ABC for copyright infringement. Wade claims to hold certain rights to films made by Ed Wood. The late critic Joel Siegel was doing a riff on why aliens in movies always have a lot of human characteristics for the *Good Morning America* show on ABC. He used clips from three movies filmed by Ed Wood. You can see why Wade was upset when you read the dialogue that played over the clips. Here it is:

A clip of *Robot Monster* with this voice-over: "In *Robot Monster*, the second worst movie ever made, they couldn't afford an alien costume, but the director happened to have a gorilla suit and a diving bell helmet in his garage."

A clip of *Plan Nine from Outer Space* with Joel Siegel's voice-over: "In *Plan Nine from Outer Space,* the worst movie ever made, the alien beings look suspiciously like bad actors."

A clip of *Queen of Outer Space* with Siegel's voice over. "In *Queen of Outer Space* the alien looks suspiciously like a bad actress." And for the first time, the film dialogue comes up as an actor in a very strange costume says to Eva Gabor, "We're the only men on the whole planet?" and she gives a big smile and says, "Yes."

You can see that these uses fall safely within the doctrine of fair use as described in the above section. But Wade had an ace up his sleeve. He found out that ABC had licensed other clips for this show and for a lot of other shows. He brought stacks of signed licenses into court and waved them triumphantly at the judge. The court was not impressed.

Wade Williams was silenced, but probably only temporarily. He really likes to license out clips from the Ed Wood films.

TO PAY OR NOT TO PAY ACTORS, DIRECTOR, AND WRITER? THAT IS THE BIGGER QUESTION

When you license a film clip from a film made pursuant to one or more union contracts (SAG, DGA, or WGA), you have to pay the members of that union who worked on the film what is called a **reuse fee**. A **reuse fee** is a payment that is required by union contracts when a piece of a film made after 1960 is taken and used in another work. The details of this requirement are set out in Chapter 18 about licensing film clips. So the question is frequently asked of me, "If I use a film clip pursuant to fair use, do I still have to pay the reuse fee?"

The answer is "No." You do not pay a reuse fee when you use a film clip pursuant to fair use.

The logic requires a little explaining, but you should understand the logic (or keep this book handy) just in case you have to explain it to someone else.

The requirement to pay a reuse fee comes from the union contracts that SAG, DGA, and WGA negotiated in 1960. These provisions, which remain in the contracts today, require the producer to pay a fee if a portion of the film is used in another work. The idea came up to cover a lot of the situations. For example, characters in a new film or television program might be watching television and an old TV show would be playing on the set. The unions wanted their members who worked on the "old television show" to be paid on the theory that the studios ought to be hiring new folks to create the show being watched by the cast members, rather than re-using a clip. Thus, if the producer licenses the right to you to do the same thing, the requirement to pay the reuse fee is triggered. And the actors don't have to agree. If you use a clip under fair use, the producer isn't licensing the clip and the reuse fee isn't triggered.

Now the studios are not dumb. Getting the permission of actors can take time. The cost can be uncertain. So, rather than bothering with all of that, they merely tell you that the cost will be two times astronomical plus you have to pay the reuse fees, whatever they turn out to be. Basically, they push their contractual obligation on to you as a condition of licensing the clip to you. Those requirements will be fully discussed in Chapter 19.

AND WHAT ABOUT CREDIT????

Always give credit where credit is due. Didn't your mother tell you that? When you use a clip or photo or snippet of music pursuant to fair use, you are exercising your constitutional right to tell your story. Of course, you give credit to the source material.

Most of my clients give credit in the lower left-hand corner of the clip as it is showing and then in a list in the end roll. Do not mislead. Just give the credit. Don't say something like "with thanks to" or "clips obtained from" or—worst of all—"licensed from." All those phrases indicate some sort of permission was given.

Credit is particularly important outside the U.S. where *droit attribution*, as the French say, is an integral part of the copyright law. It is one of the rights held by an owner of a copyright on the same foot as the right to control the copying and distribution of a work. The failure to give credit is an infringement of copyright in many countries. And when you give credit, always include the director for a film clip, no matter who owns the copyright. That, too, is part of the law when your film to travels into many territories outside the U.S.

FAIR USE IN THE FILM DOES NOT NECESSARILY MEAN FAIR USE IN ADVERTISING

Let's assume that you have completed your film and there are certain fair use items within the film. You showed good faith by asking permission, which was denied. You gave credit where credit was due. You can breathe a big sigh of relief. You don't have to worry about anything else.

Wrong.

You need to be very cautious about using the fair use items in the advertising of your film. Whether it is fair use to use a certain item in advertising is a whole new analysis and it is much more difficult to show fair use in advertising.

The most common scenario in which this is an issue is the creation of a trailer for your film. The trailer maker might very well want to use a clip from your film that contains within it a clip that you used pursuant to fair use. This situation has come up several times in my practice and, to date, the analysis has always come out the same: It simply doesn't work. The fair use clip has typically been shortened, but there is no reason to use the clip except to sell the underlying film. Be creative. Find something else. This use of the fair use clip to promote your film simply falls outside of the parameters of fair use in every case that has come across my desk.

However, it is not impossible to have fair use in advertising. You may remember Bob Tur from the above section. He won two lawsuits against television stations that used his video of the Reginald Denny beating that helped ignite the 1992 race riots in Los Angeles. That seminal, one-of-a-kind footage was used in news programs the very night of the incident, but the court found no fair use. Later, when the trial was on cable's Court Television, Court TV used a shorter clip of that very same footage to promote its coverage of the trial and later to promote a special dedicated to the trial.

Tur sued.

This time, Tur lost.

In going through the four factors, the court found that Court TV's purpose was entirely different from the fast-breaking news purpose for which the footage was originally shot. The amount used was very, very brief—no more than necessary to let the viewer know what the trial was about and did not interfere with the prime market for the footage, which was licensing to news outlets.

More importantly the court also held that this use was highly transformative. Most advertising is not so transformative. The purpose is to sell, sell, sell—to call attention to the movie or book they are trying to promote. In order to pass the fair use test, such uses need to be highly transformative. Here are a few **screen grabs** from the Court TV promotion that was found to be so transformative that it was fair use in spite of the fact that it was pure promotion.

Promoting *Williams & Watson trial coverage on Court TV.*

Split-screen shot of original video & Court TV trial footage, which was considered "transformative" with the witness voice-over and very different purpose.

These principles were well illustrated in a case involving two books about the video game Pac-Man. The game was a sensation when it came out. Almost three decades later it seems like a tame—maybe lame—antique. It was the forerunner of today's chase-'em, catch 'em, destroy 'em games. Not so many people play the Pac-Man game anymore, but we all have to play by the rules that decided that case.

The company that owned the copyright to the game and to the little figures that chased each other around the game wanted to stop the distribution of two books that were designed to teach folks how to win at Pac-Man. Here are pictures of the covers of both books. Look them over and take a guess as to how the court ruled with regard to these two books. Think about the reasoning behind your guess.

There were a lot of issues in the case, and the court did issue an injunction against further printing of the books until some changes were made on the inside. But as to the two covers that are shown below, the court decided that one was okay and one was not okay. Check your own guess now that you have that monstrous hint.

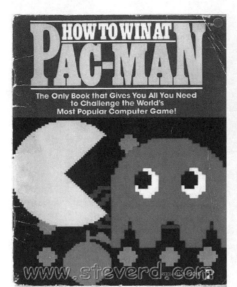 

The cover on the right was the one that was okay. The court held that "the illustration of the Pac-Man characters on the cover is useful in alerting the browser that the book does concern itself in part with the Pac-Man game . . . the very modest use of [the] copyrighted figures on the cover can be justified in terms of explaining to the would-be reader what he may find by picking up this book and examining it further."

The cover on the left was not okay. In the transcript of the proceedings, the court is reported to have said, "It is the merit of the comment, criticism, or review which should sell the publication. That, after all, is the reason for the exception; namely, that we should permit in a free society comment, criticism, and review, not only for purposes of political freedom, but for purposes of the general welfare of society and the improvement of whatever enterprise might be involved. But there is nothing in that view which justifies the appropriation of a copyright for strictly marketing purposes."

Bottom line: The court allowed the publisher of the two books to show enough of the copyright to let readers know what was in the book (on the right), but not more than that because then the prime purpose would appear to be to lure readers to buy the book (on the left.)

ADVERTISING THAT SELLS YOUR FILM CAN KILL YOUR FILM

Even advertising that does not use one single little snippet of the fair-used material that was in your film can still impact your film. For example, take the 16-hour Elvis documentary, *The Definitive Elvis*. It was enjoined because a myriad of clips were not fair use. According to the law, the court is supposed to consider "all relevant factors." And the court did. In fact, the first thing the court mentioned was the packaging right after the court identified who the various plaintiffs were. Here it is:

"On its box, *The Definitive Elvis* describes itself as "an all-encompassing, in-depth look at the life and career of a man whose popularity is unrivaled in the history of show business and who continues to attract millions of new fans each year. This ground-breaking, sixteen hour series is brimming with classic clips, rare home movies, [and] never before-seen photos. . . . Every Film and Television Appearance is represented in this series as well as Rare Footage of Many of Elvis' Tours and Concerts." The *Definitive Elvis* employs these clips, in many instances, repeatedly. And the advertising was specifically and prominently discussed in the opinion:

"Passport seeks to profit directly from the copyrights it uses without a license. One of the most salient selling points on the box of *The Definitive Elvis* is that "Every Film and Television Appearance is represented." Passport is not advertising a scholarly critique or historical analysis, but instead seeks to profit at least in part from the inherent entertainment value of Elvis' appearance on such shows as *The Steve Allen Show, The Ed Sullivan Show,* and the *1968 Comeback Special*. The purpose of showing these clips likely goes beyond merely making a reference for a biography, but instead serves the same intrinsic entertainment value that is protected by Plaintiffs' copyrights."

The message to you is that your job is not finished when you turn over your film to a distributor or broadcaster. Watch carefully how your project is promoted. If the advertising says anything close to, "Buy this video and you get to watch all the cool stuff that someone else owns," you know you are in trouble. The advertising for *Elvis* should have said in essence that *Elvis* was the definitive biography of Elvis with little or no mention of the clips. If you entice people to buy your video because of the clips you are using, instead of the story you are telling, you better license the clips.

Insurance to the Rescue

Until February of 2007, the standard insurance policy covering the content of a film specifically excluded anything for which you did not have a written release. Fair use was not considered and was not covered unless you happened to have stumbled over an entertainment attorney who had the reputation and the moxie to negotiate with the insurance company. Even then the coverage was often provided on a handshake or side letter but not part of the policy itself. All that changed when leading insurance companies announced a fair use rider that would be sold as part of the errors and omissions insurance policy for filmmakers. All of this is discussed in some detail in Chapter 21.

DOES FAIR USE AVOID THE NEED TO CLEAR MUSIC?

Many people who have a general notion of fair use think that there is some magic amount of a song that you can use without receiving permission or paying a fee. "Eight bars?" they ask. "Two bars?" they ask. They think that fair use dictates a specific amount of music that can be used without clearance and thus save a lot of work and some money.

Not so.

The rap group The 2 Live Crew went all the way to the Supreme Court for their parody recording of the song "Oh, Pretty Woman." They won on the parody issue, but the Supreme Court sent the

case back to the trial court because they used a bass riff from a
Roy Orbison recording. It was only a single riff, yet the Supreme
Court held that it was archetypical of Orbison's music and not
necessarily part of the parody. Therefore, it was not automatically
fair use. See the next chapter for a full discussion of parody in
general and the "Pretty Woman" case in particular.

It used to be that fair use was virtually no help to you in
the music area. You had to clear all music. To illustrate the
importance of this point, Evan M. Greenspan, a music clearance
company, used to send out a button with materials about their
company that read, "USE A NOTE, GO TO JAIL."

Today, there still is a real dearth of cases involving music,
but with the *Statement of Best Practices* and more fair use cases
in related areas, it is easier than ever before to qualify music as
fair use under certain circumstances. I will list four situations
in which I have been successful in obtaining E&O insurance
coverage, even though a specific case covering this exact situation did not exist. Note that each of these examples is for a
documentary film.

1. Music is playing in the background. You did not arrange
   to have it play and have minimized the sound to the
   extent possible. You did not cut to the music and did not
   use the music outside of the scene in which it existed
   naturally. This is the third example set out above in the
   Best Practices chart, and there actually is one case on this
   point, which I'll tell you about below.

2. A portion of the soundtrack of a film that is part of a clip
   that was used pursuant to fair use. This is in contrast to
   third-party music that is on a clip used pursuant to fair
   use.

3. A short portion of a piece of music that is discussed in
   the film and played to illustrate the point that is being
   made about the music is not necessarily fair use, but can
   be, if used very conservatively.

4. A short portion of a piece of music in a biographical documentary in order to illustrate that the performer of the music played or sang the music at a certain time and place.

There are very few cases that have allowed a use of copyrighted music to be fair use in a film or program. One involved a television film crew covering an Italian festival in Manhattan. The soundman picked up snippets of a copyrighted song as the cameras rolled on a band marching by. The music was replayed on the news that night. This use was held to be fair use, in part because of the transitory public interest in the news event of which the music was an integral part and the small portion of the song that could be heard on the broadcast.

In the late '90s, there was a Michigan case that found fair use of music. There were 35 seconds of a song used in a half-hour anti-violence episode on a series on public television targeted at teenagers. No lyrics were used, and half of the 35 seconds that were used were inaudible. The court went through the four-step analysis.

Unfortunately, the first published opinion about "sampling" lists of music went very sour. It was correctly decided on the facts, but it wasn't "sampling" as you and I might think of it. The case involved the first eight bars of Gilbert O'Sullivan's hit song "Alone Again (Naturally)." The eight bars were continuously looped so that the same 10 seconds are heard throughout the recording. The recording in question was on Biz Markie's rap album *I Need a Haircut*. The rapper's courtroom presentation wasn't the greatest. In fact, the judge was so incensed that, in his written opinion, he accused the rapper of theft and referred the entire matter to the U.S attorney to consider criminal prosecution.

The prosecutor declined to file criminal charges, but who wants to come that close? Certainly, no record company or reasonably successful recording artists want to take that kind of risk. A lot of time and energy goes into clearing the sampling rights. In fact, a few specialty music-clearance houses flourished in Los Angeles and New York to obtain the rights to sample.

Along came the Beastie Boys in a case that clarified and underscored this case. The Beastie Boys had licensed a three-note, six-second musical sequence contained in a recording of jazz scholar James W. Newton's "Choir." The exotic sounding tidbit was looped more than 40 times into the Beastie Boys hit song "Pass the Mic."

The Beastie Boys licensed the sampling rights from the owner of the master recording and thought that they had licensed the sampling rights from Newton, but the check was returned and nobody ever followed up.

The composer sued.

The composer lost.

The court correctly held that it was only the sounds taken from the sound recording that needed to be licensed. The unique sound is what the Beastie Boys were after, not the composition. The court went on to add that even if the Beastie Boys were after the composition, they didn't take enough to be recognizable, let alone copyrightable all by itself. Therefore, the use of the composition was fair use and the composer lost the case.

It was a big clarification for those who want to put together a rap record based, in part, on the recordings of others. This is the first case in which a judge analyzed the differences between copyrights in sound recordings and copyright in musical compositions. The conclusion in this particular situation was that the license from the owner of the master recording was enough. Had the Beastie Boys taken more, perhaps the result would have been different, but the court correctly figured out that these are two different rights' holders with different results, even for the same rap recording.

One important lesson to be drawn from the Beastie Boys' case is the difference between the composition and recording in a fair use situation. Fair use of the composition doesn't necessarily mean fair use of the recording which carries its own separate copyright. There are circumstances in which you might be better off making your own recording of a song you want to use. It will often be cheaper. It will also be safer.

And just as I was proofing this chapter, a new and important case came down from the New York federal court. The court found the use of 15 seconds of a master recording of John Lennon's song "Imagine" to be a fair use. Previous cases allowing fair use of music were limited to the composition. In fact, one other court had hinted that sampling might be an exclusive right of the copyright owner of a master recording.

The film using "Imagine" was called *Expelled*. It dealt primarily with the harsh treatment of anyone in the academic community who wanted to promote the concept of intelligent design as it applies to the creation of earth and man. The film also explored the position of some scientists who think that the role of religion should be reduced or eliminated. To illustrate the role of this thought in pop culture, Ben Stein (the narrator of the documentary) comments that the thought is nothing new and in fact "takes a page from John Lennon's playbook." Immediately after those words, the 15 seconds from "Imagine" plays with the lyric printed out on the screen over four stock shots: "Nothing to live or die for and no religion, too."

Our office issued the opinion that this use of a master recording was a fair use. Not only did we think it was a fair use, we thought it fit into the safe harbor that is discussed above. Take another look at the chart describing the spectrum of fair use cases. The particular clip of music is the best proof of the point that Ben Stein was making, so the filmmakers needed it to make the point. They only used as much as necessary to make the point. And the point they were making would be clear to anyone viewing the film without any further outside explanation. The film was released on a thousand screens. Immediately, a storm of discussion raced across the Internet, most of it by people who did not understand fair use.

Yoko Ono sued.

Yoko lost.

In the thoughtful chambers of a federal court in New York, the judge's careful analysis resulted in a finding that we were right in our fair use assessment.

CLEARANCE LOG FOR _____

	Time code (in & out)	Type of item (Clip/ Photo/ Poster/ Original Footage)	Description	Contact Person	Status & Notes (specify territory & terms if not universal, in perpetuity)
1					
2					
3					
4					
5					
6					
7					
8					
9					
10					
11					
12					
13					
14					

You can download this form at www.clearanceandcopyright.com

Use the code: ibotCC3

CHAPTER 3

PARODY, SATIRE, AND JOKES

This chapter covers three different and distinct concepts—parody, satire, and jokes—that are often confused in people's minds. A parody comments *directly* on a copyrighted work and therefore is allowed to take quite a bit from the work that is the *subject* of the comment. A satire comments on some broad aspect of society. Often, it is usually evaluated liberally under the fair use doctrine. Neither one has to do with humor, although, more than not, they both evoke a laugh—or at least a smile. Therein lies the confusion. A joke gets no special break under copyright law. The issues raised by jokes are usually all about the person who is the object of the joke and what rights they have, as in, "How did they get away with saying that?"

DEFINITION OF PARODY

This is a very misunderstood area. You are not exempted from obtaining clearance of a copyrighted material just because the material is used in a humorous way. A parody is a very specific thing with very specific requirements. There is no humor defense for copyright infringement. There is only a parody defense, which is a subset of the fair use defense.

The first time the Supreme Court ruled on the importance of parody was in what has become known as the Gaslight Case. It concerned a parody on television of a then-famous and serious movie. The 1985 Gaslight Case ended with four justices deciding one way, four justices deciding the other, and a ninth judge abstaining. This equally split decision did not help at all since the Supreme Court affirmed the lower's courts decision without issuing an opinion. My legal definition of a parody—drawn from an examination of the cases in this area—is the following:

1. A new, copyrightable work

2. based on a previously copyrighted work

3. to such an extent that the previous work is clearly recognizable

4. but not taking more from the copyrighted work than is necessary,

5. that criticizes or comments on, at least in part, the subject matter or style of the previous work, and

6. is not likely to hurt the value of the previous work.

Did you see any requirements regarding humor? Statistically speaking, most examples of parody turn out to be humorous. Certainly, commenting on an underlying work generally comes out in a way that puts a smile on the face of the listener. However, humor is absolutely not a requirement, and judges often go out of their way to say that they don't think that the parody before them is funny. Heaven forbid that the judge might have a sense of humor.

A TRUE PARODY DOES NOT HAVE TO BE CLEARED

The Supreme Court had not issued a controlling decision on parody until The 2 Live Crew case in 1994. Irving Azoff and The 2 Live Crew were sent back to the trial court so that a jury could decide if a single bass riff constituted fair use. The real reason for the lawsuit, however, was the fact that the song that The 2 Live Crew wrote, recorded, and released was a parody of "Oh, Pretty Woman." The Orbison estate, not surprisingly, was upset. Here are selected lyrics from Orbison's "Oh, Pretty Woman" compared to The 2 Live Crew's "Pretty Woman."

"Oh, Pretty Woman" by Orbison and Dees vs. "Pretty Woman" by The 2 Live Crew version:

Pretty Woman, walking down the street,	Pretty woman, walkin' down the street,
Pretty Woman, the kind I like to meet,	Pretty woman, girl you look so sweet,
Pretty Woman, I don't believe you,	Pretty woman, you bring me down to that knee,
You're not the truth,	Pretty woman, you make me wanna beg please.
No one could look as good as you.	Oh, pretty woman.
Mercy.	
Pretty Woman, won't you pardon me,	Big hairy woman, you need to shave that stuff
Pretty Woman, I couldn't help but see,	Big hairy woman, you know I bet it's tough
Pretty Woman, that you look lovely as can be.	Big hairy woman, all that hair it ain't legit
Are you lonely just like me?	'Cause you look like Cousin It.
Pretty Woman.	Big hairy woman.

The 2 Live Crew won their case on the parody issue. Compare the lyrics used by The 2 Live Crew's against Orbison's "Oh, Pretty Woman" and then go down the six points in the definition I set out at the top of this chapter. You'll find that the work is clearly a parody.

In fact, the first three factors in my definition fall clearly in the favor of The 2 Live Crew. These lyrics are (1) a new creation (2) that is based on Roy Orbison's "Oh, Pretty Woman" (3) to such an extent that the original "Oh, Pretty Woman" is clearly recognizable—even on the written page without the music.

The fourth factor brings in some subjective judgment as to whether The 2 Live Crew did or did not take more from Orbison's "Oh, Pretty Woman" than was necessary. Courts tend to lean toward a finding that the taking was not excessive. Perhaps The

2 Live Crew could have taken a little less, but that is basically a creative judgment. The courts try not to second-guess that creative judgment if they find that all the other requirements are satisfied. I think the better reading of the fourth factor is that the taking was not unreasonable or, maybe even more accurately, that they added more than they took. As we have more litigation and therefore more decisions, this factor will be clearer. Right now, the test is whether the amount taken is "no more than necessary."

The fifth factor concerning social commentary is very broad. Almost any commentary can qualify. It does not have to be particularly funny. In fact, I am not aware of a single case in which the judge admitted to liking the humor of the parody. I know of many cases in which the judges made it clear that the parody was not all that funny—in the official view of the court.

Once you get this far in the analysis, it almost always follows that the new work seeks a different audience from the audience sought by the previous work. While courts spend a lot of time on this factor and most scholarly writers believe that this finding is essential, I view it as much less bothersome than the rest of the elements since it is hard to imagine a circumstance in which the parody would be seeking the same market as the previous work. To me, one result of creating a parody of a work is an appeal to a different audience.

There are two relatively recent cases from the book publishing area that really help to shed some light on the concept of parody and how the factor of social commentary on the underlying work (not humor) is the key factor in deciding whether a work qualifies as a parody and therefore does not need the permission of the owner of the copyright of the work that has been borrowed from (or pilfered from, if you are the owner of the underlying work).

Humorous Book but Not a Parody

Not too long after O.J. Simpson's criminal murder trial and before a civil jury found him responsible for killing his ex-wife, several books came out about the case. Simon & Schuster had what they thought was a parody all printed and being shipped to stores when a court enjoined the delivery. Very few copies ever saw the light of day. The book was called *The Cat Not in the Hat* and purported to be a parody based on Dr. Seuss's famous *The Cat in the Hat*.

The publisher's problem is obvious to anyone who has read the beginning of this chapter. Let's hold the book up to the six-point Donaldson test set out at the beginning of the chapter. Keep in mind that the fifth factor is the key, and that is exactly where Simon & Schuster lost their case. Although lawyers tried to argue that *The Cat Not in the Hat* was a commentary on the innocence of the Seuss book, it was crystal clear that the book was trying to take a humorous look at the murder trial. And the thing that made it humorous was the relentless, start-to-finish taking of the style and rhyming of Seuss and even the look of the illustrations in Seuss's book.

The commentary was not on the Seuss book, it was on the O.J. trial. If the authors wanted to write humorously—or otherwise—on the O.J. trial, they would have to create their own work, not "borrow" someone else's work. They merely rewrote the Seuss text, preserving many of the phrases of the original in order to create a wry look at what the authors believed was a miscarriage of justice. That point of view had sufficient support to guarantee sales, but the authors needed to write their own work, not try to piggyback someone else's creativity.

Once that factor went against the authors of *The Cat Not in the Hat*, nothing else mattered much. One could view the taking as excessive. After all, even the Seuss drawings were copied into the new work. And there is a strong argument that the existence of this work would have been very confusing to the young audience of *The Cat in the Hat*. Certainly, it would have been easy for someone to grab the wrong book because of the similarity in how they looked. It would have been natural for someone to believe that there was some sort of endorsement or approval from the Seuss estate for the new work. But the important reason that the copies of the new book had to be destroyed was that the social commentary was not on the underlying work, it was on a completely different subject . . . no matter how hard the lawyers tried to twist things after the fact.

The court mentioned this case when they sided with Columbia Pictures against Miramax. Miramax made a trailer and poster for Michael Moore's documentary film *The Big One* that they intended as a parody of the highly successful *Men in Black*. The court said that Miramax's poster and trailer were not targeted at *Men in Black*, but merely incorporated features of Columbia's work to "get attention" and "avoid the drudgery in working up something fresh."

Ridicule Is Not Always a Parody

As I stated earlier, the ridicule of a work or humorous commentary on a work doesn't necessarily constitute parody. Take for example a case involving *The Daily Show* on Comedy Central. The format of the show clearly mimics all news and entertainment magazine shows. The show itself might very well be considered a parody. However, a New York court found that a segment on *The Daily Show* ridiculing another program was not a parody. In the segment, various clips were displayed from public-access television, one of which was from *The Sandy Kane Show*, which featured Ms. Kane dancing in a bikini and singing a sexually explicit song. The segment was mockingly dubbed "Public Excess." An announcer on *The Daily Show* introduces the clip by saying, "How about a little cheesecake with Sandy Kane?" and then calls the clip "offensive" as it is played.

Obviously, Ms. Kane took offense! She sued.

The court stated that the use of the clip did not involve an "altered imitation of a famous work," but instead was a "presentation of an obscure, original work in a mocking context."

The only similarity the court found between a parody and the "Public Excess" segment was the element of ridicule. In the end, even though the court did not find a parody, it found in favor of Comedy Central on the basis of fair use, since their commentary was unquestionably critical of *The Sandy Kane Show*.

Serious Book Was a Parody

The Wind Done Gone is a small and powerful novel about the slaves who populated Tara, the cotton plantation in Margaret Mitchell's *Gone With the Wind*. In Mitchell's book, however, the only characters who came alive on Tara were white. The furniture was described in more detail than the many black people who made the place run. The Mitchell estate sued—and won an injunction at the trial court level—on the theory that this book was an unauthorized sequel. However, the estate lost on appeal and *The Wind Done Gone* was allowed to be published.

When you compare the two books using the test at the beginning of the chapter, it is easy to see why *The Wind Done Gone* is available for purchase today. It clearly makes commentary on the subject matter of *Gone With the Wind*. It takes characters right out of *Gone With the Wind* and tells their rich stories, including—and maybe especially—the pain of being treated as less than human by the book's white characters who loom so large in American literary life. So the fifth factor—the key factor—is very much in favor of *The Wind Done Gone*. Having read both books, my personal opinion is that *The Wind Done Gone* could have used more material from *Gone With the Wind* than it did: The plantation name was changed, and most, if not all, of the character names were changed.

This case also illustrates the powerful forces that seek to broaden the fair use area. The following news organizations all joined the fight on behalf of *The Wind Done Gone*: Cox Enterprises, Cable News Network, and the owners of *The New York Times* and the *Boston Globe*, *The Wall Street Journal*, the *Chicago Tribune*, the *Los Angeles Times*, and *The Tampa* (Fla.)

Tribune. They filed so-called friend-of-the-court briefs. Friend-of-the-court briefs are filed by someone who has an intense interest in the outcome of a case, but is not a party to the case, so they have no right to appear. These briefs are filed with the appellate court after the court grants permission to the organization to file the brief. The court has to be convinced that the filer has something important to say and that they have a legitimate interest in the outcome of the case.

These news organizations own a lot of copyrights, so you might think that their interests lay more closely with the Mitchell estate. However, the money they lose by expanding fair use (of which parody is a subset) pales in comparison to the money they make by having ever greater freedom in using the copyright-protected work of others as they race to gather and disseminate the news.

Parody and Personal Rights

If you parody a person, the chances of upsetting that person are substantial. Public figures in America have learned to grin and bear it because they have a higher requirement of proof in order to win their cases. Political cartoons are a good example of parody because they distort a person's features in making a point about the person's views or attitudes. As we go to press, cartoonists are having a field day with Obama's big ears, Hillary's stern look, and anything and everything that stresses McCain's age. Political candidates are so used to this, they generally just shake it off, but not everyone can. Take, for example, Jerry Falwell, a well-known Evangelical pastor who was featured in a parody advertisement in *Hustler* magazine.

Falwell sued *Hustler* for defamation and intentional infliction of emotional distress when the porno mag featured a fictitious Campari liquor ad with a mock interview of Jerry Falwell talking about his "first time." The *Hustler* ad was a parody of a series of liquor ads in which celebrities spoke about the first time they consumed Campari, which, oftentimes sounded like they were speaking about their first sexual experiences. The *Husler* ad quoted Jerry as saying that his first time was during a drunken incestuous rendezvous with his mother in an outhouse. Falwell was quite upset, but the court did not take his side. The trial court ruled that no reasonable person could have believed the advertisement to be true but found *Hustler* liable for intentional infliction of emotional distress. This case went all the way up to the Supreme Court, which affirmed the lower court's ruling regarding the defamation claim—but reversed the ruling regarding Falwell's claim for intentional infliction of emotional distress. The Court said that public figures and public officials may not recover for this claim without showing that the defendant maliciously made a false statement of fact.

Public figures have also tried to assert publicity rights violations in order to curb these unflattering parodies. The Winter brothers were very offended by their portrayal in the fictional comic book series Jonah Hex. The brothers are well-known musicians in Texas who have albino features. The series depicts the brothers as villainous half-worm, half-human offspring born from their human mother, who was raped by a worm. Even though the characters in the comic book are clearly fictional, they have similar long white hair and their names are also very close to the names of the brothers.

Unflattering? Yes.

A violation of their publicity rights? No.

The court said that it doesn't matter whether it is a parody, satire, or caricature, the test is whether the product is so transformative that it becomes primarily the defendant's own expression rather than the celebrity's likeness. The court said that the caricatures did not violate the brothers' publicity rights because the depictions contained a significant amount of expressive content other than their mere likenesses.

The point of the story is that you have to be careful when choosing to parody someone. Hurt feelings result in lawsuits. Just be sure to have a sold legal justification for your parody before you show it to the world and check in with copyright counsel to be sure it's a parody.

TRADEMARK PARODY

Yes, it is possible to parody a trademark. In fact, the courts have been increasingly tolerant of those who would make fun of a product by parodying its trademark. A couple of the best cases of this involved the good old-fashioned Barbie doll. Remember the catchy "Barbie Girl" song that repeatedly refers to Barbie's ability to party and undress anywhere? I'm sure it's a tune Mattel won't ever forget. Mattel is very protective of their doll and jumped at the chance to sue MCA Records.

Unfortunately for Mattel, the court didn't agree with their arguments. The court reasoned that there was little likelihood that consumers would think Mattel had anything to do with the song, and the song was a parody because it targeted the doll as opposed to any other subject.

This didn't stop Mattel. Tom Forsythe was also a victim of a trademark infringement suit by Mattel. He photographed a series of images featuring Barbies in a variety of nude and provocative of poses. Some of the photos showed the dolls sitting in martini glasses and rolled up as enchiladas in an oven. Tom said he wanted to convey the message of "crass consumerism." The court agreed with Tom.

The court said Tom parodied Barbie even though his ultimate goal was to describe his own work.

The courts' tests for finding a trademark parody are a bit convoluted, so please be sure to consult an attorney if you plan to use a trademark in this manner.

At the time of this writing, I haven't been able to find a case of a film parody of a trademark. You don't want to be the test case. No matter how much confidence you have in the possibilities of breaking new legal ground, the holders of trademarks are very aggressive in protecting their marks. Mighty corporations, such as Mattel, go after any parody, no matter how inconsequential, out of fear that a small parody may birth a larger parody. Their complacence toward a small parody can be used against them when they are faced with a larger parody.

Another reason to be cautious is that defending this kind of litigation tends to be even more expensive than other types of litigation. That is because of the deep pockets of corporate plaintiffs and because of the need for evidence of the public's state of mind.

WHAT PARODY IS NOT

The above discussion is designed to give you a pretty good idea of what constitutes a parody. To be absolutely clear, the following items are pointed out because they are not parodies. Some people think that they are and make the mistake of not clearing the music before putting it in their film. The result is that they have to take the song out of their film or negotiate a payment under the adverse circumstance of already having it in the film or risk litigation.

•   A copyrighted song presented in a funny way. A torch song sung by someone in drag or by a drunk character slurring through a song or by a singer performing a song intentionally off-key may be intended as a joke. These may (or may not) bring laughs, but they fail as parodies and therefore must be cleared. They are not parodies because they are not new works and do not make any commentary on the original lyrics. Rather, the humor is in the presentation. You must clear this music.

•   Changing a song slightly to fit your purposes. Changing "Happy Birthday" to "Happy Anniversary" to make that song appropriate for the occasion or changing "Michelle" to "Miquel" to make it appropriate to a character's name may be necessary, but it is not a parody. The song must be cleared. There is no parody because it does not meet the definition. Changing just one word does not make a new work, and it certainly would not be copyrightable. The previously copyrighted work is recognizable, but there is no social commentary and the audience is essentially the same as the audience for which the song was written.

•   A parody is not created when an impersonator or impressionist sings a song (without changing it) in a style of someone other than the person who made it a hit. Dana Carvey imitating President Bush singing "The Party's Over" is not a parody. If the words and music remain the same and the humor is derived from the notion of former President Bush singing that song, there is no parody. The song has to be cleared.

PARODY IN A FILM SCORE

Note that one of the reasons that true parody is allowed without permission from (or payments to) the original copyright holder is that to do otherwise would eliminate the art form. If someone creates a serious work, they do not want someone else to take the heart of the work and poke fun at or belittle its core message.

Your problem as a filmmaker is that a music soundtrack is not like a single record, which can be pulled from the market. No producer wants to be in a position of losing the rights to a song after it is recorded into a film production. Be sure to check in with a copyright specialist if you want to proceed without permission to use a particular song on the theory that you are using a parody of the song. Remember that parody is one of those rare clearance areas where there is no harm in asking. You are almost always denied permission, but since it does not take a great amount of time, you might just be surprised

SATIRE

A satire tends to mock social conventions. Unlike a parody, a satire can stand on its own and make a statement without borrowing from an original work.

When courts are presented with a satire case, they don't say, "This is a satire, so we will give it extra latitude." Rather, they painstakingly set out the manner in which the new work comments on some social condition and use that as a significant factor in their analysis. For the purposes of this chapter, I wanted to break out satires as a separate subject because of the frequent confusion among parodies, satires, and jokes.

Courts haven't said much about the intersection of satire and fair use, although several cases provide insight into how it might be treated if the court were to consider the issue:

A good example of the protection a trademark enjoys from satire is the familiar Dallas Cowboys cheerleader outfit. The distinctive white vest decorated with three blue stars on each side of the front and white fringe around the bottom, white vinyl boots, white shorts, a white belt decorated with blue stars, and a blue bolero blouse is their trademark. The trademark is owned by The Dallas Cowboys Cheerleaders, Inc.

The year was 1979. The Dallas Cowboys were having a great year, and were headed to the Super Bowl again. Unfortunately, the cheerleaders were not having such a great year. The Pussycat Cinema was playing the self-rated XXX *Debbie Does Dallas*. An outfit almost identical to the trademarked outfit appeared in key parts of the film, either on or off the actresses featured in this now-famous film. The sport was purely sexual.

The Dallas Cowboys Cheerleaders, Inc., sued. They had spent a lot of money and effort to create a certain image of the Dallas Cowboy Cheerleaders. The girls in the film did not fit that image.

The Cheerleaders won.

As the court correctly pointed out, "Trademark law not only serves to avoid the likelihood of public confusion, but also serves to protect the right of a trademark owner to control the product's reputation."

The court stopped Pussycat Theaters from all further showings of the film.

Pussycat appealed.

Pussycat lost again. The result was that the entire movie was worthless to Pussycat. There was no way to save it. The trademark was infringed throughout the film, even if the entire outfit was not worn in every scene and the court made it quite clear that porno was not a satire. Interestingly, the cheerleaders failed to ask for an injunction against video distribution, so the film is still available to the persistent video aficionado.

Let's look at an example that you may remember. Almost every reference to *Animal House* declares it to be a satire on college fraternity life. The film depicts two freshmen attempting to join a fraternity. The students are turned away from the clean, elitist, predominantly Catholic and conservative Omegas and then try their luck at the Delta Tau Chi house. The Delta house party includes typical fraternity debauchery like broken bottles, urinating on people, and household items strewn across the front lawn. The freshmen are quickly accepted by Delta because the fraternity needs the money. The remainder of the film serves as a forum to comment on the fraternity culture and their rivalries. So, as you can see, the film did not need to borrow from a copyrighted work to make its point, but it definitely could have! The several lawsuits concerning this film did not address these issues. They mention it only as an archetypical example of satire.

Another, more recent case, involved the artist Jeff Koons. He was paid $1.6 million to create a series of paintings entitled the "Easyfun-Ethereal" for Germany's Deutsch Bank. He culled advertising images and his own photographs, scanning them into a computer and digitally superimposing the scanned images against backgrounds of pastoral landscapes to comment on the ways in which our most basic desires are depicted in popular images. In one particular instance, Koons scanned a photo by Andrea Blanch, titled "Silk Sandals by Gucci," which was, as the title suggests, a photo of a pair of woman's feet wearing Gucci sandals. Blanch had shot the photo for a Gucci ad. Koons incorporated part of the photo into his own artwork, which depicted four pairs of women's feet and lower legs dangling over images of various dessert dishes.

Blanch recognized her photo. She was not happy. She sued.

She lost.

The court explained the satire in detail by describing the social comment being made, rather than sticking the satire label on the painting. In fact, the court doesn't mention the word. The court focused on the first fair-use factor (the purpose and character of use), and said it weighed in favor of Koons' appropriation because the use of the photo was transformative and because its purpose was to demonstrate how advertising whetted our various appetites, not to sell shoes for Gucci. Koons used Blanch's work to comment on its social meaning rather than to exploit its creative virtues.

The court concluded that Koons used Blanch's photograph in a transformative manner to comment on its social meaning rather than to exploit its creative virtues. Koons wanted to "comment on the ways in which some of our most basic appetites for food, play, and sex are mediated by popular images." Doesn't this sound like the very definition of satire?

This wasn't the first time that Koons was sued for using someone else's work to create his own pricey pieces. In the previous cases, he did not fare so well because the courts did not totally buy in to his social commentary argument. I guess he learned how to present his point of view from those earlier cases.

Before the Blanch case, Koons directed the creation of a sculpture called "String of Puppies" based exactly on a photograph of puppies. Koons' work was an enlarged three-dimensional sculpture of the puppies painted in different colors. Aside from the size and color changes, the photograph and sculpture were essentially identical. Although Koons argued that he intended "to comment satirically upon contemporary values," the court stated that to qualify as fair use, the allegedly infringing work must comment or criticize the allegedly infringed underlying work. Confusing, right?

The main difference is when Koons used Blanch's photograph in "Niagara," the artwork was commenting on how that photograph, along with other popular images, mediates society's basic appetites for food, play, and sex. When Koons copied elements of the puppies photo to create "String of Puppies," the resulting piece did not comment on or criticize the original photo or any social norms in any way. That was obvious to the casual observer, which made it harder for him to argue convincingly that he was making some broader social commentary.

As you can see, using copyrighted works for satire under the fair use doctrine may be difficult to do, so please seek legal counsel before doing so. There is a fine line that can't be crossed, and it is always best to allow an expert to determine when you can and can't do so.

Flip back to the previous section about parodies and look at the case involving *Cat Not in the Hat*. You can see that book about the O.J. Simpson trial was clearly a satire. The lawyers didn't go there because the authors took way too much from the famous Dr. Seuss book to pass muster under a straight fair-use test. That is why they tried (unsuccessfully) to convince the court that *Cat Not in the Hat* was a parody.

THE CASE OF THE JOKE

Many of my clients tend to confuse parodies and satires with jokes. A **joke** is something that is said or done to evoke laughter or amusement. It can be a one-liner or an amusing story with a long-awaited punch line. A parody or satire does not have to be funny. The difference between a parody or satire on the one hand and jokes on the other is crucial, since jokes are not generally copyrightable whereas a parody is. I say "generally" since there are instances of a joke being copyrightable, but generally jokes are considered to be ideas, and copyright law only protects expressions of ideas fixed in tangible form.

So what about all of those comedians accusing each other of stealing jokes? In 2006, a group of comedians, including Jay Leno and Rita Rudner, filed a lawsuit claiming copyright infringement when a woman compiled jokes performed by the comedians into several books and sold them to the public. The court didn't have to decide this case because it settled, but the point of the matter is that comedians can be very protective of their work and they may have a valid claim, albeit tough to prove, if they can show that their jokes are expressions of ideas similar to an original literary work.

Foxworthy's Redneck Humor—A Case of Its Own

A custom T-shirt company produced a line of T-shirts bearing redneck jokes with lines like, "If you've ever financed a tattoo . . . you might be a redneck." Unfortunately, this was too similar for Jeff Foxworthy, who is known for his redneck humor. The only difference with his jokes and the jokes that appeared on the defendant's shirts was in its format. Foxworthy's jokes started with the redneck line—"You might be a redneck if . . . you've ever financed a tattoo."

The T-shirt company didn't deny the allegation that they duplicated the redneck jokes found in Foxworthy's books. Instead, they argued that Foxworthy's jokes were not original and, thus, he could not claim authorship. The court disagreed. It sided with Foxworthy, holding that he established that the jokes were not only his ideas, but his own expression, which the defendants copied verbatim.

There is very little case law that suggests jokes are copyrightable, and I haven't seen any case since Foxworthy which supports this concept. Nevertheless, it is important to note that they may be rare instances where a joke is indeed protected under the copyright law.

Most of the legal claims on jokes occur when someone really doesn't like to be made fun of. Most people don't want to be laughed at. But there is not much they can do about it. Chapter 13 deals with all the personal rights, but for the purposes of this present chapter, we will just look at them quickly. The personal rights are the right of privacy, the right not to be slandered, and the right not to be put in a false light. There is also the right of publicity. The over-arching reason that none of these rights are invaded is because no one is misled into thinking that the comic is making a statement of fact. The comic couldn't possibly be slandering someone or putting them in a false light if everyone who hears the joke understands that it is a joke rather than a statement of fact. No privacy is invaded if no facts about the person are revealed and since none of the content of a joke is taken as fact. The right of publicity is an individual's right to control the exploitation of his or her name and likeness, but Joe Blow can't object to a joke being told about him, unless there is a big sign outside that says, "Come on in. Tonight we are telling a lot of jokes about Joe Blow."

Note that the key in all of this is that the comment is intended to elicit a laugh (whether it does or not) and all the listeners understand the comment that way at the time that it is uttered. That is why it doesn't help at all when someone says, "I was just joking" after making a racial slur, a sexually inappropriate comment in the workplace, or a mocking comment aimed at someone's physical disability. No, no, no. Such comments have just landed the speaker in hot water, in spite of the attempted "save."

CHAPTER 4

PUBLIC DOMAIN

An old saying goes, "A little knowledge can be a dangerous thing." Many people seem to know just enough about public domain to be dangerous. **Public domain** literally means "owned by the public." No individual or corporation owns the copyright in the material, so they don't need to be asked to use it. As a member of the public, you are as free to use the material as anybody else. This chapter explains the concept and provides some contemporary examples to help you understand public domain and its best use in making your film.

WHAT IS PUBLIC DOMAIN?

Let's assume a work qualifies for protection under the copyright law. That is, it is original, created by an author, and has been reduced to a tangible form. How is it that some or all of such a work might still be in the public domain? The law says that there are five ways a property can become public domain:

1. Facts and events are already in the public domain. No one can "own" the date of an election, or the fact that the grass is green, or the fact that 2 + 2 = 4. BUT if you write about any of these facts in an original way, your

original writing is protected by copyright. If you hear or read an account of a true event, you can use the facts to your heart's content: You just can't use the other person's way of telling about those facts.

2. Very old works for which the copyright has expired are in the public domain. How old? Well, it is quite complicated because many factors come into play besides pure age, such as whether the work was published or not and where it was first published. But there is a safe harbor. If a work was created prior to 1923, it is in public domain. No doubt about it. However, a later translation or remake or recording of that work could still be well-protected by copyright. For instance, copyright might protect a revised edition of a book or a remake of a film.

3. Technical flaws are a big reason some works are in the public domain. Some works created and published before 1978 may have fallen into the public domain because they did not meet the formalities under the old U.S. Copyright Law or because application for term renewal was not timely filed.

4. Publications and other works created by employees of the United States government and its agencies, as part of their job, are in the public domain. The documents may be unavailable for your use because they are classified or because of privacy considerations, but they are still in the public domain.

5. **Abandonment** has always been a possibility. **Abandonment** in copyright law is not just leaving the rights unused and unattended for years, like a toy slowly rusting in the rain. It requires some clear, unequivocal, affirmative act by the copyright owner. I didn't bother to mention this in the first two editions because it was such a rare occurrence, having happened only a few times over the hundreds of years we have had a copyright law here in the U.S. I would not mention it in this third edition except for the fact that something akin to abandonment has been recently developed, and its popularity is growing.

At the same time that the clearance culture was demanding higher and higher prices for the use of the smallest snippet and the anti-piracy efforts were reaching new global and litigation heights, a movement was mushrooming to share works without paying fees and without having to ask permission. The one that has gained the most traction consisted of some licenses created by Creative Commons. They don't thrust works in the public domain, but sharing of otherwise protected works is encouraged and facilitated by these licenses, so they will be discussed in this chapter in a separate section below.

Remember that "familiar" does not mean public domain. "Rudolph the Red-Nosed Reindeer" is very familiar and has been around a long time, but the song and the Rudolph character are protected property. Should you try to use this classic character, born in a song, without permission, you will quickly be contacted by my former law partner Dixon Dern, who is Rudolph's lawyer.

Before you conclude that a work is in the public domain, you should purchase a copyright report. A **copyright report** is a detailed history of the work and related registered items. Unless the answer is obvious, you should review the copyright report with a lawyer to decide whether copyright protects the work or not. While you are free to search the records of the Copyright Office yourself, the task can be daunting. Such a search also omits reports published in the trade newspapers about the piece you are searching, which are included in private reports. The Copyright Office does not issue any such reports. It just records and organizes material that is submitted. Copyright reports can be obtained from the following companies:

Thomson CompuMark
1750 "K" Street N.W., Suite 200
Washington, DC 10006
(800) 356-8630
www.thomsoncompumark.com
dc_orders@t-t.com

Law Offices of Dennis Angel
1075 Central Park Avenue, Suite 306
Scarsdale, NY 10583
(914) 472-0820; (212) 239-4225
www.lawyers.com/dennisangellaw
dangelsq@aol.com

Even if a photo or a piece of film is in the public domain,
be careful. Chapter 13 discusses the rights of the people who
appear in public domain photos and film clips. Other elements
in a film clip, such as music, might also have protection. See a
lawyer before you spend a lot of money on a project that relies
on what you believe are public domain elements.

FACTS AND EVENTS

If you have an urge to buy life story-rights, it is generally because
of someone involved in an interesting and publicized story. The
facts of the story are in the press, and, as stated above, facts
are public domain. So, why do people devote so much time and
energy to buying these rights if everybody is free to use the
facts because they are not protected by copyright?

Even when something is in the public domain, it is often a
good idea to acquire an underlying property. It makes studios and
financiers feel more comfortable. You can sign a contract directly
with the person whose story you wish to tell, or you can purchase
the film rights to a book or magazine story about that person. The
reasons are severalfold. First, E&O Insurance (see Chapter 20) is
generally easier to obtain if you purchase such underlying rights.
The insurance companies feel that if the story was published,
and therefore available to the public and no lawsuit followed, it
is less likely that the film will draw a lawsuit.

The second advantage of buying underlying rights is that
the writer of such a story may very well have some juicy, hard-
to-find piece of information that was not used in the article
that they may share with you if you purchase the film rights

to the story. In fact, the person who lived the story always has such information. Simply put, you make a better movie with the participation of these people. Finally, it often helps to have a spokesperson for publicity purposes who is familiar with, or directly involved with, the subject, but is not a direct participant in making the film. Purchasing film rights from a person usually makes them available for such promotional purposes.

Also note: People possess rights of privacy and publicity that you cannot invade, and a right not to be put in a false light (as set forth in detail in Chapter 13). When you purchase someone's life-story rights, they waive the right to file a lawsuit based on a violation of those rights.

The Amy Fisher Story

One of the best examples of the interplay between public domain facts and life-story rights is the Amy Fisher story. You may recall that Amy Fisher was a 17-year-old girl who claimed to have had an affair with Joey Buttafuoco. Three different television networks made her story into three different movies. Here is the chronology:

May 19, 1992	Amy goes over to Joey's split-level house on Long Island with a gun. Joey's wife, Mary Jo Buttafuoco, answers the door and takes a bullet to the head.
May 20, 1992	The story is fast becoming the hottest tabloid tale of the moment.
June, 1992	NBC purchases the life-story rights of Amy Fisher. Tri-Star purchases the life-story rights of Mr. and Mrs. Buttafuoco. ABC purchases nothing: They rely on public domain material.
Dec. 1, 1992	Amy Fisher enters a plea bargain and is sent to jail for five to fifteen years.
Dec. 28, 1992	NBC airs *Amy Fisher: My Story*, starring Noelle Parker. This is the tale told through the eyes of Amy herself.

Jan. 3, 1993   ABC airs *Beyond Control: The Amy Fisher Story*, starring Drew Barrymore. They base it exclusively on public domain facts as they were reported in the transcripts of the trial and in the press.

Jan. 3, 1993   CBS airs *Casualties of Love: The Long Island Lolita Story*, starring Alyssa Milano. This is the Buttafuoco side of things.

As you might guess from the above, NBC portrayed Joey as an adulterous lover and portrayed Amy more kindly. CBS portrayed Joey as an innocent victim of Amy's obsession. ABC, relying on public domain material found in news accounts, didn't draw conclusions about who was right or wrong or good or evil. One thing is for sure: Amy shot Mary Jo and for that she sat in jail.

Astonishingly, each made-for-television movie was a genuine rating success. But ABC had the best ratings because they were able to hire Drew Barrymore with the money they saved on life-story rights.

Sensational Criminal Stories

This feeding frenzy raises two other issues about films based on sensational criminal activities. One is the "Son of Sam" statute passed in many states, including New York. The other issue is that your money may be better spent on stars or really good writers or directors for your film, rather than acquiring rights that are available to you through the judicious use of matters in the public domain.

The Son of Sam statute began in the State of New York in response to some hefty payments made to a notorious convicted murderer for his—you guessed it—life story rights. The public outcry demanded a legislative response. The idea was to prevent felons from selling their stories. However, the legislative response was not uniform among the states, partly because it is difficult to devise a scheme that survives constitutional scrutiny. The schemes generally apply only to persons who have been convicted. If you feel the urge to pay a felon for life-story rights, see a lawyer. At least you won't run afoul of the law. Personally, I have never and will never pay money to a felon for his or her story.

ABC's telling of the Amy Fisher tale garnered the highest rating of the three networks without buying any life story-rights. They saved their money and spent it on a star, Drew Barrymore. One of the hottest movies made for television was HBO's *The Positively True Adventures of the Alleged Texas Cheerleader-Murdering Mom*, starring Holly Hunter. That film was based on public domain matter, including a tape-recorded conversation with "Mom" that was originally taped for the police investigating Mom. The conversation was spoken verbatim by the actors in the film.

Events during the O.J. Simpson murder trial inspired the California Legislature to pass a related law. This one prohibits witnesses to a crime from selling their stories to the media before the end of the trial. That law has not been tested, but look for some court decisions, and look for the spread of this kind of statute throughout the country.

If you are creating a script based on facts that are in the public domain, be sure that you keep copies of all the research materials that support your script. Be sure that you have two sources for each factual assertion, (e.g., 8/8/89 interview with Joe Blow, court transcript of Jane Smith p. 7671). You cannot fictionalize any aspect of a person's life just because you have the right to portray the public domain facts about that person. (For information about people and their rights, read Chapter 13.)

If you are going to create this type of script, you should require the writer to prepare an annotated script. An **annotated script** has references to the various sources the writer relied on when writing the script. You annotate a script by inserting numbers directly on the factual assertions in the script. These numbers correspond to numbers arbitrarily assigned to the various sources used by the writer as the basis for the script. Members of the Writers Guild have the protection of some relatively new rules about annotated scripts. If you require a WGA member to submit an annotated script, you must inform the writer at the beginning of the assignment because it is a lot of extra work to save all the research in an orderly manner and then to go through and annotate a script. At the end of this chapter, there is an Annotation Guide for Scripts Based on Facts. You can attach it to the contract of any writer you hire to write the script for a film based on factual events.

Here is a good piece of news for those of you who are researching scripts based on facts. The author of the "true crime" books *Where Death Delights* sued the producers of the television series *Quincy* for infringement of the copyright of some fictional stories that the author wrote. Even though the stories were totally fictional, the author represented them to the reading public as true. Therefore, the reading public could treat them as true, putting the stories in the public domain.

In court, as a plaintiff, the author said that any reader should have known that the works were fiction because of their absurdity. The court held the author to his original representation of his stories as "true crime" stories. The moral is that you do not violate copyright law when you retell a story or a fact that you find in a book or article if the author of the book or article said that it was true. An author cannot promote a book as true and then claim that it is a work of fiction in order to pursue a lawsuit for copyright infringement when someone uses the story. This is true even when a typical reader would not necessarily view the contents of the book as plausible.

One case even involved stories supposedly told to the author by aliens from outer space. When the stories were copied, the courts found the representation on the jacket and in publicity about the book's truthfulness to be controlling; therefore, there was no copyright infringement. This is also true for "fictionalized" elements of biographies. The author of a biography of the actress Frances Farmer found that out when he sued the producers of the movie *Frances*. "Too bad" said the court. "You presented the book as true, so even the pseudo-facts are in the public domain." Of course, you should see a lawyer if you are planning a film based on material you did not purchase.

Facts—An Exception

One area that is particularly relevant to television producers is "hot news," although it has no relevance to someone involved in the longer, more leisurely, process of creating a documentary film, feature film, or other project with a less-pressured process. A hot news exception protects facts for a short period of time.

If a newsgathering agency spends resources and energy to gather fast-breaking news, the facts that it collects are protected from organizations who would like to piggyback on that effort, without spending the bucks to gather the news themselves. To cite a specific case, the International News Service was prohibited from taking factual information from Associated Press news articles and then reselling this information to its own subscribing newspapers. All of this falls in the area of unfair competition.

The National Basketball League tried to use the AP case to stop Motorola from sending out its sports scores to pager subscribers. The court said, "Oh, no, no, no." The NBA doesn't spend energy collecting this data. The scores and stats that result from NBA games are facts and, therefore, free for anybody to use. It was Motorola's team of fact-gatherers that did the work of collecting the data and sending it out to subscribers.

OLD PROPERTIES

If a tale like the Grimm brothers' *Snow White* is in the public domain, what rights must be acquired, and from whom, if you want to create your own Snow White? You could ask the same question for Mary Shelley's *Frankenstein* and many other books.

The Grimms' fairy tale *Snow White and the Seven Dwarfs* is in the public domain. Disney's copyright is in their film based on that book. The Disney copyright applies only to the items that Disney created independent of the underlying work. For instance, the Grimm brothers describe Snow White to the tiniest detail in the book, so she must have a certain appearance to be faithful to the book. It turns out that Disney's *Snow White* looks very much like the Grimm brothers described her. Disney added very little new to the Snow White character. The Grimms only describe the seven dwarfs in the book as seven "friends," and they are otherwise quite amorphous. These "friends" were not necessarily human or living and did not have names, sex, or a description of any kind. Disney owns the copyright on those dwarfs, their names, appearances, and personalities. In the book, the mirror itself is the talking beauty consultant. In Disney's film, it is the mirror frame that talks back to whomever listens. This is why Disney sued Lou Scheimer and Filmways when he created an animated film using some of those elements, but they did not sue Spike Jones for his humorous version of *Snow White* that used none of Disney's elements.

If you are creating something based on an old work in the public domain (such as Mary Shelley's *Frankenstein*), be sure you go back to that work to create your derivative work. Universal is very protective of the cinematic *Frankenstein* they created many years ago. Several elements in Universal's creation are quite different from Shelley's original physical description. Shelley wrote about skin stretched tight over the bone structure, thin black lips, and extended arms. Universal's distinctive bolt through the neck, the flat head, the jacket that does not fit, the visible stitching of the skin, and other elements—when taken together—create a distinctive, protected character. Universal is very aggressive in protecting its copyright, but you are free to create your own monster based on Shelley's work. Shelley's *Frankenstein* is in the public domain all over the world because it was created in the 19th Century. Kenneth Branagh held close to the original book in his film *Mary Shelley's Frankenstein*, which protected him from any claims by Universal.

Technical Flaws

Before 1978, the copyright term had a life divided into two parts. The first part was 28 years long. After 28 years, copyrights had to be properly and timely renewed or the work would fall in the pubic domain. As you know from Chapter 1, you don't need any formalities today. Copyright attaches as soon as an original work is created in tangible form.

Determining if and when a work was **published** can be quite tricky. A work is **published** when copies of the work are distributed to the public via sale, lease, or other ownership transfer. Publication also occurs when copies are offered to a group of persons for the purpose of further distribution, when copies are distributed to a group of persons for public performance, or when an authorized offer is made to transfer any of the ownership rights. A song is not published when it is sung, a film is not published when it is shown at a festival, and a play is not published when it is performed. Digital transfers via the Internet are considered a form of publication. However, note that publication typically requires the author's consent.

For works protected by foreign copyright, the length of the copyright can be an exotic search of a crosspatch of laws. A foreign work no longer must meet these formalities of notice and renewal for works created before 1978 and first published after March 1, 1989, in order to have copyright protection in the U.S. See a lawyer if you have a question that falls in this area.

When a picture or the screenplay that it incorporates falls into the public domain, anybody is free to make a derivative work from either one. This is true of any public domain work. Courts have held that each of the following methods of creating new works that are derivative of existing public-domain films can produce a copyrightable property. However, the new elements are protected by copyright. The public domain film is still in the public domain, but, as you can see, the following techniques created a new, protected, highly exploitable film:

1. A colorized version of a black-and-white film. Ted Turner gained protection for his colorized versions of a number of classics, including *Asphalt Jungle*.

2. A new version of a public domain motion picture can be newly registered and protected by copyright when you pan and scan the public domain version. **Pan and scan** refers to the process by which motion pictures are adapted from the wide-screen theater format to a narrower format fitting on the old-style television screens. Pan and scan shows only a portion of the original film frame. The heirs of John Wayne won a summary judgment on this issue (without a trial) when they sued UAV for infringing the copyright of their derivative version of their dad's 1963 film, *McLintock!* Note that anybody can pan and scan a film, and, for better or worse, the pan-and-scan copy is protected. Note also that if you try to register a pan-and-scan film, be sure to identify the new film as a pan-and-scan version, because a mere change in format is not copyrightable. If the Copyright Office cannot tell from your application whether your new version is copyrightable, correspondence will ensue that can chew up a lot of time.

3. One can always redo the soundtrack with new music or obtain exclusive rights to the music in the film instead of the usual non-exclusive rights that are traditional for film music. In the case of *McLintock!*, the heirs were successful in obtaining copyright protection after they digitized the soundtrack of the 1963 movie, remixed it, stereoized (the court's word, not mine) the previously monaural sound, and upgraded its quality. The court said that all of this added up to a "creative mixing and balancing of sounds."

Government Properties

Any document created by a government employee while working for the government is in the public domain because the employer is the government, which means that the public owns the document.

But not every government document was created by a government employee. It is not uncommon for the government, at any level, to contract out for services. Before you incorporate a government document or property into your work, be sure that you're dealing with a government document that was prepared by a government employee during the course and scope of his or her employment. Once you have made such a determination, you may use the document without worry, unless it is classified or otherwise protected.

The array of government documents that are available to you is truly bewildering. Documentary filmmakers have long enjoyed the use of clips from films created for the government by government employees.

Creative Commons

In the '80s and '90s, gatekeepers became more and more insistent that filmmakers and authors obtain written permission for every scrap of material they used in their works, whether the law required such clearance or not. This "clearance culture" spawned rising prices for clips, music, photos, and anything else you might need or want from a creative point of view.

To paraphrase Sir Isaac Newton, "For every action, there is a reaction."

Sure enough, in response to the clearance culture, various movements have recently risen to promote the freer exchange of creative material than allowed by the copyright law. The granddaddy of these movements and the strongest survivor is Creative Commons. They have created six different licenses that an author can use to make his or her materials more freely accessible to others. Each of the licenses grants certain rights to use material without seeking written permission. But certain restrictions apply.

These licenses are loaded with legalese. One would expect that a license birthed from a populist movement might have been written in plain English. Obviously, you should have your lawyer review the license before you use it to acquire material or before you apply it to your own creation. First we will discuss whether you want to use a work that carries with it a Creative Commons license.

If you have found a photo or clip or something else that you would like to incorporate into your film or book, and it has a Creative Commons license, here is what you do. Read the title of the license. Four of them contain the words "non-commercial" or "no derivatives" or both. Stay away from them. "Non-commercial" means just what it says in many, many more words in the body of the license. This license does not allow any commercial exploitation of the work you are creating if it includes one of these Creative Commons licenses. Forget it. If you are reading this book, you are smart enough to want the option of commercially exploiting your work. "No derivatives" mean that you cannot create a derivative work, and they define that a bit more broadly than most people. The license says that if you incorporate the item into a film or book, you are creating a derivative work, which—for the purposes of this license—is a no-no.

That leaves two remaining licenses. They are entitled Attribution 3.0 U.S. and Attribution Share Alike 3.0." At least those are the titles at the time of this writing. Stay away from the Attribution Share Alike 3.0" license. Very far away. This license says that you will let others use your creation on the same basis that you are obtaining their license. No film distributor or book publisher is going to work with you if you allow others to freely use your work on this basis. At least I don't know of any at the time of this writing. Selling your work is going to be problematic when people can get it for free. If you have commercial aspirations for your project, don't use this license, even if your own view of social justice and the higher good make you want a world where everything is shared between loving people who are focused on helping their fellow humankind.

That leaves us with Attribution 3.0 U.S. Basically, it allows you to use the item you want as long as you identify the source and spell out that it is being used pursuant to this particular Creative Commons license. It does not require you to allow others to use your work in the same way. Pretty cool. And there are folks who have put this license on photos and other works. Good for them. Even better for you. But the license is not without its drawbacks.

There is one great, big stumbling block. The license says that you may not use a digital-rights management system (or DRM) on your work, if you use this license. (This stipulation is in all Creative Commons licenses.) DRMs are the digital locks that distributors put on DVDs so that no one can copy them. Under a new law that was passed in the '90s called the Digital Millennium Copyright Act (DMCA), it is a crime to break these locks even to copy public domain material that might be on the DVD, although Professor Jennifer Urban and other scholars doubt that provision would withstand a robust challenge in court. Your grandmother could break these locks with a wink of her eye, but the penalties for doing so are mighty scary. Most distributors want to use these locks on their DVDs, so using any Creative Commons license could be an impediment to your getting a DVD deal. At a minimum, it will raise an issue for discussion. If you are distributing yourself over the Internet, this license is fine.

Having said all the above, we turn to which of the Creative Commons license you would put on your project if you were inclined to let others use it to its maximum effectiveness. The first ones discussed yield the least amount of copyright ground to a subsequent user. The last one discussed yields the most copyright ground to someone who incorporates your work into theirs. Which one you choose is a function of your own personal worldview. If your vision for the work you just created includes commercial exploitation, have your lawyer review the agreement first.

Orphan Works

An **Orphan Work** is any work for which you can't find the legitimate owner after you have made a substantial search. You really want to use that special photo in your book or that terrific clip in your documentary or that snippet of music in your film and you are willing to pay for it, but you just can't find the owner. This situation has been the nemesis of the creative community for generations.

A lot of people confuse orphan works with works in the public domain or with fair use. Orphan works present a very different problem from either public domain or fair use.

Under the copyright law as it has existed for more than 200 years and as it existed at the time of this writing, it is not safe to use an orphan work, no matter how hard you tried to find the owner. If the owner later appears and files a claim against you, he or she has the right to all the remedies that any other copyright owner has: injunction, damages, and the ability to tie up you and your film for a very long time in court. This is not a parade of imaginary horribles. This is the law as it has been in this country since the copyright law was first passed.

Relief is in sight.

Senators Leahy and Hatch saw the problem. They understand the problem. As the leaders of the Senate Committee that oversees copyright legislation, they had the Copyright Office study the problem and proposed The Orphan Works bill to correct this situation for members of the creative community who want to use true orphan works. I say "true" orphan works, because you cannot give a wink and a nod to the effort of finding the owner. But if you have made a substantial effort and you still cannot find the owner, you have a "true" orphan work. I (and a lot of other people) think you ought to be able to use such works and if the owner shows up later, his or her remedies ought to be limited.

The pending legislation says that if the owner of an orphan work shows up after you have already used the work, they are owed a reasonable license fee, but the more draconian remedies available to copyright owners are eliminated. Various stakeholders are weighing in on exactly what the remedies should be. The details keep changing. Progress is glacial. But progress there is and relief is truly in sight.

As this legislation moves through Congress, there are a few things that you should know. You will have to make a substantial search for the owner in order to come within the protection of the Orphan Works bill.

You can't just rely on someone else's search.

You have to keep a written record of your search.

You may have to file your search with some third party as future evidence of its authenticity.

Progress on this legislation will be regularly posted on the website for this book, and it will not require the special codes that give you access to the forms in this book. Just go to www .clearanceandcopyright.com and you will be able to find out the status of this legislation. In the meantime, understand the risks you are taking when you use an orphan work. Coverage under your E&O policy can sometimes be negotiated with the insurance companies, but the results are most uneven.

The biggest issue being debated around orphan works at the time of this writing is the knottiest of them all: What constitutes such a substantial search that you are justified in putting the label of orphan works on any particular item?

Whether a search qualifies as substantial will be different for each and every project. Different techniques for finding owners of films are discussed in Chapter 18 (Clearing Film Clips). Various search tools are given in that chapter. How many of the tools you would need to use in any particular case would be a function of what you discovered along the way, the budget of your project (a James Bond picture should make a greater effort than a low-budget documentary), the nature of the work you are seeking to identify (a home movie and a known studio film would require different efforts), and other factors unique to your project. If you find yourself in orphan work land, you should check with a professional before locking picture.

RECAPTURE

Taking steps that have the practical effect of recapturing works from the public domain is an interesting area. Everyone knows of the enormous potential value in the monopoly granted by the law of copyright. Millions of dollars hang in the lawful ownership of the copyright to the most inane creations. As mentioned above, prior to 1978, some creations fell into the public domain in the U.S. through an inadvertent noncompliance with the old technical requirements. The new Copyright Act provides for the recapture of certain foreign creations that failed to meet these technical requirements. The feeling in Congress was that some foreign owners were unfairly penalized because they were unaware of the technicalities of U.S. law. Shrewd lawyers often work to come up with schemes that give their clients similar control over the use of their film, even if they do not give the clients the copyright itself.

The company controlling the name and likeness of the Three Stooges tried to exercise copyright-like control over their old public domain films by asserting that people who wanted to use clips from those films had to pay for use of the name and likeness of the Three Stooges. In fact, the company convinced most of the studios to pay up. They had a pretty good deal going. But New Line went ahead and used a clip from a Three Stooges movie, playing it on a television in the background of a scene in the feature film *The Long Kiss Goodnight*. The jig was up. The court said that as long as the clip from the public domain film was used purely as a clip, then the owners of the Three Stooges could not block the use of their name and likeness.

Images of the Three Stooges on T-shirts, mugs, and other items would produce a different result, but the clips could be used—as clips—without payment of any sort. That's why some of the actors on *Cheers* sued the folks who bought the rights from the producers of *Cheers* to build bars in airports that looked like the *Cheers* set. These bars' use of big dolls that looked like the actors implied an endorsement of the airport bar by the actors. And similar non-copyright considerations allowed the illustrator of the public domain Peter Rabbit books to sue when those famous illustrations were redrawn, photographically reproduced, and used in a manner different from how they appeared in the original work. The court found that the illustrator's trademark in the character illustrations had been infringed, even though the books themselves are in the public domain.

Documentary filmmakers frequently pay archives for the privilege of using clips from public domain films. The reason they pay a fee is for the archive's time and trouble. It costs the archive money to store the films and to service a request for a clip from the film. It also costs money to catalog the various shots in the films so that you can find them easily. So you can expect to continue paying for clips from archives, even if the film from which the clip comes is in the public domain.

With domestic films, there are ways to "recapture" something very similar to the copyright, even if the film itself is in public domain. Consider *It's a Wonderful Life*. That classic film, starring Jimmy Stewart and my longtime client Donna Reed, was seen nonstop during the Christmas season because it was in the public domain. However, the music was not in the public domain. Films contain music that has a separate copyright and a separate ownership. *It's a Wonderful Life* contains a considerable amount of pre-existing music, licensed for use in the film. Though the film itself fell into the public domain, the music was still protected. A team of very clever copyright specialists contacted the copyright holders of some of the music in the film and made exclusive licensing deals with them. That act provided the working equivalent of a copyright recapture for

It's a Wonderful Life through the music contained in the film. Chapter 16 explains how that recapture happened.

BEWARE OF SHORTCUTS

Beware of lists that claim to set forth works that are in the public domain. Beware of people who claim that the copyright for a master recording or the photo they want to sell you is in the public domain if they do not provide carefully documented proof. Take the information they provide to an experienced copyright lawyer. You may want to buy your own copyright report. The question of whether a given work is in the public domain can occasionally be cut and dry, but it is more often than not a sophisticated and entangled question for which you should receive the best possible advice.

There are many twists and turns. For instance, being in the public domain in one country does not mean that a work is in the public domain in all countries. The laws of various countries are becoming more homogenized, and the countries without any copyright law are virtually nonexistent today. Nevertheless, there is still a large variation around the world. For instance, Peter Pan is in the public domain in the United States due to its age. However, the Parliament of Great Britain has given it special status so that it has permanent copyright protection. Therefore, Steven Spielberg had to make peace with the Great Ormond Street Children's Hospital in London, which owns the copyright to *Peter Pan*, before he could distribute the film *Hook* (which is clearly a derivative of *Peter Pan*) in Great Britain.

4.01 ANNOTATION GUIDE FOR SCRIPTS BASED ON FACTS

Annotated scripts should contain for each script element, whether an event, setting, or section of dialogue within a scene, notes in the margin that provide the following information:

1. Whether the element presents or portrays:

    a) Fact, in which case the note should indicate whether the person or entity is real; with respect to a person, whether (s) he is alive; and, with respect to all of the foregoing, whether a signed release has been obtained

    b) Fiction, but a product of inference from fact, in which case the information described in 1.(a) should be provided; or

    c) Fiction, not based on fact

2. Source material for the element:

    a) Book

    b) Newspaper or magazine article

    c) Recorded interview

    d) Trial or deposition transcript

    e) Any other source

NOTE: Source material identification should give the name of the source, page reference (if any), and date (e.g., *The New Yorker* article, page 27, August 1, 1988). To the extent possible, identify multiple sources for each element. Retain copies of all materials, preferably cross-indexed by reference to script page and scene numbers. Coding may be useful to avoid repeated, lengthy references.

Descriptive annotation notes are helpful (e.g., setting is hotel suite because John Doe usually had business meetings in his hotel suite when visiting L.A., *New York Times*, Section 1, page 8, April 1, 1981).

CHAPTER 5

CHARACTERS AND COSTUMES

Frequently, an identifiable and sometimes valuable character lies within the underlying properties and the films that are produced based on these works. The law defining what constitutes a protectable character and actually protecting it can be quite muddy. In this chapter we'll try and clear it up as best as one can, given the murky state of the law. We will also talk about costumes in this chapter because you will want to put them on the characters in your film, and they may help identify protected characters. Besides, where else would we put that subject in this book?

TWO TYPES OF CHARACTERS

Character copyrights are muddy because the courts have not always distinguished clearly between two different kinds of characters. This book and some articles are beginning to point out the distinction between these distinctly different kinds of characters: visual characters and story characters. We'll start with visual characters because they are easier to understand for you and me and judges who write decisions in cases involving these characters. We will then move on to the characters who are defined by the story they are in because story characters are more difficult for the courts and for you and me.

VISUAL CHARACTERS

Visual characters usually start out as drawings. That's why some legal commentators refer to them as **drawn characters.** When that is the case, they are not so much characters as copyrighted drawings, figures, or images. Visual characters can also be described in words as long as their descriptions are so detailed and vivid that they substitute for drawings.

The most famous of these characters are highly profitable: Mickey Mouse, Superman, E.T., and Freddy Krueger—they would be recognizable in any context. You see them at an amusement park, on a magazine page, or in the theater and you know who they are. These characters each have a persona that the owners want to protect, and the owners get very upset with any misappropriation of their property.

Well-known visual characters are rarely available to independent filmmakers for use in their projects. They are widely licensed for use on merchandise that generates a royalty payment to the copyright holder pursuant to a written agreement that contains quality-control provisions. If you as a producer want to hire an artist to help you create a new visual character of your own, be sure to have that done pursuant to a work-for-hire agreement. A good example of a work-for-hire agreement with an explanation of its terms is found at the end of Chapter 7. If you are an artist or writer, creating your own character, you may want to make a drawing or gather the written description together and register them with the Writers Guild (see Chapter 11) to establish the fact that you created this character on a certain date.

A visual character may appear many different times in many different stories without diluting the character in any way. Having a story or a plot is not necessary for the character to be recognizable. The strongest visual characters can be printed on a mug or baseball hat and are still recognizable. The facial and bodily characteristics are the physical embodiment of that character.

A Nightmare of a Case

DJ Jazzy Jeff and the Fresh Prince can tell you all about it. In 1988, they put out an album that contained a song entitled *A Nightmare on My Street.* The album was an immediate hit, and MTV loved the song and wanted to make a music video to play on their channel. Meanwhile, New Line Cinema was getting ready to put out a fourth installment of the *Nightmare on Elm Street* series starring the ever-popular character of Freddy Krueger. The parties tried to come to an arrangement so that DJ Jazzy Jeff and the Fresh Prince could use Freddy Krueger in their video to cross-promote their album with the upcoming movie, but the artists wanted too much money, and New Line decided to go with a different rap group.

Jazzy Jeff and the Fresh Prince decided to go ahead and make their video anyway, with a character who looked a lot like Freddy Krueger. He had burnt skin, and a low, raspy, threatening voice; and a gloved hand with sharp implements protruding from the fingers. He appears in DJ Jazzy Jeff's dream and then becomes real to chase after people, just as Freddy Krueger does in *The Nightmare* films.

New Line decided they needed to stop this video from being shown because it infringed on their copyright of Freddy Krueger as a character, separate and apart from any story.

They sued for a preliminary injunction.

They won.

The court decided that the character of Freddy Krueger was sufficiently delineated to be copyrighted apart from the movies in which he appeared. His character traits—burnt skin, and the sharp objects coming off his gloved hand, and the method he uses to kill people (inhabiting their dreams and then becoming real)—were specific enough to give Freddy a copyright of his own. The court then decided that the villain in the music video was substantially similar to Freddy Krueger. They granted the preliminary injunction.

Freddy single-handedly took care of his infringers, and they were barred from showing the video to the public.

Initially, we are not surprised by this outcome. Freddy Krueger is an immensely popular character, and merchandising rights to his name and likeness are worth millions of dollars per year. His character has been established over several years and several films. Face off against Freddy Krueger? No way. Of course the courts were going to side with him.

Rocky Prevails

A similar thing happened to a writer named Timothy Anderson. Anderson liked the first three *Rocky* movies so much that he decided to write a fourth one himself, without permission from the rights-holders of the first three movies. He came up with a 31-page treatment, and even got as far as pitching it to MGM. He never heard anything back, but one day saw Sylvester Stallone discussing his plans for a fourth *Rocky* movie on national television. Even Anderson's friends called him, telling him that Stallone was talking about Anderson's story on TV. Anderson didn't think it was fair that he was not compensated for his story treatment, and decided to do something about it.

He sued.

He lost.

The court first looked at the various characters involved in *Rocky*. They had been well-developed over the course of the first three movies—not just Rocky, but Adrian, Apollo Creed, Clubber Lang, and Paulie, too. Rocky himself is so well-delineated that his name is the title for all four movies, and his character has become identified with specific traits ranging from speech mannerisms to physical characteristics. The court decided that the group of main characters taken as a whole is protected by copyright, and that Rocky taken alone would also be protected by copyright. Moving on to the second part of the test, they ruled that the fourth movie was not substantially similar to Anderson's treatment. Thus, Rocky and his fellow characters were protected by copyright, and Anderson loses his case because he did not have permission to use them from the copyright holder.

As if that wasn't enough, the court then moved on to analyze Rocky as a story character. They thought that the focus of these movies was the characters—their development and relationships with the other characters. The movies were not focused around intricate plots or storylines. Thus, the characters were protected no matter how you looked at them.

Since Anderson did not receive permission to use the copyrighted characters, his work was infringing on the character copyrights held by Stallone. Accordingly, his treatment was copyright infringement, meaning Anderson was left without any copyright in the treatment. And without a valid copyright, you cannot sue if someone else infringes on your work. Even though Rocky wasn't the underdog in this fight, he still delivered a knockout blow, and Anderson got nothing for his troubles but a large legal bill.

Now You See It, Now You Don't

On the other hand, not all visual characters are protected by copyright. They also have to be sufficiently original—that is, distinctive—to qualify for copyright protection. Robert Rice learned that the hard way. Back in 1986, Rice created a home video entitled *The Mystery Magician*, in which an unknown magician performed magic tricks while wearing a mask, and then informed viewers of the "trick" behind the trick, revealing how to perform several well-known magic tricks and illusions. Over the next 13 years, about 17,000 copies of the video were sold around the world.

Then toward the end of 1997, and continuing through 1998, Fox Broadcasting Company aired a series of specials featuring a masked magician who revealed the secrets behind famous magic illusions.

Rice thought the specials bore an uncanny resemblance to his video, and the masked magician seemed an awful lot like the one he created in 1986.

He sued.

He lost.

The court looked at Rice's magician. He wore standard magician garb—black tuxedo, white shirt, black bow tie, and a black cape with red lining. His role was limited to performing and revealing magic tricks. He had only appeared in one video that sold 17,000 copies. The court did not think the magician was distinct from a lot of other magicians, except for a mask, and that wasn't enough for this particular magician to be copyrightable.

So Rice tried to argue that the magician was defined by the story. He claimed the video was all about this "renegade magician" risking his career by revealing secrets of the trade. The court did not like this, either. The real story, they said, concerns the public dissemination of secrets behind famous tricks and illusions. All the magician does is perform the tricks and do a few voice-overs explaining how they are done. For the lawyers reading this book, you will see the court used different language to describe what it was doing. We will touch on the court's language in a section later on in this chapter.

Furthermore, the court pointed out, any similarities between the magician in the video and the one on television are generic and common to all magicians. There are only a few ways to express a magician revealing magic secrets while disguising his identity, and Rice cannot claim protection from the use of a mask to disguise a magician's identity. That would be entirely too broad and unfair to others.

STORY CHARACTERS

Story characters are first created in works of literature. Typical examples are two characters created in books a century apart: Frankenstein and James Bond. Dialogue, plot, and interaction with other characters define these characters. Various actors have played these two roles over the years. In spite of the different physical attributes of the actors, the characters are the same. Physical appearance is rarely at the heart of a story character.

That being said, literary characters that have been subsequently visually depicted (like James Bond) are much more likely to gain copyright protection than a strictly literary character. Courts find it easier to see the unique expression necessary for copyright in a visually depicted character than in one that is only depicted on the page.

James Bond Always Wins

Honda found out about story characters the hard way. In 1994 they decided they wanted to sex up the image of the sporty little two-seater they called the del Sol. They created a terrific television commercial. Picture it: A handsome dark-haired man with his gorgeous female companion in their finest clothes cruise along in the twilight. A helicopter drops down behind them in full pursuit. A man with metal-encased arms jumps from the helicopter onto the top of the moving car. The driver looks coolly at his companion while the villain viciously tries to claw his way into the car from above. Our hero reaches over and calmly releases the car's detachable roof, dispensing the villain and the roof with a flick of the wrist and speeding safely off into the night with his lovely lady friend.

Honda loved the commercial. They loved it so much they decided to air it during the 1995 Super Bowl.

MGM, however, seemed to think that the television ad drove a little too close to James Bond, one of the most lucrative franchises in motion picture history.

They sued.

They won.

The court said Honda had illegally copied the James Bond character and were infringing on MGM's copyright. The court looked at the case in two different ways. First, they said that the character of James Bond was protected, separate and apart from the movies themselves, because people went to each Bond movie to see the character himself, not to see the storyline unfold. Second, the court said that James Bond is copyrighted because his character is fully developed and especially distinctive.

The court ruled that Honda's hero was a copy of Bond, and they were using him to sell cars. Britain's most famous secret agent triumphed yet again, and Honda was forced to pull the commercial off the air. Again, the courts usually use a slightly different way to explain all of this. We will get to the courts approach shortly.

For me, it violated my "too cute" rule. The Honda people must have known exactly what they were doing. Why didn't they dream up their own hunk to sell the del Sol? That's the Donaldson test. Don't trade off other people's hard work. Create your own characters. And try not to face off against James Bond, because you know he always wins in the end!

Character Doesn't Have to be Visually Depicted to Get Copyright

Although it is much more difficult to copyright a character who is strictly represented in literary form, it is possible. The iconic cowboy character of Hopalong Cassidy appeared in 26 different novels before being turned into a film character. In a later court battle over television rights, the court ruled that certain characters in the books were sufficiently delineated to be copyrightable, even without any film appearances taken into account. Another court ruled that the long-standing radio characters of Amos and Andy were sufficiently delineated in the original radio scripts to be copyrightable at that time, before they were turned into television fare and given visual representations.

It requires a substantial amount of literary material to gain copyright in a literary character apart from the works the character appears in. The threshold may be lower than requiring that a character appear in dozens of novels or years worth of radio scripts, but is certainly higher than what is needed for a drawn comic book or cartoon character to gain protection. Superman provides a terrific example of the ease that a drawn character has in gaining copyright protection versus the difficulty that a story character has—even if it is the same character! In finding that the comic book character of Wonderman was a rip-off of Superman, the court compared the strength and speed of the characters, their costumes, their mutual abilities to stop bullets and leap from building to building, and their goals of battling against "evil and injustice." The court ruled that the Superman drawn character "embodied an arrangement of incidents and literary expressions original with the author that could be properly copyrighted."

If this subject of characters is of special interest to you, you might want to refer back to Chapter 4 on Public Domain to read about Frankenstein and Snow White. Frankenstein is in the public domain but is ill defined in the initial writing. Universal owns the specific rendition of that character as depicted in their films. Snow White is in the public domain and very well-defined by the Brothers Grimm, so all Disney owns is their contribution to the story such as the seven dwarts. Still, it is a good idea to follow the tips below when you want to use any literary characters for a film. It is always better to spend a little time and money now to cover your bases than to risk losing your rights altogether (and incurring substantial legal fees while you are at it).

Tips for Dealing With Story Characters

Often, a series of books based on a character, such as Sherlock Holmes, exists before you become interested in the character. In that case, you should obtain an option on the entire series if possible. If that is not possible, arrange a **holdback period** and

right of first negotiation with regard to those other books or articles in which the character appears. A **holdback period** is a period of time during which the other party will not do something because you don't want the competition. In this case, it would be a period of time in which the owner of the character doesn't let anyone else develop a film for a certain period of time so that you can get your movie off the ground. A **right of first negotiation** means that if the owner of the right plans to sell it to anyone, he or she has to first negotiate in good faith with you. It is generally tied to a **right of last refusal.** A **right of last refusal** means that if you don't reach agreement during the negotiation you have as a result of your right of first negotiation and the owner eventually is ready to make a deal on better terms than you offered, he or she has to come back to you and give you a very short time to make a deal on those revised terms. That protects you from somebody insisting on tough terms with you and then giving the project to someone else on much better terms.

To obtain rights to a story character from a story, book, or article, you must option and purchase the entire work because this type of character is defined by dialogue, plot, and character interactions. It is not recognizable without these defining elements. If you option the film rights in someone else's property, be sure that you have optioned the film rights in the characters in that property. You will be well served to have your agreement state explicitly that you have the right to use the characters in future movies. Central characters often become the focus of a franchise. In the film business, a **franchise** is a character, concept, or title that is supposed to guarantee a good opening weekend for a film. It is the brass ring that everyone is reaching for. A franchise in the movie business is the most valuable thing you can possibly control. James Bond is the most lucrative box-office franchise character in the history of film.

If your work provides so much of the physical conception of a character that you think you have created a distinctive work, create a drawing of the character and register it with the Copyright Office using Form PA in this book.

TWO WAYS OF LOOKING AT THINGS

There are two main tests that the courts use to determine whether or not a specific character is protected by copyright separate and apart from any copyrighted story or film in which they may appear.

The first and currently most favored is the **character delineation** test. First, the court looks at whether the expression of the original character is sufficiently delineated to be copyrightable. Then they ask if the expression of the allegedly infringing character is substantially similar to that of the original character. This test is as confusing to judges as it probably is to you. In essence, it has charged judges with the responsibility of subjectively determining each case individually. In reality, things like popularity and longevity of a character have a lot of influence in the outcome. The more people know of the character, and the more copyrighted works the character has appeared in, the more likely the character will be copyrighted apart from those works.

The second test is the **story being told** test. It is used less than the character delineation test, but some courts will still take it into consideration. If the character in question constitutes the "story being told," rather than just being a vehicle through which to tell the story, then the character is protected by copyright. At first, this might seem to limit protection to characters in stories that are essentially character studies, where the work is all about the character and has very little plot to speak of. In reality, courts have been more liberal in applying this test. Similar factors as the character delineation test come into play, like popularity and/or longevity of a character. In practice, this test more suitably becomes a question of whether audiences seek out a work specifically to see the particular character in action, or whether they go more because of the underlying plot.

COSTUMES

You have seen how costumes might help define a character for purposes of copyright in some of the examples above. This short section deals with costumes that you might want to put on your characters in a film. I couldn't find a case directly on point; however, there are general principles to be applied.

The question of clearance for the clothing you purchase to use in your film arises in three possible situations: the manufacturer's or designer's logos, copyright material appearing on clothing (mostly T-shirts), and seeing either one of these in scenes that might discredit the logo. Sadly, nervous (usually fairly low-level) producer types—drive costumers crazy with a blanket rule that no clothing can bear a logo or image that could be susceptible of copyright protection. These seem a bit extreme to costumers and certainly raises the bar higher than a court is likely to. In discussions with insurance companies, I have determined that their legal departments tend to agree with the following general observations, which—at this point—are just my own professional opinion.

If a logo of the manufacturer or designer appears on a piece of clothing, a court should have no problem with that as long as the clothing was being used in the manner in which it was intended to be used. Chapter 14 on Trademarks explains all of this in detail. That chapter also explains why you should think twice about prominently displaying such logos if the character is a heinous slasher of little children.

When artwork appears on clothing in a film, the same rules should apply, even though the law of copyright instead of the law of trademark is the source of such rules. This would be especially true if the film in question is a documentary. A documentary filmmaker should not alter reality by requesting someone to change their clothing for fear that the picture on the front of the T-shirt or the back of a jacket is a picture protected by copyright. In a fictional film, the use of such clothing helps define the character and should be permissible, but we have not found a case to confirm that position which itself is a piece of information that should give you comfort.

Court cases regarding the fair use of costumes do not come up often. But, Ted Giannoulas was an exception to that statement. He debuted as the mascot-like character The Chicken in the '70s at many professional sporting events. The Chicken became a national celebrity and performed all over the world. Ted decided to change it up a bit by adding a Barney character to his routine. His Barney costume was quite similar to the real Barney. It featured a rounded purple body with an oversized head. The Chicken and Ted's "Barney" participated in a dance-off. Barney, with his happy demeanor, tries to pick up some moves from The Chicken but then reverts to his characteristic fairylike dancing. The Chicken continues teaching Barney, who finally picks up some cool moves and out-dances The Chicken. This results in the ultimate smack-down by The Chicken of the fraudulent Barney, who is pushed, slapped, sacked, and flipped.

The owner of the Barney trademark, which included the costume, was quite upset.

They sued.

They lost.

The court stated that the whole act was a parody. Despite the obvious similarities between the defendant's Barney costume and the actual Barney costume, the court found that the new costume was a transformative work through its comic effect and ridicule of Barney. The costume was used simply to recognize the character (which is necessary for a parody) and then the act ridiculed the character once it was recognized.

Ted's victory was slim payback for the time, effort, energy, and money that it takes to fight a lawsuit. Be careful whom you ridicule, even though the law may ultimately be on your side.

PART II

GETTING A COMPLETED SCRIPT

There are only four ways to obtain a script:

Write it alone

Hire someone else to write it

Write it with someone else

Buy a completed script

Of course, you could steal it, but if that is your plan, why would you be reading this book?

CHAPTER 6 — **ACQUIRING RIGHTS TO EXISTING PROPERTY (INCLUDING LIFE-STORY RIGHTS AND RELEASES)**

CHAPTER 7 — **HIRING A SCRIPTWRITER—WORK FOR HIRE**

CHAPTER 8 — **WRITING WITH A PARTNER**

CHAPTER 9 — **BUYING SOMEONE ELSE'S COMPLETED SCRIPT**

CHAPTER 10 —**PROVISIONS COMMON TO MOST AGREEMENTS**

CHAPTER 11 —**REGISTERING COPYRIGHT OF THE SCRIPT**

ACQUIRING THE RIGHTS TO SOMEONE ELSE'S PROPERTY

Producers are often inspired to make a film after they have read a book or seen a play or been exposed to some other kind of property, including an old movie. They say to themselves, "Wow, that would make a great movie." Many times that thought is followed with the thought: "... and I'm the right person to make it." To do so, you will have to obtain the right to make the movie from the person or company that created the film or play or book or other item of inspiration.

WHAT RIGHTS TO ACQUIRE

Each property mentioned above is known as an underlying property. An **underlying property** is the source material used as the basis for a script that is not wholly original with the author. **Underlying rights** are the foundational rights that you must control in order to have the right to make and distribute a film based on a previously existing property. Underlying property refers

111

to the book or play or story or life rights or previous film upon which a later film is based.

All of the rights you need to make and exploit a film are called film rights or motion picture rights. **Film rights** and **motion picture rights** are interchangeable industry terms—a sort of shorthand—for a collection of different rights. Those rights include the right to make a film for initial exhibition on television or in theaters, the right to make sequels and remakes of that film, and the right to distribute the film on home video and other media, even if it is not invented yet. Some people prefer the term audio-visual rights. **Audio-visual rights** are the same as film or motion picture rights, but, as a descriptive phrase, seem to better describe the possible development and use of future technologies. You also want to acquire related rights such as the right to use the title of the underlying work and the right to use the name and likeness of the author of the underlying work for publicity purposes. For instance, if you don't own the film rights to the play *My Big Fat Greek Wedding*, you cannot make a film from a script based on that play. It is also true that even if you have the film rights, when your ownership of the underlying rights runs out, you no longer have the right to exploit the picture you made.

Universal Studios learned that lesson when the U.S. Supreme Court took away its right to distribute Alfred Hitchcock's *Rear Window*. The film was made in 1945 from a script based on a short story by Cornell Woolrich published in 1940 in a magazine. This was when the term of copyright was much shorter, but the copyright could be renewed. When Woolrich assigned the film rights to his original story to Universal, he also agreed to assign the renewal at the appropriate time. But Woolrich died before the renewal time arrived. Due to unique provisions in copyright, the law did not bind his heirs to the original agreement regarding renewal, so when the successor to the rights (Sheldon Abend) offered to resell Universal the underlying rights that they felt they had already paid for, Universal refused. They felt that they had previously paid Woolrich for such rights, and they didn't like the additional price Abend was asking, so they went ahead with their plans to re-release *Rear Window*.

Abend sued.

Abend won.

The court ruled that Universal could not do anything with their film during the story's renewal term until they purchased the underlying rights from Mr. Abend.

The point of the *Rear Window* story is that you must own the film rights to an underlying work to have the right to do anything with a film based on that work. Luckily, the nasty renewal right and all its fascinating problems are becoming less prominent in the copyright landscape. If the underlying work you are interested in was created before 1978, you should consult an experienced copyright attorney to help guide you through the copyright-renewal thicket. For works created after 1978, there are still reversion issues and transfer issues, but there aren't renewal problems.

Assume that you have found a property on which you want to base a script for a film. Rarely can you (or do you want to) pay the entire purchase price of those rights before you even have a script or the commitment of a financier. This is why producers like yourself option the property. An **option** is the exclusive right to purchase something in the future, on fixed terms and conditions.

Options are common in many businesses, including the film business. Instead of laying out a large sum of cash up front, the filmmaker offers a small cash amount to the owner of the property. This guarantees that you (the filmmaker/option holder) can purchase the film rights, in the future, under certain specified conditions. You can think of it as buying time.

No matter what kind of property you are optioning, the important thing is to *always, always get it in writing.*

Even experienced attorneys who option property often and communicate clearly need to "get it in writing." Things change, and when they do, you will find that memories change. Take the sad, but true, story of Frank Konigsberg, a highly experienced producer of award-winning movies for television.

In 1987, after a lunch meeting with Anne Rice, the author (and inveterate letter-writer), Konigsberg and Rice entered into an oral agreement by which he optioned the rights to her upcoming book *The Mummy*. They agreed that she would create a bible. A **bible** is an industry term used primarily in television for a detailed story description, more detailed than the typical treatment but less detailed than a full script. They agreed that Konigsberg could use this bible to interest television networks in a movie made for television. His plan was to set up the television project while Rice wrote the novel. His option was to commence on the date a television network promised to develop the bible into a script and was to run for two years thereafter. Drafts of a contract were exchanged, but never signed. Rice delivered the bible, Konigsberg paid her $50,000, but still no written contract was signed. Konigsberg assumed that the exchange of money sealed their agreement. Wrong.

Although the novel became a bestseller, Konigsberg was not able to convince a network to proceed with a movie. He tried to extend his still-unsigned option, but Rice refused.

Konigsberg sued to establish co-ownership of the bible and a license to the film rights. Rice denied that Konigsberg had an option agreement and asserted that even if he did, his efforts to extend the rights were not timely.

The court tossed Konigsberg's suit out of court. "No agreement signed by the author," the court intoned. "I know what she said, but what did she sign?" This was the question that hung in the air as the gavel cracked against the small, round, wooden block to mark the end of the matter.

Nevertheless, the wrath of Frank Konigsberg is not so easily squelched, even by a court decision. Worse, such victories often produce some gloating by prevailing plaintiffs. So it was that Anne Rice, feeling too smug to let Konigsberg's defeat go undocumented, wrote Konigsberg a letter. In addition to the expected paragraphs that added salt to his wounds, it contained the following admission of an agreement: "As far as I'm concerned," she proclaimed, "these contracts, though never signed, were honored to the letter. . . . You got exactly what you paid for—a bible script and the television rights to the novel, *The Mummy*, for more than two years." Rice claimed that the only thing Konigsberg failed to do was "pick up your option, or extend it."

Not only did her letter fail to shame Frank, it seemed to provide his case with a missing link: an admission of an agreement. So Frank appealed.

In addition to all the other reasons for reversal, he added this letter as new evidence. "A writing?" he railed. "It's a writing you want? I've got a writing. Look at this!" he must have chortled as he added the letter to his legal brief. Surely the court would accept the affirmation of Konigsberg's position by the defendant herself.

The appeal failed. The court's decision states that Konigsberg and Rice were "doing lunch" and "not doing contracts." Why didn't Rice's salty letter to proclaim her vindication after the court's ruling breathe life into the unsigned contracts from the original lunch meeting? "Too late," the court responded. That is not the kind of writing they wanted. You must have a contract signed *reasonably contemporaneously* with the making of the agreement. Rice's letter was too late, too much after-the-fact. Once again, Frank lost. This time Anne Rice did not write a letter.

It is still hard for me to believe that the courts allowed the letter-writing Ms. Rice to stand on a technicality. Often, in this type of case, the court will say to a litigant, "Yes, you are right. The letter of the law is on your side, but your behavior prevents you from using the letter of the law to your advantage. It would be unfair. We do not allow you to assert these technicalities, because to do so would produce an unfair result." Obviously, the courts do not always do this. They didn't do it for Konigsberg and they may not do it for you.

Be sure to put your agreement to writing.

CHARACTER(S)

Characters are separate, independently copyrightable works of creation. They are discussed in depth in the previous chapter. This is a reminder that, if you option the film rights in someone else's property, be sure that you have optioned the film rights in the characters in that property. You will be well served to have your agreement state explicitly that you have the right to use the characters in future movies. Central characters often become the focus of a franchise. A franchise is a character, concept, or title that is supposed to guarantee a good opening weekend for a film. It is the brass ring that everyone is reaching for. A franchise in the movie business is the most valuable thing you can possibly control. James Bond is one of the most lucrative franchises in the history of film.

WHOM TO CONTACT

Most producers know instinctively that they are better off talking to the person who created the work than to the agent or other representative of that person. When you talk directly to the creative force, you can share visions, and you can convince the work's creator, who has the ultimate decision-making power, that you are the best person to protect the project.

A good place to turn for information on how to reach a specific person is your local library. Most libraries have a research librarian to help you. Extensive biographical information exists on almost anybody who has done anything. There are *Who's Who* for almost every endeavor. These books routinely list addresses for the personalities in their pages.

Another source for locating someone is the Internet. You need to have access and some knowledge about how to find your way around. Once you are into the Internet, there is virtually no one of note about whom there is not a great deal of information.

The remainder of this section deals with specific types of properties. You will find guidance on how to contact the right person for a wide variety of properties on which you might want to base a film. No matter what type of property you are after, the more direct your contact is with the actual rights-holder, the better off you are.

Fictional Books and Stories

You are reading a book. In your mind's eye you are seeing the movie; it pops right up in your head without an invitation. You have to buy the film rights. Whom do you call?

You can always call the publisher. They are easy to find. That is what the cash-rich studios do. However, in 30 years of practice, I have never heard of a case in which the publisher said, "No, we don't own or control the film rights." Whenever you call a publisher to ask who has film rights, you will receive one of three answers: "Yes, you called the right place, we do own those rights" or "The agent for those rights is X" or "I'll get right back to you." When the publisher calls you back, they tell you that indeed they control the rights, so you should negotiate with them. What happened was that if they didn't already own or control the rights, they contacted the author and gained control of, or at least the right to represent, the film property's rights. This puts another person, and possibly another commission, between you and the original owner.

Most book authors control the film rights to their books. Even if they allowed the publisher or agent to negotiate those rights, they still retain ownership, and generally retain approval rights over any film deal, so you still want to talk directly to the author. The issue is finding them.

The best place to start your search for an author of a book is in the book itself. There is almost always a biography of the author, which often includes the author's city or town of residence. Try the telephone directory for that town. Fortunately, many authors have decided to live in small towns where a mere telephone call or two finds them easily. Acknowledgments often give many clues that can help you find the author. If all else fails, write to the author in care of the publisher. Such letters are generally forwarded unopened to the author.

Fictional magazine stories remain an important source for film material. Fictional magazine stories can be easier to adapt than a full-length book because they do not contain a lot of extra information and plot lines that could not possibly fit into a feature film.

Finding the author of a magazine article is a simple matter of dropping a line to the magazine. The magazine will almost always forward the letter to the author. Most magazines include at least a two- or three-sentence biographical note that will help you find the author directly.

Normally, a magazine story requires both a grant of rights from the author of the story and a release from the publication. The author of an article signs a grant of rights to a magazine much like the agreement signed by the author of a book. The magazine's publisher rarely owns the film rights to articles that they publish, but insurance companies want to be sure. A simple letter from the publisher, saying that it is okay for you to go forward, is sufficient.

Although there is no union for people who write books and magazine articles, there are some organizations to which most authors of books belong:

The Newspaper Guild: (212) 575-1580
www.nyguild.org
The purpose of the Newspaper Guild is to advance the economic interests and to improve the working conditions of its members and to raise the standards of journalism and ethics of the industry.

American Society of Journalists and Authors:
(212) 997-0947
www.asja.org
"The nation's leading organization of freelance writers." AJA offers benefits and services focusing on professional development

and the opportunity for members to explore professional issues and concerns with their peers.

National Writers Union: (212) 254-0279

www.nwu.org

The purpose of the National Writers Union is to organize writers to improve professional working conditions through collective bargaining action and to provide professional services to members.

PEN (Poets, Essayists, and Novelists): (212) 334-1660

www.pen.org

A fellowship of writers working for more than 75 years to advance literature, to promote a culture of reading, and to defend free expression.

Author's League of America: (212) 564-8350

The Author's League is the oldest and largest group of professional, published authors in the nation. Membership in the League supports advocacy initiatives on copyright, free expression, and tax-law matters that affect writers.

Authors Guild: (212) 563-5904

www.authorsguild.org

staff@authorsguild.org

The Authors Guild, the nation's largest society of published authors, is a leading advocate for fair compensation, free speech, and copyright protection.

One of these approaches almost always puts you in touch with the author. Once you find them, you can put the question to them directly. At some point, the author usually refers you to someone negotiating on their behalf, but you benefit by having direct initial contact. You can convince the author that you are sincere, hardworking, talented, and the best thing that ever happened to the book's film prospects.

Comic Books

When buying the film rights to a comic book, think "graphic novel" to bring clarity to the process. Generally, the copyright to each element that makes up the comic book is held by the comic book's publishing company. There are several reasons for this. One is that the characters have the potential for becoming so valuable that the ownership of the characters is the biggest asset of a successful comic-book company. Comic-book publishers generally require the writers of the stories and the illustrators and all the other designers who work on a successful comic-book series to assign their creations over to the publishing company.

As explained in Chapter 7, comic books cannot be works for hire unless the people who created the comic books were employees of the company. The comic-book publishing company usually has to obtain assignments. Therefore, your contract generally will be with the publishing company and the terms are similar to a book deal, except for the representations and warranties section and the merchandising section. There are special notes covering all these points in the Sample Option and Purchase Agreement at the end of Chapter 9.

Non-Fiction Books, Magazine Articles, and Newspaper Stories

Books and periodicals often contain articles about true-life events. In such a case, you might decide to leapfrog over the publication and the writer and go directly to the subject of the book or article. This would involve a life-story rights agreement that would be exactly like the agreement discussed in Chapter 4. The safest thing to do is to sew up the rights to both the life story from the person who lived it and the magazine article from the person who wrote it.

When dealing with two tiers of possible ownership (such as the author of an article and the subject of an article), you have to be very careful about how much you agree to pay any single entity. You do not want the total price to be so high as to make the production package unattractive to a studio or financier. Remember, these are underlying rights.

View this situation both offensively and defensively. You want to tie up as many rights as possible if the story is particularly newsworthy, especially if there are other producers seeking these rights. On the other hand, you still must be careful about overspending. Remember, if a story has truly grabbed the imagination of Hollywood, competing projects are often developed—and sometimes produced—no matter how many people you may pay for life-story rights.

Review Chapter 4 for the story of the unseemly spectacle of all three major networks broadcasting three different movies-of-the-week about young Amy Fisher, who shot the long-suffering wife of Joey Buttafuoco. Two of the movies were based on the purchase of story rights from different individuals, and the other relied on public domain material.

Songs

Acquiring the right to base an entire film on a song is not too common, but it happens. (*Ode to Billy Joe* and *Harper Valley P.T.A.* are two examples.) These rights are rarely held or administered directly by the songwriter. Because of this, it takes extra effort to talk directly with the songwriter. Songwriters either establish their own publishing company or agree to work with an existing one. A **publishing company**, in the music business, is the company that administers the various rights that flow from ownership of the copyright to a song.

A publishing company administers synchronization rights, mechanical rights, publishing rights (the right to print the music in folio form), and receives the payments for performance rights (the right to sing the song in public or play a record of it over the air or, outside of the U.S., to perform it as part of a film soundtrack). The right to make a film from a song is a separate right and would not normally be given to the publishing company, but it is a good place to start.

Of course, a song can be in the public domain (see Chapter 4), but be careful. Do not assume that a song is in the public domain. Even "Happy Birthday" is protected by copyright and must be licensed.

It is hard to imagine anyone wanting to make a movie from a song, unless the song was extremely well known. Think of the songs that have been made into movies, such as *Yellow Submarine* and *Harper Valley P.T.A.* (television series). Each of these songs was very well established before anybody wanted to make a movie on the strength of their titles or content. The prices for such rights are therefore high and the profit participation substantial. An independent producer would have to be prepared for this financial challenge.

Plays

Again, the most effective way to begin to option film rights in a play is usually to talk directly with the playwright. If you cannot find the playwright after doing similar research as outlined above, try the Dramatists Guild. It is the only national organization for playwrights, and most successful playwrights belong to it. Member services can verify that the playwright is (or is not) a member of the Dramatists Guild. If so, tell them that you are trying to reach the playwright and ask for the correct contact information.

Dramatists Guild, Inc.
1501 Broadway, Suite 701
New York, NY 10036
(212) 398-9366
www.dramatistsguild.com

If this does not work, remember that most playwrights are affiliated with specific theaters. This is generally a very informal arrangement, but can rise to the level of a compensated position known as "playwright-in-residence" or "artist-in-residence." No matter what the formality of the relationship, the theaters with which a playwright is associated almost always know a way to contact the playwright. You can identify the affiliated theaters by determining where workshops or world premiers of the playwright's works regularly occur. When you contact a theater, you want to talk to the theater's artistic director or assistant to the artistic director.

If all this fails, look at a program for the play you want to option. Usually the source for permission to produce a play (as a play) is printed on both the program and any published version of the play. Contacting that person or entity should lead you to the holder of the film rights to that play.

One last way to contact "someone official" is to contact the company that licenses the play's amateur performing rights. Fortunately, there are only a few companies in the business of licensing these rights, but note that musicals are generally represented by different companies from straight plays. The oldest and largest licensor:

Samuel French, Inc.
In New York: (212) 206-8990
In Los Angeles: (323) 876-0570
www.samuelfrench.com
samuelfrench@earthlink.net

A couple of other companies with a nice catalogue of plays:
Dramatic Publishing Company
Woodstock, Illinois
(800) 448-7469
www.dramaticpublishing.com
plays@dramaticpublishing.com

Dramatist Play Service
New York, NY: (212) 683-8960
www.dramatists.com
postmaster@dramatists.com

When you call any of the above, do not ask, "Who owns the film rights to the play *XXXXXX*?" They will normally just say that they don't know and that they do not have anything to do with film rights. Ask, "Do you handle performing rights for *XXXXXX*?" If the answer is "no," keep trying until you find the company that does handle those rights. When you reach the right company, merely ask for a contact number for the author directly. You are usually given the contact number for the playwright's agent.

Old Movies

If what moves you to make a movie is someone else's movie, you want to obtain both the sequel and remake rights to that movie (or television series). A **remake** is a movie in which you recast and reshoot essentially the same script that formed the basis for a previous film. You use the same characters, in the same story, during the same time period, in the same locale (although sometimes a remake updates the time period). A recent example of a remake was Sydney Pollack's remake of the Billy Wilder classic *Sabrina*.

A **sequel** is a story that uses one or more of the same characters in a different story, set in a different time. Notice that sequels cover events written to occur after or before (a prequel) the "original" story. **Prequel** is something of a slang term to describe the sequel that is set earlier in time than the original story.

When you wish to make a television series into a film, you will almost certainly be working with a studio. The huge box-office revenues resulting from these films when they are well done has driven up their budgets (and the cost of acquiring character rights) into the studio range. Such a sequel usually takes the characters out of the television series and places them in a new story in a new location and a new time period.

The hard part is figuring out who owns the original film rights. Many old contracts were not so clear, and most older films have had their rights splintered and sold off in many different directions. Rarely were the sequel or remake rights the focus of attention when older films were bought and sold because they are often sold as part of a library. A **library** is a group of films whose copyright is owned by one entity. Remember when Ted Turner bought the MGM library? Many people thought that he had grossly overpaid for it, but he laughed all the way to the bank.

The Turner organization had specific instructions not to sell off the library or even the remake and sequel rights of films in the library. Turner felt that he could make a lot of money by colorizing the old films, and he wanted to protect their value for exhibition after he colorized them. He also knew that someday he wanted to be in production, and owning remake and sequel rights would form a rich vein to mine for new pictures. All of those early dreams are being played out today.

In looking for sequel or remake rights to a film, you can start by ordering a copyright report. Chapter 4 tells you how to obtain such a report, which can be anything from two pages to twenty pages long. Note that the original copyright owner of the film almost always owns the remake and sequel rights until those rights are transferred. Examine each of the transfers to create a chain of title as described in Chapter 21. Remember that the sequel and remake rights can be held back or sold separately, so do not make any assumptions. There is one situation in which the copyright holder of the original film will not necessarily own sequel and remake rights to that film. This exception exists if the old film was based on some underlying property (such as a book or a play) and the filmmaker only obtained rights to make a single film.

6.01   OPTION AND PURCHASE AGREEMENT

UNDERLYING RIGHTS

THIS AGREEMENT, effective as of _____, ___, is made by and between _____ [name of producer] located at _____ (the "Producer") and _____ [name of owner] located at _____ (the "Owner"), concerning the rights to a _____ [e.g., book, play, unpublished story] entitled "_____" and the materials upon which it is based. The following terms and conditions shall apply:

> **Date:** *By using an effective date right at the beginning of the contract, you eliminate disputes over when a contract was signed and therefore when an option lapses. Few contracts are signed by all parties on the same day, so avoid using the date of signature.*
>
> **Producer:** *You, as the filmmaker, are the "Producer."*
>
> **Owner:** *The author of the book is the "Owner," as in an owner of the rights you want to acquire. If there is more than one owner/ author, be sure to list all of them here and have all of them sign as parties to the deal.*

1.   **DEFINITION OF "WORK":** For purposes of this Agreement, "Work" means the _____ [nonfiction/original work/unpublished manuscript] entitled "_____" written by _____ and any and all other literary materials, titles, themes, formats, formula, incidents, action, story, dialogue, ideas, plots, phrases, slogans, catchwords, art, designs, compositions, sketches, drawings, characters, characterizations, names, and trademarks now contained therein, as well as such elements as may at any time hereafter be added or incorporated therein, and all versions thereof in any form.

> **Work:** *Pick the best description of the property you are optioning. If there was a previous title, include that also by saying, "and previously entitled _____." If the Work has been registered with the Copyright Office, you might give that registration number by way of further identification. In the list of included items, be sure to include characters.*

2.   **GRANT OF OPTION:** In consideration of the mutual promises contained herein, and the payment to Owner of $_____ (the "Option Price"), Owner hereby grants to Producer the exclusive, irrevocable right and option (the "Option") for _____ months (the "Option Period") to acquire the exclusive motion picture, television, videocassette, and all subsidiary, allied, and ancillary rights in and to the Work pursuant to the terms set forth below.

> **Option Price:** *You want this to be as low as possible. Sometimes you can even negotiate a free period. Do not be surprised if you run into someone (like me) who says: "No Free Option!" That is my mantra when representing the owner of a property, although I obtain "free" options all the time for my independent producer clients. My argument: It's not "free!" My client will be working, writing (maybe), (if not) hiring someone to write, shopping the project, and generally spending time, effort, and money on the project.*
>
> **Hint:** *Since you do <u>not</u> have the deep pockets of a studio, your first job is to convince the author of your passion for the work. Listen to the author's dreams and hopes. You will be the protector of those dreams and hopes. As self-serving as it may sound, it truly is <u>not</u> about the money at the option stage. Except in big studio deals for hot properties, the initial payment is simply not large enough to be the most important aspect of the deal. The likelihood of the film getting made is the important thing. However, the emotional hook—the sizzle that closes your negotiation—can be a simple promise from you: "If you entrust your property to me, I will be as faithful to your work as possible. I will keep you advised every step of the way, and I will do my best to protect you."*
>
> **Option Period:** *A year or 18 months is standard for this first period.*

3. **EXTENSION OF OPTION:**

(a) Producer shall have the right to extend the Option Period for one (1) period of twelve (12) months for $_____ non-applicable. For the right to the extension of the first Option Period there must be one of the following:

> (i) letter of commitment to direct from an established director;
>
> (ii) the project is set up at a company, major studio, or mini-major studio able to fund the project;
>
> (iii) substantial negotiations in progress for complete financing of the film;
>
> (iv) letter of commitment to act in the film from one star;

or

> (v) a full-length feature-film script has been completed.

(b) Producer shall have the right to extend the Option Period for one (1) additional twelve (12) month period for $_____ non-applicable. In order to have a right to a second extension, Producer must secure at least two (2) of the above five (5) items.

Option Extension: It is standard that you have the right to extend the option. This is important because it takes a very long time to get a film made. Even three years total, as provided here, is a short time. Inexperienced producers often think that they will get their movie made more quickly than anybody else. Based on what? Be realistic. Writers are reluctant to have their material off the market for a long period of time. Frequently, the amounts paid for the second and third years are substantially higher than the amount paid for the initial period . . . and they are non-applicable.

Non-Applicable: Whether subsequent option payments apply or do not apply to the final purchase price is often a point of negotiation. The initial payment is usually applicable (i.e., deductible). More often than not, additional option payments are not deducted from the purchase price and are therefore labeled non-applicable. The money must be paid before the time elapses under the current option. This payment acts to keep the option open for the extended period of time. If you let your option expire, you no longer have any right to buy the work or to extend the option. The original owner is then free to option the work to another party.

Progress Requirements: One way to soften the length of time and/or to get more time is to have your right to renew the option be a result of progress made on the film. That is the approach used above. But do not make those barriers too high. The last sentences of Subparagraph (a) and Subparagraph (b) might work for you— though you don't have to include them in your first draft. If no such demand is made, you can strike this language. (Be sure to tailor the language to your needs.) No studio ever makes this kind of deal. Studios simply pay option prices. Therefore, if you use this approach, you must provide alternatives if the project is set up at a studio. After that, the option may be renewed with a cash payment only.

4.   **EXERCISE OF OPTION:** Producer may exercise this Option at any time during the Option Period, as it may be extended, by giving written notice of such exercise to Owner and delivery to Owner of the minimum Purchase Price as set forth below. In the event Producer does not exercise said Option during the period as it may be extended, this Agreement shall be of no further force or effect whatsoever. All rights granted hereunder become property of Owner. Upon exercise of the option, Producer shall have the right to file the Assignment, Exhibit A, with the Copyright Office.

Hint: This paragraph is what gives you the ability to purchase the rights you have optioned. It is standard.

5. PENDING EXERCISE OF OPTION: Producer shall have the right to engage in all customary development and pre-production activities during the option period as it may be extended.

> **Hint:** *The fact that you optioned the film rights infers this to be true. Stating the fact clearly is better. Often people add "including but not limited to" and then go on for a page or two. That's overkill.*

6. GRANT OF RIGHTS: Effective upon Producer's exercise of the Option, Owner does hereby exclusively sell, grant, and assign to Producer all rights in and to the Work not reserved by Owner, throughout the universe, in perpetuity, in any and all media, whether now existing or hereafter invented, including, but not limited to, the following: all motion picture rights, all rights to make motion picture versions or adaptations of the Work, to make remakes and sequels to and new versions or adaptations of the Work or any part thereof, to make series and serials of the Work or any part thereof; the right, for advertising and publicity purposes only, to prepare, broadcast, exhibit, and publish in any form or media, any synopses, excerpts, novelizations, serializations, dramatizations, summaries, and stories of the Work, or any part thereof; and all rights of every kind and character whatsoever in and to the Work and all the characters and elements contained therein.

> **Hint:** *This is exactly what you are purchasing. This is why you are making the payments. This paragraph can also run on for pages, but the above is all-inclusive. It puts the burden on the Owner to be specific about reserved rights.*
>
> **Hint:** *If you obtain sequel rights at the same time you buy the film rights—as you always should—you can take any story character out of the film and use that character in another film. The author of the book usually retains the right to write a sequel to the book being optioned. Comic books always retain that right. Note that the language here says that you also purchased the film rights to the characters. A very sharp owner will not allow you to own the characters without a hefty additional payment.*
>
> **Caution:** *Some Owners want to approve the final script. The studio <u>will not</u> allow the author of the book to have approval over the screenplay. In fact, a studio will not allow <u>you</u> to have the final approval over the screenplay. Do not make this type of promise to a writer. At most, you can allow the Owner to read the final shooting script and to have a short period of consultation.*

7. PURCHASE PRICE: As consideration for all rights and property herein granted, and all warranties and covenants herein made by Owner, Producer agrees to pay Owner the following sums not later than the commencement of principal photography of a production:

(a) $_____ if the final budget for the motion picture based on the Work does not exceed two million dollars ($2,000,000), less any moneys paid as option exercise money and less the option payment for the initial period;

(b) If the final budget exceeds two million dollars ($2,000,000), one percent (1%) of the final budget for the motion picture based on the Work less any amounts paid for option exercise; however, in no event shall the amount of such payment exceed fifty-thousand dollars ($50,000).

> ***Purchase Price:*** *Price can be a flat fee or a percentage of the film's budget, or a combination. Most film budgets allow 1% of the budget for purchase of the book, with a floor and ceiling. The floor is the minimum price you pay, regardless of the budget. The ceiling is the maximum price you pay, regardless of the budget.*

8. ADDITIONAL COMPENSATION:

(a) **Contingent Compensation:** Producer also agrees to pay Owner ___ percent (__%) of one hundred percent (100%) of the net profits from any production based on the Work for which Owner receives any other payment under this Agreement. "Net Profits" shall be defined, accounted for, and paid in the same manner for Owner as for Producer, whether Producer's contingent compensation is called Net Profits, Adjusted Gross Profits, or otherwise.

> ***Note:*** *Net Profits have gotten a bad name. Try using Contingent Compensation. The language in this agreement avoids all accusations of Hollywood accounting, at least by you, because Owner gets a piece of what you get. If you are going to pay for the film yourself or through your family and friends or a company you own or control, be sure to spell out your definition of Contingent Compensation. Be as specific as possible to avoid future conflicts. 1% to 1.5% is common. 2.5% is about as high as is ever paid.*

(b) **Bonus Compensation:** Producer shall pay Owner $_____ in addition to any other money due Owner under this agreement upon the happening of the following: _____
_____.

> **Performance Bonus:** *Often there are bonuses if a film grosses over a certain domestic box office as reported in* Weekly Variety *or* The Hollywood Reporter *(e.g., $10,000 if the film grosses $100 million in domestic box office). Usually such performance bonuses are advances against contingent compensation. Do not grant bonuses for things like awards or Oscar nominations. These events do not always translate into money for you.*
>
> **Books:** *Best-seller Bonuses are common. You want to be sure to put a cap on such bonuses and specify the list that qualifies. "$10,000 per week for each week on* The New York Times *Best Seller List up to 10 weeks" would be a common provision.*
>
> **Plays:** *Often, there are Broadway production or Pulitzer Prize-winning or Tony Award-winning bonuses. These provisions persist in spite of the clear diminution of Broadway's importance to the national theater scene. This is due in part to the fact that there is no shorthand substitute by which to measure success. The Mark Taper Forum in Los Angeles birthed back-to-back Pulitzer Prize-winning plays, but still does not rate the mark of success that a Broadway production rates. More film rights are optioned from productions in Los Angeles than from Broadway, but this is over-looked and underrated. Broadway stoically remains the hallmark of a play's success and the trigger for bonus payments.*
>
> **Magazine Story or Song or Comic Book:** *There are rarely bonuses involved with songs or magazine stories or comic books. The merchandising aspects of anything related to a comic book are very important, and may be difficult to secure for a film. They are usually reserved by or at least shared with the publisher.*

9.   MERCHANDISING: Owner shall be entitled to receive a royalty equal to ten percent (10%) of Net Merchandising Receipts attributable to the use of any character in the Work in Merchandise of any kind, it being the intent of the parties to create the broadest possible definition to Merchandise. Such amounts shall be reducible by the aggregate amount paid on account of all royalties to other performers for use of such other performers' names, likenesses, or images or Producer's Logo or other intellectual property that receives a royalty on any given piece of Merchandise to not less than seven and one-half percent (7½%) of Net Merchandising Receipts. Net Merchandising Receipts are all receipts of any kind of nature received by Producer less only third-party sales commissions not to exceed twenty-five percent (25%).

10. CREDITS:

(a) In the event a motion picture based substantially on the Work is produced hereunder, Owner shall receive credit in the following form:

Based on the book by _____

or if the film has a different title from the Work, then:

Based on the novel "_____" by _____

> **Hint:** *This is a standard source-material credit. A **source-material credit** is the credit that acknowledges the original material upon which the first-draft script was based. The title of the underlying work is not listed unless it is different from the title of the film.*

(b) Such credit shall be accorded on a single card in the main titles on all positive prints of the picture and in all paid advertising in which the director has received credit, except for advertising of eight (8) column inches or less; group and list advertisements; teasers; publicity; special advertising; billboards; television trailers; film clips ("excluded ads"). Nothing contained in this Paragraph shall be construed to prevent the use of so-called "teaser," trailer, or other special advertising, publicity or congratulatory advertising. All other matters regarding prominence, placement, size, style, and color of said credits shall be in Producer's sole discretion.

> **Hint:** *This is a very precise description of your obligations as far as credit. It is acceptable to the studios and to any legitimate distributor.*

(c) No casual or inadvertent failure to comply with credit requirements hereunder shall be deemed a breach of this Agreement.

> **Hint:** *This is very important to you, since there can always be a slip-up. Often the Owner insists (and you should agree) that you take reasonable steps to correct any mistake when it is brought to your attention.*

11. RESERVED RIGHTS: All publication rights are reserved to Owner for Owner's use and disposition, including but not limited to the right to publish and distribute printed versions of the Work and author-written sequels thereof (owned or controlled by Owner) in book form, whether hardcover or softcover, and in magazines or other periodicals, comics or coloring books, whether in installments or otherwise, subject to Producer's limited rights to promote and advertise. Producer shall have the right of first negotiation and last refusal to enter an agreement such as this one with regard to any works created by Owner pursuant to this paragraph.

> *Reserved Rights: Owners of underlying rights invariably want to reserve certain rights. The standard reserved rights for books are the rights of publication and author-written sequels that are set forth in the sample agreement. You want to get all the rights you can, but these rights are often allowed to remain with the owners of the property. Frequently, there are no reserved rights for a spec script. If you are optioning a spec script, try issuing your first contract without this paragraph. If you do that, strike the words "not reserved by Owner" from the first sentence of Paragraph 6 and eliminate the next two paragraphs as well.*
>
> *Books: Authors want sole publishing rights and the right to re-release the book using film art on the cover to coincide with the release of the film. It is up to them to raise this issue. It is ultimately the studio's decision, but this is a safe item to give away.*
>
> *Plays: Everything having to do with the play as a play will be reserved by any author with an ounce of self-esteem. That includes publication of the play, performance of the play, and the creation of any other plays that are derivatives of the play. Some producers want to require a holdback period for the performance of the play. A **holdback period** is a period during which certain rights that are possessed are not used. Personally, I don't think it is necessary, but I know that many producers ask (and many playwrights give) a holdback period of 6 to 12 months from release of the film during which the playwright will not authorize the performance of the play.*
>
> *Magazine Story: Publication rights are the only rights normally reserved by the owners of magazine articles.*
>
> *Song: There probably aren't enough of these deals done to say that anything is ironclad, but I would think that everything except the right to make a film would be reserved by the songwriter.*
>
> *Old Movies: The right to continue releasing and otherwise exploiting the previous film is always retained by the owner.*

12. RIGHT OF FIRST NEGOTIATION: If Owner desires to dispose of or exercise a particular right reserved to Owner herein ("Reserved Right"), then Owner shall notify Producer in writing and immediately negotiate with Producer regarding such Reserved Right. If, after the expiration of thirty (30) days following the receipt of such notice, no agreement has been reached, then Owner may negotiate with third parties regarding such Reserved Right subject to the next paragraph.

> *Comment: The above and below paragraphs spell out your rights when the Owner exploits Reserved Rights. It is pretty self-explanatory. This is a strong protection from anyone making a fortune on the hard work you went through to get a film made. You can shorten some of these time periods, but do not quickly give up these rights if the Owner has Reserved Rights. You don't need these two paragraphs at all if there are no Reserved Rights.*

13. RIGHT OF LAST REFUSAL: If Producer and Owner fail to reach an agreement pursuant to Producer's right of first negotiation, and:

(a) Owner makes and/or receives any bona fide offer to license and/or purchase the particular Reserved Right or any interest therein in a context other than an auction ("Third Party Offer"), Owner shall notify Producer, if Owner proposes to accept such Third Party Offer, of the name of the offeror, the proposed purchase price, and other such terms of Third Party Offer. During the period of ten (10) days after Producer's receipt of such notice, Producer shall have the exclusive option to license and/or purchase said Reserved Right upon the same terms and conditions of said Third Party Offer. If Producer elects to exercise the right to purchase such Reserved Right, Producer shall notify Owner of the exercise thereof within said ten (10) day period, failing which Owner shall be free to accept such Third Party Offer. If any such proposed license and/or sale is not consummated with a third party within thirty (30) days following the expiration of the aforesaid ten- (10-) day period, Producer's Right of Last Refusal shall revive and shall apply to each and every further offer or offers at any time received by Owner relating to the particular Reserved Right or any interest therein; provided, further, that Producer's option shall continue in full force and effect, upon all of the terms and conditions of this Clause, so long as Owner retains any rights, title, or interests in or to the particular Reserved Right, or

(b) Owner seeks to obtain bona fide offers to license and/or purchase the particular Reserved Right or any interest therein by means of auction ("Auction"), Owner shall notify Producer of the time, date, location, and rules of such Auction within thirty (30) days thereof. Owner shall be entitled to license and/or sell the Reserved Right to the highest bidder at such Auction, provided that the terms and conditions of the license and/or sale to any party other than Producer shall be at least as favorable to Owner as those terms and conditions last offered by Producer to Owner under Clause 3 above. If any such license and/or sale is not consummated with any party in the course of said Auction, Producer's Right of Last Refusal shall revive and shall apply to each and every further Auction relating to the particular Reserved Right or any interest therein; provided, further, that Producer's option shall continue in full force and effect upon all of the terms and conditions of this Clause, so long as Owner retains any rights, title, or interests in or to the particular Reserved Right.

> *Go to Chapter 8, Provisions Common to Most Agreements, to finish up this contract. You should use all the paragraphs contained there except Expenses, unless the Owner brings that up.*

CHAPTER 7

HIRING A SCRIPTWRITER— WORK FOR HIRE

Suppose you have a great idea. Maybe you have optioned the book of your dreams. However, you either do not have the time or do not have the inclination to write the script. Maybe your talents are as a producer and you know your limits as a writer. So you decide to hire someone else to do it. This chapter details the process of finding and working with the writer. It also details your best protection through the special copyright term "work for hire."

CHOOSING A WRITER

This is not as easy as it may seem. Hiring a screenwriter can be a tricky task. Too many producers hire whomever they meet or happen to know without really addressing the writing issues in a tough manner. To spend a great deal of time working on a script with a screenwriter who is not right for a project can be an enormously frustrating experience for all concerned. Take care with the selection process. The best screenwriter in the world does not hit a home run every time, and less experienced screenwriters are less predictable, partly because they have a smaller body of work for you to read before you decide whether to let them write your script.

Here are three tips to hiring a writer:

1. Interview more than one writer.

2. Read lots of the writer's scripts.

3. Check out the writer's work habits. (Talk to people who have worked with the writer.)

Be sure that the scripts upon which you make your choice have as much in common with your project as possible. Make sure that the screenwriter wrote the scripts you read without a partner, unless you plan to work with the partner also. When you read a script written by a writing team, finding out who brought what to the table is virtually impossible, especially if your only source for that information is the one team member whom you plan to hire.

WHAT IS WORK FOR HIRE?

Once you decide whom to hire to write your script, you want to structure the deal as a work for hire. A **work for hire** is defined in U.S. Copyright Law as either:

A. a work prepared by an employee within the scope of employment; or

B. a work specially ordered or commissioned for use as one of a very limited number of specified works.

Category A is easy to determine, but does not usually apply to an independent filmmaker. It is, however, the category under which a great deal of television is written and produced. Examples of employees whose job it is to create the works identified as Category A include term writers at a studio, animators at Disney, and the actors hired during principal photography. The creative works (and copyright therein) prepared by these employees are, by definition, the immediate property of the employer under the work for hire doctrine.

Category B, however, is of great help to independent film-makers. It is an anomaly of copyright law. Many people in the film business do not understand that this is a very special tool of our industry. It creates a mechanism so that certain items can be created as a work for hire, even though the person doing the creating is not a full-time employee.

To appreciate just how unusual this aspect of copyright law is, take a quick look at the specific items to which it applies. Here is the exact list of items as it appears in U.S. Copyright Law:

1. a contribution to a collective work

2. as a part *of a motion picture or other audiovisual work*

3. as a translation

4. as a supplementary work

5. as a compilation

6. as an instructional text

7. as a test

8. as answer materials for a test

9. as an atlas

Notice how they buried films among all that apple-pie stuff like newspapers, tests, and atlases? Looking at that collection of works, it is amazing that films are among them. In fact, the legislative history of this provision of the law shows that the movie tycoons pushed it through Congress. All of the other items helped to justify the request for the work-for-hire concept to apply to motion pictures.

If the work does not fall within one of the above categories, you cannot commission it as a "work for hire." For instance, a novel or a play cannot be commissioned as a work for hire. Even if a work does fall within one of the above categories, the parties must expressly agree in a written instrument signed by both parties that the work will be considered a work "made for hire." This agreement must be made before or about the same time as the work is created.

Be sure that you understand the implications of this extraordinary provision. Without this provision, the words of a writer are the copyrighted property of the writer as they are being typed. The writer can then assign or license the work to another, but the writer is always the "author" for purposes of copyright law. If the work was created as a work for hire, the words belong to the employer as they are created. The employer is the author for all purposes. There is no point in time when the words belong to the person who typed them on paper.

A work for hire is comparable to the assignment of an original work if the transaction goes well. If there is a dispute, the author who has assigned the materials to a producer would have certain remedies through which they could conceivably get the property back. This is not possible, however, if the work was a work made for hire. Since the writer never owns the property in a valid work-for-hire situation, there is no way that the person creating the words and typing the words on paper can get the ownership by bringing an action to cancel the transfer or to break the license.

It is also important to note that generally the duration of a copyright that initially resides with an individual is the author's life plus 70 years. For a work for hire, the duration of a copyright is 95 years from publication or 120 years from creation, whichever expires first. An assignment from an individual to a corporation does not lengthen the life of the copyright. The law establishes the life of the copyright at the moment of creation according to whether the person writing is doing so as a work for hire or not.

INDEPENDENT CONTRACTOR

Note that an underlying question in all of this is whether the actual creator of the work is an employee or an independent contractor. The definition of **independent contractor** is detailed below. If the actual creator is an employee and the work was created within the scope of that employment, then the work was a "work for hire." If the creator was an independent contractor under written agreement, then the work can only be a work for hire if it is one of the nine kinds of work listed above.

When the issue is contested, the courts use various factors to decide whether a person is an employee or an independent contractor. The contract between the parties is not an important factor in deciding whether a person is an employee or an independent contractor. The court recognizes that the producer and writer will often create contract language to shift income-tax burdens, to reduce unemployment insurance payments, or to gain other short-term financial benefits. The only reason that the court looks at the contract is to see if it sheds any light on the various factors that the court does consider important, such as the details of time, place, and manner for preparing the work.

When determining employment status, the most important factor is who controls the time, the place, and the manner in which a task is to be performed. If the individual writer works pretty much on his or her own, using his or her own computer and research tools, and turns in a finished draft, that person would be considered an independent contractor. Other factors the courts consider: Who owns the equipment? Does the person hired have an independent business? Does the person have employees to help achieve the goals? What remedies do you have if you are unsatisfied with the end result? As a producer, the important thing to know is that writers are almost always independent contractors. Film actors are employees and can never be independent contractors.

When you plan to commission a work to be created as a work made for hire, follow the Golden Rule of Filmmaking:

ALWAYS, ALWAYS GET IT IN WRITING.

You read earlier how important it is to have options in writing. It is even more important when it comes to agreements to create a work for hire. The requirement to have something in writing is part of this unique anomaly of copyright law. The courts have been very strict in interpreting that requirement. They say, when it comes to a work for hire, you must:

1. have a written agreement (in legalese, often known as "a writing"),

2. signed by the person against whom it is to be applied,

3. at substantially the same time as the writer commenced the work.

What the court seems to say is that under the Copyright Law, the written agreement does not merely prove the contents of your agreement, it changes the character of the thing being created. In that sense, it is part of the creation and so must be in a tangible form, just like the work itself must be reduced to a tangible form in order to receive copyright protection. As an intellectual abstraction, the court's reasoning cannot be faulted. But the erasure of all the normal defenses of estoppel or waiver or the inability to prove an agreement by performance (or reliance) seems an extremely harsh result in some circumstances. Your job is to know that you're working in a profession controlled by a very special area of the law—you are dealing in intellectual property. Only rarely do courts allow an oral transfer of copyright licenses to be confirmed in writing after the fact.

WRITERS GUILD OF AMERICA (WGA)

As a producer, you must sign the Minimum Basic Agreement (MBA) of the WGA if you plan to hire a writer who is a member of that union. There is absolutely no reason to sign the MBA if you do not plan to hire a union writer. By signing this agreement for any given project, it does not mean that all of your other projects need to be brought under the MBA requirements. Merely create a separate corporation to sign the MBA. You then have two companies or producing entities, and you are considered double vested. **Double vested** means that you control two (or more) production or development entities, one of which is a signatory of the MBA and the other of which is not. Almost all independent producers become double vested at some point in their lifetime. Even the major studios have figured out ways to be double vested.

Once the MBA is signed, the signatory company must create and produce all its properties under the terms of the union agreement. However, you as an individual can be involved with, own, or control other companies that remain non-signatories. Caveat: Once you bring a project within the MBA, you cannot then assign it back and forth for the purpose of having a non-guild writer work on it for a while and then switch it back later. This is a cardinal rule of conducting yourself as a double-vested producer. Once you have made a WGA project out of any given script, it stays a WGA project.

Although one occasionally meets a writer who is able to earn a living as a screenwriter without being a member of the WGA, it is safe to say that most television and studio film writers are members of the WGA. It is equally true that many independent films are written by non-union members. However, writers often request that there be a provision in the contract that if they qualify and join the WGA, any future writing services from them to you will only be rendered after you have signed the MBA. Even as an independent producer, you should have no real problem with such a request and it does help the screenwriter.

THE WORK FOR HIRE AGREEMENT

When you're ready to hire a writer, the contract at the end of this chapter should serve your needs to ensure that you are complying with the work-for-hire provisions of the United States Copyright Law.

Although copyright laws usually don't allow you to copy things out of books for your own use, this book is full of contract forms for your use. Just make any changes to the contract form that suits your needs and then type it up, or just download it from the website (www.clearanceandcopyright.com).

A work-for-hire contract need not be overly long, although studio contracts for such work can be 20 to 40 pages. What follows is a simple, straightforward agreement, which comes with a Certificate of Authorship. As in the case of the Assignment provided as part of the Option and Purchase Agreement at the end of Chapter 9, this one-page document can be registered with the Copyright Office without disclosing the financial details of the relationship. Note that the Certificate of Authorship, therefore, is much more than a mere statement of who wrote a certain script. It also confirms the work-for-hire arrangement and provides the "fail-safe" assignment discussed in the text. You may see Certificates of Authorship that include a lot of extra things. Legally, they add almost nothing to the basic contract.

7.01 WRITER AGREEMENT—WORK FOR HIRE

THIS AGREEMENT, effective as of _____, 20__, is made by and between *[NAME OF PRODUCER]*, located at *[PHYSICAL ADDRESS]* ("Producer"), and *[NAME OF WRITER]*, located at *[PHYSICAL ADDRESS]* ("Writer"), concerning the Writer's writing services in connection with the motion picture project entitled "_____" ("Picture"). The following terms and conditions shall apply:

> **Date:** *By using an effective date right at the beginning of the contract, you eliminate disputes over when a contract was signed and therefore when an option lapses. Few contracts are signed by all parties on the same day, so avoid date of signature.*
>
> **Producer:** *You, as the filmmaker, are the "Producer."*
>
> **Writer:** *The author of the script is the "Writer," and the owner of the rights you want to acquire. If there is more than one author, be sure to list all of them here and have all of them sign as parties to the deal. See Chapter 8 for more information on how to protect yourself when two or more writers have collaborated to write a script.*

1. ENGAGEMENT:

(a) Writer shall render all services customarily rendered by writers in the motion picture industry and at all times promptly comply with Producer's reasonable instructions with respect to writing the screenplay for the Picture ("Screenplay").

(b) First-Draft Screenplay: Writer shall write the first-draft screenplay ("First Draft") based upon material supplied to Writer by Producer (the "Assigned Material"). Writer shall commence writing services upon execution hereof and shall deliver the First Draft to Producer within ten (10) weeks thereafter.

> **Schedule:** *This paragraph and the ones that follow present a carefully thought-out model that tracks the writing schedules set forth in the WGA agreement. You can modify the schedule according to your discussions with the writer you hire, but keep a schedule in your contract. Many of the problems that come up between a writer and a producer are a function of different expectations and attitudes about time. You have a much better chance at a good, working relationship with the writer you hire when you start out with a written schedule.*
>
> **Hint:** *Many contracts concerning writing services refer to the minimum payments or other minimum rights set forth in the MBA, even though the producer is a non-signatory. This a common way to shorthand such things as wages, credits, and creative rights even when the writer is not qualified to enter the guild. For instance,*

> *in the above paragraph, you could replace the last sentence with "Writer shall perform services according to the minimum schedule of payments contained in the MBA of the WGA." If the contract is to be pursuant to the WGA, state that clearly and require the Writer to become or remain a member in good standing.*

(c) Option For Rewrite and Polish: Producer shall have an irrevocable and exclusive option ("Option"), for a period of three (3) weeks after delivery of the First Draft, to engage Writer to write and deliver to Producer a rewrite of the First Draft ("Rewrite") and a polish ("Polish") thereof. Producer may exercise said Option by written notice to Writer at any time during the Option period. Writer shall commence Writer's services with respect to the Rewrite upon exercise of the Option, and shall deliver the Rewrite to Producer, incorporating such changes to the First Draft that Producer may require, no later than four (4) weeks after commencement of services.

Producer shall have a period of three (3) weeks from the date of Producer's actual receipt of the Rewrite (the "Reading Period") to study the Rewrite and to confer with Writer regarding any changes to the Rewrite which Producer may require. Writer shall commence Writer's services with respect to the Polish on or before the expiration of the Reading Period, and Writer shall deliver the Polish to Producer, incorporating such changes to the Rewrite that Producer may require, no later than two (2) weeks after commencement of services.

> **Hint:** *By stating that this is an option, you have the right, but not the obligation, to obtain additional services from this writer.*

(d) Postponement of Services: Producer may require Writer to postpone writing either the Rewrite or Polish for a maximum period of six (6) months, provided that Producer pay Writer the applicable fixed compensation for such services as if the services had been timely performed. Writer shall render such postponed services when required by Producer, subject only to Writer's professional availability.

> **Comment:** *This is a fair balancing of interests of the producer to pace progress during development and of the writer not to be hassled by a producer who can't decide what to do.*

(e) Time of the Essence: Time of delivery is of the essence to Producer.

2. EXCLUSIVITY: At all times during the writing periods hereunder, Writer's services shall be furnished by Writer to Producer on an exclusive basis. At all other times, Writer's services shall be furnished on a non-exclusive, but first-priority, basis with no other services to materially interfere.

> *Hint: This paragraph does not add much in most situations, since writers work at home, but it does give you certain rights in case of a flagrant violation. Writers have to avoid contractual conflicts, but as a practical matter most writers don't work exclusively on a single script. They are always noodling about multiple projects.*

3. COMPENSATION: Upon condition that Writer shall fully perform all material services required to be performed by Writer and that Writer is not in default of this Agreement, Producer agrees to pay to Writer, as full consideration for all services to be performed by Writer hereunder, and for all rights herein granted, and all representations and warranties made, the following sums in the following manner:

(a) Fixed Compensation:

(1) First Draft. $_____, payable one half (½) upon execution of this Agreement and one half (½) upon delivery to Producer of the completed First Draft.

(2) Rewrite. In the event Producer exercises Producer's Option hereunder, Producer shall pay to Writer $_____, payable one half (½) upon commencement of Writer's services and one half (½) upon Writer's delivery to Producer of the completed Rewrite.

(3) Polish. In the event Producer exercises Producer's Option hereunder, Producer shall pay to Writer $_____ in connection with the Polish, payable upon commencement of Writer's services in connection therewith.

(b) Additional Compensation: If the Picture is produced, writer shall receive two and one-half percent (2.5%) of the final locked budget of the picture (less overhead, insurance, bond, and interest charges) with a ceiling of $_____ and a floor of $_____, less any amount previously paid to writer, payable on or before the first day of principal photography.

> *How much?: For experienced writers, there are quotes that are used as a basis for payment. A **quote** is merely the price that a writer received for a past assignment. Such quotes tend to establish a floor for the price that the writer accepts in the future. If one of those past scripts was produced and did very well at the box office, that fact usually increases the price. If the film made from the script was a bomb, that fact can soften the price from the past quote. Be sure to verify that the quote given to you was legitimate.*
>
> *Hint: If you don't have much money up front, be prepared to pay more when principal photography begins. However, there are limits. Every film has its own economics. No matter how much money there is to spend on a production, there is a limit to the*

> *amount of the film's budget that goes to the script. That is why this paragraph is structured as a percentage of budget. The real test of a script is whether it is made into a movie. You can never afford to pay up front for the full value of the script if the picture isn't actually made. Even studios do not throw around the big bucks unless they are sure that the film is going to be made. Instead, there is a standard paragraph calling for additional payments to the writer in the event that the film is made. If you are on a real shoestring, even these will be deferred until money comes in as in the next paragraph.*

(c) Contingent Compensation: An amount equal to five percent (5%) of one hundred percent (100%) of the Producer's share of Net Profits, if any, from the Picture, if Writer receives sole "screenplay by" credit in connection with the Picture, or an amount equal to two and one-half percent (2.5%) of the Producer's share of Net Profits, if any, from the Picture, if Writer receives shared "screenplay by" credit in connection with the Picture. "Net Profits" shall be defined, accounted for, and paid in the same manner for Writer as for Producer whether Producer's contingent compensation is called Net Profits, Adjusted Gross Profits, or otherwise.

> ***Note:*** *The word "profit" in the film industry has become a joke due to some ingenious studio accounting practices. "Contingent compensation" avoids much of the negative reaction triggered by the word "profit."*
>
> ***Hint:*** *More for reasons of history than logic, the contingent participation that goes to writers has settled in at 5% for sole writing credit, reducible to 2.5% for shared writing credit. That is the standard in the industry in spite of the fact that the contingent compensation is not mentioned in the MBA of the WGA. So, if a writer asks for such participation, it is hard to argue against it. In a situation where a screenwriter is also your partner, you might go above that, but you would be doing so as a function of the role that the screenwriter plays as a partner, not for the screenwriter's role as a screenwriter. The key is the definition of net profits. The language above leaves everything to be negotiated in the future. The most generous language you can possibly agree to is a definition that links the writer's definition to the producer's. For example: "Net Profits shall be defined, calculated, and paid on the same basis as Producer's contingent compensation, whether such compensation is designated Net Profits, Adjusted Gross Profits, or otherwise." This is a generous provision because all of the various categories of profit participation are treated as one.*

4. CREDIT:

(a) In the event the Picture is produced and Writer has performed all services required of Writer hereunder, Writer shall be entitled to "screenplay by" credit in connection with the Picture as determined pursuant to Exhibit A. All other matters regarding prominence, placement, form, size, style, and color of Writer's credits shall be in Producer's sole discretion. Any paid ad credit to which Writer is entitled hereunder shall be subject to Producer's and any distributor's usual and customary exclusions. Nothing herein shall be construed to prevent so-called award or congratulatory or other similar advertising with respect to the material or Picture that omits the name of the Writer.

> **Hint:** Note the deferment to Exhibit A. Read it carefully to understand the process being proposed. Do not commit irrevocably to the writer's credit unless you are planning to finance the movie yourself, or you have the financial commitment well in hand. The WGA requires producers who sign their agreement to follow the guidelines they have adopted. Even if you are not a signatory, it is best to use their guidelines. The WGA provides a well thought-out, detailed guideline to determining credits, which ought to hold down disputes. It is difficult for a writer to argue against the use of the WGA credit guidelines. Exhibit A was prepared by one of the oldest and largest law firms based in Los Angeles and avoids the pitfalls of merely referencing the WGA agreement, which carries with it certain procedural requirements not available to you unless you sign the WGA agreement.

(b) Inadvertent Non-Compliance: No casual or inadvertent failure to comply with the provisions of this Paragraph shall be deemed to be a breach of this Agreement by Producer unless writer gives Producer notice of a failure to comply hereto and Producer fails to exert good-faith efforts to correct prospectively such within a reasonable time thereafter.

> **Comment:** This is a standard, important provision.

5. WORK-MADE-FOR-HIRE:

(a) Writer hereby acknowledges that all of the results and proceeds of Writer's services produced for the Picture hereunder shall constitute a "work-made for-hire" specially commissioned by Producer and Producer or Producer's assignee shall own all such results and proceeds. Producer shall have the right to use Writer's name and approved likeness with respect to distribution and exploitation of the Picture. Producer may make such use of the Picture and distribution of the Picture as Producer, in its sole discretion, shall deem appropriate.

(b) If Writer's services are not recognized as a "work-made-for-hire," Writer hereby irrevocably grants, sells, and assigns to Producer, its successors and assigns, all of Writer's rights, title, and interest of any kind and nature, in and to the Picture, including, without limitation, all copyrights in connection therewith and all tangible and intangible properties with respect to the Picture, in perpetuity, whether in existence now or as may come into existence in the future.

> **Hint:** *This paragraph is at the heart of a writer's agreement. It says that you own everything that the writer writes. As a Work for Hire, you (or your production company) will be listed as the Author for copyright purposes.*

(c) Certificate of Authorship: Writer will execute and deliver to Producer in connection with all such material the Certificate of Authorship attached hereto as Exhibit B.

> **Hint:** *See comments on that form.*

6. WRITER'S INCAPACITY: If, by reason of mental or physical disability, Writer shall be incapacitated from performing or complying with any of the terms or conditions of this Agreement ("Writer's Incapacity") for a consecutive period in excess of five (5) days or an aggregate period in excess of seven (7) days during the performance of Writer's services, then:

(a) Suspension: Producer shall have the right to suspend Writer's services hereunder so long as Writer's Incapacity shall continue, but in no event shall any suspension hereunder exceed sixty (60) days.

(b) Termination: Producer shall have the right to terminate this Agreement and all of Producer's obligations and liabilities hereunder upon written notice to Writer; except, however, said termination shall not terminate Producer's obligations and liabilities hereunder with respect to any drafts of the Screenplay delivered by Writer to Producer in conformance with the terms and conditions hereof (including, without limitation, any obligations and liabilities that may have accrued relating to the payment of Additional Compensation and the according of credit hereunder).

> **Comment:** *The above paragraph and the next four paragraphs all deal with your rights when you believe the writer is in default. Some independent producers think this all looks too ominous and leave these provisions out. Because the money involved is so much less than that involved in studio deals, it is usually okay just to "cut your losses" and go to another writer. You have the right to terminate even if it is not spelled out in the contract.*

7. WRITER'S DEFAULT: If Writer fails or refuses to write, complete, and deliver to Producer any material herein provided for within the respective periods herein specified, or if Writer otherwise fails or refuses to perform or comply with any of the material terms or conditions hereof other than by reason of Writer's Incapacity ("Writer's Default"), then:

(a) Suspension: Producer shall have the right to suspend Writer's services hereunder so long as Writer's Default shall continue, but in no event shall any suspension hereunder exceed a duration of thirty (30) days.

(b) Termination: Producer shall have the right to terminate this Agreement and all of Producer's obligations and liabilities hereunder upon written notice to Writer; except, however, said termination shall not terminate Producer's obligations and liabilities hereunder with respect to any drafts of the Screenplay delivered by Writer to Producer prior to Termination in conformance with the terms and conditions hereof (including, without limitation, any obligations and liabilities that may have accrued relating to the payment of Additional Compensation and the according of credit hereunder).

(c) Anticipatory Default: Any refusal or statement by Writer implying that Writer will refuse to keep or perform Writer's obligations and/or agreements hereunder shall constitute a failure to keep and perform such obligations and/or agreements from the date of such refusal or indication of refusal and shall be a Writer's Default hereunder.

8. TERMINATION RIGHTS: Termination of this Agreement, for any reason whatsoever, shall:

(a) Compensation: Terminate Producer's obligation to pay Writer any further compensation; except, however, said termination shall not terminate Producer's obligation to compensate Writer as provided hereunder with respect to any drafts of the Screenplay theretofore delivered by Writer to Producer in conformance with the terms and conditions hereof (including, without limitation, any obligation that may have accrued relating to the payment of Additional Compensation hereunder).

(b) Refund or Delivery: If termination occurs prior to Writer's delivery to Producer of the material on which Writer is then currently working, then Writer shall either immediately refund to Producer the compensation which may have been paid to Writer as of that time for such material, or immediately deliver to Producer all of the material then completed or in progress, to be decided in Producer's sole discretion.

9. SUSPENSION RIGHTS: No compensation shall accrue or become payable to Writer during the period of any suspension. If Producer shall have paid compensation to Writer during any period of Writer's Incapacity or Writer's Default, then Producer shall have the right (exercisable at any time) to require Writer to render services hereunder without compensation for a period equal to the period for which Producer shall have paid compensation to Writer during such Writer's Incapacity of Writer's Default; unless Writer immediately refunds to Producer said compensation paid to Writer, upon receipt of notice from Producer to commence such services hereunder.

10. WRITER'S RIGHT TO CURE: If any Writer's Default is inadvertent and reasonably curable, Writer shall have a period of three (3) calendar days from the date of notice of default to cure (one time only) such Writer's Default; provided that if such Writer's Default occurs during principal photography of the Picture, Writer's cure period shall be reduced to twenty-four (24) hours. Any such cure by Writer shall not preclude Producer from exercising any rights or remedies Producer may have hereunder or at law or in equity by reason of Writer's Default.

Go to Chapter 10, Provisions Common to Most Agreements, to finish up this contract. Each one of the provisions set out there ought to be included in this contract for all the reasons listed next to those provisions, except the Ownership paragraph that duplicates one of the paragraphs above. In fact, the signature block is located among those provisions—no signatures, no agreement. (All of those paragraphs refer to "Owner." Change "Owner" to "Writer" to make the language match.)

EXHIBIT A
CREDIT DETERMINATION

A.   Screen credit for the screenplay authorship of a feature-length photoplay will be worded "Screenplay By" or "Screenplay _____."

B.   Except in unusual cases, screen credit for the screenplay will not be shared by more than two (2) writers and in no case will the names of more than three (3) be used, provided, however, that two (2) established writing teams, recognized and employed as such and of not more than two (2) members each, may share screen credit for the screenplay. The intention and spirit of the award of credits being to emphasize the prestige and importance of the screenplay achievement, the one (1), two (2), or at most three (3) writers or two (2) teams chiefly responsible for the completed work will be the only screenwriters to receive screenplay credit.

C.   The only exception to the foregoing shall be a photoplay on which one (1) writer (or a team) writes both the original story and screenplay. In this case, the credit may be worded "Written By."

D.   The term "screenplay" means the final script (as represented on the screen) with individual scenes, full dialogue and camera setups, together with such prior treatment, basic adaptation, continuity, scenario, dialogue, added dialogue or gagging as shall be used in and represent substantial contributions to the final script.

E.   The term "photoplay" means a feature-length photoplay.

F.   No production executive shall be entitled to share in the screenplay authorship screen credit unless he does the screenplay writing entirely without the collaboration of any other writer.

G.   When more than one (1) writer has substantially contributed to the screenplay authorship of a photoplay, then all such writers will have the right to agree unanimously among themselves as to which one (1) or two (2) or, in exceptional cases, three (3) of them, or two (2) teams of the nature above mentioned, shall receive credit on the screen for the authorship of the screenplay. If at any time during the course of production all such writers so agree, then the Producer will not be obligated to issue the notices specified in Paragraphs K through R of this schedule.

H.   The Producer shall have the right to determine in which of the following places the screenplay credit shall appear on the screen:

    1.   On the main title card of the photoplay,

    2.   On a title card on which credits are given only for the screenplay,

3. On a title card on which credits are given for the original story,

4. On a title card on which credits are given for the sources of the material upon which the screenplay was based.

I. A writer whose contribution is judged by the Producer to represent a substantial portion of the completed screenplay shall, for the purpose of this Agreement, be considered a substantial contributor. As a substantial contributor, he shall be entitled to participate in the procedure for determination of screen credits.

J. The screen credits and also the work of writers making substantial contributions but not receiving screen credit may be publicized by the Producer.

K. Before the screen credits for screen authorship are finally determined, the Producer will send a written notice to each writer who is a substantial contributor to the screenplay. This notice will state the Producer's choice of credits on a tentative basis, together with the names of the other substantial contributors and their addresses last known to the Producer.

L. The Producer will make reasonable efforts in good faith to communicate with such writers. No notice will be sent to writers outside the United States or writers who have not filed a forwarding address with the Producer. In the case of remakes, the Producer shall not be under any obligation to send any notice to any writer contributing to the screenplay of the original production unless such writer received screen credit in connection with the original production.

M. The Producer will keep the final determination of screen credits open until a time specified in the notice by the Producer, but such time will not be earlier than six o'clock, p.m., of the fifth business day following dispatch of the notice above specified. If, by the time specified, a written notice of objection to the tentative credits or request to read the script has not been delivered to the Producer from any of the writers concerned, the tentative credits will become final.

N. However, if a protest or request to read the script is received by the Producer from any writer concerned within the time specified in Subdivision M hereof, the Producer will withhold final determination of credits until a time to be specified by the Producer, which time will not be earlier than forty-eight (48) hours after the expiration time specified for the first-notice mentioned in the foregoing paragraphs.

O. Upon receipt of a protest or request to read the script, the Producer will make a copy of the script available for reading at its place of business. The Producer will also notify by fax the writer or writers tentatively designated by the Producer to receive credit, informing them of the new time set for final determination.

P.   If, within the time limit set for final determination of credits, exclusive of any writer or writers waiving claim to screen credit, all of the writers entitled to notice have unanimously designated to the Producer in writing the name of the one (1) or two (2) or, in exceptional cases, three (3) writers or two teams to whom screenplay credit shall be given, the Producer will accept such designation. If such designation is not communicated to the Producer within the time above mentioned, the Producer may make the tentative credits final or change them as the Producer sees fit within the requirements as to wording and limitation of names.

Q.   The writer shall have no rights or claims of any nature against the Producer growing out of or concerning any determination of credits in the manner herein provided, and all such rights or claims are hereby specifically waived.

R.   Any notice specified in the foregoing paragraphs shall be sent by the Producer by faxing, mailing, or delivering the same to the last known address of the writer or may be delivered to the writer personally.

S.   In the event that after the screen credits are determined as hereinabove provided, material changes are made in the script or photoplay that, in the sole and absolute discretion of the Producer, justify a revision of the screen credits, then the procedure for determining such revised credits will be the same as that provided for the original determination of credits.

T.   The writer shall not claim credit for any participation in the screenplay authorship of any photoplay for which the credits are to be determined by the procedure herein provided for prior to the time when such credits have in fact actually been determined, and no writer shall claim credits contrary to such determination.

U.   No casual or inadvertent failure to comply with any of the provisions of this Exhibit shall be deemed to be a breach of the contract of employment of the writer, or entitle him to damages or injunctive relief.

EXHIBIT B
<u>**CERTIFICATE OF AUTHORSHIP**</u>

I, _____, hereby certify that, for good and valuable consideration, receipt of which is hereby acknowledged, I have been commissioned to perform writing services in connection with a motion picture presently entitled "_____" pursuant to an agreement (the "Agreement") between me and _____ ("Producer"), dated as of _____, 20__, and that any and all stories, screenplays, and other material created, composed, submitted, added, or interpolated by me (the "Work") in connection therewith are "work made for hire" for Producer. I further certify that Producer is the "author" of the Work for all purposes, including, without limitation, the copyright laws of the United States, and the owner of the Work and all of the results and proceeds of my services arising out of or in connection with the Agreement, including, without limitation, the theme, plot, characters, ideas, and story contained in, and all copyrights (and all extensions and renewals of copyrights) in and to the Work, and all rights therein and thereto, including the right known as "droit moral," and the right to make such changes therein and such uses thereof as Producer may from time to time determine. I hereby waive the benefit of any provision of law known as "droit moral" or any similar or analogous law or decision in any country of the world.

I further represent and warrant that the Work (except material furnished to me by or on behalf of Producer) is original with me or in the public domain throughout the universe; to the best of my knowledge does not defame, infringe upon, or violate the rights of privacy, rights of copyright, or other rights of any person or entity; and is not the subject of any litigation or to the best of my knowledge claim that might give rise to litigation.

IN WITNESS WHEREOF, I have executed this Certificate of Authorship as of this _____, 20__.

_____

(Writer)

> *Hint:* *Many people add provisions that turn this simple Certificate of Authorship into a contract of its own. The agreement to which it is attached controls all the terms and conditions of the work. Therefore, it is not necessary to clutter this simple certificate with other terms and conditions. Also, it is never a good idea to repeat subject matter because you could end up with internal inconsistencies in your contract.*

You can download this form at www.clearanceandcopyright.com Use the code: ibotCC3

CHAPTER 8

WRITING WITH A PARTNER

For a variety of rational and irrational reasons, you may want to write with a partner rather than hire someone to do all the writing. Usually, the notion is rooted in common dreams at a minimum and more often in a strong friendship. You should know that you are entering territory that all too often ends in heartache, anger, and litigation. This chapter deals with the pitfalls and preventions.

A SPECIAL KIND OF PARTNERSHIP

This writing relationship almost always begins with a great deal of passion and commitment and enthusiasm. It rarely begins with an agreement that covers what happens after the hot, Oscar®-quality script is completed, because both parties know that it will sell instantly for a bucket of money. But what if it doesn't?

When hard choices are faced, the parties usually struggle individually and collectively to figure out what to do with the script. I have seen many examples of this situation turning sour, ripping apart long-standing friendships and leaving both writers feeling used, misunderstood, and unappreciated. Even though you are sure it would never happen to you, it is better to avoid the possibility by reaching an early agreement. If you have a problem making these decisions before you even start writing, imagine how difficult it would be if the choices you face are a series of unhappy choices concerning a completed script that did not sell or if you have just been offered that bucket of money, but your partner thinks the work on the script was not 50/50.

Copyright law controls your relationship with a writing partner, unless you have a written collaboration agreement. Most people are quite surprised at the absolute power of a writing partner when there is no written agreement. A writing partner can stop a deal "deader than a doornail," as my grandmother used to say.

"But that does not make any sense," you protest. "My partner would never do that," you say. Actually, it happens every day— and it is a heartbreaker for everyone involved. Save yourself a lot of grief. Sign a collaboration agreement up front for a happier experience with your writing partner, unless you are willing to completely let go of all control of the finished project.

The dispute can be a completely good-faith dispute based on an honest difference of opinion between two intelligent people. When a script sells, one writer might want terms that the other writer does not care about. Often, one writer would like to do business with a producer with whom the other writer is not comfortable. Often, one writer wants to walk away from a deal if the money is not enough while the other writer wants to go forward, just to get the picture made.

The example at the end of this chapter is a simple collaboration agreement that spells out each partner's rights. It overrides the sometimes dire circumstances imposed by copyright law.

But we can't rush to the contract without a story or two.

Just as I began revising this book, I was hired as an expert witness in the last of the James Bond litigation concerning Ian Fleming and his collaborator on *Thunderball*, Kevin McClory. Ian Fleming had written a half dozen thrillers about a fictional member of Her Majesty's Secret Service, James Bond. Fleming had tried to sell these books to Hollywood to no avail. There was a short period of hope when one of the books was optioned for a television show, but that never went anywhere.

Fleming hooked up with Kevin McClory to write a script. Kevin had some conditions. It would be a new story, not based on any of the books. There would be a new antagonist—a worldwide, world-threatening criminal organization, not some individual satisfied with individual crimes. It would be a new James Bond—witty, urbane, who loved and used plenty of high-tech gadgets, not the stodgy, somewhat sour character of the novels. And there would be women galore, beautiful world-wise women, the likes of which had never before made an appearance in the Fleming novels.

Ian Fleming and Kevin McClory wrote *Thunderball*. They never wrote out a collaboration agreement. They sold *Thunderball*. Still no collaboration agreement.

Fleming thought their deal was for the script only and wrote a novel based on the script called, surprisingly enough, *Thunderball*. Since they had written *Thunderball* together, McClory thought they jointly controlled all rights in the script and that he should receive credit and income from the novel.

McClory sued in England. There was a settlement reached midway through the trial that was reduced to two pages. It settled the particular lawsuit, which is why to this day you will see Kevin McClory's name on every copy of the *Thunderball* novel that was printed after the suit was settled. But still no collaboration agreement!

The very next Bond film produced another lawsuit and another settlement. That was 1976, and the two have been at it ever since, at least until the year 2000, long after Fleming was dead, and the battle involved those who acceded to Fleming's rights. Finally, it is over. Or have I spoken too soon? After such a long period of rancor between the two sides, it is hard to imagine that there will be a truce that counts. The last couple of lawsuits ended in a whimper. McClory has very few legal options left. The court ruled that after his initial victories, McClory should have kept up the legal challenges. Instead, he chose to carry on the fight mostly in the press.

He (and the studio claiming through him) lost the last lawsuit on the theory of laches. **Laches** is a legal theory that says that even if you have a technical right to bring a lawsuit, if you waited too long to bring your suit, you lose.

McClory's position was that he and Fleming had created a new, cinematic James Bond that shared only a name and occupation with the James Bond of the first six novels, and therefore he was entitled to share in the income stream earned from that character. Bond is the most profitable character in movie history. It is a real puzzlement that McClory chose the court of public opinion instead of a court of law to wage most of his battles. After a couple of early wins, he seems to have lost his stomach for the whole thing, but he was still angry enough to take out full-page ads from time to time.

So, even when the script does sell and the movie is made, there can be something other than a happy ending. Please, for your own sanity and happiness, prepare this simple collaboration agreement.

JOINT WORK

What does the law say when you write a script with someone and you do not have a written agreement or—even more common— you have not really discussed the issue? You just assumed that you two would co-own the resulting script. You assumed that you would get some proportional share, if not 50%. First rule to remember in the area of copyright is that your agreement has to be in writing or it does not count for a thing. That is also true as between joint authors. Without any written agreement to the contrary, each joint author receives the right to an equal, undivided interest in the copyright and the right to deal in any of an author's rights, subject only to an accounting to the other author and payment of his or her share.

The trick is to figure out if you are really joint authors under the copyright law. The copyright law defines a joint work as "a work prepared by two or more authors with the intention that their contributions be merged into inseparable or interdependent parts of a unitary whole." The disputes usually arise when one person thinks the activity was co-writing and the other person thinks the activity was a friend being a producer or a director or a dramaturge. When the suggestion is made that the activity was co-writing, hurt and indignation flare. That leads quickly to anger and shortly thereafter to litigation. The courts have protected authors from claim-jumping by overreaching research assistants, editors and former spouses, lovers and friends, and other people whom authors talk to about what they are writing.

In the past, courts primarily focused on whether the plaintiff made some separately copyrightable contribution in order to have any ownership right in a script or film. This is difficult to determine in many cases in which there are true collaborators. The two writers sit in a room talking all day, one of them pecking away occasionally on the computer, but they are creating together. The person not at the computer is comfortably making a 50% contribution, even though the other person is the only one typing in the information.

The courts are also looking at whether the parties shared mutual intent when the writing or filming was taking place, to create a work of joint authorship. Without that intent, the courts say, there cannot be a work of joint authorship. Since that almost always takes both parties admitting that fact and you would not be in a dispute if you agreed, these cases have become very hard to win. Sometimes, how the parties are credited on the project at various stages helps to determine the intent of the parties.

All of these cases seem to grow out of people not reducing their expectations to writing. Worse yet, there is a strong undercurrent to the cases that the person thinking they were treated badly never articulated what they thought was a fair treatment in the first place.

Malcom X, like all movies, was the result of a lot of contributions by a lot of people. One of them was Jefri Aalmuhammed, who was credited in the end-roll credits as Islamic Technical Consultant. He sued Spike Lee and Warner Bros. and a lot of people, claiming joint authorship in order to obtain credit on the film and to share in the profits. Everyone agreed that he had made enormous contributions to the film, its dialogue, and even some characters. Even a couple of scenes that he wrote found their way into the finished film. But Warner Bros. was the copyright holder. They didn't even share copyright ownership with Spike Lee, so any effort to say that they *intended* to share the copyright with anyone else was going nowhere.

Let's be clear. If Aalmuhammed had spoken up earlier and tried to reach an agreement whereby he would share the copyright or even screen credit for co-writing the script, he would have—in all likelihood—failed in his efforts. However, that would have been much better than waiting for the film to be complete and then spend a lot of time and money and psychic energy on a lawsuit. He could have been totally aware of the situation and chosen how he wanted to behave, given the fact that he was not going to receive credit or ownership. This book is rife with examples of the virtue of expressing your needs and wants clearly and early.

The court also talked a lot about superintendence in the *Malcom X* case. The court's opinion focused on who had the final say. Joint authors have an equal say. If all the suggestions of one person can be accepted or rejected without any reason by the other person, that other person has superintendence over the script or film. It is that superintendence that identifies a sole author as opposed to someone who is co-authoring.

The notion of superintendence also played a central role in the decision in the musical *Rent*. After a seriously flawed workshop production of *Rent*, Ms. Thomson was brought in to help fix it, and fix it she did. However, all of her suggestions and input were subject to the approval of the author. Even though she wrote up to 9% of the final dialogue for the show, not a word went in without Larson's approval. And there were no other indicia of authorship ever discussed, such as shared credit, so Ms. Thomson lost her claim to co-ownership of *Rent*, although she retained ownership of the lines in *Rent* that she wrote. Her only alternative was to pull out her 9% of dialogue. Those words would have been fairly useless to her and harmful to *Rent*, so the parties were able to reach a financial settlement after the decision was rendered, but the result was dissatisfying to everyone. It would have been much better to settle all of this up front.

However, you should know that not all courts give the same importance to superintendence. Some federal courts look solely at the parties' shared intent and whether they made separate, copyrightable contributions. One federal court has said that this rule is better than the Ninth Circuit rule used in the *Malcolm X* case, reasoning that the concept of superintendence is susceptible to manipulation. The court found that the plaintiff wrongfully denied the defendant from exercising control over the project. The court said that such a situation exposes a flaw in the Ninth Circuit's rule because strict application of the rule would reward parties who wrongfully prevent a true collaborator from exercising control.

SILENCE IS GOLDEN

While you always want to give credit where credit is due, never ever put someone's name on a script without the intent that the script is indeed co-authored. More than once I have been consulted by someone who placed someone else's name on a few copies of a script "to make them feel good," "to send to their family," or "to get them off my back about the credit thing." What better proof of co-authorship could there possibly be than if you, yourself, put someone else's name on a script? Be clear about the connection between the credit that you ultimately intend to use and the credits that show up on all those interim drafts.

Mike Batt, the British composer and producer, discovered the importance of credit when he included a track of absolute silence on the debut album entitled *Classical Graffiti* by The Planets. They were a group of eight sexy young adults looking to become crossover successes as violinist Vanessa Mae and Bond, the handsome string quartet. Batt called the track "A One Minute Silence" and then, in homage to the late John Cage, the composer of a "silent" musical composition entitled *4'33"*, Mike Batt listed the composers of "A One Minute Silence" as "Batt/Cage."

It's all a joke, right? Wrong. The Mechanical-Copyright Protection Society, the British organization that collects royalties for composers and publishers of music, sent a license form to Batt on behalf of Cage's publishing company. They wanted half of the mechanical royalties for that track of the CD, since a separate payment is made for each track of a CD. Batt's rejoinder (and the ironic observation of more than one otherwise serious music critic in London) was that Batt's silent minute was very different from John Cage's four minutes and thirty-three seconds of silence he had recorded years earlier. Hmmmm. Sometimes, the law of copyright and the money flow that it controls can lead to some Byzantine results. After a brief splash in the press, this particular dispute was settled privately.

HIRING COLLABORATORS

As a producer, you may hire a team of writers or option a script written by two or more writers. In these instances, a collaboration agreement not only protects the writers. It can also protect you.

If the writers get in a squabble after you become involved as a producer, you will be drawn into the controversy, your project will be affected. This is not what you want. Making a movie is hard enough without the writers being at war.

If you are dealing with a team of writers, ask to see their collaboration agreement. More often than not they will not have one. In that case, be very careful that your option and purchase agreement spells out carefully your rights vis-à-vis the writers.

You must be sure that you have the right to move the script along; that if you hire them to write as a team, you can fire them as a team for the breach of either one; that you can hire someone else to write in the future; the order of names for purposes of credit is settled or under your control; and that it is clear how the money is to be paid to them. Don't get involved in their problems. Quietly cover all of these issues in your option and purchase agreement.

The collaboration agreement that follows is structured in response to the fact situation in which you as the producer will be co-writing with another person who will be carrying the laboring oar with regard to the writing. If you are two writers starting out on a script without any purchaser in mind, there will be a few variations that are pointed out in the comment sections to the agreement.

8.01 COLLABORATION AGREEMENT

This Agreement, effective as of _____, 200__, is made by and between [NAME OF 1ST WRITER] (Writer A), located at [PHYSICAL ADDRESS], and [NAME OF 2ND WRITER] (Writer B), located at [PHYSICAL ADDRESS], regarding collaboration on a proposed script for a feature-length film entitled "_____ _____" ("Work").

> **Comment:** *Fill in the names in the agreement in the same order as you want them to appear in the credit. The credit paragraph is on the next page, but you will want to start off the agreement in the same way. Fill in the most permanent address available for each writer, which is often not his or her current residence.*
>
> **Hint:** *This agreement will be more user-friendly if you use the writers' last name rather than Writer A and Writer B.*

1. Each Writer will provide the other with access to all material prepared to date on the Work. The Writers agree to be available to each other at convenient times to supply additional information and for consultations, conferences, and story meetings.

2. Writer A will write the script of the Work. In writing the Work, Writer A agrees to adhere to material supplied to Writer A by Writer B or by others to whom Writer B introduces Writer A and not introduce any extraneous incidents or anecdotes without first obtaining Writer B's personal approval. Notwithstanding anything to the contrary contained herein, Writer B shall have personal approval over the contents of the script. Writer A shall deliver the first draft screenplay on or before _____, _____.

> **Comment:** *Both the paragraph above and the paragraph below assume that you are clearly the producer on this project and you have entered into this collaboration agreement because you have a great idea, but no money; these paragraphs also assume that you will be helping and performing some writing service, especially with regard to the idea and developing the story, but that "Writer A" will be doing most of the work at the computer. If you are two friends starting out to write a script together, you can describe your working relationship in the above paragraph and modify the next paragraph to cover the situation if one of you wants to quit or, worse, starts slacking off on the work.*

3. Should Writer A be unable to deliver a complete and satisfactory script because of Writer B's failure to cooperate with Writer A, Writer A shall have the right to terminate this Agreement, but Writer A may retain any moneys already paid to him or his designee for his work, and Writer B retains all rights in and to the material created. Should Writer A deliver a script that is unacceptable for any reason directly relating to the quality of Writer A's work, Writer B

may terminate this Agreement, and Writer A shall have the obligation to return any moneys paid to Writer A under this Agreement. If this Agreement is terminated for any of the aforementioned reasons, it is specifically understood that Writer B shall have the unencumbered right to enter into an agreement with regard to the Work with another writer.

4. If either party shall be unavailable for the purposes of collaborating on such revision or screenplay, then the party who is available shall be permitted to do such revision or screenplay and shall be entitled to the full amount of compensation in connection therewith, provided, however, that in such a case wherein there shall be a revision in the original selling price, the party not available for the revision or screenplay shall receive from the other party $_____ or _____% of the total selling price.

> **Comment:** *Often, when a script is sold, the purchase agreement contains a provision that the writer is obligated to write one or more revisions to the script. If you are writing with someone else, it is a good idea to have that number separated out in the purchase agreement so that you do not have to get into an argument with your co-writer if you end up doing all the work on the rewrite or vice versa.*

5. Upon completion of the Work, it shall be registered with the Writers Guild of America, West, Inc. ("WGA") as the joint work of the parties. If the work shall be in the form such as to qualify it for copyright protection under the Copyright Act, it shall be registered for such copyright protection with the United States Copyright Office in the names of each of the parties, and each party hereby designates the other party or parties as such party's true and lawful attorney-in-fact to so register such Work on behalf of the other party or parties, which right is coupled with an interest.

> **Comment:** *The last sentence of the above paragraph contains a new phrase that you might not be familiar with, "a right coupled with an interest." A right coupled with an interest refers to a legal concept concerning making someone your agent, representative, or attorney in law or attorney-in-fact. When you appoint someone as your representative and that person has an interest in the subject, you cannot cut off that representation so easily. It is not impossible, but it certainly is not as easy as when you would normally just be able to write a letter and withdraw the power to represent you.*

6. The credit on the Work where credit appears, and in any and all forms and in any and all media in which the Work is used or licensed, will be the same size, color, and boldness and shall read as follows:

Written by [A] _____ and [B] _____

7. Writer A and Writer B represent and warrant that each is free to enter into this Agreement, and that insofar as material created by each is concerned, the work is original, it does not contain any libelous or other unlawful matter; and it does not invade any right of privacy or publicity nor infringe any statutory or common-law copyright. Each writer agrees to hold the other harmless from and against any and all claims of libel or of copyright infringement or of invasion of privacy or similar rights arising out of material created by each writer in the Work.

8. The parties agree that all income received from the world-wide sale or disposition of any and all rights in and to the Work (including, but not limited to, print publication rights, dramatic motion picture, television and allied rights) shall be divided between the parties as follows: __% to Writer A and __% to Writer B. Neither party shall enter into any other agreement or dispose of rights in or to the Work unless it is done so under this Agreement. The parties will each be paid directly by any third party.

> **Hint:** *Without an agreement to the contrary, the law imposes an even split, no matter how uneven the contributions are. The last sentence benefits everybody by eliminating future accounting disputes.*

9. Neither party may enter into any agreement for any of the rights in and to the Work without the written consent of the other party. Co-signature of agreements for the disposition of any such rights shall constitute written agreement by both parties.

> **Hint:** *This language reflects the law without an agreement. As a producer, you will probably want to replace this language with the following, which shifts control to you: "Writer B has the right to market, develop, and exploit the work so long as Writer A is kept fully informed and all receipts are divided as provided herein."*

10. If the parties cannot agree on how to exploit the Work after one or both of them have completed the Work or cannot agree on how to complete the Work, then Writer A will take over the project for two years to complete and market the property and may enter any agreement with a bona fide third party, so long as Writer A keeps Writer B advised of all significant activities, advises Writer B before entering into an agreement transferring rights of any kind in the property, and provides in the agreement of transfer for direct payment to Writer B of Writer B's share of the proceeds as provided in this Agreement. After the two-year period elapses, Writer A's rights pursuant to this paragraph will shift to Writer B, subject to all the same conditions for the next two years. The right to complete, market, and exploit the work will continue to switch back and forth until the work is sold.

> **Comment:** *This is a scheme that prevents the script from being the victim of a disagreement between two collaborators. The project can still move forward. It is not ideal, but then the situation is not ideal either. This paragraph creates a workable solution where none else might be available. Feel free to craft your own solution to this problem.*

11. If any disposition is made for any rights in or to the Work, this Agreement shall be in force and effect and continue for the life of the copyright therein.

12. The parties agree that Writer B shall be responsible for all expenses incurred in the preparation of the Work until such time as funds are received from any source, at which time expenses shall be reimbursed after payment of commissions and before the agreed to split between Writer A and Writer B.

> **Comment:** *This is the standard agreement when Writer B is a producer. If you two are writers who will be looking for a producer once the script is completed, you should each bear your own expenses. If the script requires a research trip somewhere or some other substantial expenditure, the party making the expense should be reimbursed off the top. Off the top means that the reimbursement is made before the agreed split of proceeds.*

13. Any controversy between the parties hereto involving the construction or application of any of the terms, covenants, or conditions of this Agreement shall, on written request of one party served on the other, be submitted to arbitration before a single arbitrator in Los Angeles, California, according to the Rules of the Independent Film and Television Alliance ("ITFA"). The cost of arbitration, including attorney fees, shall be borne by the losing party.

> **Comment:** *The virtues of arbitration are many to the independent producer. Whatever you do, you want to stay out of court. Many people like to have mandatory mediation before going to arbitration. Mediation is the process by which the parties to a disagreement agree to talk through the problem with a neutral third party who is trained to bring people into agreement. Mediation is a good idea, but often involves some money, always involves some time delays, and is something that many people would like to decide upon when a dispute arises. If it is appropriate, mediation is easy enough to institute.*

_____   _____
Writer A   Writer B

You can download this form at www.clearanceandcopyright.com
Use the code: ibotCC3

CHAPTER 9

BUYING SOMEONE ELSE'S COMPLETED SCRIPT

Every movie starts as a gleam in someone's eye ... a hope, a dream. A good script is hard to find, and when you find one, it screams out to be made. If you are planning to option a completed script and have therefore skipped Chapter 7, review it now. There is a lot of helpful information there about options in general and why you need them in writing. To be fully prepared for your negotiation, you should also read both the previous chapter and the following chapter, which cover related deal points.

SPEC SCRIPTS

Many writers will submit their completed spec script to you in the hope that you will produce it. A **spec script** is a script written on speculation—the speculation that you or some other producer will want to option and/or purchase the script and make a movie based on it. No one paid the writer, so the writer owns all rights in the script.

The script will have been brought to your attention by either its writer or a go-between, such as an agent, a manager, or a lawyer. Either way, you should talk directly to the screenwriter about the film you want to make, if you can.

If by any chance the screenwriter's address and phone number are not on the cover of the script, you can call the Writers Guild of America, West at (323) 782-4505 or the Writers Guild of America, East at (212) 767-7821 and ask for member-contact information. This service tells you the name and phone number of the person to contact for any writer who is WGA member. If the writer you wish to contact is not a WGA member, try the phone book. Again, talk directly to the writer if at all possible.

If the script is written by co-authors, review the information in Chapter 8 about collaboration agreements. Even on the option and purchase of a simple script by one author, you need to be sure that you are dealing with the correct person. You'll note that within the boilerplate provisions discussed in Chapter 11, there are certain representations and warranties. But you still are better off making a personal inquiry rather than relying on the "boilerplate" guarantees that an anxious author might not even read.

When you talk to the author, ask about all the details of the creation of the work. You need to be sure that the writer is the exclusive owner of what they are attempting to sell you. You must be totally comfortable that you are dealing with everyone who needs to be dealt with. If you were to ask, "Did you get any help on this script?" or, "Did anyone help you write it?" the answer is usually "no." So ask the question a little differently to get a more complete answer. Ask, "Who did you work with on this script?" Make notes on this conversation, keep it in your chain-of-title file. Again, you should review the information on collaboration agreements and rights of co-authors.

The actual option and purchase agreement is fairly simple and straightforward. The tough part is finding a really good script that is worth the effort and energy needed to turn it into a film. That takes a lot of reading and a firm knowledge of what you like and why. Before laying out any money or energy or time on the project, you want to be sure that you have in mind the same film that the writer has in mind. Find out if you share a vision of the ultimate film: What is the tone of the film? Who would be a good director and why? What actors do you see in the lead roles? What budget are you going to try for? Where do you want the film to be shot?

Once you have purchased a script, you have the legal right to take it in whatever direction you want, but you and your project are better off if everyone starts out headed in the same direction. For one thing, if you like the script so much, you probably want any script changes to be made by the original writer. (Even if no additional writing is indicated, a polish is almost always required when the director and the stars become attached.) Generally, you can negotiate a better deal with the original writer involved because the original writer knows the material and the original writer is more motivated to see the film made than a replacement writer would be.

A sample Option and Purchase Agreement can be found at the end of this chapter. It has all the standard provisions and explanations, or useful hints concerning many of them. This agreement can be typed into your system or downloaded from the Internet by visiting www.clearanceandcopyright.com. Then you should modify it for your particular situation before you line up your money. It is straightforward and shorter than many option and purchase agreements used in Hollywood. One reason is that the "option agreement" and the "purchase agreement" are combined into one document. This combined approach seems more natural for most people. A short-form assignment is attached as an exhibit to use as needed. This is a very important document. Be sure to have that assignment signed right along with the main agreement, even though you will not record it with the Copyright Office until you complete the purchase of film rights. The purchase of the property usually happens just before the commencement of principal photography. Things are moving fast at that point in time and you can't afford any delay. You certainly can't afford to deal with a rights-holder who wants to hold you up for their own nefarious reasons. Get the copyright holder's signature early. It would not hurt to have a lawyer review your changes, but common sense is your biggest ally. As soon as you complete the paperwork on this (or any other) option agreement, mark your calendar with at least two important dates: the date that the option runs out and one month before. This may be the most valuable tip in this book.

Once an option terminates—once its time runs out—there is nothing you can do to revive it without the owner's agreement. The option is dead after the last day of its existence. You cannot revive it without the owner allowing you to do so. It is not like an agreement with a contractor who shows up a day late with paintbrush in hand and paints your house. In that case, you owe the painter the agreed-upon amount of money. If you show up a day late with your extension check in your hand, nothing happens. The option is dead. Nothing you do replaces the act of extending your option in a timely fashion. The writer is under no legal or moral obligation to grant you a new option or to revive the old one.

PROTECTING YOURSELF AGAINST UNSOLICITED SCRIPTS

Writers are submitting their scripts all over town. As a producer, you may receive dozens of spec scripts that are not what you are looking for. If you later produce a film that in any way resembles a spec script that a writer submitted to you, that writer might very well file a claim of infringement. (See Chapter 1 for an example involving Warren Beatty and his film *Shampoo*.)

You can gain some protection against unsolicited scripts (and those who send them to you) by the use of a submission agreement. A **submission agreement** provides that if you read a script, the writer will not bring a claim against you for copyright infringement if you produce a similar movie without the writer's participation. The use of these agreements grew out of the cases discussed earlier in this book. There is a handy example of an agreement at the end of this chapter. Print it out and address it to yourself. You can then have the writer sign it.

Most studios, the independent producers who occupy offices on their lots, and other established people do not want to read scripts that come to them "over the transom." If the script is not from an agent or a known entertainment attorney, they do not want to receive it in their offices, much less read it. Not only are the odds against it being much good, the long shadow of litigation looms over every uninvited project that creeps into one's office.

If you are reading scripts by writers who are not represented, you should have the writers of these scripts sign some type of submission agreement. The writer has very little choice—the signing of these documents is generally nonnegotiable. There are simply too many new scripts registered with the Writers Guild each year. It usually doesn't make sense to read scripts from writers you don't know or who do not even have an agent. You do not care if the writer chooses not to sign the agreement and therefore not to submit the script to you. By refusing to sign, the writer has just saved you the trouble of reading one more (probably bad) script.

The submission agreement is an egregious document. In fact, some of these agreements go so far that they are not enforceable. The writer is between a rock and hard place on this one. On its face, it says that you can do anything you want with the submitted material, but obviously, an overt act of plagiarism would not be protected. Infringement cases are hard to win, but you do not want to be sued. Submission agreements give you some protection.

BUYING
SOMEONE
ELSE'S
COMPLETED
SCRIPT

173

9.01   OPTION AND PURCHASE AGREEMENT

THIS AGREEMENT, effective as of _____, 20__, is made by and between [NAME OF PRODUCER] ("Producer"), located at [PHYSICAL ADDRESS], and [NAME OF WRITER] ("Writer"), located at [PHYSICAL ADDRESS], concerning the rights to a motion picture script entitled "_____" and the materials upon which it is based. The following terms and conditions shall apply:

> **Comment:** *Refer to Chapter 7 if you have any questions as to how to fill out this introductory paragraph.*

1.   DEFINITION OF "WORK": For purposes of this Agreement, "Work" means the motion picture script entitled "_____" written by _____ and any and all other literary materials, titles, themes, formats, formula, incidents, action, story, dialogue, ideas, plots, phrases, slogans, catchwords, art, designs, compositions, sketches, drawings, characters, characterizations, names, and trademarks now contained therein, as well as such elements as may at any time hereafter be added or incorporated therein, and all versions thereof in any form.

> **Work:** *Pick the best description of the property you are optioning. If there was a previous title, include that also by saying, "and previously entitled _____." If the Work has been registered with the Copyright Office, you might give that registration number by way of further identification.*

2.   GRANT OF OPTION: In consideration of the mutual promises contained herein, and the payment to Writer of $_____ (the "Option Price"), which shall be applicable against the total Purchase Price, Writer hereby grants to Producer the exclusive, irrevocable right and option (the "Option") for _____ months (the "Option Period") to acquire the exclusive motion picture, television, DVD, Internet, and all subsidiary, allied, and ancillary rights in and to the Work pursuant to the terms set forth below.

> **Option Price:** *You want this to be as low as possible. Sometimes you can even negotiate a free period. Do not be surprised if you run into someone (like me) who says: "No Free Option!" That is my mantra when representing the owner of a property, although I obtain "free" options all of the time for my independent producer clients. My argument: It's not "free!" My client will be working, writing (maybe), (if not) hiring someone to write, shopping the project, and generally spending time, effort, and money on the project.*
>
> **Hint:** *Since you do not have the deep pockets of a studio, your first job is to convince the author of your passion for the script. Listen to the author's dreams and hopes. You will be the protector of those*

dreams and hopes. As self-serving as it may sound, it truly is not about the money at the option stage. Except in big studio deals for hot properties, the initial payment is simply not large enough to be the most important aspect of the deal. The likelihood of the film getting made is the important thing. However, the emotional hook—the sizzle that closes your negotiation—can be a simple promise from you: "If you entrust your property to me, I will be as honest to your work as possible. I will keep you advised every step of the way, and I will do my best to protect you."

Option Period: *Twelve (12) months to eighteen (18) months is standard for this first period.*

3.   EXTENSION OF OPTION:

(a) Producer shall have the right to extend the Option Period for one (1) period of twelve (12) months for $_____ non-applicable. For the right to the extension of the first Option Period there must be one of the following:

(i)   letter of commitment to direct from an established director;

(ii) the project is set up at a company, major studio, or mini-major studio able to fund the project;

(iii) substantial negotiations in progress for complete financing of the film; or

(iv) letter of commitment to act in the film from one star.

(b) Producer shall have the right to extend the Option Period for one (1) additional twelve- (12-) month period for $_____ non-applicable. In order to have a right to a second extension, Producer must secure at least two (2) of the above four (4) items.

Option Extension: *It is standard that you have the right to extend the option. This is important because it takes a very long time to get a film made. Even three years total, as provided here, is a short time. Inexperienced producers often think that they will get their movie made more quickly than anybody else. Based on what? Be realistic. Writers are reluctant to have their material off the market for a long period of time. Frequently, the amounts paid for the second and third years are substantially higher than the amount paid for the initial period . . . and they are non-applicable.*

Non-Applicable: *Whether subsequent option payments apply or do not apply to the final purchase price is often a point of negotiation. The initial payment is usually applicable (i.e., deductible). More often than not, these additional payments are not deducted from the purchase price. The money must be paid before the time elapses under the current option. This payment acts to keep the*

BUYING
SOMEONE
ELSE'S
COMPLETED
SCRIPT

175

option open for the extended period of time. If you let your op-tion expire, you no longer have any right to buy the work or to extend the option. The original owner is then free to option the work to another party.

Progress Requirements: *One way to soften the length of time and/or to get more time is to have your right to renew the option be a result of progress made on the film. That is the approach used above. But do not make those barriers too high. The last sentences of Subparagraph (a) and Subparagraph (b) might work for you— though you don't have to include them in your first draft. If no such demand is made, you can strike this language. (Be sure to tailor the language to your needs.) No studio ever makes this kind of deal. Studios simply pay option prices. Therefore, if you use this approach, you must provide alternatives if the project is set up at a studio. After that, the option may be renewed with a cash payment only.*

4.   EXERCISE OF OPTION: Producer may exercise this Option at any time during the Option Period, as it may be extended, by giving written notice of such exercise to Writer and delivery to Writer of the minimum Purchase Price as set forth below. In the event Producer does not exercise said Option during the period as it may be extended, this Agreement shall be of no further force or effect whatsoever. All rights granted hereunder become property of Writer. Upon exercise of the Option, the date of exercise shall be inserted in the blank space provided in the short form copy-right assignment, attached hereto as Exhibit A. Exhibit A shall be and will become a binding agreement between the parties hereto without any further execution or delivery. In the event Producer does not exercise said Option within the time and in the manner herein set forth herein, Exhibit A shall be of no further force or effect whatsoever.

> ***Comment:*** *This paragraph is what gives you the ability to purchase the rights you have optioned. It is standard.*

5.   PENDING EXERCISE OF OPTION: Producer shall have the right to engage in all customary development and pre-production activities during the option period as it may be extended, including the right to revise the work.

> ***Hint:*** *The fact that you optioned the film rights infers this to be true. One of the things you want is to be able to change the script. That means creating a derivative work, which requires permis-sion of the copyright owner who is the writer. This is where you obtain the writer's permission. Stating the fact clearly is better. Often people add "including, but not limited to" and then go on for a page or two. That's overkill.*

> **Comment:** *Many writers will want a guarantee that they will write the first revision, if any, of the script. Fair enough. If you don't think the writer is up to taking the script to the next level, look at this payment as part of the cost of the script.*

6. GRANT OF RIGHTS: Effective upon Producer's exercise of the Option, Writer hereby exclusively sells, grants, and assigns to Producer, Producer's successors, licensees, and assigns all rights in and to the Work not reserved by Writer, throughout the universe, in perpetuity, in any and all media and by any means now known or hereafter devised, including, without limitation, all forms of theatrical and non-theatrical distribution and exhibition (including, without limitation, free broadcast, pay television, cable, subscription, pay-per-view, video-on-demand, DVD, and Internet), including, without limitation the following: all motion picture rights, including the right to make remakes, new versions or adaptations of the Work or any part thereof; to make series and serials of the Work or any part thereof; the right, for advertising and publicity purposes only, to prepare, broadcast, exhibit, and publish in any form or media, any synopses, excerpts, novelizations, serializations, dramatizations, summaries, and stories of the Work, or any part thereof; and all rights of every kind and character whatsoever in and to the Work and all the characters and elements contained therein.

> **Hint:** *This is exactly what you are purchasing. This is why you are making the payments. This paragraph can also run on for pages, but the above is all-inclusive. It puts the burden on the Writer to be specific about reserved rights.*

7. PURCHASE PRICE: As complete consideration for all services to be performed by Writer hereunder, for all rights herein granted, and all representations and warranties made, Producer agrees to pay Writer two and a half percent (2.5%) of the final locked budget for the motion picture based on the Work with a floor of $_____ and a ceiling of $_____, if Writer receives sole credit; reducible to one and a quarter percent (1.25%) if Writer receives shared credit, with a floor of $_____ and a ceiling of $_____. Such amount shall be paid no later than the commencement of principal photography of the production.

> **Purchase Price:** *Price can be a flat fee or a percentage of the film's budget, or a combination. Most film budgets allow about 2.5% or 3% of the budget for purchase of the script, with a floor and ceiling. The floor is the minimum price you pay, regardless of the budget. The ceiling is the maximum price you pay, regardless of the budget.*

BUYING
SOMEONE
ELSE'S
COMPLETED
SCRIPT

177

8. ADDITIONAL COMPENSATION:

(a) Contingent Compensation: Producer also agrees to pay five percent (5%) of one hundred percent (100%) of the Producer's share of net profits if Writer receives sole credit; reducible to two and a half percent (2.5%) if Writer receives shared credit. "Net Profits" shall be defined, accounted for, and paid in the same manner for Writer as for Producer, whether Producer's contingent compensation is called Net Profits, Adjusted Gross Profits, or otherwise.

> *Comment: Net Profits have gotten a bad name. Try using Contingent Compensation. The language in this agreement avoids all accusations of Hollywood accounting, at least by you, because Writer gets a piece of what you get. If you are going to pay for the film yourself or through your family and friends or a company you own or control, be sure to spell out your definition of Contingent Compensation. Be as specific as possible to avoid future conflicts. The standard is 5% for sole credit, 2.5% for shared credit.*

(b) Bonus Compensation: Producer shall pay Writer $_____ in addition to any other money due Writer under this agreement upon the happening of the following: _____

_____.

> *Performance Bonus: Use this paragraph only after the Writer requests it! Often there are bonuses if a film grosses over a certain domestic box office as reported in* Weekly Variety *or* The Hollywood Reporter *(e.g., $10,000 if the film grosses $100 million in domestic box office). Usually such performance bonuses are advances against contingent compensation. Do not grant bonuses for things like awards or Oscar nominations. These events do not always translate into money for you.*

9. CREDITS:

(a) In the event a motion picture based substantially on the Work is produced hereunder, Writer shall receive credit in the following form:

Written by _____

unless the credit guidelines of Writers Guild of America would produce another result, in which case the credit will be determined according to those guidelines.

(b) Such credit shall be accorded on a single card in the main titles on all positive prints of the picture and in all paid advertising in which the director has received credit, subject to Producer's and any distributor's usual and customary exclusions. All other matters regarding prominence, placement, size, style, and color of said credits shall be in Producer's sole discretion. Nothing herein shall be construed to prevent so-called award or congratulatory or other similar advertising with respect to the material or Picture that omits the name of the Writer.

> **Comment:** *This is a very precise description of your obligations as far as credit. It is acceptable to the studios and to any legitimate distributor.*

(c) No casual or inadvertent failure to comply with credit requirements hereunder shall be deemed a breach of this Agreement.

> **Hint:** *This is very important to you, since there can always be a slip-up. Often the Writer insists (and you should agree) that you take reasonable steps to correct any mistake when it is brought to your attention. If asked, you should agree to add, "provided Producer takes reasonable steps to prospectively cure upon written notice from Writer."*

> *Go to Chapter 10, Provisions Common to Most Agreements, to finish up this contract. You should use all the paragraphs contained there except Expenses, unless the Writer brings that up.*

BUYING
SOMEONE
ELSE'S
COMPLETED
SCRIPT

179

EXHIBIT A
ASSIGNMENT (Short Form)

FOR good and valuable consideration, receipt of which is hereby acknowledged, the undersigned Writer does hereby sell, grant, assign, and set over unto _____ (hereinafter referred to as "Producer"), and Producer's heirs, successors, licensees, and assigns, forever, the sole and exclusive motion picture rights, television motion picture, and other television rights, DVD, and Internet rights, and certain subsidiary, allied, and ancillary rights, including merchandising rights and limited publication rights, for advertising and exploitation purposes only, throughout the universe in perpetuity, in and to the script (e.g., original literary/musical) described as follows:

Title: "_____"

By: _____

including all contents thereof, all present and future adaptations and versions thereof, and the theme, title, and characters thereof. The undersigned and Producer have entered into a formal option and purchase agreement dated _____, 20__, relating to the transfer and assignment of the foregoing rights in and to said Work, which rights are more fully described in said Option and Purchase Agreement. This Assignment is expressly made subject to all of the terms and conditions of said Agreement.

IN WITNESS WHEREOF, the undersigned has executed this assignment on _____, 20__.

WRITER: _____

> **Hint:** This document is signed along with the main agreement so that you don't have to obtain it later. You do not use it until you actually exercise the option agreement and own the film rights to the Work (book, song, article). When you exercise the option and own the Work, one of the first things you do is to file the assignment with the Copyright Office for all the reasons stated in the Chain of Title chapter (Chapter 21). Use the Cover Sheet provided in Chapter 21 to record the assignment.
>
> **Comment:** Consideration is legalese shorthand for whatever is of value that you give up for what you get. Money is the "consideration" that most people think of. Your promises can also be consideration. It is okay to reference the fact of consideration without spelling out details, especially in a document like this that will be open to the public.

You can download this form at www.clearanceandcopyright.com
Use the code: ibotCC3

9.02   SUBMISSION AGREEMENT

[date]

[Producer's name]
[Producer's address]

Dear [Producer's name]

I desire to submit to you for your consideration the following described material (herein called "Submitted Material"), written, composed, owned, or controlled by me and intended to be used by you as the basis for one or more theatrical motion pictures:

I recognize the possibility that the Submitted Material may be identical with or similar to material which has or may come to you from other sources. Such similarity in the past has given rise to litigation so that, unless you can obtain adequate protection in advance, you will refuse to consider the Submitted Material. The protection for you must be sufficiently broad to protect you, your related corporations, and your and their employees, agents, licensees, and assigns and all parties to whom you submit material. Therefore, all references to you include each and all of the foregoing.

As a material inducement to you to examine and consider the Submitted Material, and in consideration of your so doing, I represent, warrant, and agree to the following terms and conditions:

1.   I acknowledge that the Submitted Material is submitted by me voluntarily, on an unsolicited basis, and not in confidence, and that no confidential relationship is intended or created between us by reason of the submission of the Submitted Material. Nothing in this agreement, nor the submission of the Submitted Material, shall be deemed to place you in any different position from any other member of the public with respect to the Submitted Material. Accordingly, any part of the Submitted Material that could freely be used by any member of the public may be used by you without liability to me.

2.   You agree that you shall not use the Submitted Material unless you shall first negotiate with me and agree upon compensation to be paid to me for such use, but I understand and agree that your use of material containing features or elements similar to or identical with those contained in the Submitted Material shall not obligate you to negotiate with me or entitle me to any compensation if you have an independent legal right to use such other material which is not derived from me (either because such features or elements were not new or novel, or were not originated by me, or were or may hereafter be independently created and submitted by other persons, including your employees).

BUYING
SOMEONE
ELSE'S
COMPLETED
SCRIPT

181

3.   I represent and warrant that I own or control individually, or together with those other persons signing this letter, the Submitted Material, that the Submitted Material is free of all claims or encumbrances and that I have the exclusive right to offer all rights in the Submitted Material to you.

4.   I agree that no obligation of any kind is assumed or may be implied against you by reason of your consideration of the Submitted Material or any discussions or negotiations we may have with respect thereto, except pursuant to an express written agreement hereafter executed by you and me that, by its terms, will be the only contract between us.

5.   Any claim, controversy, or dispute arising hereunder shall be settled by arbitration before a single arbitrator in accordance with the rules of IFTA. The award of the arbitrator shall be binding upon the parties and judgment thereon may be entered in any court. The prevailing party shall be entitled to all arbitration costs, and reasonable attorney fees.

6.   I have retained a copy of the Submitted Material. I assume full responsibility for any loss of the Submitted Material, irrespective of whether it is lost, stolen, or destroyed in transit, or while in your possession, or otherwise.

7.   Except as otherwise provided in this agreement, I hereby release you of and from any and all claims, demands, and liabilities of every kind whatsoever, known or unknown, that may arise in relation to the Submitted Material or by reason of any claim now or hereafter made by me that you have used or appropriated the Submitted Material, except for fraud or willful injury on your part.

8.   No statements or representations have been made except those expressly stated in this agreement. This agreement may be modified only by subsequent written agreement signed both by you and me.

Very truly yours,

_____

Writer
[Writer's address]
[Writer's phone number]

Encl.: Submitted Material as Described Above.

You can download this form at www.clearanceandcopyright.com
Use the code: ibotCC3

CHAPTER 10

PROVISIONS COMMON TO MOST AGREEMENTS

Many independent filmmakers think that boilerplate means one of the following: "I don't have to read that." "Skip over this; it's lawyer stuff." "Boring." "I never understand that stuff." "I'll never need to use that stuff." There is an element of truth to each one of these reactions. However, these sections in a contract are the ones that come into play almost every time there is a problem. These paragraphs are the ones you turn to in most disputes.

CONTRACTS AND NEGOTIATION

A short course on contract law is well beyond the scope of this book, but you should understand a few key points (besides the importance of getting everything in writing) if you ever negotiate any of the deals on your film.

A deal closes when the parties agree to the extent that they can move forward with the performance of the deal. Everybody is bound to perform. The tradeoffs have been made. The compromises have been made. The deal is closed.

Unless you have a specific agreement to the contrary, no deal is closed until all the points of the deal are closed. This truth about the way American law works has given rise to various catchphrases you may have heard: "It ain't over till it's over." "It ain't over till the fat lady sings." "I'll trust it when the check clears the bank."

Even if you are aware of this truth, you will still be upset if you think that you have a deal on all points except one, and then find the other party backing off on some of the points of the deal where agreement had been reached.

To have an enforceable contract, you have to have agreement on four elements:

1. What you are getting.

2. What you are paying for what you are getting.

3. How long the contract will last.

4. Whom the contract is between.

You can work out everything else along the way.

Offers and Counteroffers

If you receive a written offer, you can write "accepted" across it and the deal is done. Be careful when you counteroffer. There is a widely held misconception that you can always accept an offer. When you make a counteroffer to someone who has made an offer to you, the law looks at the transaction in a very particular way. The law says that you rejected the offer that was made to you and put a new offer on the table. The other party may let you accept a previous offer, but they are not bound to do so. You do not have a legal right to demand that the other party's old offer stay on the table.

Written vs. Oral

Samuel Goldwyn once boomed, "An oral agreement isn't worth the paper it's written on." When it comes to matters of copyright, you must get it in writing. There are no exceptions. It is required by the Federal Copyright Law. The law requires a few other contracts to be in writing, but for contracts in the other areas of law there are some exceptions. Examples of contracts that "must" be in writing include contracts that sell land and contracts lasting longer than one year. The major exception is when there has been reliance on an oral agreement. For contracts that convey an interest in a copyright, even reliance does not excuse the need for a writing. Otherwise, contracts do not have to be in writing. The problem with an oral agreement is the enforcement of it. If you get into a dispute, you can be sure that the other side will remember the agreement differently from the way you remember it.

Remember, the paper does not fulfill the agreement—people do. No contract can protect you against bad people who are determined to do bad things to you.

The Structure of a Contract

No matter what the subject of a contract is or how much money is involved, a contract ought to be well organized and easy to read. In fact, you should never sign (or present) a contract that you don't understand. Here are some rules of thumb for you to remember when you are putting together your own contracts:

The first paragraph should name the parties, provide their addresses, and identify them in parentheses. Once identified, you always refer to the party by the short identifier instead of the long name. Most of the agreements in this book are between the Producer and the Owner. Be sure that the identifiers are consistent throughout the contract. The first paragraph also gives an effective date for the commencement of the contract.

Note that the words Producer and Owner are capitalized in the paragraph above and in the paragraphs that are at the end of this chapter. That is because they are defined terms. A **defined term** is a term (or word) that is defined somewhere in the contract and has a special meaning throughout the contract. For instance, Owner refers to the specific person identified as such in the first paragraph of the contract. Always capitalize the word throughout the contract to show that you are not referring to any old owner, but rather to a specific person. Never use the word in the contract in its generalized meaning. If you absolutely must use the word in a nonspecific way (i.e., not referring to the Owner defined in paragraph one), be sure to use it in lower case. When you use the word as it has been defined in the contract, it should be capitalized.

Number your paragraphs in the order in which they appear.

Put captions on your paragraphs. **Captions** are the titles of the paragraphs. They can help you quickly find specific subject areas in the contract.

Be sure to limit each paragraph to one subject.

Don't discuss any subject in more than one place.

Try not to refer to other paragraphs in the contract by number. As you work on a contract, paragraph numbers can change without all the references to the paragraphs changing, which can create confusion later.

Describe the basic deal early in the contract in clear, easy-to-understand language. Follow the basic deal with the less important things. Then move on to termination provisions and close with the provisions common to most contracts that are at the end of this chapter.

Always, always, always be sure that the signatures on the bottom of the contract match the parties at the top. There is a huge difference between an agreement with a corporation and an agreement with an individual. If a person is signing for a corporation, be sure they set out their position with the corporation. If a person is signing as an individual and you are going to be paying that person more than $600, it is a good idea to have that person include his or her social security number.

A few of the agreements in this book are complete in and of themselves. Most of them only have the introductory paragraphs containing the basic deal terms. In order to form a usable contract, they need to also contain the provisions that are provided at the end of this chapter. When they need these provisions, that is noted below the basic deal terms of each contract.

International

If you are to make money from your film, it must be sold around the world. This activity is normally handled by a foreign-sales agent, but you might like to know something about how it works to sell rights to distribute your film all over the world. Put your contract in English. English has become the language of international commerce in general. In the film business, even people from non-English-speaking countries will generally put their film contracts in English.

BOILERPLATE

Take a few minutes to read through the language and the legal explanations in this chapter, and then you can use them in your agreements without thinking through them for each individual contract. You should have a smattering of knowledge about these important provisions, and now is a good time to acquire that knowledge. Too many producers wait to learn about these paragraphs until there is a crisis or dispute that boilerplate controls!

Having some background in these matters also makes the negotiation go more easily. It discredits you and your position if you have never read the language or do not understand it yourself. You are the filmmaker. You are supposed to be taking care of all these details. The writer, the director, the actors, and the crew all look to you for leadership on the business side of things. Be informed and you will make better deals, and those with whom you work will have more confidence in you and you will sleep better at night.

Some of the clauses are included merely because they are so common. Some, such as the arbitration clause, can be extremely important to you. Others define what happens in certain circumstances and are therefore helpful in keeping you out of controversy.

It is always good to have these things spelled out so that there are no future misunderstandings. Why should you get into an argument? A good contract does more than protect you from scoundrels. A good contract helps both parties avoid future confrontations. Be sure to add the appropriate "boilerplate" provisions to the agreements you take from other parts of this book. These provisions are so important that you are directed to this chapter by several other chapters.

Do not include any special heading (such as "boilerplate provisions") for these paragraphs. Just number them in sequence, starting with the next number available to you in the contract you are creating.

10.01   BOILERPLATE PROVISIONS

> **Comment:** *Number these paragraphs sequentially from the last paragraph in the contract in which they are being attached. If they are being applied to a writer-for-hire agreement, change Owner to Writer throughout. Note that the parties are Producer and Owner, which matches most of the other contracts in this book. These defined parties must remain consistent throughout a contract. Also, the subject of the contract is Work in these provisions. If the subject of your agreement is something else (e.g., Script), change that term throughout as well.*

EXPENSES: Producer shall reimburse Owner's actual, out-of-pocket expenses for all travel requested to be made by Owner to the extent pre-approved by Producer.

> **Comment:** *This is usually a deal point. It shows up in virtually all contracts for personal services. This is the best language because it puts you in control. Studios usually spell out a specific dollar amount to be paid as per diems. Per diem is a specific amount paid on a daily basis to cover all expenses (typically excluding airfare and hotel) without any need to provide receipts or an accounting. Another approach is to say, "Owner shall receive expenses on a favored nations basis with Producer when asked by Producer in writing to travel more than fifty (50) miles from home on behalf of the project."*

NAME AND LIKENESS: Producer shall have the right to publish, advertise, announce, and use in any manner or medium the name, biography, and photographs or other likenesses of Owner in connection with the exhibition, distribution, advertising, and promotion or other exploitation of any film created as a result of the exercise by Producer of its rights hereunder, including merchandising, if merchandising rights are granted herein.

> **Comment:** *You must acquire these rights to advertise the picture with the name of the Owner. Otherwise, you cannot use the Owner's name in your advertising. What a strange poster that would be. Some Owners will want the right to approve photographs of themselves. If so, you should insist that they approve at least half of those presented to them.*

MERCHANDISING/COMMERCIAL TIE-UPS: Producer shall not use Owner's name (other than in the billing block), likeness, biography, or voice in connection with any merchandising without Owner's prior written approval. Owner shall receive royalties on any approved merchandising, to be negotiated in good faith. There shall be no use of Owner's name (other than in the billing block), likeness, biography, or voice in connection with any commercial tie-ups or endorsements.

> *Comment: This language is standard in most agreements. You can leave it out of your initial draft, but if the other party is represented by a lawyer, agent, or manager, they will almost always ask you to put in this clause.*

PUBLICITY RESTRICTIONS: Owner agrees that, except as merely incidental to Owner's personal publicity endeavors, Owner shall not issue or authorize or permit the issuance of any advertising or publicity of any kind or nature relating to this Agreement, Producer, the material, any exercise of any rights in the Work, or any versions or productions based in whole or in part thereon, without the prior written consent of Producer.

> *Comment: Studios like to control all publicity. These provisions are desirable. Studios will accept an assignment without these provisions in the agreement, but they are preferred.*

NO OBLIGATION TO PRODUCE: Nothing herein shall be construed to obligate Producer to produce, distribute, release, perform, or exhibit any production based upon or suggested by the results of Owner's services hereunder.

> *Comment: Totally unnecessary from a legal point of view, this paragraph cuts off any claim or misunderstandings. Even if you think that you have the money lined up, this is a good paragraph to have in your agreement in order to avoid future disagreements.*

REVERSION: If Producer exercises the option and fails to commence principal photography within seven years thereafter, Owner may send Producer written notice that the rights will revert to Owner unless principal photography commences within ninety (90) days of such notice. If Producer fails to so commence principal photography, the rights shall revert to Owner. If a picture is subsequently produced by another producer, Owner shall reimburse Producer all out-of-pocket costs paid by Producer plus interest at a rate of ten percent (10%) per annum out of first monies received by Owner in connection with the Picture, but no later than the commencement of principal photography.

> *Hint: You can leave this paragraph out of your first draft and put it in when the Owner asks for it. (If you hire a member of the WGA, the member will obtain something very near to the above rights through the WGA Minimum Basic Agreement.) The length of time is, of course, subject to negotiation.*

REMEDIES: Owner acknowledges and agrees that Owner's sole remedy for any breach or alleged breach of this Agreement by Producer shall be an action at law to recover monetary damages.

In no event shall any of the rights granted or to be granted and/ or the releases made herein revert to Owner, except as provided herein, nor shall Owner have a right of rescission or right to injunctive or other equitable relief.

> **Comment:** *This sounds harsh, but it is absolutely necessary in a studio deal. You should have this protection so that you have maximum flexibility on how and where to set up your film for financing and distribution, because no studio will take on a project without it.*

FORCE MAJEURE: If the development or production of the Picture is materially interrupted or delayed by reason of epidemic, fire, action of the elements, walkout, labor dispute, strike, governmental order, court order, or order of any other legally constituted authority, act of God or public enemy, war, riot, civil commotion, or any other cause beyond Producer's control, whether of the same or of any other nature, or if because of the illness or incapacity of any principal member of the cast, any unexpired portion of the term hereof shall be postponed for the period of such interruption or interference.

> **Comment:** *Things happen. When they do, your rights should be spelled out. This simple paragraph helps to avoid the basic issue of whether you have the right to extend your agreement if some catastrophe happens that delays your project. Smart Owners will want to put some limit on the time a contract can be extended before it is terminated.*

ASSIGNMENT: Producer has the right to assign this contract to any person or entity in Producer's sole discretion. Owner shall have no right to assign this contract.

> **Comment:** *Stating that you have a right to assign the contract is unnecessary legally, but it makes it clear that you can do this. Even if you are going to pay for the production of the film yourself, you want this ability since the actual production entity might be a corporation or other company that you control rather than you as an individual. You may need it when it comes time to distribute the film.*

REPRESENTATIONS AND WARRANTIES: Owner represents, warrants, and agrees that it has the right and authority to enter this agreement and that:

(a) The Work itself is original with Owner and no part of the Work is in the public domain;

(b) Owner has not and will not enter into any agreements or activities which will hinder, compete, conflict, or interfere with the exercise of any of the rights granted to Producer. Owner has no knowledge of any claim or potential claim by any party that might in any way affect Producer's rights herein;

(c) The Work does not, and no use thereof will, infringe upon or violate any personal, proprietary, or other right of any third party, including, without limitation, defamation, libel, slander, false light, or violation of any right of privacy or publicity or any copyright law.

(d) The exercise of the rights herein granted to Producer will not in any way, directly or indirectly, infringe upon any rights of any person, or entity whatsoever.

> **Comment:** *We see these so often that we forget how important they are. Read them over. Of course, your deal is premised on these understandings, but without them in the contract, the other party could say otherwise.*

INDEMNIFICATION: Owner agrees to defend, indemnify, and hold Producer, and Producer's employees, agents, successors, licensees, and assigns, harmless from and against any and all claims, damages, liabilities, losses, or expenses (including reasonable attorney fees and costs) suffered or incurred by Producer on account of or in connection with the breach or alleged breach of any of Owner's representations, warranties, or covenants set forth herein.

> **Hint:** *This puts teeth in the Representations and Warranties paragraph. Some producers issue the initial contract without binding themselves to a similar indemnification. If you do that and the other party complains, put it in a paragraph that mirrors this one and binds you as Producer to indemnify Owner.*

PUBLIC INFORMATION: Producer, and Producer's successors, licensees or assigns, shall have no less rights by reason of this Agreement to material in the public domain than any member of the public may now or hereafter have.

> **Hint:** *This clause allows you to make a film in this milieu, even if you don't make a film based on this particular script or book or life story. Wise owners and writers resist such a clause in the agreement with the following argument: "If you want public domain information, go ahead, but I won't help you get started."*

ARBITRATION: Any claim, controversy, or dispute arising hereunder shall be settled pursuant to California law by arbitration before a single arbitrator in accordance with the rules of the Independent Film and Television Alliance (IFTA) held in Los Angeles, California. The award of the arbitrator shall be binding upon the parties and judgment may be entered in any court. The prevailing party shall be entitled to collect all arbitration costs and reasonable attorney fees.

> **Hint:** This is very important to independent producers. Many studios, with their large legal staffs and deep pockets, like to avoid arbitration, but will not turn down a project based on arbitration provisions in the underlying contracts. Unless you designate arbitration, you are stuck with expensive, time-consuming litigation in the courts. Arbitrations avoid lawsuits. An arbitration is cheaper and faster. You can even present your evidence yourself and do all the paperwork yourself, although you would be well-advised to consult an attorney. The negative is that there is virtually no appeal from the decision of an arbitrator. An arbitration award can be confirmed in court in a very simple process, and then the award becomes a court judgment without taking many dollars and much time to obtain.
>
> **Hint:** There are other recognized arbitral agents besides IFTA. IFTA is my preference because the panel of arbitrators is particularly knowledgeable in independent filmmaking. IFTA arbitrations can be held anywhere in the world. The largest panel of IFTA arbitrators is in Los Angeles. If the other side does not want use the IFTA, try the American Arbitration Association (AAA).
>
> **Hint:** The designation of a city can be important in an actual dispute. If you cannot agree on a city in advance, at least narrow the choices down to two cities, either one of which can be used. This way you do not have a surprise trip to Iowa when you least expect it.

NOTICE: Any notice to be given hereunder shall be in writing and sent by either: U.S. mail and faxed or e-mailed, a recognized courier service such as Federal Express, or personal courier service to the party receiving notice at the address written above. Notice shall be effective on the date faxed or e-mailed or three days after mailing, whichever is earlier.

ADDITIONAL ASSURANCES AND DOCUMENTS: This Agreement is irrevocable and is not only for Producer's benefit, but also for the benefit of any other party to whom Producer may sell, assign, and/or license the rights, privileges, powers, or immunities granted herein. Owner, to the best of Owner's ability, will prevent the use by others of the rights granted hereunder in a manner inconsistent with the grant of rights to Producer. Producer may prosecute, and Owner irrevocably grants to Producer full power and authority to do so, in Owner's name, and to take any and all steps as Producer, in Producer's sole discretion may elect, to restrain and prevent others from so using such rights. Owner further agrees to execute, acknowledge, and deliver to Producer any and all further assignments and other instruments, in form approved by counsel for Producer, necessary or expedient to carry out and effectuate the purposes and intent of the parties as herein expressed. If Owner shall fail to so execute and deliver any such assignment or other instruments within ten (10) days of being presented, Producer shall be deemed to be, and Owner irrevocably appoints Producer, the true and lawful attorney-in-fact of Owner to execute and deliver any and all such assignments and other instruments in the name of Owner, which right is coupled with an interest.

> *Hint:* *Although this is standard, it gives you a lot of power. Sharp writers/owners are going to want to restrict this. Do not eliminate it all together. The following paragraph is acceptable as an alternative:*

OTHER DOCUMENTS: Owner agrees to execute such assignments or other instruments as Producer may from time to time deem necessary or desirable to establish, or defend, its title to any material created hereunder or rights granted hereunder. Owner hereby irrevocably appoints Producer the true and lawful attorney-in-fact of Owner (which right is coupled with an interest) to execute, verify, acknowledge, and deliver any and all such instruments or documents that Owner shall fail or refuse to execute, verify, acknowledge, or deliver within ten (10) days of receipt thereof. Producer shall provide Owner with copies of any such instruments or documents executed, verified, acknowledged, and delivered by Producer on Owner's behalf hereunder.

COMPLETE AGREEMENT: This agreement constitutes the entire agreement between the parties with respect to all of the matters herein and its execution has not been induced by, nor do any of the parties hereto rely upon or agreed as material, any representative.

PRODUCER   OWNER

_____   _____
BY: BY:
ITS: SSN:

> *Comment:* *Note that there is no requirement for date and address because they are covered in the introductory paragraph. Also, be sure to obtain the Owner's social security number at this point. You will need it for tax reporting, so obtain it early.*

You can download this form at www.clearanceandcopyright.com
Use the code: ibotCC3

CHAPTER 11

REGISTERING COPYRIGHT OF THE SCRIPT

Copyright attaches to a script as soon as it exists in tangible form. Copyright does not require registration. Nevertheless, you should register your script for several important reasons. This chapter gives you the reasons and benefits to registration along with a step-by-step registration guide.

WHEN TO REGISTER

The latest you should register your script is commencement of pre-production. However, you will continue to rewrite your script during pre-production and even during principal photography. Most of you will continue to rewrite the script during post-production.

The most important reason to register your script as soon as you are sure you will commence principal photography is that SAG requires proof of copyright registration of the script before you can use a SAG actor in your film. A copy of the application and the signed registered-mail receipt is the minimum they require.

You might be thinking that you will not use SAG actors in your low-budget digital film. Think again. SAG has made it so attractive to use their members that even student films tend to use SAG actors. There are now special student film contracts, experimental film contracts, and low-budget contracts that virtually eliminate the financial considerations from the use of union talent. And let's face it: Any actor with any experience at all is going to be a member of the union.

Even if you do not use SAG actors, as hard as that is to imagine, the commencement of pre-production is still a good time to register your script with the Copyright Office.

To register earlier could be a waste of time because of substantial subsequent revisions. If you wait until later, you are spending an enormous amount of time, energy, and money to create a film without clearly and publicly stating your claim to do so. Many independent filmmakers mistakenly delay this important item. This is not a good practice, especially when it is so easy and cheap to register both the script and the chain-of-title documents. Don't delay.

Registering your script with the Copyright Office brings a number of other legal protections. They are discussed in the next section, in order to give you an overview of the legal benefits that still flow from copyright registration. None of these reasons is strong enough to cause you to register your script prior to the commencement of principal photography.

LEGAL BENEFITS FROM REGISTERING YOUR SCRIPT

The author of the script (either the writer himself or herself or the employer if it is a work for hire) owns the copyright to the script as it is being created. No registration is necessary. No declaration on the cover of the script is necessary. All of those formalities were done away with when the copyright law underwent a major revision in the late '70s.

However, formal copyright registration of the script with the Copyright Office provides additional protection to the copyright owner beyond that which is automatically granted as the script is being written. By registering your ownership of copyright, you gain several protections: You give notice to the world of your status as the copyright owner. You can file a lawsuit to protect your rights. If you register before an infringement occurs, you qualify for statutory damages and attorney fees when someone infringes your copyright.

You must register your copyright with the Copyright Office before you can bring a lawsuit for infringement. If you want to file a lawsuit but haven't registered the copyright, it is easy to file for the registration so that you can proceed, but you do not receive the benefit of obtaining attorney fees for any infringement that occurs before you register. When you hire an attorney, the ability to obtain attorney fees if you win is a big incentive for a lawyer to take your case.

The most serious problem with registering your copyright after it has been infringed is the limit on damages. **Damages** is the money a court awards you at the end of your lawsuit if you win. Without copyright registration, you can only receive actual damages. Actual damages are the losses that you proved in court with witnesses and accounting statements. If you have registered your copyright, you are also eligible for statutory damages.

Statutory damages are awards granted by a court when a copyright owner's work has been infringed, but the owner cannot prove the actual losses or the losses are quite small. Under these circumstances, the court may feel that the amount of actual damages that an infringer would have to pay the copyright owner is not a satisfactory amount to pay for the infringement. Statutory damages give the court a stronger deterrent to use against infringers.

To be eligible for statutory damages and attorney fees, you must have registered the copyright in your property within 90 days after its publication or one month before it is infringed.

If not, your recovery will be limited to actual damages. Actual damages are the actual provable dollars you lost or the defendant gained on account of the infringement. Proving actual damages is very time-consuming and expensive.

If a copyright owner is eligible to receive statutory damages, he may elect any time before final judgment is rendered to receive the statutory award of a sum to be determined by the court of not less than $750 or more than $30,000, for all infringements involved. If the infringement is shown to be willful, statutory damages can be increased to $150,000. Because of the way courts interpret the word "willful," chances are good that the infringement will be found to be willful. However, in the case of an innocent infringer, the court may choose to reduce the award to a sum of not less than $200.

The impact of all this is clear. In my early days as a litigator, I represented the litigious Bob Tur, who you can read about in the chapter about fair use. As a freelance reporter he had shot some news footage that he licensed to a local television station for the six o'clock news. A service copied the news off air and offered to make copies for anyone interested for $89 apiece. My client knew this activity was going on, on a regular basis. People who were on the news, their publicists, and folks pursuing legal claims were all potential customers of this off-air copying service. One day my client sent a friend in to the service and purchased two copies of one of his reports for $89 each. The evidence indicated that there were probably a few more tapes made, but my client, the copyright owner, could not prove this claim. Considering that only two illegal copies were confirmed, an award of actual damages ($89 per tape less costs) would have been an inappropriate remedy under the circumstances. The court awarded $10,000 in statutory damages plus attorney fees for each of two videotapes that were illegally copied off air. **Off air** means from a television set as the program is coming across the cable or over the airwaves.

IN WHOSE NAME DO YOU REGISTER THE SCRIPT?

You are about to start principal photography. The copyright to your script should be registered in the name of the production company that will be producing the film. This is done because it insures that the copyright ownership will clearly reside with the production company, which is exactly what SAG requires.

Generally speaking, that company is a single-purpose production company. A **single-purpose production company** is a production company that is formed solely and exclusively for the purpose of producing a film and has not performed any other business before producing the film.

The preferred kind of company used to be a corporation. Today, most people use a limited liability company. A **limited liability company** is a form of business entity—usually referred to by its initials, LLC—that was legislated into existence in the '70s and has grown very steadily in popularity with professionals and filmmakers since then. An LLC protects you from liability in the same way as a corporation protects you from liability, but has the advantage of working like a partnership as far as passing profits and losses through to the members.

Generally speaking, the LLC will also exploit the film after it is completed and disburse deferments and profits to those who are to receive them. This function can be assigned to a CPA or some other company. The completed film will be turned over to a studio or other financier when it is completed if the film is produced as a negative pick-up. A **negative pick-up** describes the situation in which a studio agrees to pay for your finished film and, in exchange, you deliver all rights to the studio when you literally deliver the negative.

Script registration should be in the name of the LLC (the production company) to make it very clear to SAG that the company is the current title holder and to pave the way for easy assignment of the various rights necessary to distribute the completed film. Be sure that all of your chain-of-title documents are in order, as is more fully described in the next chapter.

INSTRUCTIONS TO FILL OUT COPYRIGHT FORMS

Overview

It is easy to register your script with the Copyright Office. Just follow these steps:

A. OBTAIN a copy of FORM PA from the Copyright Office website at www.copyright.gov/forms or by calling (202) 707-9100. They have many registration forms, each for a different type of work. Make several photocopies. **Form PA** is the correct form for the registration of a published or unpublished script or treatment or script outline. (PA stands for performing arts, which includes film and television.) You can print them out to your heart's content. Be careful, though—if you do not photocopy the form exactly, it will be sent back to you by the Copyright Office! The Copyright Office is currently moving toward electronic registration for all applications. When this happens, there will be only one form (Form CO) that will be used for all types of works. This form is streamlined and even easy to fill out. Payments and deposits will also be made electronically.

   As of the time of this writing, you can submit your application online by becoming a "beta tester" for the Office's online registration service. Just visit the Office's website and click on "What's New?"

B. FILL OUT the form following the easy instructions in this chapter. (A sample completed form is included at the end of this chapter.)

C. Prepare a cover letter like the one at the end of this chapter. You can send your letter certified with a return receipt requested so that you know your letter was received or you can include a return postcard.

D. Include a CHECK or MONEY ORDER payable to the "Register of Copyrights."

E. Include one copy of your SCRIPT.

F. MAIL TO: Library of Congress
                Copyright Office
                101 Independence Avenue SE
                Washington, DC 20559-6000

G. WAIT. Be patient. It will be months before you hear back.

Eventually, you either receive your application back with a registration number stamped in the upper right-hand corner, or you receive a call or letter from someone in the Copyright Office who is reviewing your document. Answer their questions satisfactorily and your registration will show up quickly. If things get sticky, call your attorney.

Your Certificate of Copyright is a copy of the actual form you filed, with a number stamped in the upper right-hand corner. The registration number begins with the letters PA, followed by two digits identifying the year and a sequential number identifying your work.

Be sure that the copyright symbol "©" is affixed to every copy of the work, together with the year of creation and the owner's name as follows:

© 2008 Michael C. Donaldson

or

Copyright 2008 Michael C. Donaldson

In the United States, the copyright notice is no longer required, but it is still a good idea. People are used to seeing this notice, and if you do not include it, they may erroneously assume that you are not claiming copyright. It also gives them the name of a contact for your script.

Step-by-Step Guide

SPACE 1: Title of Work

You must provide a title. This information is important and permanent. The title must be in letters and/or numbers in the English language. If the script that you attach to your registration form has a title page (or an identifying phrase that could serve as a title), write those words completely and exactly in this space on the application. Indexing depends on the information you write in this space.

Previous or Alternative Titles

Complete this space if there are any additional titles for the script under which you could reasonably anticipate that someone searching for the registration might look, or under which a treatment or option or other document pertaining to the script might be recorded. If there are none, then write the word "none." Do not write down titles that you merely played with in your mind. (Note: Do not write down the name of an underlying property that your script is based upon. You are asked to give that information later in the form.)

Nature of the Work

Write this word in the space provided: "screenplay." The word works whether your script is for a feature film, a movie made for television, a short, or a documentary.

SPACE 2: Author(s)

While the answer is usually simple enough, there can be a variety of interesting issues raised by this deceptively simple question. Important legal rights are determined by the answer to this block. Answer these carefully because rights can easily last 100 years or more. Don't forget that you will have to record all the documents needed to show the transfer(s) from the author to the production company that is listed as the copyright claimant. This will create a good chain of title as explained in the next chapter.

a. *Name of Author*

First, decide who is or are the "author(s)" of this work. You may want to review the guidelines in Chapter 7, regarding work made for hire. In the case of a work made for hire, write the full legal name of the employer or person for whom the script was written. You may also include the name of the employee along with the name of the employer (for example: "Elster Production Co., employer for hire of John Ferguson") on the first line of this blank.

If someone helped create the work, be sure to read the next section to find out if that person should also be listed. If you wrote the script by yourself, this space has your full name alone. This tells the Copyright Office and the world at large that you were the sole and individual creator of the specific script that you are submitting to the Copyright Office.

Information about the author's date of birth is optional, but useful to identify the author further. If the author is dead, the year of death is mandatory. This is because the life of the copyright is measured from the death of the author.

Anonymous means that the author is not identified on the copies of the script. If the author is anonymous, state "anonymous" on the "name of author" line or, if you choose, reveal the author's identity on this form. Note that the identity of the claimant is revealed in Space 4. The claimant must always be revealed, even if an author is anonymous or pseudonymous.

Pseudonymous means that the author is identified on the copies of the script under a fictitious name. If the author is pseudonymous, either give the pseudonym and identify it as such (example: "Huntley Haverstock, pseudonym") or, at your option, reveal the author's name, making clear which is the real name and which is the pseudonym (for example: "Judith Baton, whose pseudonym is Madeline Elster").

Nationality or domicile must be given even if the author is anonymous or pseudonymous. Domicile is the place of permanent residency of the person(s) who wrote the script or the employer of that person in the case of a work made for hire. If only one of these is the United States, fill in that one. You do no harm by filling in both of these lines.

b. *Nature of Authorship*

Give a brief general statement of the extent of the original contribution the author made, such as: "Wrote the entire script." If this author contributed anything less than the entire script, give a brief, but accurate, description of that contribution, such as "added several scenes to the first draft" or "created the character WOODY" or "English translation of original Swahili script." If you used someone else's copyrighted material in your script, make sure you are clear that your claim does not cover material you did not create.

c. *Name of Author (again)*

Filling in this blank declares that the registered work has joint authors. Be sure this additional person has the legal status as a joint author before listing him or her on your registration form. Even if someone contributed a whole scene and characters, they may not achieve the legal status of a co-author. If a person is a co-author, that person has substantial legal rights. Unless there is a written collaboration agreement that says otherwise, the co-author has an equal right to control every aspect of the exploitation of the script. This is true even if the contributions to the script are highly unequal. See the section regarding collaboration agreements in Chapter 9 for more information on joint authorships.

If you need further space for additional authors, use Continuation Sheets. Follow the same instructions as above for each additional author you list.

SPACE 3: Creation and Publication

This information is required. A mistake as to the date does not invalidate your registration as long as there is no intent to deceive.

a. Do not confuse creation with publication. A script is created when it is written on paper for the first time. You must state the year in which creation of the script was completed. The date you give here should be the year in which the person who physically wrote the words completed the particular version you are registering, even if other versions exist or if further changes or additions are planned.

b. You will almost always leave this space blank (date of publication). **Publication** is the distribution of copies of the script to the public by sale or other transfer of ownership, or by rental, lease, or lending. Publication does not occur as a result of a private use of a script or even shopping a script, because that is private activity designed to ultimately sell the script. You do *not* have to amend the registration when and if publication ever occurs. Under certain circumstances, the court will consider a script published when the film based on the script is published. So it is easy to see why this space is usually left blank.

SPACE 4: Copyright Claimant(s)

a. *Claimant(s)*

Since I recommend registering in the name of the production company at the beginning of pre-production, this will rarely be the person who actually did the writing. By this time, the copyright claimant is a person or organization to whom the copyright has been transferred in order to produce the film.

b. *Transfer*

If the copyright claimant is not the author, write a brief statement of how ownership of the copyright was obtained. One of the following phrases covers almost all circumstances: "By written contract"; "Transfer of all rights by author"; "Assignment"; "By will."

The documents that evidence these transfers must be recorded with the Copyright Office so that they become public records. The next chapter covers the recording of these documents (Chain of Title).

SPACE 5: Previous Registration

Basically, only one copyright registration can be made for the same version of a particular work. That is why "no" is by far the most common answer, and you can skip the rest of the discussion of space 5. If there are other works out there that are tempting you to check "yes," read the next chapter about recording Chain of Title documents before you go farther.

a. Why Re-Registration

If this version of the script is substantially the same as a script covered by a previous registration, a second registration is not generally possible. There are only three situations in which you can successfully file a second registration:

1. The work has been registered in unpublished form and a second registration is being sought to cover the first published edition. This would rarely apply to a film script. When it does, it is because the movie was made and becomes such a hit or such a classic that someone wants to publish the screenplay. If so, check box "a."

2. Someone other than the author is identified as copyright claimant in the earlier registration, and the author is now seeking registration in the author's own individual or corporate name. Such a situation indicates someone probably already has a lawyer. If you are in this situation, check box "b."

3. If the work has been changed and you are now seeking registration to cover the additions or revisions, check box "c" and complete both parts of Space 6. As you know, I recommend one registration at the commencement of pre-production.

b. Previous Registration Number

The number to be filled in on this blank is the number that appears on the top right-hand corner of the earlier registration certificate. If more than one previous registration has been made for the work, give the number and date of the latest registration.

SPACE 6: Derivative Work or Compilation

a. Derivative Work

Your script is a derivative work if it was based on one or more pre-existing works, such as a book, a play, or a magazine article. Sequels, prequels, and remakes are derivative works of the previous film. If there is a previously registered version of the script, the current version is a derivative work. Such a script would be an infringing work if the material taken from the pre-existing work had been used without the consent of the copyright owner. Do not disclose pre-existing works that merely influenced or inspired your script or served as a source of factual information if there has been no substantial copying from the pre-existing work. If you have obtained life-story rights from someone, the script is still considered original, and not a derivative work.

If your script is a derivative work, be sure you listed the scriptwriter as author in Space 2, not the author of the underlying work. The year of completion in Space 3 is the completion of the script, not completion of the underlying work.

Complete both Space 6a and Space 6b for derivative works. In Space 6a, identify the pre-existing work that has been recast, transformed, or adapted. Include the copyright registration number if you know it.

b. *Material Added*

The copyright in a script that is a derivative work covers only the additions, changes, or other new material appearing for the first time in that script. It does not extend to any pre-existing material, such as the dialogue of characters first appearing in a book. Therefore, describe the new material broadly, such as "entire script, except selected story points and eight of the thirty characters, from the book" or "entire script except selected plot points."

c. *Compilation*

Though this form raises the issue, scripts are rarely a compilation. A compilation is defined as "a work formed by the collection and assembling of pre-existing materials." Even *The Civil War* by Ken Burns was not a compilation for copyright law purposes, although pre-existing photos comprised most of the footage. Thirteen authors working one after another or all in the same room do not make a compilation. A compilation is a gathering together of independent materials. The creative work is in the selection and arrangement. I cannot imagine how a screenplay could be a compilation. Therefore, do not check the box indicating a compilation without talking to a lawyer!

SPACE 7: Deposit Account and Correspondence

a. *Deposit Account*

Leave this space blank. Lawyers and studios that do a lot of registrations deposit money in advance with the Copyright Office. Their accounts are debited for their individual registrations. That will generally not apply to individuals reading this book. You will send a check for total fees due with your application.

b. *Correspondence*

You must provide the name, address, area code, and daytime telephone number of the person to receive correspondence about this application. If you are registering this yourself, use your name or company name. If you want questions about your application to go to someone else, such as your lawyer, provide their name.

SPACE 8: Certification

The application cannot be accepted unless it bears the date and the *handwritten signature* of the person filing the application. You must put an "**x**" or "✓" in one of the four boxes to let the Copyright Office know your status. Because you will generally be registering the script at commencement of pre-production in the name of the producing entity, you will almost always check the second box. If you are the author, check the first box. If you are not the author but are the copyright claimant, check the second box. By the time pre-production starts, the author is rarely still paying for everything out of pocket, so this box will rarely be checked. The entity producing the film is the copyright claimant, so you would not usually check the first box. Read the next chapter carefully to find out what documents need to be recorded at the Copyright Office in order to show exactly how the production company became the copyright claimant. As producer (or author), you will not check the third box for owner of exclusive rights. This would be a distributor in most cases. If you are signing on behalf of your corporation, because you were authorized to do so by the author or the copyright owner, check the "authorized agent of" box, which is the fourth box at the bottom of the list. (Note: You must be a corporate officer to sign on behalf of your corporation or the manager to sign on behalf of a limited liability company.) This is the box I always check when I sign these copyright registration forms as the lawyer for clients.

SPACE 9: Address for Return of Certificate

This address block must be completed legibly. The Copyright Office uses a window envelope to mail back your application after the registration number is assigned.

Fees

Each individual application must be accompanied by a fee. At the time of this writing, the fee is set at $45. It increases every five years based on the Consumer Price Index.

The Deposit Requirement

Every application to register a copyright must contain a deposit of the materials being registered. It is the specific item attached to the application that is registered with the Copyright Office. Include a complete copy of the version of the script you are registering, even though there may be many versions before the one you are registering and many more changes to come.

Registering the Book, Article, or Story
That Your Film is Based On

When your film is based on a book, article, or story, you want to be sure that the copyright for that work has been registered so that you can record your transfer of the film rights from the author or owner to you. Or maybe you have written a book, article, or story that you want to base a film on. Either way, that requires a different form. Use form TX to record the transfer. Basically, filling out this form is the same as described above except:

SPACE 1: Title of Work

The last section in this space asks you to identify whether the book, article, or story being registered is a contribution to a periodical, serial, or collection. If this is the case, write the title of the contribution in the line headed "Title of this Work" and then give information about the collective work containing your contribution in the line headed "Publication as a Contribution."

SPACE 6: Derivative Work or Compilation

There is only a slight chance that a book, article, or story is a compilation. An example of a compilation would be a collection of certain 1917 speeches by Woodrow Wilson.

There is a sample form TX at the end of the chapter.

SO WHAT IF I MAKE A MISTAKE?

It's very important to make sure your copyright registration form is 100% accurate. However, we all know mistakes happen. If there is an error on the initial form that you file, you can fix it by filing a Form CA with the Copyright Office. A Form CA is a form that allows the copyright owner to either correct or add additional information to a previously filed registration form. This does not eliminate the initial form. Rather, the Form CA is added to the registration, so if someone looks for the owner of your work, they will find both the incorrect or incomplete original form and the form with the corrected information. So that you know what it looks like, there is a copy of the form at the end of this chapter.

11.01 FORM PA FOR A SCRIPT

Copyright Office fees are subject to change. For current fees, check the Copyright Office website at *www.copyright.gov*, write the Copyright Office, or call (202) 707-3000.

Form PA
For a Work of Performing Arts
UNITED STATES COPYRIGHT OFFICE

REGISTRATION NUMBER

_____

PA   PAU

EFFECTIVE DATE OF REGISTRATION

_____

Month   Day   Year

DO NOT WRITE ABOVE THIS LINE. IF YOU NEED MORE SPACE, USE A SEPARATE CONTINUATION SHEET.

1

TITLE OF THIS WORK ▼

PREVIOUS OR ALTERNATIVE TITLES ▼

NATURE OF THIS WORK ▼ See instructions

2

a

NAME OF AUTHOR ▼

DATES OF BIRTH AND DEATH
Year Born ▼   Year Died ▼

Was this contribution to the work a "work made for hire"?
☐ Yes
☐ No

AUTHOR'S NATIONALITY OR DOMICILE
Name of Country
OR { Citizen of _____
Domiciled in _____

WAS THIS AUTHOR'S CONTRIBUTION TO THE WORK
Anonymous? ☐ Yes ☐ No
Pseudonymous? ☐ Yes ☐ No
If the answer to either of these questions is "Yes," see detailed instructions.

NATURE OF AUTHORSHIP Briefly describe nature of material created by this author in which copyright is claimed. ▼

NOTE

Under the law, the "author" of a "work made for hire" is generally the employer, not the employee (see instructions). For any part of this work that was "made for hire" check "Yes" in the space provided, give the employer (or other person for whom the work was prepared) as "Author" of that part, and leave the space for dates of birth and death blank.

b

NAME OF AUTHOR ▼

DATES OF BIRTH AND DEATH
Year Born ▼   Year Died ▼

Was this contribution to the work a "work made for hire"?
☐ Yes
☐ No

AUTHOR'S NATIONALITY OR DOMICILE
Name of Country
OR { Citizen of _____
Domiciled in _____

WAS THIS AUTHOR'S CONTRIBUTION TO THE WORK
Anonymous? ☐ Yes ☐ No
Pseudonymous? ☐ Yes ☐ No
If the answer to either of these questions is "Yes," see detailed instructions.

NATURE OF AUTHORSHIP Briefly describe nature of material created by this author in which copyright is claimed. ▼

c

NAME OF AUTHOR ▼

DATES OF BIRTH AND DEATH
Year Born ▼   Year Died ▼

Was this contribution to the work a "work made for hire"?
☐ Yes
☐ No

AUTHOR'S NATIONALITY OR DOMICILE
Name of Country
OR { Citizen of _____
Domiciled in _____

WAS THIS AUTHOR'S CONTRIBUTION TO THE WORK
Anonymous? ☐ Yes ☐ No
Pseudonymous? ☐ Yes ☐ No
If the answer to either of these questions is "Yes," see detailed instructions.

NATURE OF AUTHORSHIP Briefly describe nature of material created by this author in which copyright is claimed. ▼

3

a YEAR IN WHICH CREATION OF THIS WORK WAS COMPLETED This information must be given in all cases.
_____ Year

b DATE AND NATION OF FIRST PUBLICATION OF THIS PARTICULAR WORK
Complete this information ONLY if this work has been published.
Month _____ Day _____ Year _____ Nation

4

See instructions before completing this space.

COPYRIGHT CLAIMANT(S) Name and address must be given even if the claimant is the same as the author given in space 2. ▼

TRANSFER If the claimant(s) named here in space 4 is (are) different from the author(s) named in space 2, give a brief statement of how the claimant(s) obtained ownership of the copyright. ▼

APPLICATION RECEIVED

ONE DEPOSIT RECEIVED

TWO DEPOSITS RECEIVED

FUNDS RECEIVED

DO NOT WRITE HERE
OFFICE USE ONLY

MORE ON BACK ▶   • Complete all applicable spaces (numbers 5-9) on the reverse side of this page.
   • See detailed instructions.   • Sign the form at line 8.

DO NOT WRITE HERE
Page 1 of _____ pages

You can download this form at www.copyright.gov

PREVIOUS REGISTRATION Has registration for this work, or for an earlier version of this work, already been made in the Copyright Office?

☐ Yes ☐ No If your answer is "Yes," why is another registration being sought? (Check appropriate box.) ▼ If your answer is No, do **not** check box A, B, or C.

a. ☐ This is the first published edition of a work previously registered in unpublished form.

b. ☐ This is the first application submitted by this author as copyright claimant.

c. ☐ This is a changed version of the work, as shown by space 6 on this application.

If your answer is "Yes," give: **Previous Registration Number** ▼   **Year of Registration** ▼

5

DERIVATIVE WORK OR COMPILATION Complete both space 6a and 6b for a derivative work; complete only 6b for a compilation.

Preexisting Material Identify any preexisting work or works that this work is based on or incorporates. ▼

a **6**

See instructions before completing this space.

Material Added to This Work Give a brief, general statement of the material that has been added to this work and in which copyright is claimed. ▼

b

DEPOSIT ACCOUNT If the registration fee is to be charged to a Deposit Account established in the Copyright Office, give name and number of Account.

Name ▼   **Account Number** ▼

a **7**

CORRESPONDENCE Give name and address to which correspondence about this application should be sent. Name / Address / Apt / City / State / Zip ▼

b

Area code and daytime telephone number   (   )   Fax number   (   )

Email

CERTIFICATION* I, the undersigned, hereby certify that I am the

Check only one ▶
☐ author
☐ other copyright claimant
☐ owner of exclusive right(s)
☐ authorized agent of _____

Name of author or other copyright claimant, or owner of exclusive right(s) ▲

8

of the work identified in this application and that the statements made by me in this application are correct to the best of my knowledge.

Typed or printed name and date ▼ If this application gives a date of publication in space 3, do not sign and submit it before that date.

Date _____

Handwritten signature (X) ▼

x _____

Certificate will be mailed in window envelope to this address:	Name ▼
	Number/Street/Apt ▼
	City/State/Zip ▼

9

*17 *USC* §506(e): Any person who knowingly makes a false representation of a material fact in the application for copyright registration provided for by section 409, or in any written statement filed in connection with the application, shall be fined not more than $2,500.

Form PA – Full   Rev: 07/2006   Print: 07/2006 — xx,000   Printed on recycled paper   U.S. Government Printing Office: 2006-xxx-xxx/60,xxx

You can download this form at www.copyright.gov

Continuation Form · Form RE/CON

For Renewal Registration · United States Copyright Office

REGISTRATION NUMBER

EFFECTIVE DATE OF RENEWAL REGISTRATION (MM/DD/YYYY)

COMPLETE ONLY THE SPACES THAT APPLY TO YOUR CLAIM.

FORM RE/CON REC'D:

DO NOT WRITE ABOVE THIS LINE.

PAGE _____ OF _____

A   Title at line 1a of Form RE: _____

B   Continuation of title in line   ☐ 1a   ☐ 1b   ☐ 1c: _____

C   Additional original copyright claimants (line 1g): _____

D   Additional authors who contributed to the work or material claimed (line 2b)

Name: _____   This author created: _____
Date of death, if applicable: _____   _____
(MM/DD/YYYY)

Name: _____   This author created: _____
Date of death, if applicable: _____   _____
(MM/DD/YYYY)

Name: _____   This author created: _____
Date of death, if applicable: _____   _____
(MM/DD/YYYY)

Name: _____   This author created: _____
Date of death, if applicable: _____   _____
(MM/DD/YYYY)

E   Additional statutory claimants (line 3a)

Name: _____   as the: _____
Address: _____   ◄ OR ► Year of death: _____

Name: _____   as the: _____
Address: _____   ◄ OR ► Year of death: _____

Name: _____   as the: _____
Address: _____   ◄ OR ► Year of death: _____

Name: _____   as the: _____
Address: _____   ◄ OR ► Year of death: _____

FORM RE/CON   REV: 10/2007   PRINT: 10/2007—XX,000   Printed on recycled paper

U.S. GOVERNMENT PRINTING OFFICE: 2007-330-945/60,XXX

You can download this form at www.copyright.gov

11.03   SCRIPT REGISTRATION COVER LETTER

Date:

**CERTIFIED
RETURN RECEIPT REQUESTED**

Register of Copyrights
LIBRARY OF CONGRESS
101 Independence Ave., SE
Washington, DC 20559-6000

RE:

Dear Register:

Enclosed please find the following elements to register the above-referenced script:

1. Check in the amount of forty-five dollars ($45.00) for the Copyright Registration;

2. Completed PA form;

3. Script; and

4. Return postcard

Please register the above items immediately. We understand that the stamped original Form PA will be returned to this office.

Thank you for your assistance in this matter.

Very truly yours,

MICHAEL C. DONALDSON

Enclosures: as listed

You should type this letter on your letterhead.

11.04 POSTCARD

The Copyright Office will date stamp and sign and return to you a self-addressed, stamped postcard (not a letter, a postcard). That is your proof of receipt. Use the following language on the back part of the postcard and you will have your proof.

BACK

This postcard shall act as a receipt for the following items:

Form PA to register the Script entitled:

_____

By: _____

Together with a check in amount of $30.00 and a copy of the script for Registration of Copyright

FRONT

Your Name
Address

Your Name
Address

Copyright Office fees are subject to change. For current fees, check the Copyright Office website at *www.copyright.gov*, write the Copyright Office, or call (202) 707-3000.

Form TX
For a Nondramatic Literary Work
UNITED STATES COPYRIGHT OFFICE

REGISTRATION NUMBER

TX   TXU

EFFECTIVE DATE OF REGISTRATION

Month   Day   Year

DO NOT WRITE ABOVE THIS LINE. IF YOU NEED MORE SPACE, USE A SEPARATE CONTINUATION SHEET.

1

TITLE OF THIS WORK ▼

PREVIOUS OR ALTERNATIVE TITLES ▼

PUBLICATION AS A CONTRIBUTION If this work was published as a contribution to a periodical, serial, or collection, give information about the collective work in which the contribution appeared.   **Title of Collective Work ▼**

If published in a periodical or serial give: **Volume ▼**   **Number ▼**   **Issue Date ▼**   **On Pages ▼**

2   **a**

NAME OF AUTHOR ▼

DATES OF BIRTH AND DEATH
Year Born ▼   Year Died ▼

Was this contribution to the work a "work made for hire"?
☐ Yes
☐ No

AUTHOR'S NATIONALITY OR DOMICILE
Name of Country
OR { Citizen of ▶
     Domiciled in▶

WAS THIS AUTHOR'S CONTRIBUTION TO THE WORK
Anonymous?   ☐ Yes   ☐ No
Pseudonymous?   ☐ Yes   ☐ No

If the answer to either of these questions is "Yes," see detailed instructions.

NATURE OF AUTHORSHIP Briefly describe nature of material created by this author in which copyright is claimed. ▼

NOTE

Under the law, the "author" of a "work made for hire" is generally the employer, not the employee (see instructions). For any part of this work that was "made for hire" check "Yes" in the space provided, give the employer (or other person for whom the work was prepared) as "Author" of that part, and leave the space for dates of birth and death blank.

b

NAME OF AUTHOR ▼

DATES OF BIRTH AND DEATH
Year Born ▼   Year Died ▼

Was this contribution to the work a "work made for hire"?
☐ Yes
☐ No

AUTHOR'S NATIONALITY OR DOMICILE
Name of Country
OR { Citizen of ▶
     Domiciled in▶

WAS THIS AUTHOR'S CONTRIBUTION TO THE WORK
Anonymous?   ☐ Yes   ☐ No
Pseudonymous?   ☐ Yes   ☐ No

If the answer to either of these questions is "Yes," see detailed instructions.

NATURE OF AUTHORSHIP Briefly describe nature of material created by this author in which copyright is claimed. ▼

c

NAME OF AUTHOR ▼

DATES OF BIRTH AND DEATH
Year Born ▼   Year Died ▼

Was this contribution to the work a "work made for hire"?
☐ Yes
☐ No

AUTHOR'S NATIONALITY OR DOMICILE
Name of Country
OR { Citizen of ▶
     Domiciled in▶

WAS THIS AUTHOR'S CONTRIBUTION TO THE WORK
Anonymous?   ☐ Yes   ☐ No
Pseudonymous?   ☐ Yes   ☐ No

If the answer to either of these questions is "Yes," see detailed instructions.

NATURE OF AUTHORSHIP Briefly describe nature of material created by this author in which copyright is claimed. ▼

3   **a**

YEAR IN WHICH CREATION OF THIS WORK WAS COMPLETED   This information must be given
◀ Year   in all cases.

b   **DATE AND NATION OF FIRST PUBLICATION OF THIS PARTICULAR WORK**
Complete this information ONLY if this work has been published.
Month ▶   Day▶   Year ▶
◀ Nation

4

See instructions before completing this space.

COPYRIGHT CLAIMANT(S) Name and address must be given even if the claimant is the same as the author given in space 2. ▼

TRANSFER If the claimant(s) named here in space 4 is (are) different from the author(s) named in space 2, give a brief statement of how the claimant(s) obtained ownership of the copyright. ▼

DO NOT WRITE HERE
OFFICE USE ONLY

APPLICATION RECEIVED

ONE DEPOSIT RECEIVED

TWO DEPOSITS RECEIVED

FUNDS RECEIVED

MORE ON BACK ▶   · Complete all applicable spaces (numbers 5-9) on the reverse side of this page.
· See detailed instructions.   · Sign the form at line 8.

DO NOT WRITE HERE
Page 1 of _____ pages

You can download this form at www.copyright.gov

DO NOT WRITE ABOVE THIS LINE. IF YOU NEED MORE SPACE, USE A SEPARATE CONTINUATION SHEET.

PREVIOUS REGISTRATION Has registration for this work, or for an earlier version of this work, already been made in the Copyright Office?

☐ **Yes** ☐ **No** If your answer is "Yes," why is another registration being sought? (Check appropriate box.) ▼

a. ☐ This is the first published edition of a work previously registered in unpublished form.

b. ☐ This is the first application submitted by this author as copyright claimant.

c. ☐ This is a changed version of the work, as shown by space 6 on this application.

If your answer is "Yes," give: **Previous Registration Number ▶**   **Year of Registration ▶**

5

DERIVATIVE WORK OR COMPILATION

Preexisting Material Identify any preexisting work or works that this work is based on or incorporates. ▼

a

6

Material Added to This Work Give a brief, general statement of the material that has been added to this work and in which copyright is claimed. ▼

b

See instructions
before completing
this space.

DEPOSIT ACCOUNT If the registration fee is to be charged to a Deposit Account established in the Copyright Office, give name and number of Account.
Name ▼   **Account Number ▼**

a

7

CORRESPONDENCE Give name and address to which correspondence about this application should be sent.   Name/Address/Apt/City/State/Zip ▼

b

Area code and daytime telephone number ▶   Fax number ▶

Email ▶

CERTIFICATION* I, the undersigned, hereby certify that I am the

Check only one ▶ ⎨ ☐ author
☐ other copyright claimant
☐ owner of exclusive right(s)
☐ authorized agent of _____

of the work identified in this application and that the statements made
by me in this application are correct to the best of my knowledge.

Name of author or other copyright claimant, or owner of exclusive right(s) ▲

8

Typed or printed name and date ▼ If this application gives a date of publication in space 3, do not sign and submit it before that date.

                                                                      Date ▶

Handwritten signature ▼

Certificate will be mailed in window envelope to this address:	Name ▼
	Number/Street/Apt ▼
	City/State/Zip ▼

9

*17 *USC* §506(e): Any person who knowingly makes a false representation of a material fact in the application for copyright registration provided for by section 409, or in any written statement filed in connection with the application, shall be fined not more than $2,500.

Form TX – Full   Rev: 11/2006   Print: 11/2006 — 30,000   Printed on recycled paper   U.S. Government Printing Office: 2006-xx-xxx/60,xxx

You can download this form at www.copyright.gov

11.06　FORM CA

Copyright Office fees are subject to change. For current fees, check the Copyright Office website at *www.copyright.gov*, write the Copyright Office, or call (202) 707-3000.

Form CA
For Supplementary Registration
UNITED STATES COPYRIGHT OFFICE

REGISTRATION NUMBER

TX	TXU	PA	PAU	VA	VAU	SR	SRU	RE

EFFECTIVE DATE OF SUPPLEMENTARY REGISTRATION

Month　Day　Year

DO NOT WRITE ABOVE THIS LINE. IF YOU NEED MORE SPACE, USE A SEPARATE CONTINUATION SHEET.

A

Title of Work ▼

Registration Number of the Basic Registration ▼

Year of Basic Registration ▼

Name(s) of Author(s) ▼

Name(s) of Copyright Claimant(s) ▼

B

Location and Nature of Incorrect Information in Basic Registration ▼

Line Number _____ Line Heading or Description _____

Incorrect Information as It Appears in Basic Registration ▼

Corrected Information ▼

Explanation of Correction ▼

C

Location and Nature of Information in Basic Registration to be Amplified ▼

Line Number _____ Line Heading or Description _____

Amplified Information and Explanation of Information ▼

MORE ON BACK ▶　• Complete all applicable spaces (D-G) on the reverse side of this page.
　　　　　　　　• See detailed instructions.　• Sign the form at Space F.

DO NOT WRITE HERE

Page 1 of_____ pages

You can download this form at www.copyright.gov

217

FUNDS RECEIVED DATE

EXAMINED BY

CORRESPONDENCE ❏

REFERENCE TO THIS REGISTRATION ADDED TO
BASIC REGISTRATION   ❏ YES ❏ NO

FOR
COPYRIGHT
OFFICE
USE
ONLY

DO NOT WRITE ABOVE THIS LINE. IF YOU NEED MORE SPACE, USE A SEPARATE CONTINUATION SHEET.

Continuation of: ❏ Part B *or* ❏ Part C

D

Correspondence: Give name and address to which correspondence about this application should be sent.

E

Phone (_____)_____ Fax (_____)_____ Email _____

Deposit Account: If the registration fee is to be charged to a Deposit Account established in the Copyright Office, give name and number of Account.

Name _____

Account Number _____

Certification* I, the undersigned, hereby certify that I am the: (Check only one)

❏ author   ❏ owner of exclusive right(s)

❏ other copyright claimant   ❏ duly authorized agent of _____

Name of author or other copyright claimant, or owner of exclusive right(s) ▲

of the work identified in this application and that the statements made by me in this application are correct to the best of my knowledge.

F

Typed or printed name ▼   **Date ▼**

Handwritten signature (X) ▼

Certificate
will be
mailed in
window
envelope
to this
address:

Name ▼

Number/Street/Apt ▼

City/State/ZIP ▼

YOU MUST:
• Complete all necessary spaces
• Sign your application in Space F
**SEND ALL ELEMENTS
IN THE SAME PACKAGE:**
1. Application form
2. Nonrefundable filing fee in check or
   money order payable to *Register of
   Copyrights*
MAIL TO:
Library of Congress
Copyright Office
101 Independence Avenue SE
Washington, DC 20559-6000

G

Form CA–Full   Rev: 07/2006   Print: 07/2006—••,000   Printed on recycled paper   U.S. Government Printing Office: 2006-•••-•••/••,•••

You can download this form at www.copyright.gov

PART III

PRINCIPLE PHOTOGRAPHY

Often you will have to make quick decisions about clearance issues that come up during principal photography. This part is designed to aid you in these decisions. Keep this part handy during the shoot.

CHAPTER 12 — **OTHERS WHO MAY HAVE RIGHTS IN YOUR FILM**

CHAPTER 13 — **ALL THOSE PESKY PEOPLE WHO SHOW UP IN YOUR FILM**

CHAPTER 14 — **TRADEMARKS**

CHAPTER 15 — **SETS AND SET DRESSING**

CHAPTER 16 — **CLEARING ALL MUSIC IN YOUR FILM**

CHAPTER 17 — **HIRING A COMPOSER TO WRITE ORIGINAL MUSIC**

CHAPTER 18 — **CLEARING FILM CLIPS**

OTHERS WHO MAY HAVE RIGHTS IN YOUR FILM

This chapter discusses the rights of writers and other individuals who contribute some creative or financial element to your film. Once principal photography begins, a myriad of other people will work on, invest in, give you opinions about, and generally "help" you on your film. They all make—or think they make—creative contributions to the total effort. Some of those contributions could be registered for their own separate copyright. This chapter discusses the most important among these people and provides the language you should include in your deal memos and agreements to be sure that you retain all the rights in your film that you need (and deserve). If you are making a documentary or shooting on the street, review Chapter 13, which discusses people who are actually depicted in your film.

WRITERS

The first and most obvious group of people who would have an interest in your film, absent some written agreement to the contrary, is the writers. The first couple of chapters in this section deal almost exclusively with the written agreement between you, as the producer, and the writer. You must have a written agreement with the writer for a variety of reasons, not the least of which is that without a written agreement, the writer of the film would have a slam-dunk claim for copyright infringement against your film.

Fortunately, everybody is alert to the importance of having a written agreement with the writer of the screenplay before the commencement of principal photography. In fact, SAG will not allow their members to start work on your film until you can show them that the script has been registered with the copyright office and that you have an enforceable agreement with the writer and that you have paid the writer. Usually, a canceled check will do, but you have to satisfy SAG that the writer is under contract and fully paid whatever is owed as of that date, or your SAG actors will not be cleared to work on your film.

THE DIRECTOR

The primary person—besides you and the writer—who contributes creative efforts to the film is the director. In fact, in much of the world, the creation of the director is considered so major that the director has rights that cannot be taken away by any contract. These are called moral rights. Throughout Europe, they are known by their French name, *droit moral*.

The term **droit moral**, or **moral rights**, covers a group of rights that protect the work from being changed without permission of the person who holds droit moral or moral rights.

For example, John Huston's 1950 black-and-white film *Asphalt Jungle* was one of the greatest crime films of all time. Sterling Hayden and a near-perfect cast created one of the real gems in the MGM library. When Turner Broadcasting acquired the MGM films, the package included this Huston classic.

Shortly thereafter, Turner colorized the film. By then John Huston had died, but Huston's estate wanted to prevent the colorization. They didn't bother to sue in U.S. courts because the U.S. doesn't recognize moral rights. The estate sued in French courts to prevent the exhibition of the film in France under the moral rights, which French law says cannot be waived by an artist. Even if the artist signs a contract saying that they waive their moral rights, the moral rights are not given up or waived. The Huston estate won. The colorized *Asphalt Jungle* cannot be exhibited or sold in France.

As a producer, you want to be sure that the contract with your director has language to minimize the impact of droit moral. You also want the contract to affirmatively grant to you all the rights that you need. Here is what you need:

> **Grant of Rights:** All of the results and proceeds of Director's services shall constitute a "work made for hire" for Producer. Accordingly, Producer shall be deemed the author and the exclusive owner thereof and shall have the right to exploit any or all of the foregoing in all media, whether now known or hereafter devised, throughout the universe, in all versions, in perpetuity as Producer determines at Producer's sole discretion. Director waives any so-called moral rights.

Note how the waiver of moral rights is at the end of the paragraph. Some producers like to have a separate paragraph so that there is no question about the waiver. Remember that under the law of many countries, the "author" of a work of art cannot waive moral rights. There is a substantial movement in this country, led by the Directors Guild of America and The Artists Rights Foundation, to lobby Congress for some movement toward the European model concerning artists' rights. Interestingly, at the time of this writing, Dreamworks, which was founded by Steven Spielberg, Jeff Katzenberg, and David Geffen, announced at its formation that it would not require artists to waive moral rights. However, Dreamworks—like everybody else—uses work-for-hire language, so the concession may not be of much value to the individual artists until the U.S. law is changed. It does make for good public relations, however.

OTHERS
WHO MAY
HAVE RIGHTS
IN YOUR
FILM

223

ACTORS

If you use a Screen Actors Guild (SAG) actor, the Standard Day-Player and Standard Weekly contracts have a clause that incorporates the SAG Basic Agreement into each deal. The rights and responsibilities of that agreement include ownership by the production company of the performances rendered by the actors. If you are using non-union actors or are writing a more comprehensive contract, be sure to include the following language:

> **Rights:** Producer shall own all rights of every kind in the results and proceeds of Actor's services hereunder. Producer shall have the unlimited right throughout the universe and in perpetuity to exhibit the Motion Picture in all media, now or hereafter known. Actor's services are a work for hire.

COMPOSER

On independent films, the composer of the film's soundtrack often retains a financial interest in the copyright for the music composed for the film. Sometimes composers retain actual ownership of the copyright. This is fully discussed in Chapter 17. The only reason to make this sharp departure from the comprehensive grant of rights discussed here for everybody else is to pick up music for your film at a good price. Do not lightly give up ownership of the music in your film if you can avoid doing so. If you do, make sure you have a license in perpetuity throughout the universe to use the music in your film.

CREW

Many crew members create things that could be registered for copyright except for their agreement with you, the filmmaker. For instance, a propmaker, a set designer, the costume designer, and the cinematographer routinely create items that could be registered for copyright protection in their own name. Under current copyright, even choreography is protected by copyright.

Many crew deal memos fail to take this into account. This is particularly true with independent filmmakers. One very famous filmmaker working on a documentary said, "Hey, man, these guys are cool. We're all friends. They're not going to hassle me." He was *probably* right. Besides, this crew frequently worked on his high-visibility features. They weren't about to "hassle" him. The film was a labor of love by people who had known each other for a long time.

However, consider the small Michigan filmmaker Hi Tech Video, who made a wonderful documentary about Mackinaw Island. When ABC ripped off 38 seconds of their work for a network piece and refused to pay for it, even after they were asked nicely to do so, Hi Tech sued. Slam dunk, right?

Wrong! ABC defended itself on the grounds that there were no written agreements with crew members who worked on the documentary. Therefore, the crew who created the documentary were the authors under the copyright law, not Hi Tech Video. The crew would have to collectively sue, not the company that organized the shoot but did not create the film. ABC won.

Few crew members attempt to acquire an independent copyright on their work, but they could if they wanted to. Here is the language you need:

> **Services and Rights:** All of Employee's work performed hereunder shall be a work for hire. Producer shall be the sole and exclusive owner of all the results and proceeds of Employee's services, and Producer shall have the right to exploit said results and proceeds and all rights of every kind therein in all media throughout the universe in such manner as Producer elects.

OTHERS
WHO MAY
HAVE RIGHTS
IN YOUR
FILM

225

NAME AND LIKENESS

This is another important consideration that should be addressed in your crew and talent agreements. In addition to being able to use the proceeds of the work of all of the above people, you also want the right to use their names and likenesses in the publicity and the advertising of your film. It would seem that most people involved in a film want credit, but sometimes how much credit, or credit for what, becomes an issue. Size, placement, and relative position are all hotly negotiated items for the cast and crew.

The credit provisions are so carefully negotiated that you might forget the flip side of the credit equation—you need permission to use names in advertising. Take the case of *Stephen King's Lawnmower Man*. The film was inspired by a short story by King. After script development and filming, King was convinced that the film was such a departure from his original short story that it was no longer "Based on the Short Story by Stephen King." So as not to mislead his fans, he sued to have this credit removed and to remove his name from in front of the title. He won a partial victory. The court was persuaded that the federal Lanham Act prevented attributing the film to King's story when it didn't relate. So King's name came off the title. The "based on" credit remained because there was a written contract that specifically provided for a "based on" credit, and the producer did start with King's short story.

Be sure to include the following in all of your contracts with creative personnel:

> **Name and Likeness:** Producer shall have the right to publish, advertise, announce, and use in any manner or medium the name, biography, and photographs or other likenesses of Owner in connection with the exhibition, distribution, advertising and promotion, or other exploitation of any film created as a result of the exercise by Producer of its rights hereunder, including merchandising, if merchandising rights are granted herein.

INVESTORS

OTHERS
WHO MAY
HAVE RIGHTS
IN YOUR
FILM

227

This group is the one that you have to be the most careful about. The investor(s) often seeks to own or co-own the copyright to your film. It's hard to argue against that effort because:

They are involved early, at a time when you have the rights to give away.

They can argue that you really are not losing anything since you wouldn't own the copyright if you made your film through the studio system.

You need them.

They have lawyers. In fact, most entertainment law offices represent a number of investors.

So what do you do? You argue against the request with the following:

As an investor, their real interest is a financial return. You can give them the exact same amount of money from profits as they would receive from the same percentage of ownership. Investors shouldn't have to take on the obligation of a copyright owner. The copyright owner can be sued for infringement of copyright. Investors don't need the worry of copyright owner-ship. If something happens to the investor, you don't want to co-own a copyright with heirs you don't know.

If you go through the hassle to make a film independently, of raising the money, of working without the safety net of a studio, of trying to sell it, of mortgaging your home to get it completed, you want to control the copyright. Copyrights last a long, long time. The copyright to film is your retirement. A copyright has the potential for throwing off income for the life of the copyright. By their statutory term, they will outlive you. Even though new films are made every year, the appetite of new media gobbles up more than the supply. Films are constantly being dusted off for re-release, remakes, video release, or sale to cable. As new media are coming on line in the next decade, more films will be needed. New production cannot fill this need.

Take the case of the original videotapes of the wedding of Nicole Brown and O.J. Simpson. When the company that shot that footage sold the business to a new owner, the new owner threw all the old master tapes of weddings into a trash bin behind the building without going through them. A passerby raided the bin for the tapes and used them to tape programs for his own pleasure at home. After viewing one such private home recording, he caught a glimpse of the wedding activities underneath, and recognized the participants as O.J. and Nicole Simpson. The murder trial had not begun, but he knew that he had something of value and was able to sell the master (not the copyright). The purchaser of the master also had to acquire the copyright to this film from the original photographer before it could be used, so the copyright owner received a substantial payment. (Even at the height of public interest in all things O.J., the "wedding tapes" did not sell well.)

In a more traditional scenario, Jack Hill produced a number of low-budget action films in the '60s and '70s. None of them was tremendously successful. In 1995, Hill discovered the negative to one of his films, *Switchblade Sisters*, in an old garage. Shortly thereafter, to Hills's amazement and surprise, he received a call from Miramax. The gentleman advised him that Miramax wanted to make *Switchblade Sisters* the initial release under Quentin Tarantino's banner, Rolling Thunder. Hill's shock turned to joy when he confirmed that he still owned the copyright and the print he found could be used by the lab to generate a negative from which release prints could be struck. The premier in Los Angeles was June 7, 1996—more than 20 years after its initial release. You'd better believe that Jack has since verified his ownership of the copyrights of other films he produced.

Be sure that you maintain ownership or control of your copyright. Let your investors participate to the full extent of your agreement in the cash generated by the film. You do not want to chase down co-owners in order to react to an opportunity for you to exploit your film. If you owe someone money as a result of the exploitation, you can always put that share into a savings account until you find that person's heirs. You don't have that leisure when opportunity knocks on your door. You need to answer the door!

The most common investment documents for independent films take care of this problem for you. The Limited Partnership (LP) used to be the single most-used method for raising equity investment for an independent film. In the LP, investors are limited partners with limited liability that they can only hang on to if they do not exercise control over the business of the limited partnership. In this case, the limited partnership would own the film, and you or your corporation would be the General Partner. The General Partner exercises all the control over the assets of the limited partnership. This gives you what you need.

Recently, the Limited Liability Corporation (LLC) has become very popular. A **Limited Liability Corporation** is a hybrid entity that provides the shared responsibilities of a partnership with the protection from personal liability of a corporation. The allocation of control is contained in the Operating Agreement. If you use an LLC, be sure that your lawyer builds in the same amount of control for you that you would have if you used a limited partnership. The control provisions of the LLC should be written in clear English so that your investor knows that you will be calling the shots with regard to the exploitation of the film.

BANKERS

"Bankers? Bankers? We don't need no *!@#* bankers!" you might cry. But bankers—such as creditors, vendors, and investors—might well acquire an interest in your film through the mechanism of a security interest in your copyright. In order for someone to have a security interest in your film, you will have to have signed a specific document to that effect. A **security interest** is like a mortgage on your house in that it allows someone to foreclose on the copyright in your film if you don't do what you say you are going to do, which usually is pay money.

The name of the document you sign is **Mortgage of Copyright**. People who obtain such interests have to file the papers correctly in all the right places. They usually know the ropes and get all their paperwork lined up correctly. Every bank that loans money in connection with a film will insist on obtaining a Mortgage of Copyright. If your film is partially financed through foreign sales contracts, a bank loan will almost always be involved.

A security interest in your film is also the way that the Screen Actors Guild (SAG) likes to insure that you keep your promise to pay residuals to actors. They will often ask you, as an independent filmmaker, for a security interest in your film to secure the payment of residuals. In this way, they act very much like a bank. Their security interest gives SAG an effective enforcement mechanism for those who slack on their payment of SAG residuals.

Investors could ask for a security interest also, to insure that any money due them is paid. However, most people who invest in independent film are not sophisticated enough to ask you for this particular piece of paper.

CHAPTER 13

ALL THOSE PESKY PEOPLE WHO SHOW UP IN YOUR FILM

People have rights, too! In the third decade after George Orwell's *1984*—which was supposed to have been the watershed for dehumanization—legal protections for individual rights and the number of rights that are protected seem to be on the rise. Just because you have the right to use a photo does not necessarily mean that you have the right to use the likeness of the person depicted in the photograph. That is a question that you must analyze and answer separately. The right to use a film or video clip does not necessarily give you permission to use the likeness of the person(s) appearing in the clip. And what about all those pesky people who wander into a shot or grant an interview and then fail to sign a release?

RIGHTS OF PEOPLE

Personal rights are the rights held by individuals to protect and safeguard their body and their personality. Generally, they were created by the courts based on the writings of legal scholars. Most states have legislated them into existence. Personality rights, which include the right of publicity and the right of privacy, are based on the notion that every person has the right to control the way they are presented in public, unless they have placed themselves in the public eye or are participants in matters of public interest. Even then, individuals have the right to insist on accuracy and the right to prevent the commercial exploitation of their names or likenesses.

Fictional films usually do not run afoul of the rules about the rights of publicity and privacy, unless they identify a real person in their films. That is just one reason why the script-clearance procedures discussed in Chapter 15 are so important. Through those procedures, you learn if you are inadvertently identifying a living person, and, if you are, you can change the name of the character before you start shooting.

Producers of fact-based films—such as documentaries, biopics (biographical motion pictures based on the life of a famous person, living or dead), or historical films—need to be very aware of the rights of individuals.

Right of Privacy

The Right of Privacy is an individual's right to be left alone. This is the personal right that a filmmaker is most likely to invade innocently. Intent is rarely considered by courts in this case, meaning that it doesn't matter who you were aiming at, it only matters who you hit. If you violate someone's right of privacy, your innocent state of mind generally is of no help in avoiding liability and not much help in reducing damages. However, if the person happens to be a public official, an innocent mind (or lack of intent as the courts like to say) helps a lot. In America, public officials and celebrities enjoy much less of a right of privacy because they have voluntarily placed themselves in the public eye. It may reduce what you owe, but you will still owe something.

The Right of Privacy can take several forms. For your purposes, it covers several traditional items: You cannot "out" someone in any way. You cannot reveal the private facts of someone's life. You cannot intrude into someone's private space in the course of your filmmaking. These activities invade someone's right of privacy.

Everyone has a bubble of privacy around them. That privacy bubble can be burst in various ways. One is the disclosure of private facts. Not lies. Not distortions. Facts. These private facts, however, must be of a kind that, when disclosed without permission, would be highly offensive to a hypothetical ordinary and reasonable person—you know, the kind that exists nowhere except in the minds of judges and the high-priced lawyers who try to persuade them. There is no interest in protecting any shrinking soul who is abnormally sensitive about such publicity.

So I went in search of the cases that could show us fact situations that did and did not qualify as "highly offensive" (not just slightly offensive) to the masters of our litigation fates. I think I have a feel for what some judges are thinking, but I offer no guarantees—and there is no clear and simple way to describe the definitional watershed. Probably the simplest way to express the demarcation of "offensive" is to say that you should be highly sensitive to religion, sex, and politics—that is, views on matters of social importance. Why? Because that is where normal people are sensitive and that is where lawsuits are spawned and that is where filmmakers most commonly lose.

Since the right of privacy protection slams hard into the First Amendment right of free speech, free press, and the public's right to know, there is a well-known exception: If the matter is of public interest, you can reveal it. There is something intuitive about all of this. If a congressman is diddling an intern, that is of public interest and can be mentioned, even though an office affair between consenting adults in a nongovernmental workplace would probably not be fair game. In practice, the courts have stripped elected officials of virtually all of their privacy rights based on the public's right to know.

Crimes are always reportable. The California Supreme Court used to have an exception for stories about former criminals who have long been rehabilitated and are living a life of quiet obscurity. The courts said such folks had a right of privacy. However, based on some U.S. Supreme Court cases, the court reversed direction and said that the right to free speech trumps this aspect of the right to privacy. Writers and filmmakers can tell their stories (based on official public records) even if the stories are painful reminders to the rehabilitated criminal.

Producers of documentaries and magazine shows on television are most likely to run afoul of someone's right of privacy, but the producer of a fictional film could do the same thing in a two-step process. First, someone is convinced (and their friends and family are convinced) that a certain character in a film is really them and, second, that the movie reveals private facts about them. The most common problems come up in movies that are admittedly based on true-life stories.

The best way to avoid accidentally tripping over the right of privacy is to obtain a Script Clearance Report. The companies that prepare such reports check out names and locations against real people and places in the area of your film's setting. If you cannot afford such a report, then go through your script yourself and see if a normal viewer could reasonably identify a real person based on the information they observe in your film. If you are shooting in a fictional store in Queens, pick up the phone book and see if an establishment exists by the same name anywhere around the New York area. Better yet, seek out generic names for use in your film. Don't give your characters full names when using a first name only would do. Details, such as both a first and last name, are rarely essential to cinematic storytelling, and if handled improperly, they can get you into trouble.

This is an area where you must exercise extreme care. Frederick Wiseman, the well-known, award-winning documentary director, ran into a brick wall at the beginning of his career. The court enjoined his masterpiece film *Titicut Follies* from being commercially exhibited for 30 years. When a court **enjoins** something, it issues an order for people not to do a certain thing—in this case, Wiseman was stopped from commercially exhibiting *Titicut Follies*. Few people saw it after its initial public screenings because of flawed releases. Well, that was the official reason. There is a whole book on the litigation alone.

ALL THOSE
PESKY PEOPLE
WHO SHOW UP
IN YOUR
FILM

235

The film depicted the inner workings of a Massachusetts hospital for the criminally insane. The head of the hospital signed on behalf of the hospital and on behalf of most of the patients depicted. The hospital administration liked the film when they screened it privately, but when they showed it publicly, an understandable outcry followed. The emotionally brutal treatment depicted in the film was very different from what the public expected.

The state arranged for legal guardians for some of the patients, enabling them to sue on the grounds that the hospital did not have authority to waive the patients' rights of privacy. The result of the lawsuit was technically correct. The film languished, virtually unseen, on the shelf until the last patient went to the grave with the right to privacy well intact. Since those rights die with a person, the film can now be seen more widely. Wiseman now gets all of his releases on audio tape, usually at the end of the interview.

When Do You Need a Release for People in Public Places?

What happens when you're filming in a public place? Do you need to get a release from every person who gets in your shot? The answer to this question requires a knowledge of a person's right to privacy. The answer turns on whether the person has a reasonable expectation of privacy. Therefore, when you are asking about shooting in a public place, the answer is no. There is no general right to privacy for someone who is in a public place. There have been lots of cases about this. Here are two of my personal favorites.

My absolute favorite case involved a CBS news crew. They were filming one of those wonderful It's-Spring-and-everybody-is-in-love stories. The camera crew filmed a construction worker named Carl (still wearing his hard hat) walking down the street holding hands with his girlfriend (also wearing a hard hat.) Carl immediately told the camera crew that he did not want to be on television and even spoke with the production manager and demanded that the tape be destroyed. They could have easily excluded him. The hard hat was hard to miss. Not only was there no permission, he had done everything reasonable to prevent being included in the piece. He REALLY did not want to be on television, at least not in that way. Despite Carl's protests, the footage was used during the news broadcast that night. As you might imagine, not only was Carl unhappy, but so was his girl-friend, and so was his wife (oops), and so was his girlfriend's fiancé (double oops).

Carl sued CBS for invasion of privacy.

Carl lost.

The court said that Carl had no expectation of privacy in a public place and CBS had a right to videotape him and air the footage. Carl argued that since he demanded the film not be used, CBS should not be permitted to show it. The court didn't agree and said that imposing such "prior restraint" on the news media could affect dissemination of unfavorable news.

In short, the filming of persons in public places does not constitute an invasion of privacy, even if the disclosure is embarrassing to the subject and the subject takes active steps to prevent it.

Now let's add another factor: the hidden camera. In this case, Dateline produced a news report investigating the practice of charging for services on so-called toll-free or 800 numbers. In connection with their investigation, Dateline reporters met with representatives from a company that was looking for investors for its programmed 800 and 900 telephone lines. The pitch where plaintiffs discussed their product was held on an outdoor patio at a restaurant in Malibu in the presence of waiters and other people. The folks from NBC did not disclose that they worked for a television station or that they were taping or that the video would be broadcast on national television. When the footage aired, the company was mighty unhappy with NBC.

The company sued for invasion of privacy.

The company lost.

The court granted summary judgment to Dateline because there was no legitimate expectation of privacy on that public patio. Waiters and other customers were within hearing distance. The fact that the company reps thought they were making a pitch to legitimate potential investors didn't phase the court. The company reps should have been more careful. Note that the result might have been different if the reporters had used super-sensitive microphones or cameras that could see through walls or the like.

Now let's add one more factor that pushes the case over the line and produces a different result. In this case the broadcaster lost because deception was used in order for the reporters to gain access to shoot their footage. The year was 1992, ABC's PrimeTime Live program was doing an investigative piece that focused on the Food Lion grocery story chain and how they handled or mishandled meat products. Two reporters went under-cover, created false resumes and got hired to work at the Lion King deli counter. They used the same sort of hidden cameras that Dateline used in the above case. They shot footage from the public deli counter and in the less public areas like the meat cutting room, break room and manager's office. The problem for ABC and the single reason that they lost the case was that the employees gained their positions through an elaborate hoax. It wasn't just a matter of not revealing their true employment as in the Dateline case, but they created false resumes with false references, addresses and work history. None of this sat well with the courts. The courts said the employees were trespass-ing because they got their jobs under false pretenses. They also violated the duty of loyalty to their employer.

The lesson is that you can shoot in public places without permission as long as you don't make affirmative misrepresenta-tions. But each of these cases—and many more on the subject

ALL THOSE
PESKY PEOPLE
WHO SHOW UP
IN YOUR
FILM

237

—is very fact-specific and also addresses other aspects of the activity. The written court decisions are much more nuanced than my descriptions. If you are going to take part in any activity involving hidden cameras, be sure that you are working with a lawyer who is knowledgeable in this particular field and that you use lots of personal integrity. Don't tell lies to get the story you want!

Even fictional films have taken advantage of this truth. When Summit and Fox Searchlight acquired the film *Once,* our office was called on to render an opinion on all those folks on the streets of Dublin who were included in various scenes without permission and certainly without signed releases. We gave a favorable opinion and the film went into theaters across America without incident and eventually won an Oscar for Best Original Song. But don't try that at home. No distributor would ever touch a fictional film, shot in America that included folks who appeared without permission. It is just not going to happen.

Also, you should know that the use of these images in advertising involves an entirely separate analysis. To a limited extent, however, you are entitled to advertise a film that contains images of folks who have not signed a release if you are entitled to use the image in the film itself. James Aligo found this out the hard way. His image appeared on screen for about four seconds in a Time Life Books infomercial promoting a rock anthology that they had published. He sued under the right of publicity discussed in the next section and lost. The court, among other things, said that the advertisement would be allowed because it was advertising the underlying work and was a fleeting image. There are a lot of restrictions on the use of an image without permission in an advertisement, but it is possible.

So, why all the signs at some shoots and why do broadcasters demand all those signed releases? Broadcasters want releases to reduce the risk of having to deal with this kind of claim. Signs are erected for the same reason. People are much less likely to complain if they were warned. If you put up a sign at a shoot, make a tape of it for your files that shows clearly where it was posted. An announcement at the event also helps and some indication of where the shooting will take place within the venue. Keep your signs simple. I laugh when I see a warning sign that is so densely worded that no casual passerby would read it. The idea is to inform. Something like this works:

ALL THOSE
PESKY PEOPLE
WHO SHOW UP
IN YOUR
FILM

239

A documentary is being filmed
today.
If you don't want to be in it, please
stay out.
If you enter this area, you are agreeing to be filmed.

Or something like this:

The XXXX television show
is filming here today.
If you enter this area, you are agreeing to be filmed.

Now let's add the celebrity factor. As the paparazzi know, celebrities are like everyone else when they are out in public. They have no right of privacy. But they do have a right of publicity which limits how those photographs can be used. Read on to gain an understanding of this important right.

Right of Publicity

Professor J. Thomas McCarthy, a leading authority in the use of name and likeness, succinctly defines an individual's Right of Publicity as the inherent right of everyone to control the commercial use of his/her identity. In his book, he says, "The right of privacy protects the soul. The right of publicity protects the pocket book." The right of publicity has to do with using someone's face or name to sell your product without permission to use that particular face or name. Be sure that you have permission for all the things you use in your advertising. In the body of your film, you have every right to accurately portray a public figure.

The rule is: "You have to pay up before you put someone's mug on a coffee mug and try to sell it to the public." The same thing goes for your movie poster. That is the bottom line. Professor McCarthy's treatise (mentioned above) is over a thousand pages with cases and history and theory and explanation. All you need to know is that different rules apply to the advertisements for your film than apply to the content of your film. You are much more likely to need permission before you use someone's name or likeness in your movie poster or other advertising than for the underlying film.

Misuse of a star's name and likeness has produced much litigation in what are called pre-sales. **Pre-sales** refers to selling the right to distribute a film in a certain territory before the film is complete—usually before filming has even started. That is one of the main activities at the film market that takes place during the Cannes Film Festival held in France during May of each year, the American Film Market (now shortened to AFM) held in November in Santa Monica, California, and European Film Market held in February in Berlin, Germany. If you pursue your dream of being an independent producer, you will be spending a lot of time at these markets, because this is where a lot of production financing is arranged and is completed when films are sold.

As you wander around these markets, you will see many posters for films that have not been shot. The producers are trying to raise the money for these productions through pre-sales. The posters, however, can only list a name if you have written permission from the actual actor—not from his or her agent or lawyer.

If you do not have written permission to include someone's name in the publicity for your picture, you are on safe ground to include a factual statement about the involvement of a certain person in the production of your picture. You can say: "So and so directed the film." The more you include in addition to a simple factual statement, the more it looks like you are using the person's name to help sell your film, which, of course, you are. As your press release talks more and more about a person, it moves along a spectrum of safety from the very safe, simple statement to the unsafe area of invasion of the right of publicity.

ALL THOSE
PESKY PEOPLE
WHO SHOW UP
IN YOUR
FILM

241

In negotiating the permission to use an actor's likeness on a poster, you will generally run into a request for approval over the likeness by the person you are negotiating with. Try to limit the approval right by requiring the actor to approve at least 50% of the photographs contains his/her likeness within a fairly short period of time. Only the biggest stars are entitled to 100% approval over their likeness, and only the biggest stars have more than three or four days to give that approval. Also, approval should be deemed given after the third batch of photos is sent. The actor should not be allowed to unreasonably extend his or her legitimate request for an approval right to trump your need to advertise your picture. There is no extra charge for the right to advertise someone in your picture—the cost is wrapped into the overall cost of the services to be rendered.

The negotiation on the use of a name in advertising comes in the credit paragraph of a contract struck with just about everybody who will work on your picture. The toughest name-use negotiations are always with the above-the-line personnel. **Above-the-line personnel** are the key creative elements of a picture and the key financiers. These generally include all producers, lead actors, the director, and the writer. The issues most commonly encountered in name use in advertising are placement, prominence, and appearance in the main titles of the motion picture and in all paid advertising for the picture, except congratulatory ads and award campaigns. It is a little easier going with the below the line personnel. **Below-the-line personnel** include everybody who isn't above-the-line personnel: the crew, non-star actors, suppliers, and licensors. There the credit provision is usually the assurance of appearance in the end-roll credit on all positive prints of the picture. These people's names usually do not appear in paid ads. The actual line that separates above-the-line from below-the-line personnel is a line across the page of the budget that separates the budget into two parts. The bottom part for other cast, crew, locations, equipment, and suppliers is fairly stable and predictable. The cost of the major talent and the script in the top part is subject to heavy negotiation and escalation, depending on whom you are able to attract to your project.

Usually an entirely separate paragraph dealing with publicity will appear in your contracts with the writer and the director and lead cast members. It sets out when the person must be mentioned in publicity and sets forth some restrictions on the artist issuing their own publicity. These restrictions are particularly important in the early stages of the project. The producer must maintain some degree of control so that word does not go out into the world before the producer is assured that all the elements are lined up. Sometimes a sensitive negotiation can be sidetracked by premature publicity about a picture—especially premature publicity that identifies attached creative elements before their attachment has been firmly cemented with a contract.

Note that the right of publicity is in the nature of a property right. Every citizen has it whether they are a celebrity or not. Obviously, it is a right that is more relevant and comes up more often in the life of the rich and famous than in the lives of the rest of us, but the right of publicity is a right that we all have. We all have the right to control the commercial exploitation of our name and likeness.

Many states have passed laws to protect one's right of publicity. However, it is the courts, not the legislatures, that have created most of the law in this area. You, of course, must be guided by the most protective state in the union.

Because the right of publicity is a property right, it lives past an individual's death and may be passed on to one's heirs. In contrast, the invasion of the right of privacy and false light and defamation are personal rights, so the injury is personal and dies with the person. You can't defame a dead man, but you can violate a dead man's right of publicity. In fact, all the state laws dealing with the right of publicity make it clear that the right can be left in a will and that the right lasts for a long time after death. Most of the statutes provide for terms that are 50 to 70 years in length after death.

SOUNDALIKES AND LOOKALIKES

ALL THOSE
PESKY PEOPLE
WHO SHOW UP
IN YOUR
FILM

243

Sometimes you cannot sign up the performer you want, so you are tempted to hire someone who sounds like or looks like the person you wanted to hire in the first place. They are called soundalikes and lookalikes. Not a good idea. Unless you are scrupulously accurate and forthcoming about the fact that you are using a soundalike or a lookalike, you are in trouble. Given the high cost of litigation, a good rule to follow is, "When in doubt, don't."

Don't think that you can skirt around these problems by invading someone's right to publicity with less than a picture and name splashed all over the place. Sometimes, the use of a distinctive voice, such as the one owned by Bette Midler or Tom Waites, is sufficient to identify the performer, even if an imitator supplies the voice. This is especially true in the context of advertising. Waites recovered $200,000 from Frito-Lay when it used someone who sounded so much like him that everyone thought it was him, even though he had always been very out-spoken about not endorsing products. Soundalikes and lookalikes are of no help to you if you are using them to trick the public into thinking that you have the endorsement or the backing of a celebrity when you don't really have their backing.

Those whom the courts have punished for using soundalikes or lookalikes have really crossed the line. Take the Bette Midler case. The advertising agency for the Ford Motor Company really wanted Bette Midler to sing their song for a commercial. Midler did not want to do it. So they hired one of her former backup singers and paid her to sing as much like Bette Midler as she could. Having shared the stage with Midler for many years, she came very close. The advertising agency was happy. Ford was ecstatic. The public was confused. We all thought that Bette Midler was singing the Ford song. That little bit of intentional deception cost Ford and its ad agency a bundle. And rightly so. Honesty, accuracy, and disclosure are the guideposts to staying out of trouble, especially when dealing with rights of people.

I have warned you not to ask unless you are sure that you need the permission that you are seeking. Nowhere is this advice more important than in the area of using soundalikes and lookalikes. The reason is that an early inquiry is a tangible piece of evidence that, at the inception of the project, you wanted the star. It is easy for a jury to believe that when you did not get the star, you hired a cheap substitute.

When your purpose is to save money and you cannot get the star you want, go in a different direction altogether—do not try to fool folks. It's not nice, and it can be much more expensive than hiring the star in the first place. It is certainly more expensive than going in an entirely different direction. Don't you really think that they could have sold just as many Fords with another campaign or another talent in the campaign they did run?

Even political figures, who have virtually no privacy rights, have publicity rights. You cannot imply a commercial endorsement of your product or film by a political figure without the permission of the political figure. Speech and comment about political figures are among the most protected areas of free speech, as long as there is no endorsement of a product implied.

DEFAMATION: LIBEL AND SLANDER

Defamation is the publication of anything false that is injurious to the reputation of another or which tends to bring them disrepute. A defamation designed to be read is **libel**. An oral defamation is **slander**.

Growing up, we all learned that it is not nice to tell lies. When the lies are about other people, they can cost you big bucks.

As a filmmaker, libel and slander issues do not come up often unless you are making a documentary or a biopic, or some other type of film that is offered up as a truthful version of the facts. Television movies often wander into this territory.

If you are offering your film as truthful, you want to have double sourcing on everything. **Double sourcing** simply means that you have two separate and independent sources for each factual assertion in your script. This is especially important for anything that might offend anyone, but especially the subject of the remark or representation. The second source should be truly independent of the first source. For instance, two different newspaper articles written from the same press conference or press release is not really a double source. The same fact verified by a second person not at the press conference would be a double source.

False Light

It used to be that the law only punished lies that damaged a person. Clint Eastwood fought one of his many battles with one of the grocery-store tabloids. *The Star* reported that he was romantically linked with someone other than the woman he had been involved with for many years. It was untrue. Everyone in Clint's life knew that it was untrue. On the face of it, this created a "no harm, no foul" situation. Clint felt deeply wronged by this false report.

He sued.

He won.

The courts created a new tort called false light. **False light** means that the statements were not true and caused some harm or embarrassment to Eastwood. In this situation, he was falsely reported to be dating someone else. Because he was a public figure, the court said that he had to show that there was gross negligence in their reporting of the situation. The rest of us only have to prove ordinary negligence.

Even if you are making a documentary and you accurately depict a person in context, you can still put them in false light in the editing room. Consider Michael Moore, whose *Roger & Me* offered many a good laugh. Unfortunately, some of those laughs were at the expense of certain persons who thought that the humor came from putting them in a false light. Remember the scene shot at the Great Gatsby Garden Party? One guest came off as an arch-conservative, insensitive to the evicted. In actuality, he was the liberal chairman of the Democratic Central Committee and had helped Michael in the past.

He sued.

The jury agreed with him. The jury found that Michael Moore had put the plaintiff in a false light. Michael didn't feel the need to obtain a formal release to use the man in the documentary because the man knew Michael, knew about the documentary, and consented to be in it. Everything would have been fine, but the way the film was edited put this man in a false light. Michael needs all the protective language he can get to protect against false light claims.

Defenses to Defamation and False Light

There are a number of common defenses to a suit for defamation. None of them is as good as never getting sued in the first place. Be careful when you make statements about individuals who are living and identifiable.

Truth: This is the classic defense. Everybody seems to know that truth is a defense. Even if a statement is not completely true, you should win with a public figure if you have checked the facts out and you have a reasonable basis for believing they are true. Unfortunately for you, reasonable people may differ on what amounts to a reasonable basis for believing anything. Check the facts carefully. Double source any dubious or inflammatory claims.

Opinion: Everybody has a right to his/her opinion. If you are stating an opinion, make it very clear that it is an opinion. "Jack is a thief" is libelous. "I don't trust Jack" is an opinion. This can be tricky. The courts don't let you off the hook with merely a perfunctory statement such as, "It is my opinion that . . ." and then go on with a string of libelous statements. It must be clear to the reasonable listener that the statement is an opinion, not a fact.

Humor: Humor is a defense because, if everyone hears a comment as a joke, you have not damaged the reputation of whatever or whomever is the butt of your joke. However, there is a big difference between something that draws laughs or chuckles from most listeners and something that insults someone—and, upon realizing that your words insult the person, you say, "It was only a joke" or, "I was only kidding."

In some ways, humor as a defense is a variation on the opinion defense. In both cases, you are not stating a fact and you do not want your statement taken as factual.

THE ON-CAMERA VERBAL RELEASE

Here is the good news for documentarians. You can obtain valid and binding verbal releases on film. The key is to make sure that the subjects give a full and informed release. While the camera is rolling, tell the subject of your interview that you are making a documentary film. Tell them what it is going to be about. Then explain that with documentaries, you never know how they are going to be distributed, but television, home video, and libraries are the most obvious and likely methods of distribution. Let the person know that you will try to enter the film in film festivals, and if you are successful, there is a chance for a theatrical release. (Don't forget to tell your subject that you may sell clips from your documentary for use on news programs or in other documentaries.) This explanation takes time, but if the interview continues—as it usually will—you have recorded a valid release by the person's continued participation after your careful explanation.

Lily Tomlin learned this the hard way. She allowed documentary filmmakers to prepare a documentary about her Broadway show, *The Search for Signs of Intelligent Life in the Universe.* Tomlin allowed the crew backstage during rehearsals building to opening night. Tomlin did not ask that they leave or turn off their cameras when tensions were high and some participants revealed more of themselves than they intended.

Tomlin hated the result. She tried to stop distribution of the film on the grounds that she never signed a release and neither did any of the people around her. The court watched a good portion of film in which Ms. Tomlin and everyone involved in the show acknowledged that they were being filmed for a documentary. No objections were made when they thought a flattering portrait was being prepared, and no objections were made even at less flattering times. The court said that if they wanted to retain approval rights, they should have spoken up at some time during the process. The court felt common sense dictated that it was too late to complain after the film was finished and ready to be sent out into the world.

THE WRITTEN RELEASE

It is best to have a written agreement. With a written agreement, you can specify the scope of the rights being granted. You can obtain specific waivers. That is good, of course. But it still isn't complete protection.

When you ask folks why they want long, convoluted releases, the answer is usually, "We don't want to get sued!" Long or short, legalese or plain English, a written agreement never stopped someone from suing if they are hurt, angry, or overcome with greed. Consider the raft of lawsuits filed after *Borat* became a smash hit. Several folks who signed long, written, studio releases sued anyway on any one of several theories. The strongest theory (which was not strong enough to win or trigger major settlement offers from Fox) was that they were misled into signing the releases. After *Fahrenheit 9/11* was released, the soldier who was interviewed and signed a long release said that he was defamed because he had changed his mind after the interview. His case was thrown out of court. But the lawsuits still come. Even if you have folks sign a release, it does no harm to add a statement on camera about your project while they are in the shot so that it is clear that the persons who appear on camera knew what they getting into.

What follows is a so-called Life-Story Rights Agreement that you can use when you want to obtain the right to produce a movie based on someone's life story. This document is not an acquisition of an underlying right in the sense of the Chapter 6 acquisitions. Rather, it is a person's waiver of certain personal rights and an agreement by them to cooperate and consult in the making of the film of which they are a subject.

The Agreement is formatted like a normal acquisition of underlying rights because that is the tradition in Hollywood, and because most laypersons have the notion that they own something called life-story rights.

I have also provided a simple release in letter form after the Life-Story Rights Agreement below.

13.01   LIFE STORY RIGHTS AGREEMENT

THIS AGREEMENT, effective as of _____, 20__, is made by and between [NAME OF PRODUCER], located at [PHYSICAL ADDRESS], ("Producer") and [NAME OF OWNER], located at [PHYSICAL ADDRESS], ("Owner"), concerning Producer's acquisition of all motion picture, television, and allied rights worldwide, in and to Owner's name, likenesses, life story, and background materials as follows:

> **Comment:** *Refer to Chapter 7 if you have any questions as to how to fill out this introductory paragraph.*

1.   **DEFINITION OF LIFE STORY:** For purposes of this Agreement, "Life Story" shall mean the irrevocable, exclusive, perpetual, and universal rights to use Owner's name, likeness, sobriquet, voice, and biography; depict, portray, impersonate, or simulate Owner in any way whatsoever, and make use of all the incidents of Owner's life preceding, surrounding, following, and otherwise in any way relating to incidents about the Owner's life that the Producer deems in its sole discretion necessary or appropriate to produce one or more motion pictures, whether wholly or partially factual or fictional; and use any and all information and materials in Owner's possession or under Owner's control, which Owner shall, at Producer's request, disclose and provide to Producer freely, completely, and candidly, in such forms as, without limitation, copies of any newspapers or magazine clippings, photographs, transcripts, journals, notes, recordings, home movies, videotapes, or other physical materials relating to Owner's life story and all Owner's thoughts, observations, recollections, reactions, and experiences surrounding, arising out of, concerning all those events, circumstances, and activities relating to Owner's life story (all the aforementioned rights hereinafter collectively referred to as "Life Story").

> **Comment:** *This paragraph defines the "Life Story" that you purchase. A living person seldom wants you to have the rights to make a picture of that portion of their lives that they have not yet lived. On the other hand, you seldom need any rights to the future. Whatever attracted you to this person's life has already happened. Therefore, feel free to narrow the above by describing that part of a person's life that you want to option. Insert the description you need in place of the second appearance of the words "the Owner's life." Use plain English and you are on safe ground. Note that personal photos, notes, and journals are also pulled into this agreement. Also note that if the Owner wrote books or articles, it is important to obtain those also. Add a description of such books just before the final parenthetical statement and the books will be included in the definition of Life Story. If you don't include such books, you may have bought the cooperation of the person*

ALL THOSE
PESKY PEOPLE
WHO SHOW UP
IN YOUR
FILM

251

and certain waivers, but someone else can buy the film rights to the book. The money you spend in this area must put you ahead of the person who relies on facts in the public domain or there is no reason to spend the money. You will want this paragraph to be as inclusive as possible. Also note "or more" in that first long sentence. Very few people will want to give you the rights to make more than one movie. If they do, they will definitely want more generous payments than the ones provided in paragraph 9b. At a minimum, they will want (and deserve) payments that are equal to the payments for the first motion picture. If you take out "or more," be sure to take it out of paragraph 5 (a) (2) also.

2.   GRANT OF OPTION: In consideration of the payment of _____ ($__) to Owner, and of the mutual promises contained herein, receipt and sufficiency of which is hereby acknowledged, Owner hereby grants to Producer for twelve (12) months from and after the effective date of this Agreement (the "Option Period") the exclusive, irrevocable right, and option (the "Option") to acquire the exclusive motion picture, television, home-video, Internet, and all subsidiary, allied, and ancillary rights in and to the Life Story, as defined above.

> ***Hint:*** *This is the first money you spend on the long journey of developing a screenplay and then making a movie. Even established companies try to get 90 days free. This gives you a chance to set the project up with a company that can fund development activities.*

3.   EXTENSION/EXERCISE OF OPTION: Producer shall have the right to extend the Option Period for an additional twelve (12) months by sending notice to Owner prior to the expiration of the previous period, along with an additional payment of _____ ($___). Producer may exercise this Option at any time during the Option Period, as it may be extended, by giving written notice of such exercise to Owner. The sums paid under this Agreement, with respect to the initial and extended Option Period, shall be credited against the first sums payable as compensation under the terms of the Compensation clause below. If Producer fails to exercise this Option, then the sums paid to Owner hereunder shall be and remain the sole property of Owner.

> ***Hint:*** *Many projects based on life-story rights are for television. The range of prices for television projects is narrow. Most projects pay $35,000 to $100,000 for life-story rights, whether there is one person or several persons to receive this money. Cable outlets generally pay less than broadcast networks.*
>
> ***Comment:*** *Try to get three years if you can. It always takes longer than you think to get a movie made. Note that the second payment*

is generally not applicable, meaning that there is no deduction on account of the first payment, so if you are asked for this concession, you should feel comfortable in granting it.

4.   PENDING EXERCISE OF OPTION: Producer shall have the right to prepare screenplays, budgets, teleplays, treatments or other material, and engage in other customary development and pre-production activities. It is understood that if the Option is not exercised, Producer shall have no further right in and to the Life Story, but Producer shall own all rights of every kind in and to material Producer prepared.

5.   RIGHTS GRANTED:

(a) Upon exercise of the Option by Producer, Producer shall acquire and Owner shall have assigned, conveyed, sold and transferred to Producer all motion picture, television, home-video, Internet, allied, subsidiary and ancillary rights in and to the Life Story for use by Producer, and Producer's successors and assigns, throughout the world and in perpetuity, including, without limitation, the following rights:

1) the right to develop one or more scripts based on the Life Story;

2) the right to make one or more motion pictures based on the Life Story, any part thereof or any sequences or characters therein (including, without limitation, theatrical productions, television series, and made-for-television movies and made-for-home-video productions);

3) the right to distribute, exhibit, and otherwise exploit any such motion pictures in any and all media and by any means now known or hereafter devised, including, without limitation, all forms of theatrical and non-theatrical distribution and exhibition (including, without limitation, free broadcast, pay television, cable, subscription, pay-per-view, video-on-demand, DVD, and Internet);

4) the right to manufacture, distribute, and otherwise exploit all forms of videocassettes, DVDs and similar devices of any such motion pictures and to combine such motion pictures with other programs on such videocassettes, DVDs, and similar devices;

5) the right to make changes to the Life Story, to create fictional episodes, characters, and/or dialogue for dramatic purposes, and to use any portion or portions of the Life Story for any purpose of this Agreement;

6) the right to edit and alter any motion pictures based on the Life Story and to make foreign versions thereof;

7) the right to publicize, advertise, or otherwise promote any such motion pictures and in connection therewith to prepare and use synopses (not to exceed 7,500 words each) of the Life Story;

8) the soundtrack recording, music publishing, legitimate stage, live television, radio broadcasting, and merchandising rights to the Life Story, to any such motion pictures based thereon and to any of the characters contained therein;

9) the right to make remakes and sequels to any such motion pictures;

10) the right to copyright any such motion pictures, sound recordings, musical compositions, and all other copyrightable works based on or derived from the Life Story, and to secure copyright and trademark protection to all works based on or derived from the Life Story; and

11) the right to sublicense or authorize others to exercise any of the foregoing rights, subject to Producer's obligations hereunder provided.

> **Comment:** *Well, finally, one of those long, interminable grant-of-rights paragraphs. I thought that you ought to see one, and if you are ever going to use it, you might as well use it with someone who lives outside of Hollywood and who might need a little longer rendition of what rights are being granted. Also, you need some waivers from the holder of the bundle of rights known as life-story rights. Those waivers can be very scary when you stop and think about it. Sometimes they appear less ominous when buried among all the detail that this long version of the grant of rights paragraph provides.*

(b) Notwithstanding anything contained in this clause to the contrary, it is Producer's intention to portray Owner's and Owner's Life Story as factually as possible with the understanding that Producer has the right to deviate from the facts of the Life Story in order to enhance the dramatic value. Owner shall be entitled to review and be consulted on the final shooting scripts of the motion pictures produced hereunder, it being understood that further changes to such final shooting scripts may be made by Producer. No approval rights are granted whatsoever in connection with any scripts created or motion pictures produced hereunder, which rights shall be held solely and exclusively by Producer and shall include, without limitation, control over all dramatic elements of said scripts and motion pictures.

Comment: This is an important piece of reassurance for the owner. Your obligations are minimal. Be sure you actually consult with the owner if you promise to do so. Many producers don't offer the reassurances in paragraph (b) until asked to do so.

6. RESERVED RIGHTS: The Owner specifically reserves literary publishing rights to the Life Story (other than literary publishing rights of up to 7,500 words for use by Producer in advertising any motion picture based on the Life Story). However, if Producer produces a movie hereunder and if Owner writes a book, Producer owns all motion picture rights in book without further payments.

Comment: This is a fairly standard reserved right. You need your 7,500 words for the synopsis you send out with your publicity packet. Most producers start by asking for 10,000 words for the synopsis. The last sentence is good to ask for, but you don't always get it.

7. WAIVER: Owner hereby waives and relinquishes any rights or remedies at law, in equity or otherwise, and further releases Producer and Producer's employees, agents, successors, licensees, and assigns from, and covenants not to sue Producer, or any of them, with respect to any claim, cause of action, liability, or damages of any nature whatsoever arising out of or in connection with the exercise of any of the rights herein granted to Producer. Such liabilities include, without limitation, defamation, libel, slander, false light, false advertising, intentional or negligent infliction of mental distress, or invasion or appropriation of any right of privacy or publicity in any jurisdiction. These waivers are hereby made by Owner, both on Owner's behalf and on behalf of Owner's next of kin.

Hint: This is at the heart of a Life-Story Rights Agreement. You are obtaining the waiver of all the suits based on the personal rights held by the person whose life story you are purchasing. These rights can be violated intentionally or accidentally. There is peril in making major modifications to this paragraph.

8. CONSULTING SERVICES: Owner shall be available to Producer as consultant in connection with the first motion picture produced hereunder at mutually convenient places, dates, and times, to provide Producer with information and materials regarding the Life Story and to assist Producer in obtaining releases from any persons designated by Producer. Such consultation will involve, among other things, cooperation with Producer and any writers employed by Producer or Producer's assigns in connection with the writing of the teleplay or other forms of adaptation of the Life Story. Owner shall be entitled to compensation for the above employment in the amount of ten thousand dollars ($10,000), payable upon commencement of principal photography of the motion picture.

ALL THOSE
PESKY PEOPLE
WHO SHOW UP
IN YOUR
FILM

255

> *Hint:* *This paragraph is important in a Life-Story Rights Agreement. The only reasons to pay a person for their life-story rights are to receive their cooperation in obtaining the rich details of their story and to obtain waivers if you wander away from the literal truth to achieve dramatic impact. If you do not receive this consultation, you might as well save your money and just rely on public-domain materials. This paragraph is usually reassuring to the Owner.*

9.   COMPENSATION: As full consideration for all rights, licenses, privileges, waivers, and property herein granted, and for all warranties, representations, and covenants herein made by Owner, Producer agrees to pay Owner as follows:

(a) Guaranteed Compensation: An amount of fifty thousand dollars ($50,000), payable upon the earlier of exercise of the Option or commencement of principal photography of the first motion picture produced hereunder.

(b) Remakes and Sequels: In the event Producer, or a successor in-interest, produces any sequel and/or remake feature motion picture based on the first motion picture produced hereunder, Owner will be paid an amount equal to fifty percent (50%) of the amounts payable to Owner pursuant to the paragraph above in connection with each such sequel and/or remake.

> *Comment:* *The 50% is taken from the rather standard compensation for a screenwriter when a sequel is made from a script. However, for the owner of life-story rights, you should be willing to go to 100% if asked to do so.*

10. CREDITS: The Owner shall be entitled to receive the following screen credit in the main titles of any and all motion pictures produced hereunder: "Based on the life of _____". Owner shall be entitled to an end-roll screen credit in connection with consulting services performed hereunder, the form and placement of which shall be at Producer's discretion. Inadvertent failure by Producer to comply with these credit provisions shall not be deemed a breach of this Agreement.

> *Hint:* *You may not be able to give this credit if your film disparages a living person who has not signed a release. A credit that identifies the main character serves also to identify other people portrayed in the film, even if you change the names of those characters.*

> **Comment:** *If the Owner is not happy with the details about the words "at Producer's discretion," change these words to "subject to good-faith negotiation within customary motion picture industry parameters."*

11. REPRESENTATION AND WARRANTY

> *For this and other paragraphs, go to Chapter 10, Provisions Common to Most Agreements, to finish up this contract. You should use all the paragraphs contained there. In the Representation and Warranty paragraph, eliminate (a) and re-letter the other subparagraphs. You may have to tone down (c) and (d) for certain life stories.*

You can download this form at www.clearanceandcopyright.com

13.02   INDIVIDUAL RELEASE

ALL THOSE
PESKY PEOPLE
WHO SHOW UP
IN YOUR
FILM

257

> *Note: This has been prepared in the form of a letter to you, the Producer, to make it less formal and, therefore, less intimidating.*

[date]

To: [your name]
    [your address]

This letter shall confirm that I, the undersigned person, for good and valuable consideration, the receipt and sufficiency of which is hereby acknowledged, has granted permission to you, the producer and your successors, assignees, and licensees to use my name and/or likeness as such name and/or likeness appears in photography shot in connection with the Picture tentatively entitled _____ and in connection with advertising, publicizing, exhibiting, and exploiting the Picture, in whole or in part, by any and all means, media, devices, processes and technology now or hereafter known or devised in perpetuity throughout the universe. I hereby acknowledge that you shall have no obligation to utilize my Name and/or Likeness in the Picture or in any other motion picture.

> *Comment: Many individuals will not authorize the use of their likeness in your advertising without substantial extra payment. It is generally not worth the extra money, so you may have to take out that provision.*

Your exercise of such rights shall not violate or infringe any rights of any third party. I understand that you have been induced to proceed with the production, distribution, and exploitation of the Picture in reliance upon this agreement.

I hereby release you, your successors, assignees, and licensees from any and all claims and demands arising out of or in connection with such use, including, without limitation, any and all claims for invasion of privacy, infringement of my right of publicity, defamation (including libel and slander), false light, and any other personal and/or property rights.

Very Truly Yours,

[Releaser's signature]
[Releaser's name]
[Releaser's address]
[Releaser's Social Security no.]

> *Note: If you are paying this person more than $600, you need the releaser's social security number so that you can fill out a W2 tax form. Otherwise, leave it off.*

You can download this form at www.clearanceandcopyright.com

CHAPTER 14

TRADEMARKS, LOGOS, AND BUSINESS SIGNAGE

As long as you use a trademark or logo as it was intended to be used, and do not disparage or tarnish it in your film, you do not have to ask permission to use it. So why do so many producers insist on obtaining permission for every label, sign, or shingle that shows up on film? Read this chapter for a full understanding of this widely misunderstood area of the law.

THE BIG PICTURE

Trademarks are a kind of intellectual property that a person or company can own and prevent others from using. What makes trademarks different from copyrights is that the trademark itself—the name, logo, motto, slogan, or design—is not what's important. The important part of a trademark is what the mark represents. A **trademark** represents the source—it identifies who made the goods you are buying or who provided the services you are enjoying.

A **trademark** is the combination of words or symbols or both that identifies a product or service. One of the main purposes of trademark law is to prevent consumer confusion. If you see a "swoosh" on a piece of athletic clothing, you assume that Nike made it. You probably have expectations about quality, durability, and style acceptance that go along with identifying the clothing as Nike gear. If every piece of clothing had Nike swooshes, consumers would not know which clothing would match up to their Nike expectations and which clothing would not. In other words, they would be confused about the source of the goods. Trademark law seeks to prevent this confusion by sanctioning those who use trademarks without permission.

Another main purpose of trademark is to prevent unfair competition. Continuing the Nike example above, if non-Nike athletic gear had the swoosh on it, some consumers would be more likely to buy it because of the goodwill and favorable expectations associated with Nike products. Nike spent hundreds of millions of dollars developing their brand and educating the public about the quality of their products, and another company could co-opt all that effort for free by putting a swoosh on their products, too. The law doesn't like it when one person benefits from another person's works without paying them. It's the same logic we see in copyright law.

BUT CAN I USE SOMEONE ELSE'S TRADEMARK IN MY FILM?

This is where trademark differs from copyright. A filmmaker's right to include trademarks within a film is clear. You have a right to include them in your film as long as the trademark or the product bearing the trademark is used as it was intended to be used without any consequences of its use being abnormal or out of the ordinary.

There is one caveat: You do not have the right to commit trade libel in the name of entertainment. Trade libel occurs when a product or service is falsely accused of some bad attribute. If you showed someone eating a McDonald's hamburger or drinking a Coca-Cola and they immediately keeled over dead because the food or drink was poisonous, that would libel the trademark. This is very much like the law around libeling an individual.

Courts have only recently addressed a true parody of trademark. So far, a true trademark parody has not found its way to the U.S. Supreme Court. Federal appeals courts have written opinions on the subject that reflect very different attitudes ranging from strong trademark protection to strong protection for the right to make social commentary about a product and its trademark.

Corporations live and die by their trademarks. A filmmaker has every right to dress sets with real products, but no right to disparage a trademark. If the movie does not misrepresent the source of the product and does nothing that would have a negative impact on the value of the trademark, there is no prohibition of the use of a trademark in a film. Remember, if anybody on earth could consider your use damaging to a trademark, you'd better believe that the owner of the mark will move swiftly to correct the perceived wrong.

Congress passed a law that specifically covers this situation. It includes a so-called anti-dilution provision. In fact, the most relevant claim for trademarks being used in films is trademark dilution. While trademark infringement protects against consumer confusion, trademark dilution protects "famous marks" from being weakened or **tarnished** by third-party uses.

A trademark is **tarnished** when the mark "is linked to products of shoddy quality, or is portrayed in an unwholesome or unsavory context" or if the trademark loses its ability to serve as a "wholesome identifier" of plaintiff's product.

Trademark tarnishment by third parties is spread along a spectrum. The spectrum starts with lawful non-endorsing "non-tarnishing" use, such as a person drinking a Coca-Cola during a dinner scene, and progresses to an illegal "tarnishing" use such as a person drinking a Coca-Cola during a dinner scene and collapsing as though the Coca-Cola was poison. The middle ground contains specific factual circumstances that dictate whether the use is tarnishing or not.

Let's put these categories into context. A perfect example of tarnishment of a trademark because of a third-party's unsavory use occurred when Eastman Kodak sued a comedian named D.B. Rakow. Eastman sued Rakow because Rakow used the stage name "Kodak" while performing his comedy routine. Rakow's routine consisted of humor that related to certain bodily functions and sex. Rakow also used crude, off-color language repeatedly.

Eastman Kodak Co. didn't like that.

Kodak the film manufacturer sued Kodak the comic.

The court ruled that Eastman Kodak's mark would be tarnished because Rakow's act was excessively grotesque and crude, which was in opposition to Eastman Kodak's policy of keeping its mark separate from excessive and gratuitous sex and violence.

IS IT THE PRODUCT OR THE USER?

The mark or the product bearing the mark must be maligned, not the people who are using it. That may sound like hair-splitting, but that's what lawyers are paid to do. Here are a couple of cases that demonstrate how important those split hairs can be.

In 2003 Disney was planning to release *George of the Jungle 2*, its straight-to-DVD sequel to the original theatrical film of the same name. The villain plots to steal the deed to George's land and bulldoze the area, all in the hopes that George's wife will then run into his arms. He succeeds in stealing the deed and proceeds to move the bulldozers into position to destroy the forest when George and his animal friends fight back in the climactic battle scene. As you may have guessed, the bulldozers used were Caterpillar equipment and the Caterpillar trademark is seen on the side of the equipment, several times. The narrator in this battle scene frequently chimes in, describing these machines as "deleterious dozers," "maniacal machines," and other unflattering things. However, the bulldozers are used in their intended manner, and it is clear that the villain's henchmen are controlling the bulldozers.

Caterpillar sued Disney for diluting its trademark. Caterpillar thought that the infringement was so damaging that they wanted a temporary restraining order to stop the film from being released.

Caterpillar lost.

The court ruled that to dilute a trademark, there must be something in the movie that suggests that the product itself is shoddy or of low quality. Disney's use of the Caterpillar equipment implied nothing of the sort. The court also pointed out that even little children, for whom the movie was intended, would realize that the people driving the dozers are the bad guys, not the dozers themselves. Thus, no trademark dilution, and no restraining order. For once, *George of the Jungle* avoided smacking into an obstacle, and the movie was released as planned.

In a similar case, Wham-O—the trademark owner of the Slip 'N Slide—sued Paramount Pictures for using the Slip 'N Slide in an inappropriate manner in the film *Dickie Roberts: Former Child Star*. David Spade plays the main character in the film, and in one scene he tries to slide on Wham-O's product without first getting it wet—a usage that could be potentially harmful if someone tried it at home. Indeed, after hurting himself, the main character decides to try again, first with water on the slide, and then after coating the slide with cooking oil. With the oil well in place, he slides well past the end of the slide, colliding with a picket fence. He gets up again and calls the product "insane in the membrane."

Wham-O sued.

Wham-O lost.

The court said that the usage in the film constituted "obvious and unmistakable misuse, one recognizable by even the youngest or most credulous film viewer." Since people will know that the product is being misused, the mark will not be harmed, and the tarnishment claim should fail.

Another tarnishment case occurred when Hormel Foods sued Jim Henson Productions. In 1996, Jim Henson Productions was preparing to release its new feature-length film entitled *Muppet*

Treasure Island. One of the film's new characters was named Spa'am, a wild boar puppet purposely named after plaintiff Hormel's food product Spam. Hormel felt that the Spa'am character would tarnish Hormel's Spam trademark because even comic association with an unclean, "grotesque" boar will call into question the purity and high quality of its meat product. The court found no evidence that Jim Henson's Spa'am was unhygienic or that his character put Spam in an unsavory context because Spa'am eventually became a friend to the protagonists. Moreover, the court looked to the public perception of Spam.

> "Although SPAM is in fact made from pork shoulder and ham meat, and the name itself supposedly is a portmanteau word for spiced ham, countless jokes have played off the public's unfounded suspicion that SPAM is a product of less than savory ingredients. For example, in one episode of the television cartoon *Duckman*, Duckman is shown discovering "the secret ingredient to SPAM" as he looks on at "Murray's Incontinent Camel Farm." In a recent newspaper column, it was noted that "[I]n one little can, SPAM contains the five major food groups: Snouts. Ears. Feet. Tails. Brains." [Mike Thomas, *Ready? Set? No!*, *The Orlando Sentinel*, June 25, 1995, p. 30.] In view of the more or less humorous takeoffs such as these, one might think Hormel would welcome the association with a genuine source of pork."

New Line wasn't so lucky. In 1998 they made and wanted to release a mockumentary satirizing beauty contests in rural Minnesota. They had a great cast lined up with Kirsten Dunst, Denise Richards, and Kirstie Alley, among several other notable names. Since they characterized Minnesota as dairy country, they planned on calling the film "Dairy Queens."

American Dairy Queen Corporation (ADQ), which owns the Dairy Queen chain of fast-food restaurants, sued for trademark dilution.

ADQ won.

The court recognized that the film contained scenes that would be offensive to some people, and that there might be confusion as to Dairy Queen's affiliation with the movie since the title was so close to their trademarked name. Because Dairy Queen appeals to families, this offensive content was likely to turn people away from the restaurants, thus damaging some of the goodwill and reputation that Dairy Queen had established over many years of business. The court also ruled that New Line was primarily using the title to market, advertise, or identify the film, rather than as part of an expressive work. This put New Line even lower in the eyes of the judge. Since the harm to Dairy Queen was potentially great, and the hassle of changing the film title was relatively small, the court granted an injunction against New Line, ordering them to change the name of the film. (For you curious few, the film title was changed to *Drop Dead Gorgeous* and the film was released into theaters as planned.)

Trademark protection has exploded in the last decade well past the traditionally protected graphic labels such as Coca-Cola, Texaco, and Visa. The distinctive green-gold color of pads for dry cleaning presses were successfully registered as trademarks, giving them added protection in the marketplace. The theme songs used for Merrie Melodies® and Looney Tunes® are registered trademarks that create additional legal rights for the owners and potentially longer lives than the copyright law grants to owners. The meteorite shower passing behind the "N" in the logo for Netscape Communications has been registered as a trademark.

PRODUCT PLACEMENT

The fact that you can include trademarks without receiving permission or paying compensation has an interesting effect. As in other areas of life, this largesse follows the law. As a filmmaker, you can dress your set with any products you like. Therefore, you can charge the owner of a trademark for the privilege of being selected for use in your film. This has grown up to be known as product placement. **Product placement** is the practice of receiving some consideration from the company that owns the trademark for using the product in a film. For independent films, it is often the supplying of drinks for a cast and crew, if the actors drink that brand on-screen. For larger films, cash payments might be made. Airline or hotel rooms are often supplied in return for their logos or trademarks appearing on the screen.

At the far end of the spectrum (and what might be a new wave of film financing), a non-film company might finance an entire theatrical film so that their products are featured prominently. The first instance of this phenomenon has already happened. Adidas bankrolled a movie entitled *Goal! The Dream Begins* about a Mexican-American boy who follows his dream to play professional soccer in Europe. Of course, all the products in the film are made by Adidas, and the real soccer teams featured in the film are sponsored by Adidas in real life. (The film did not perform well at the box office in the United States, but Adidas conceived the idea as a trilogy and the next two installments are scheduled to hit theaters within the next few years.)

The reasons this might be a new wave in film financing are numerous. Companies with gigantic advertising budgets typically spend them on television commercials or print ads with a very broad reach. This means that their ads hit the eyes of a lot of consumers who have no interest in the product, and advertisers don't get the most bang for their advertising buck. And they have no expectation of recouping any money from the advertisement itself—only the hope that the ad will drive people to buy their products or services.

If they make a modest-budget theatrical film, on the other hand, they spend about the same as they would spend on a couple commercials, plus they have the possibility of recouping that money if the film does well. If the film does poorly, oh well! They would have spent the money on an ad anyway. Even if only a few people see the movie, they are much more likely to be a part of the demographic that will actually buy that company's products or services, and thus much more valuable "eyes" to the advertiser.

In most cases, there are specific requirements about use and screen time for the product that are negotiated in advance. Ten seconds of screen time is a common minimum requirement (next time you see an airline logo in a film, count the number of seconds that it appears on the screen). The value received by the filmmaker is directly related to screen time. Favorable lines from a lead actor are also valuable. Budget, cast, and projected distribution are also considered.

Most studios have someone on staff to help obtain product placements. At a minimum, the trade-outs help to hold down costs. There are companies that help independent filmmakers obtain product placement deals. Good Unit Production Managers have a list of product placement companies, such as International Promotions (*www.productplacements.com*), (818) 755-6333 and Hollywood Product Placement (*www.hollywoodproductplacement .com*), (323-205-7022).

So Why Do I Have to Clear All Those Labels and Logos and Trademarks?

Now you know that the law does not require you to obtain permission to use these items in your film or television show. There are, however, some good business reasons why some networks require that no labels or logos be shown.

Broadcast television is an advertiser-supported medium. If products were to show up with undisciplined freedom on the screen, it would be mighty hard to watch advertising for that product or any of its competitors. Also, today, networks and film studios are owned by big conglomerates that are in a lot of different businesses. They aren't going to give valuable space away to a competitor. It's not going to happen.

Any payments or considerations for including products on programming designed for initial exhibition on television is regulated by the Federal Communications Commission. However, once your theatrical movie is completed, the fact that you may have had some product placement deals does not in any way disqualify your film from television exhibition. If all this seems a bit illogical, fear not. Other areas of legislative conduct are even more difficult to bring within logic's steely discipline.

So make sure that you consider the possibility of product placement in your film if it is appropriate. You could get some free food and beverages out of the deal, and in rare cases you could get your entire budget! It's definitely worth a shot.

CHAPTER 15

SETS AND SET DRESSING

Finally we turn our attention to a number of other legal concepts that are necessary to make snap decisions on the set about clearance. This chapter pulls together a wide variety of legal concepts and applies them to everyday situations that you face as a filmmaker during principal photography. Use this chapter in conjunction with Chapter 13 on Pesky People, Chapter 2 on Fair Use, and Chapter 14 on Trademarks.

CLEARANCE

To clear or not to clear, that is the question. It is probably the question that led Shakespeare to say, "Kill all the lawyers."

It is always safest to clear. To clear means to obtain written permission from the proper individual to use a certain item in your film or to obtain a written legal opinion that permission is not necessary. Young lawyers, anxious to protect their newly licensed necks, always seem to opt to demand written releases. The problem is that it is expensive and time consuming to obtain permissions for every little item on a set. And it can be quite disruptive if you are not able to clear something in time to continue your shoot.

Studios are very conservative in this area and tend to get releases from many people who would seem to be exempted from that need by the fair use concept or the rules set out in this chapter. This is particularly true in the areas of clearing trademarks and copyrighted books, magazines, and newspapers used as set dressing. One reason for the studios' conservatism is their institutional size. Corporate size always tends to inflate urges. Another reason is that studios—with their large and stable legal departments—are reservoirs for all the bad experiences that they have had in the past and do not want to repeat.

The practice has grown up with studio legal departments clearing every piece of copyrighted or trademarked material that appears in a film. They do this out of an understandable self-defense mechanism: The studios are what are known by plaintiffs' attorneys as a target defendant. A target defendant is anyone who looks as though they have the capacity to pay big bucks to avoid being sued. Interestingly, you may also look like a target defendant if your movie is released to good reviews or enjoys even a modicum of success. Being a target defendant is in the eyes of the beholder.

The attitude of the studios is that it is cheaper to clear in advance than defend after the fact. If you can afford the time and effort, this conservative advice is sound advice. Few independent filmmakers believe that they have the resources to do that and so must take advantage of their legal right to make limited use of existing elements that are copyrighted or trademark protected. Unfortunately, the studio practice has led some people to believe that such items have to be cleared as a matter of law. Not true. Read on for the good, the bad, and the ugly.

Who to Call When You Need Help

For research to locate the owner and negotiate the licenses for anything in this chapter or for film clips, there are a small band of professionals. We often work with Barbara Gregson. Here is a list for you to chose from:

Barbara Gregson

Miller-Gregson Productions, Inc.

T: (818)996-9373

F: (818)996-9374

Email: barbara@usinter.net

Elizabeth Bardsley

3727 West Magnolia Blvd.

Burbank, California 91505

Debra Ricketts

T: (310) 586-6880

F: (310) 586-6881

Email: debricketts@gmail.com

Susan Nickerson

Nickerson Research

T: (323) 965-9990

F: (323)965-9991

Email: susan@nickersonresearch.com

East Coast Rights & Clearances:

Jessica Berman-Bogdan

Global ImageWorks

65 Beacon Street

Haworth, NJ 07641

T: (201) 384-7715

F: (201) 501-8971

Email: jessica@globalimageworks.com

Cassandra Barbour

Laura Sevier

Entertainment Clearances, Inc.

T: (562) 799-1981 or (562) 494-7240

F: (562) 799-1985 or (562) 494-7268

Email: cassandra@ent-clear.com and laura@ent-clear.com

SETS

Let's start with the sets themselves before you do anything to them. That should be simple enough, but wait—this is real life—there are always challenges. The challenges are a bit different depending on whether you are shooting on a stage or on a location, so I will discuss them separately. Let's start with the easier of the two, building your set on a stage.

Shooting on a stage

Creating a set on a stage should be completely devoid of problems, right? It's the set dressing that causes clearance problems, right? Isn't that why so much space is devoted to set dressing later on in this chapter?

Generally speaking, that is true. Most set designers take great pride in creating a new environment for a television show or movie scene. Set designers can draw on any number of sources for their inspiration. However, it's not nice to copy someone else's design and call it your own.

Consider the case of the architect who made a monkey out of the set designer for *12 Monkeys.*

The inventive architect Lebbeus Woods sued Universal Studios because a set in *12 Monkeys* copied one of Woods' drawings. Bruce Willis was suspended on a chair and interrogated. The scene was on screen for about five minutes. The trial court concluded that the set copied "substantial portions of Woods'" drawing and issued a preliminary injunction against showing the film.

Surprise! Universal settled. There is a backstory to all of this. Woods had launched a career separate from his teaching and architectural career by designing fanciful sets for films that never saw the light of day, so he was particularly upset at getting ripped off in this fashion. He wasted no time. It paid off.

Ironically, they could have hired Woods to design the set.

Shooting on location—exteriors

If you are shooting a documentary, these principles seem fairly forthright. If you are shooting a fictional film, the situation can be a bit dicey. Not so much because of a pile of cases awarding huge sums to plaintiffs who are caught on screen, but because the general public in America has a notion that they should be paid handsomely if they wander into the camera's way during a shoot. So if you are shooting a fictional film, take care that no one is included in your shot who has not signed a release. Documentary filmmakers are in a very different situation with regard to the people in the movie and should read Chapter 13, All Those Pesky People Who Show Up in Your Film.

Buildings and Their Architectural Appointments

The copyright in architectural drawings does not prevent you from including the building in a shot. You do not need the permission of the architect (or whoever else) who owns the copyright in the drawings from which the building was built. You do not need the permission of the owner of the building as long as all you do is photograph the building as it normally appears from places where it is ordinarily visible from a public place. Obviously, if you go tramping around the building with your cameras, you will need a location agreement as discussed in this chapter.

In modern buildings, there is often a fine line between what is a separate decorative sculpture and what is architecturally part of the building. Artwork that is commissioned to decorate a building can also serve as architectural features of the building.

Andrew Leicester sued Warner Bros. for using a copy of his sculpture "Zanja Madre" in *Batman Forever*. Worse, the sculpture showed up in a lot of the advertising for the picture. Warners had obtained permission from the owners of the building where the sculpture was installed to film the location, but did not obtain permission from Leicester to film his work.

"Zanja Madre," which consists primarily of four sculpted towers, was created for a building in downtown Los Angeles. You might remember them from the advertising for *Batman Forever*. However, the court found that the towers were part of a larger piece of work that defined the open space and helped direct the flow of foot traffic through the area. The court put this work on the architectural side of the architecture/decorative art divide. If that decision had gone the other way, Warner Bros. would have been looking at very large damages. Because this particular piece of sculpture was considered architectural, Leicester lost. You can photograph architectural works (from public places) to your heart's delight ... without permission ... and without payment. The problem is that it is not always easy to tell the difference between an architectural feature and decorative artwork.

There are no appellate cases directly addressing the exact situations under which you need permission to use a real location in a film, but the copyright law has an explicit statement that copyright of a building's design does not preclude photographing the building from a public location.

The general principles of law would allow you to film anything visible to the general public so long as you do not defame or disparage it. However, if you depict a business location using its real signage, be careful about trade libel. For instance, if you show a real retail store that defrauds its customers in your movie, you need a release or you might be committing trade libel against the store.

Signs and Logos

Obviously, if you are shooting commercial buildings, there is a good chance that you will include some signs in your footage. There is almost no way around it. If you are shooting on location, be sure to read Chapter 14, Trademarks, especially if you are shooting a fictional film because the chances of misrepresenting a business are much greater in a fictional film.

Shooting on location—interiors

When you rent someone's home or place of business for a shoot, it is usually because you want to set your scene in the realistic surrounding represented by that home or place or business. Obviously, you want to be sure you have access when you need it for the length of time you need, so be sure to check out the section below on location agreements. There is more to it than merely grabbing the right form.

If you are shooting a documentary, you would not move anything. You don't want to change reality. You are keeping faith with your audience by showing things as they are. Generally speaking, clearance is not necessary. The things that are in the scene when you arrive and you do not rearrange are fair game. This contrasts sharply with a photo or something that is to be used in your documentary to make a point. You will have to read Chapter 2 on fair use to make those decisions.

If you are shooting a fictional film, you will usually want to change some things, but often not everything. Studio practice is to change everything. That way you take no chances capturing a protected image that is not cleared. But that approach may not be necessary. There is a growing body of cases that would seem to indicate otherwise. Check out the section on set dressing. The cases aren't so numerous or clear-cut that you can comfortably move forward without clearing paintings and posters, but some things are safe, as you will see.

LOCATION AGREEMENTS

You should have a location agreement for each and every location you use. If your location is a public street, park, or building, you may also need a permit from the appropriate governmental authority. As a threshold issue, these location agreements serve as your permission to be there and do what you are doing. You don't want to show up with cameras and crew and be subject to delays.

If you are using a distinctive location, the location agreement also serves as a release so that you can use the trademark or tradename associated with such a location and your own signage to create a new identification for the location. Every Unit Production Manager worth their salt has a location agreement that grants the necessary permission to film at a certain location during certain hours and leave the place neat and clean when they finish. The location agreement at the end of this chapter also covers all the clearance issues we have been discussing in this book. It is a safe document for you to use. If a landlord balks at granting one of the permissions, you can then evaluate whether you need that specific permission. Simply strike out those rights that you do not need. For instance, a landowner may say that you cannot use the real signage or that you must use the real signage. If that is all right with you, just change the agreement accordingly.

Finally, be sure that you are asking the right person for the permission you need. Virtually all the location disputes I have encountered grew out of, or were complicated by, obtaining permission from the wrong person.

There are three possibilities when it comes to signatures on a location agreement: the owner, the tenant, someone who happens to be at the location such as a friend, relative, or employee. Know whom you are dealing with. Always identify the person by name and relation to the property and make sure they have the right to grant you the permission you need. A building owner usually would not have authority to grant you the right to film in someone's apartment or business. Conversely, a tenant might have the right to let you into their apartment or business, but not the right to string cables into their location.

If you need to clear the use of signage, you need to talk to the owner of the sign, since it is the owner who has the right to withhold or grant that permission. If the signage is of a trademark that you plan to malign in some way, you have to have permission from the owner of that trademark, in addition to permission from the owner of the sign on which the trademark is located.

You are the filmmaker. It is your responsibility to think through these problems. You cannot expect a busy location manager to be as completely informed as you are. You cannot expect a location manager to be familiar with all the nuances of the multi-layered law of clearances. If you suspect a problem, just tell your location manager, "Please, get the owner to sign a location agreement also."

Always beware of crew members who say that they did things a certain way last time and nothing bad happened. That kind of experiential wisdom is exactly what gets a lot of people into trouble. People say, "We used this form on the last film and it worked." More often, the truth is that the form was not tested. Let's face it, 90% of the people in the world are not jerks, and you can talk through any questions that arise. Further, the famous "last film" might not have transgressed anybody's rights. They came, they shot, they left. In those situations, the particular form that was used "worked" because everything on the set worked. This book is focusing on what rights people have, how you can avoid transgressing those rights, and how you can get those rights waived if necessary.

SET DRESSING

Getting a set just right is fun and creative and fraught with legal questions. This section lays out the law. You need to read the trademark chapter for guidance on the use of trademarks and products that bear trademarks. You have a lot more latitude than many people think. This section discusses three very different types of set dressing: decorative items that you mostly hang on the walls; books, magazines, and newspapers; and props.

Paintings, posters, photos, and other decorative items

If you work at a studio, you can skip this section. They want you to clear everything, and if you don't, you will probably be yelled at. If you are an independent producer, read on. The law allows you to use certain items without getting permission, which doesn't mean that you shouldn't try. We might as well jump right into the cases and then try to make some sense out of them.

I like to think of this section as being about works created for display. The most obvious things that you might want to use in your film that are created specifically for display are posters, paintings, sculptures, and photographs.

A QUILT, A MOBILE, A POSTER, A PAINTING

This category of decorative arts can also include things that one would normally think of as utilitarian such as a quilt or a ceramic plate, but, because of its design, construction, value, or some other reason, is clearly a work of art created for display rather than a household item created for a purely utilitarian purpose.

The leading case in this area involves a story quilt. It was the first case to clearly state a certain conclusion of law. Prior to the case, the law was either unclear or untested or both. Non-quilters don't usually think of quilters as fighters. But then they probably haven't met Faith Ringgold. Neither have I, but read on. She single-handedly—along with her hired guns—set things straight in the area of clearance for set dressing involving "decorative" works.

Faith created a quilt called "Church Picnic Story Quilt." It's no ordinary quilt. It has a painting of a 1909 church picnic and twelve panels of text incorporated into the quilt. High Museum in Atlanta owns the quilt. Faith owns the copyright.

Faith licensed the right to create a poster to the High Museum, which sold thousands of them in their gift shop. One of those posters found its way onto the set of the final scene in an episode of *Roc*, a half-hour television sitcom about a middle-class African-American family in Baltimore produced by HBO Independent Pictures. The scene took place in a church hall. The poster (sans identifying wording) hung on the back wall of the set. It was never shown in its entirety. It was not always in focus. In nine shots, it was seen a total of 26.75 seconds.

But Faith knew it was a poster of her quilt. Faith sued.

She lost in the federal trial court in New York. The court said that the use of the quilt as set dressing was de minimus. De minimus is a fancy way the courts have of saying that the injury is too trivial for the court to bother with. And just in case that didn't work, the court also said that the use as set dressing was fair use.

On appeal, Faith won. First, the court found that 26.75 seconds was not de minimus. Next, the court found that it wasn't fair use. In part, the appellate court relied on a regulation issued by the Librarian of Congress that says public broadcasting entities have to pay a license fee when a copyrighted visual work is used, even if it is displayed "less than full-screen" for more than three seconds. I bet you didn't know about that regulation. Few people do. The Librarian of Congress issues a lot of pesky, little regulations. Many of them, such as this one, are more in the nature of an advisory regulation since the Librarian has no direct enforcement mechanism.

But the same appellate court reached the opposite result just a few weeks earlier in considering 10 un-cleared photographs used in a short scene in the film *Seven* for "less than 30 seconds." In the majority of the shots, actors or furniture obstructed the photographs, and the camera did not focus on the photos. In fact, they were out of focus for much of the time. Even the plaintiff artist needed "careful scrutiny" to identify the photographs.

But prominence is in the eye of the beholder. There have been a few cases where this unstated rule did not hold true. Of course these cases were decided before the Ringgold case, so you have to take them for what they are worth. For a case that might be decided the other way today, consider what happened when Columbia made a delightful movie called *Immediate Family* about a family anxious to adopt a baby. The family builds a nursery with a mobile suspended over the crib. The mobile contained a collection of little baby bears. The mobile also contained a copyright notice.

When Carola Amsinck saw the film, she had a mixed reaction. She was pleased that her artwork, which she had licensed to the makers of the copyrighted mobile, was used in the film and shown off in such a positive light. Exactly what the copyright holder would have wanted—if she had been asked. She wasn't asked, so she wasn't pleased. She paid a visit to a lawyer. (The phrase paid a visit must be short for paid for a visit.) The lawyer, in true professional style said, "We'll sue the bastards . . . and I will do it on contingency. You do not pay me unless we win."

They lost.

The court held that indeed the mobile was copyrighted, and no permission had been sought or received for the use of the mobile in the film. The court then concluded that this use would not require permission because such depiction in a film was not the kind of copying contemplated by the authors of copyright law. Specifically, the court stated that Columbia's "display of the mobile . . . is different in nature from her copyrighted design . . . [it is] not a mechanical copy . . . [it] can be seen only by viewing the film."

If this language is adopted by appellate courts, it could be one of the clearest statements (in my own personal view) that such items do not have to be cleared as matter of copyright law. The court was saying that a copyrighted artistic creation (other than a photo, poster, or piece of film) would never have to be cleared according to the copyright law. Other laws have to be considered, but as a matter of copyright law, no clearance is necessary because a film of such a creation being used does not form a "copy" of the work under the law. Rather, the film constitutes a picture of someone using the article. Note well that this logic could not possibly apply to a film clip that you might want to use, because that is exactly the kind of copying that the copyright law was designed to prevent.

To be safe, the court added, "and if this was copying, this use was a fair use." In fact, most of the opinion discussed fair use. The court went through the statutory tests: Yes, this was a commercial use that would cut against fair use. Yes, the entire mobile was used. Yes, it was used in shots throughout the film for a total of one minute and thirty-six seconds. But it was still held to be a fair use because there was no likelihood—in the court's view—that the mobile appearing in the film would in any way diminish sales of the mobile to parents. If anything, the court reasoned, the sales of the mobile would only be helped.

If contacted in advance, the copyright owner probably would have sent several mobiles to the set for free. If not, the producer could have gone on to the next mobile. One factor that triggered the lawsuit was a feeling of being ripped off when the artist learned that the studio had contacted other copyright holders and cleared their works. "Why not me?" is a question that inspires many lawsuits. This is exactly the problem with the studios' current practice of clearing so many items.

Copyright holders who might well be flattered if asked become uniformly angry when their creation is used without being asked. Unfortunately, lawyers and their letters in response to claims often make spontaneous apologies and genuine expressions of remorse difficult if not impossible. Legal posturing sets in. Lawsuits follow. Guess what? The lawyers win—and profit—again. A little time up front can save you a lot of time and money after the fact.

A few weeks before the Ringgold quilt case, a Michigan court, in a very similar scenario, ruled in favor of fair use. Warner Bros. incorporated into their film *Made in America*, two paintings by Earl Jackson depicting rites of passage of young Africans as a set decoration in a character's home. The court said that the decorations in the character's home complemented her persona as she was very proud of her African-American heritage and owned a bookstore selling cultural books and artifacts. During two scenes in the movie, the paintings are displayed for not more than 60 seconds. In one of the scenes, the characters in the film actually bump into the painting on the wall while in a robust and passionate embrace. Even though the paintings could be clearly seen by viewers, the court relied on the Amsinck case, holding that it could not find against fair use when the paintings were displayed for less than 60 seconds and defendant's use would unlikely interfere with sales of the work. Again, there's no telling how these scenarios would play out in court today.

All of this raises serious questions for people who make documentary films. The courts have not yet been presented with the opportunity to address the difference between a documentary filmmaker who does not control what is on the walls being photographed and a feature fictional-film producer who affirmatively selects set dressing. There is clearly a difference, and the court should cut some slack for people who make documentaries and just happen to catch a piece of art in the background. Our office is of the opinion that this constitutes fair use for the documentary and filmmakers.

Are you totally confused by these cases? Don't feel bad. So are a lot of people who haven't actually looked at the footage and read the cases over and over as we have in our office. We have the clips for most of the cases we discuss, and you can see them on the website for the book. It really helps to look at the clips when you are making these decisions.

After you have read the cases over and over and looked at actual clips, some useful guidelines start to emerge:

1. If the item isn't recognizable unless you really focus on it and are familiar with it, the court isn't going to bother with it. That's easy.

2. If the item is recognizable, but not a story point and is being used as a normal item of decoration as it was intended to be used and you give credit in the end-roll credits, you should be okay. That is not for certain, because you have that pesky Ringgold case with the quilt, but that is what the other two cases say and what many related cases would indicate. You are obviously better off getting the traditional releases, but the cases don't uniformly require you to do so.

3. If the item is a focal point or used as more than mere set dressing, you should obtain a license. It's just not safe, although many scholars are of the opinion that fair use might still apply.

State Law Protection—Moral Rights for Artists

The appellate court also said that Faith Ringgold, our feisty quilt-maker discussed above, had a claim under New York state law. The law is called the New York Artists' Authorship Rights Act, and it includes "the right of the artist to have his or her name appear on or in connection with such work as the artist." The producers of the television show in question removed the museum's name and also removed Faith's name. At least you could not see her name on screen. The court did not discuss the details of her rights other than to say that the trial court had to look into the matter. Presumably, an end-roll credit would work just fine in fulfilling this obligation, but keep in mind that New York gives artists that right as a matter of state law.

New York isn't the only state that has laws to protect artists. Other states are granting visual artists a limited form of moral rights through various state laws. Since these artists do not work for the producer, they don't waive their moral rights. That is the opposite of what happens to writers. Writers routinely waive their moral rights. Studios insist on it. It has become the norm in the industry, and writers oblige because they do not have moral rights under the copyright laws of the U.S. anyway.

This right of attribution is something we talk about again and again in this book. Unless you license something pursuant to a written agreement that expressly waives credit, you should give credit. It is proper acknowledgment. It is required under the copyright law of most European countries. And now you know it is also required under the state laws of many states when it comes to works of art created for display.

Magazines, Newspapers, Books, and Other Works That Are Not Decorative

The cover of every magazine and book and the front page of every newspaper is a creative work protected by copyright. Yet, these items are frequently used in movies. As long as the use shown in your film is the normal use and you use an actual copy of the article and not a derivative work that you did not have permission to create, you should be on solid ground. None of these items is decorative. The law does not set out a list of what is and what is not a piece of decorative art and therefore protected by the cases discussed above. However, there are committee hearings and debates that take place before a piece of legislation is passed, and those contain a lot of specifics that are helpful in deciding exactly what is intended by the wording of the laws that are passed. Those documents informed both of these sections.

So strew your sets with as much authentic reading material as you like. It is protected by copyright, but this is not the kind of copying that is protected by the Copyright Act for these particular items. As long as the use is pure set dressing and not a plot point or visual focus of a scene, it is my opinion that you do not have to clear these items. No case holds to the contrary.

PROPS

I define props as anything the actors hold—not furniture, not all the things on the wall, but the things they handle: knives, magazines, letters, books, hammers, whatever might show up in their hands. Here, the rules are the same as they are for pictures, but more elastic. Even if there is a copyright in a dagger, for instance, if it is being used for the purpose for which it is intended, you do not have to clear. Most studios clear these items anyway because it is the cautious, conservative thing to do. Think of the use of these items in the same way you think of the use of a trademark and you will be in good shape. That means that you should read Chapter 14 in order to feel comfortable with the use of props that you do not create in your film.

If someone creates a prop for your film, be sure that it is an original work. Creating a new work for a prop is a good thing. Copying someone else's design and calling it your own is a bad thing . . . and an expensive thing.

WHO TO TALK TO

As with other areas, sometimes the hardest part of the clearance process is finding out who should give you the permission you are seeking. Most of the objects you photograph do not need to be cleared. However, if you decide to clear the object, you have to reach the person who owns the copyright. An extensive list of resources is contained in Chapter 18.

Typically, the person who sells the poster or picture rarely has any rights other than the right to sell you the single item you purchased. Homeowners rarely have any copyright interest in a painting or sculpture they "own." If the artist did not sign the work, inquire as to who created it. In most instances, the creator controls the copyright to the work. If you cannot determine the name of the artist, find out the name of the work. You can always do a copyright search to discover the name of the artist and the address, at least as of the time of registration. If the creator has died, you will have to identify and locate the heirs. As you can see, this is often a lot more troublesome than creating your own work.

If you still believe that you need a release, the one-page form at the end of this chapter should suffice. As with music agreements, the exact description of what you are licensing and how you are going to use it in your film are of the utmost importance.

If a jeweled dagger of exotic design is the murder weapon and is frequently photographed and handled and discussed and helps to twist (pun intended) the plot of a film, be sure to create it yourself or clear it. If the theft of a figurine of great value forms the basis of a film's plot, and is frequently photographed and discussed by the characters in the film, create it or clear it. There is no case to support this. This advice is based on my experience. The more important the use of a work, the more likely the owner of a copyright is going to press forward with a claim.

Be sure that anything you have created as a prop or piece of set decoration for your film is either a work for hire or you have a complete assignment of all the rights you need, in perpetuity, throughout the universe. In such a case, use the work-for-hire agreement for the writer of a script set out in Chapter 7 (except in Paragraph 3, use substitute language that describes the exact work you are having created).

Knock-Offs

Making a knock-off doesn't help. Knock-off is a slang term for something that has been created especially to appear very similar to another, often notable, thing. In fact, you have created new violations of the Copyright Act: You have created a derivative work without obtaining the permission of the owner of the copyrighted work from which your work derived. You might win your case if you had used the original, but you will certainly lose the portion of the case that charges you with crafting a derivative work without the permission of the copyright owner.

No matter what you are tying to knock off, there are inherent dangers. If it is an item protected by copyright, the law looks at a knock-off as a derivative work. The right to make derivative works is one of the absolute rights that the copyright holder controls. Creating one without permission is a great big "no-no" under the copyright law. If the item you want to knock off is a trademark, there are problems under the Lanham Act, which is the federal anti-trust legislation. If it is someone's voice, persona, or performance that you want to knock off, there are problems involving the misappropriation of name and likeness.

The lesson is that you should create your own wonderment. Do not mimic others. It is lazy. It is frequently unlawful. And it is almost always less interesting than what you would come up with if you let your own creative juices flow.

The sculptor Frederick E. Hart and the National Cathedral in Washington D.C. sued Warner Bros. over the use of the bas-relief sculpture "Ex Nihilo" that is over the cathedral's main entrance. The film was *Devil's Advocate*. A bas-relief that was strikingly similar to "Ex Nihilo" hung behind the desk of the satanic character played by Al Pacino, head of an ungodly successful New York law firm. It was on screen for about 20 minutes, and in a climactic scene in the third act, the figures in the bas-relief began writhing around. Hart is a devout Catholic. He sued. The church joined in. They asked the court to stop distribution!

The suit was filed just after the film went into wide release. The trial court immediately indicated that it was inclined to issue a preliminary injunction. An **injunction** is when the court says you can or can't do something. In our world, that usually means that you can't distribute your film. Not good news when you are in the middle of a wide release.

An injunction is always bad news for someone. Warners settled immediately. They agreed, among other things, to major changes in the video version of the film, in case you are wondering why you didn't see all that writhing that I described above when you rented the movie.

SCRIPT CLEARANCE

There are a number of businesses and individuals who are in the business of script clearance. Script clearance is really a misnomer since no permissions are gained. Rather, these businesses and individuals provide the very useful service of flagging all the potential clearance problems—no matter how remote—contained in the script.

It is particularly helpful with matters that seem to have nothing to do with copyright. For instance, the script clearance service checks phonebooks in the locale where your film is supposed to be set to see if you are inadvertently using the name of a real person or a real business. They also check the area for real phone numbers. If a car's license plate number is readable on screen, they can check with the state's Department of Motor Vehicles to be sure that it doesn't belong to anybody.

Big problems arise when the phone number of an unknown person is used. The annoyance is minimal: You draw a nuisance suit that won't involve a lot of money, but . . . it is a nuisance. Even a number that is unassigned today may belong to some super-sensitive soul tomorrow. You should use a number that will never be assigned to an individual or a business. They are 555-0100 to 555-0199 and (800) 555-0199. There are no 900 numbers that have been reserved for use in films.

The same is true for business names and individual names. Some people even seem to mind when you present the character in a totally positive light. You can imagine the reaction when the character is in any large or small way despicable or the business is engaged in anything mildly nefarious. Again, if you do not have someone do this checking for you, be sure to do it yourself. The safest thing is not to use a real name, or, if you do, make sure that the name is of a friend or family member and that that person signs a release. The fact that another person with the same name might surface is of less concern if you are using the name of a specific living person who has given you permission to use it.

Clearance begins with a review of the script itself. A script clearance service provides a report that sets forth everything that could possibly need to be cleared. However, the report merely points out which items might have to be cleared—leaving the responsibility of deciding what to clear or change, what to leave, and when to accept the risk or obtain permissions to you or your attorney. The report alone does not protect your production company should a subsequent lawsuit be levied against it. It merely alerts you to possible problems.

The principle of clearance is equal to that of preventive medicine: Pay a little bit now for a check-up and avoid a major hospital bill later. It is beneficial to your production company to be fully covered by script clearance to reduce the risk of settlement costs, litigation, or judgments.

Many individuals and businesses are available to write script clearance reports. The studios generally do this work in-house. Here are five places to go for script clearance:

Hollywood Script Research (818) 553-3633
448 W. Maple St.
Glendale, CA 91204
www.hollywoodscriptresearch.com
info@hollywoodscriptresearch.com

Joan Pearce Research (213) 655-5464
Los Angeles, CA
http://home.earthlink.net/~jpra
jpra@pearceresearch.com

Marshall Plumb Research (818) 848-7071
Burbank, CA
www.marshall-plumb.com
info@marshall-plumb.com

Act One Script Clearance, Inc.
230 North Maryland Ave., Ste. 206
Glendale, CA 91206
T: (818) 240-2416
F: (818) 240-2418
www.scriptresearch.com
info@actonescript.com

Mosquito Productions (818) 676-0220
7721 Twining Way
Canoga Park, CA 91304

An excerpt from a typical script clearance report is attached at the end of this chapter. You can see from that report that it just lists the potential problems. A script clearance report for a feature film generally runs 10 to 20 pages and costs about $1,500. It can be completed in a couple of weeks, unless you want to pay more for a rush job. Dealing with the issues raised by such a report is the subject of much of this chapter.

After you review the excerpt, you can understand why many makers of low-budget films decide to do this work for themselves, especially on films with a contemporary setting. With this book, you can decide what response you should have to each and every entry in the report.

As you look over the actual script clearance report, you will notice that everything possible is pointed out. Nothing is left to chance. Now that you have read the past couple of chapters, you know that the trademarks that are pointed out are not things to be concerned about so much as they are opportunities to hustle some product for your film. The buildings all have their own rules that are set out in this chapter under the location section. People and phone numbers raise issues as set out here also. Use the information in this chapter in conjunction with a thorough script-clearance service to achieve maximum protection for your film.

15.01   EXCERPTS FROM A SCRIPT CLEARANCE REPORT

<u>Research on</u>: **"TIM AND ERIC AWESOME SHOW GREAT JOB"** – ep # 206, script emailed 7/2/07, with no listed author.

We presume that this script is a work of fiction, is not based on any preexisting work, and does not reflect any data pertaining to actual persons (living or deceased) or events, unless otherwise noted.

<u>Opening notes</u>:

1.) Minor cast characters without names (e.g., "Waitress," "Old Woman," etc.) will not be mentioned in the cast list unless use might identify an actual person. Please note that it is not possible to check the name of a character who is identified by his or her given name only.

2.) We assume that all automobile use will conform to your production company's auto-use policy (if such a policy exists).

3.) Care should be taken that no actual working telephone numbers are identifiable on screen, in dialogue, as sound effects, etc. We are advised that the telephone numbers (in all area codes) ranging from 555-0100 through 555-0199 are not working numbers and will not be put into active service. We are advised that the only 800 number that will not be put into active service is 800-555-0199, and that there are no 900 numbers which have been reserved for motion picture and television use.

4.) Location agreements should be obtained for any non-studio building or site used as a location; however, such locations will be noted in our report only if any actual, specific locale is mentioned. Unless otherwise noted, we presume all set dressing and design have been created especially for production and do not reflect any copyrighted, proprietary, or protected material.

<u>Locale</u>: **Unspecified**

<u>Time</u>:   **Present**

<u>CAST</u>	<u>COMMENT</u>
Billy Williams p.1	We find numerous listings for prominent people with this name in the U.S. We find numerous residential listings for this name in the U.S. We find no conflict.

...

<u>PAGE</u>	<u>COMMENT</u>
1	**High-energy animated opening**—Presume to be created especially for production and will not reflect any copyrighted or protected material, or any data pertaining to

actual persons, firms, or organizations. Advise check music clearance.

1 **INT. STUDIO**—Advise do not identify any copyrighted or protected material, or any data pertaining to actual persons, firms, or organizations.

2 **covered in wrapping paper**—As above.

2 **It's a Robin Williams impersonator**—Possible permission for celebrity impersonation.

...

3 **welcome to Dunngeon**—We find no federal or state trademark listing for this name. We find no listing for this name with the U.S. Copyright Office. We find no listing for a television show or movie with this exact name. We find one 1922 movie with the name *Dungeon* directed by Oscar Micheaux. Advise check with legal counsel.

4 **group called Zwei Dunkel Jungen**—We find no federal or state trademark listing for this name. We find no listing for this name with the U.S. Copyright Office. We find no listing for a musical group with this name. We find no conflict.

4 **performs very short synth melodies**—Advise check music clearance.

...

5 **using a tape recorder**—Advise avoid commercial identification.

6 **High-energy animated opening**—Advise check music clearance.

7 **INT. THEATER**—Advise do not identify any copyrighted or protected material, or any data pertaining to actual persons, firms, or organizations.

7 **Capiche**—Research will be happy to provide translations, if desired, at an additional cost.

---

*You can download this form at www.clearanceandcopyright.com
Use the code: ibotCC3*

15.02 LOCATION AGREEMENT

Location of Property: _____

Description of Property: _____

Dates of Use: _____   Fee for Use: $_____

PICTURE:_____   PRODUCER:_____

In consideration of the payment of the above-indicated fee, the undersigned hereby grants to Producer, its successors and assigns, the right to enter the area located as described above (hereafter "Property") on or about the dates listed above, for the purpose of photographing by motion picture, videotape, and still photography and to make sound recordings and to otherwise use for so-called "location" purposes (the results of which are hereafter collectively referred to as "Photographs"). If such photography is prevented or hampered by weather or occurrence beyond Producer's control, it will be postponed to or completed on such date as Producer may reasonably require. Said permission shall include the right to bring personnel and equipment (including props and temporary sets) onto the Property, and to remove the same therefrom after completion of work.

The undersigned hereby grants to Producer, its successors, assigns and licensees the irrevocable and perpetual right to use the Photographs of the Property taken by Producer hereunder in connection with motion picture, television photoplays or otherwise, and all the ancillary and subsidiary rights thereto of every kind and nature in such a manner and to such extent as Producer may desire. The rights granted herein include the right to photograph the Property and all structures and signs located on the Property (including the exterior and interior of such structures, and the names, logos and verbiage contained on such signs), the right to refer to the Property by its correct name or any fictitious name, and the right to attribute both real and fictitious events as occurring on the Property and to fictionalize the Property itself. The undersigned hereby agrees and acknowledges that any and all Photographs made or to be made by Producer shall be Producer's sole and exclusive property and the undersigned shall have no claims thereto or rights therein or to the proceeds hereof.

Producer agrees to use reasonable care to prevent damage to the Property and to remove any and all property which Producer may place upon the Property in connection with its use thereof. Producer agrees to restore the Property as nearly as possible to its original condition at the time of Producer's taking possession thereof, reasonable wear and damage not caused by Producer's use excepted.

Producer hereby agrees to indemnify and hold the undersigned harmless from any claims and demands of any person or persons arising out of or based upon personal injuries and/or death suffered by such person or persons resulting directly from any act of negligence on Producer's part while Producer is engaged in the photographing of said Photographs upon the Property.

The undersigned hereby releases Producer and its licensees, successors, assigns, all networks, stations, sponsors, advertising agencies, exhibitors, cable operators and all other persons or entities from any and all claims, demands, or causes of action which the undersigned, its heirs, successors or assigns may now have or hereafter acquire by reason of Producer's photographing and using the Photographs taken of the Property, including, but not limited to, all buildings (exterior and interior), equipment, facilities and signs thereon.

The undersigned hereby represents and warrants that the undersigned is the _____ (fill in: owner, lessee or agent for the owner) of said Property and has the full right and authority to grant the license herein contained. The undersigned hereby indemnifies and agrees to hold Producer free and harm less from and against any and all liability, damages, claims, costs or fees, including but not limited to attorneys' fees, arising from, growing out of, or concerning any breach by the undersigned of this warranty.

> *Go to Chapter 10, Provisions Common to Most Agreements, to finish up this contract. You should include the Arbitration paragraph and the Signature Block. Be sure to have this form countersigned by both the landlord and the tenant, if possible. Remember, there may be signage that presents separate issues.*

You can download this form at www.clearanceandcopyright.com Use the code: ibotCC3

CHAPTER 16

CLEARING ALL THE MUSIC IN YOUR FILM

This chapter discusses clearing pre-existing music for use in your film. After reading it, you will probably be convinced that you do not want to clear the music yourself, so I will provide a list of reputable businesses that will clear such music for you. Using a composer to write original music throughout your film avoids the music clearance problems discussed in this chapter (as discussed in the next chapter).

CLEARING PRE-EXISTING MUSIC

Unless you only show your film in a classroom, clearing the music you are going to use in your film is an absolute necessity. No exceptions. Be absolutely confident that Murphy's Law exists. If only one person ever sees your film in a theater or on television or at a festival, the writers (or the owners) of the music contained in your film will hear about it. As soon as they hear about it, they call their agent. Their agent then calls you if you have not cleared the music. It happens every time!

Clearing pre-existing music involves a procedure that sounds simple, but has many pitfalls. To clear music means to obtain the permissions you need to use the music in your film. Your film cannot be exhibited publicly without a specific grant to do so from the owners of the music that can be heard in your film. This applies to the music that is intentionally included in your film and may also apply to music picked up during a location shoot. However, refer to Chapter 2, which discusses the limited situations where our firm has been able to secure insurance coverage for the fair use of music in documentaries. Either way, due to the lack of clear case law in this area, you may have to clear all uses of music. Music clearance is the producer's responsibility.

You must pay very close attention to the legalities of music clearance. The consequence of not properly clearing a song is that the rights holder can obtain a speedy and virtually automatic injunction against further exhibition of your film until the music is removed or the music rights are cleared (and paid for). At that point, the cost of those rights almost always skyrockets, because you have eliminated a lot of choices. You either pay the owner of the music rights whatever punitive price is being asked, or you take the music out of your movie. You also may be working under tremendous time pressure at that point, especially if your film is actually in release or scheduled to play at an important festival. This is a situation in which you never want to find yourself.

The steps to clearing pre-existing music sound simple enough. However, the process is so difficult and frustrating that most people use the services of someone else to perform this task. Even if you use an outside service for music clearance, you should be familiar with what they do and how they do it. It's as easy as 1, 2, 3 . . . and then you pay the fee.

STEP 1: Locate the Rights Holder(s)
STEP 2: Negotiate the Deal
STEP 3: Send Out or Request the Contract (Licenses)

This may seem mighty simplistic. Read on. Each step can be a daunting task. And keep in mind that this process only obtains the right to use the music and does NOT include the right to use a specific recording of the music. That is covered later in the chapter.

STEP 1: Locate the Rights Holder

The first step is bewildering to most filmmakers. Actual ownership of music rights can be a very complex question, since several people can collaborate to create a single composition. Further, a copyright can be divided into separate parts with each owned individually or by several parties.

Generally, a writer sells or assigns the copyright in his song to a music publisher. A music publisher manages the right to reproduce the music and collects the money for the writer from the royalties derived from its exploitation (less a fee, of course). A music publisher may be a lawyer, a manager, a person who does nothing but manage such rights for others, or a company owned by the songwriter and set up to manage a catalogue of music as a separate business. The songwriters themselves (acting as music publishers) may license their own works in their own names. You must contact the music publisher(s) of the music you wish to use in order to obtain the rights you need. One of the things that makes this process difficult is that publishers frequently buy and sell entire catalogues. The owner of the publishing rights one year may have passed them along to another company the next year. Tracking this ownership can be like following a trail of breadcrumbs.

For publisher contact information, you can try one of the three performing-rights societies. A performing rights society is an organization that monitors the performance of music and collects royalties from performances on radio and television, concert arenas, in restaurants, lounges, even bars, hotels, and retail stores playing music on a radio, and workout/dance studios playing music for aerobics classes. Representatives of one of three performing-rights societies visit all these entities to collect a fee for the performance of music in their establishment. In Europe, similar societies (usually allied with U.S. societies) collect royalties for music performance, including performances that occur when a film is shown in the theater. In America, those societies are:

ASCAP: Los Angeles: (323) 883-1000
New York: (212) 621-6000
www.ascap.com
licensing@ascap.com

BMI: Los Angeles: (310) 659-9109
New York: (212) 586-2000
www.bmi.com
LosAngeles@bmi.com
NewYork@bmi.com

SESAC: Los Angeles: (310) 393-9671
New York: (212) 586-3450
Nashville: (615) 320-0055
www.sesac.com
sjungmichel@sesac.com

These societies do not have anything to do with licensing the rights you need for feature films, even though they are at the heart of collecting the royalties for performances of music. They collect royalties for music played in public places, and music included in films when it is performed during a broadcast of the film on worldwide television, or in foreign movie theaters in Europe. They could tell you who the publisher is for most songs you want to use in your film because they mail royalty checks to these publishers. However, helping filmmakers is not their business. Such information can only be extracted with finesse and diplomacy. Ask for the Research Department and be nice to the person who answers the phone, or go online and search the database yourself.

It is most often the publisher, not the writer, who has the authority to grant permission to use music in a film, even though the publisher may have to ask for the writer's approval. Be forewarned: Obtaining all the rights you need is not necessarily one-stop shopping. There may be several publishers involved, even on a single piece of music, because each person who wrote on the song enough to co-own the copyright could have his or her own publisher.

If none of the above works out, your best bet is to contact one of the music clearance houses listed later in this chapter. They have data on many publishers, and, if they don't have data on the one who controls the rights to the music you wish to use, they have the proper contacts to find the person who controls these rights.

STEP 2: Negotiate the Deal

This section deals with obtaining the right to use the music itself, whether you arrange to have it performed or you license a specific recording of it. If you want to use a specific recording of a song, you must go through all these steps for the song itself, and then go through a similar process for the specific sound recording of the song that you want to use. Be sure to review the next section of this chapter if you also want to use a specific recording of pre-existing music.

If you are clearing the music yourself, start your search for the music publisher. They will ask you to send a request on your letterhead describing your film and listing the music you wish to use, including how you intend to use it and the approximate length of that use. Then they will provide a quote that is good for somewhere between 30 to 90 days. Be sure to obtain this written quote before the final mix. Usually, you don't sign the actual contract until after the final mix.

Remember that you are asking permission to use something that is owned by someone else. Most copyright owners want to maximize income from their music. That involves protecting it, in a certain sense, from any use that would lower its value. Sometimes that can result in a very unreceptive attitude. For instance, the rights to *Porgy and Bess* are very closely controlled by George Gershwin's heirs. The property is very close to their hearts, and the music from it is not necessarily available to you. The heirs are very protective. At the other extreme, a motivation to maximize income may cause the negotiation to focus purely on money demands, and the copyright holder hits you for everything they think that they can get. A very popular and much-used song such as "Happy Birthday" usually has a rate card with prices that depend on the budget of the film.

Your task, then, is to convince the publisher that you are making a good film, but that you do not have a lot of money. It is also important to determine the music's role in the film: whether it's playing in the background, performed in the movie by one of the characters, performed over the credits, or—like *Pretty Woman*—used as the title of the film. Each one of these uses is progressively more expensive to obtain. If you specify background music and end up using the song as a featured song, you will be in trouble. You must specify the length of the piece of music you want to use and describe the scene or scenes in which the music is to be used. Be accurate. The contract includes this information. This information defines the limit of the permission that is granted. Disclose the scenes as accurately as possible. Some owners may not want their music used as the background for certain kinds of scenes such as a suicide or a sexually explicit scene.

If you have not found your distributor, you may not be able to afford to license the music for the broad use that you want. In this case, you can obtain a much cheaper "Festival License" that grants synch licenses for limited festival exhibition. This is usually a few hundred dollars instead of a few thousand dollars. Be sure to obtain a quote for full rights and mention it specifically in your festival license agreement. That way you know exactly what your licensing budget will be if a distributor is interested in your film. You may meet resistance on this point, but press on. You don't want to be held up if you obtain distribution. Having this information is good business, and it makes you look more professional to potential distributors.

Take care in obtaining all the rights you need. Generally speaking, the rights that you want to obtain from the publisher or copyright owner can be divided into the following two broad categories: Public Performance Rights and Reproduction Rights.

These are the rights contained in a standard synch license agreement, such as the one at the end of this chapter (Form 16.01). You may want to look over that form now to learn about the various elements you will be negotiating.

Public Performance Rights

Public performance rights cover the right to perform a piece of music in public. Licensing this right allows you to recite, play, sing, dance, or act out a piece of music. (Performance of a song or other piece of music by itself, apart from a play or a film, is referred to as small rights. Performance of a song or other piece of music as an integral part of a play or a film is called grand rights.) When your movie is run in a theater, the music in your film is being performed for the paying audience that is present to watch the film. In almost all of the world, except the United States, the owner of the publishing rights in the music receives a royalty payment for these public performances independent of any money received from the producer of the film.

In the United States, because of a specific court decree, the performing rights societies do not collect performing fees from motion picture theaters. You must secure the United States theatrical performance license directly from the publisher or agent when securing a synchronization license. Outside the United States, local performing-rights societies collect a percentage of the box office receipts from theaters exhibiting your film and remit it to the proper person, usually the publisher, who turns it over to the composer or splits it between the composer and the producer, depending on the agreement between the two.

Reproduction Rights

The publisher/copyright owner has the right to control who, how, when, where, and for how much money a piece of music is reproduced. These rights to reproduce a piece of music are again divided into two categories: synchronization rights, which you always need, and mechanical rights, which are commonly—but not always—needed. You must obtain synchronization rights, which are most often referred to as synch rights. Synch rights are the rights to record music as part of your film. The name of this right comes from the fact that the music is synchronized to visual images. It always excites me to watch a studio orchestra feverishly playing music to a projected film. The conductor stares at the images on the screen. The musicians stare at the conductor. The concentration is intense. The process of synchronizing the music with the moving image is one of the most exciting parts of the whole filmmaking process. Mechanical rights are needed when the music is to be reproduced on audio records, CDs, or tapes. You definitely need mechanical rights if a soundtrack album is released. Mechanical rights are automatically granted. However, few independent films are able to support a soundtrack album, so you may decide to forego the extra expense of obtaining these rights.

Out-of-Context Rights

These are not really separate rights. They are just the above two rights when the music is used in a trailer in a way different from its use in the film. If you wish to use music from your film in the trailer for your film, you need to get specific permission to do so. You usually have to pay extra for this permission, because you are using the music to advertise your film. That tells the publisher with whom you are negotiating that the music in question has unusual importance to the success of your film. Many producers find it is cheaper and more effective to have the music for the trailer composed especially for that purpose.

Adaptation Rights

If you are going to change or add to the music or lyrics you license, you need permission to do that also. When it comes to music and lyrics, the rights holder almost always wants to see your adaptation before giving final approval. Without written permission from the owner, you do not have the right to change a note of the music or a word of the lyrics, or to add either notes or words. It's not your music. You don't own it. Therefore, you can't change it—without permission.

Other Deal Points

The price for the rights you need covers a wide range. Songs are unique, but you should make a list of acceptable alternative pieces so that you are not stuck with only one choice. You are always in a better negotiating position if you have alternatives. There are many barriers to obtaining a particular song for your film besides money: There may be a contest over ownership. Exclusivity may have been granted to someone else. You may not be able to find the publisher quickly, or the person who can negotiate the deal may be on vacation. Always, always have other choices for the music in your film.

As you negotiate, be sure that you are obtaining all the necessary film rights—worldwide—in perpetuity. Unless you are sure that you are going to give the film only a limited release, obtain all rights. Because of the use of satellites for transmission and the possibility of permanent space stations, many people like to use the phrase "throughout the universe" instead of "throughout the world."

The phrase "in perpetuity" suggests the possibility of obtaining permission to use the music for more than the life of the copyright. The current length of copyright is the life of the author plus 70 years, which could put copyright ownership into the next century. An increasing number of people believe that since most countries have a longer copyright life than we do, the copyright life in the United States ought to be lengthened. You seldom save any money on the feature film rights by obtaining a shorter license than perpetuity. In spite of the use of the word "perpetuity," such a grant cannot give you a license any longer than the license granted by the words "for the full term of the copyright, including any and all renewals and extensions," because no one can sell or license more than they own. The copyright owner does not own anything after the copyright has lapsed.

You also need to obtain all television rights for eventual domestic and foreign syndication, cable, pay TV, as well as home video rights. Interactive and multimedia rights are highly desirable but may be too expensive. If it's too expensive to obtain these rights upfront, you can negotiate a "step" deal whereby you pay for certain rights when that right is actually exploited. So, for example, you would pay an additional fee upon DVD release. A lot of producers chuckle at a phrase commonly used by entertainment lawyers: "all media whether now existing or hereafter invented." That phrase didn't exist in very early contracts. Increasingly, the potential value of newly invented media—often called new technologies—is being appreciated. For instance, the courts have ruled that television rights do not include home video rights. If the filmmaker did not have a specific grant of home video rights or the very broad grant of rights created by that catchphrase, the filmmaker is out of luck. That fine print and those silly sounding phrases can mean big bucks in the future.

Also, be sure to look out for a "most favored nations" or "MFN" clause in your music license. **Most favored nations** means that the party of the particular license you are dealing with wants to be treated the same as any other party with similar content. In other words, let's say you negotiate a license to use song X with a music publisher under certain terms at a certain price. You then negotiate with the record label to use the recording of song X under certain terms at a higher price. Now the music publisher is going to want that higher price for your use of song

X, and if there is an "MFN" clause in the agreement, you will have to pay the publisher the more favorable price.

Here is another example of how an MFN claims works. Say you license one song with an MFN clause in the license. Then you pay more for some other song. You would then have to go back and pay the higher price to the owner who inserts the MFN clause when he licensed his song to you.

STEP 3: Send Out or Request the Contract

Remember, you are dealing with rights flowing from copyright. You must have a signed agreement for your permission to have legal meaning. This is not an area in which an oral understanding can be enforced. Almost all other aspects of human conduct can be effectuated through an oral agreement. That is not true for rights that flow through copyright.

Many publishers have their own agreement. If you do this yourself, you want to use the agreement in this book. You have plenty of time now to read it over and understand it. It is fairly short, but it is complete. It does the job.

Fortunately for you, this signed agreement with its airtight indemnity clause is all that the insurance company requires. They do not require the person who grants the music license to prove their chain of title. If the custom and practice required such proof, your task as producer would be much more difficult.

CLEARING THE USE OF A SPECIFIC RECORDING

You want to use a specific recording of music. You do not want to hire musicians to play the song. You have a specific favorite recording in mind, and that is what you want to use. This situation usually occurs for specific vocalists, but it can also arise for a recording without vocals. Note that a specific sound recording of a song has its own copyright dating from the creation of the recording. This means that, even though the music itself may be in the public domain, the recording of that song still may be protected by copyright. It also means that, even though you have just gone through all the steps to obtain permission to use the music in your film, you still need to obtain the right to use the master recording in your film.

The song "Thriller" (written by Rod Temperton and controlled by Almo/Irving Music) and the recorded performance of "Thriller" (by Michael Jackson and owned by SONY Music Entertainment, Inc.) are two separate copyrights, each of which requires individual prior clearance if you want this specific recording in your film. In that case, you have to negotiate with the persons who own the copyright to the song and the copyright to the specific sound recording you want to use. To make things ever more complicated, if there is a "sampling" of music in the song, you must also contact the master rights holder who owns the sampled music.

STEP 1: Locate the Rights Holder

Usually the correct entity to contact is the recording company. The recording company is almost always listed on the record jacket, CD sleeve, or online at a digital music website. This usually makes it easier than locating the holder of the publishing rights to the underlying music. Remember that compilation CDs are third-party licenses, so you have to read the liner notes to discover the correct contact for your purpose.

STEP 2: Negotiate the Deal

Generally, this negotiation is commenced as soon as you think that you are able to close the deal to use the song. The record company often has to get the artist's approval in order to grant these rights.

All the rules and comments about negotiating for songs apply to the process of negotiating for a specific sound recording. However, you are more likely to face an inquisition about your film when you are asking for the right to integrate a specific sound recording into your film than when you are seeking the music only. Owners of the copyright of a specific recording of a song tend to be much more protective. This may be especially intense in the case of a well-known vocalist or band. Also, the holders of master-use rights do not receive performance royalties. That is why their prices are sometimes a bit higher.

Step 3: Send Out or Request the Contract

A typical contract to license a recording is called a master use license. This name refers to the fact that you are licensing the use of the master recording of a song. A short but satisfactory license can be found at the end of this chapter if the rights holder does not issue their own license agreement.

The specific description of the recording, the length of use, whether the recording will be edited, and the scenes in which it is to be used are set out in the contract. This description defines exactly what you have the right to use. You cannot use the recorded music differently from the way you describe it being used in the contract. You cannot use a different recording of the music, no matter how similar the sounds.

In *9½ Weeks*, there was a seductive food scene that is credited for making Kim Basinger a star. It contains the song "Bread and Butter" by the musical group The New Beats. Although the filmmakers had permission to use this song, the album they intended to use had a scratch, so they went to the store to get another album. They bought a K-tel album with the song "Bread and Butter" and used this track. When the band heard the song, they were angry because the K-tel version was not the recording for which the rights were granted. K-tel produces collections of various artists' hit songs, but does not always use the original recording. K-tel may have a soundalike band perform the hit or have it re-recorded. Soundalike is filmmaker slang for one group legally recording a song in the manner and style of another group. In response to claims by artists such as Bette Midler and Tom Waits (see Chapter 13), courts are beginning to move against vocal soundalike recordings in advertising but have not ruled against soundalike band music in such non-advertising uses of music as film and television.

The filmmakers mentioned above did not notice an audible difference after listening to the two recordings of the song "Bread and Butter." Nevertheless, as a matter of law, they had to correct the mistakes. They had to pay for the master they did use. They had to fix the credits. They had to mollify The New Beats (probably with cash).

Note that the innocence of the filmmaker was not much help in this scenario. Accidental or not, the uncleared sound recording was a part of the film. The choice was simply to take it out or pay whatever the owner demanded.

Music clearance is one of the most technically exacting aspects of all the clearance issues that are presented in the making of films. It is also one of the most unforgiving. You must get it exactly right or you face a claim that is usually pretty clear-cut in favor of the claimant.

Sometimes this can be used to one's advantage. The film *It's a Wonderful Life* fell into the public domain. Republic Pictures forgot to renew the copyright under the old law, which required renewal after 28 years. But they hired a copyright clearance house and a team of clever Los Angeles lawyers, who contacted the copyright holders of five songs on the soundtrack of *It's a Wonderful Life* and obtained the exclusive synchronization rights to that music. They also obtained the right to bring suit on behalf of the music's copyright owners. They used those rights to control the licensing of the film. You could still broadcast *It's a Wonderful Life*, but you would have to broadcast it with no music or create a brand-new soundtrack that does not have some of the songs contained in the original film. Not an easy task.

MUSIC CLEARANCE HELP

It is easy to understand why so many people use music clearance houses to do all the above-mentioned chores. Because they handle a volume of business, professional music-clearance people can accomplish the necessary tasks in a fraction of the time that you would take. Sometimes they can even negotiate a better price, based on their ongoing relationship with licensors. Therefore, the net costs of their services are quite reasonable.

In Los Angeles:

David Powell
The Music Bridge, LLC   (310) 398-9650
www.themusicbridge.com
thabridge@aol.com

The Copyright Clearing House, Ltd.   (818) 558-1400
www.musicreports.com

Diane Prentice—Music Clearance   (818) 830-1270

Suzy Vaughan Associates, Inc.   (818) 988-5599
www.suzyvaughan.com
srvaughan@suzyvaughan.com

Evan M. Greenspan, Inc. (EMG)   (818) 762-9656
www.clearance.com
emginc@clearance.com

Other:

B.Z. Rights (New York)   (212) 924-3000
www.bzrights.com
info@bzrights.com

Diamond Time, Ltd. (New York)   (212) 274-1006
www.diamondtime.net
jen@diamondtime.net

Copyright Music & Visuals (Canada)   (416) 979-3333
www.copyrightmv.com
info@copyrightmv.com

There are also many twists in music clearance that the professionals know about and are beyond the scope of this book. Consider the so-called *Rear Window* case from Chapter 6. In general terms, songs copyrighted in the United States before January 1, 1978, are entitled to two terms of copyright protection: a first copyright term of 28 years and a renewal term of 67 years—for a total of 95 years. If the composer died while the song you want to use was still in the first term of copyright, your licenses may be unenforceable unless you deal with the person who renewed the copyright. Furthermore, in other cases where the copyrighted work was in its first term of copyright after January 1, 1978, certain authors are entitled to a renewal and extension of the copyright in such work for the further term of 67 years, which is a total of 95 years.

Clearance houses also prepare contracts, collect the necessary fees from you, and forward these fees to various rights holders. Finally, the clearance service (for an additional fee) prepares and distributes the music cue sheet. A music cue sheet is a very important document that lists, in order of performance, each song or portion of a song and each underscore cue used in the film along with the composers, publishers, performing rights affiliations (ASCAP or BMI or SESAC), usage, and timing of each piece of music. The performing rights societies use music cue sheets to determine who receives royalties for the public performance of the music on television stations and in theaters outside the United States.

THE MUSIC SUPERVISOR

If music is going to be an important part of the film, you may want to hire an experienced music supervisor to help you achieve the right sound. A music supervisor is the person who helps select music, supervise the clearing of music, hire a composer, and supervise the recording of the score. Often this person is also a composer or musician. The music supervisor can sometimes help obtain a soundtrack album deal.

A good music supervisor, such as David Powell of MusicBridge or Nic Harcourt, perform many more functions than can be included in this book.

16.01 SYNCHRONIZATION AND PERFORMANCE RIGHTS
AGREEMENT

THIS AGREEMENT, effective as of _____, 20__, is made by and between [NAME OF PRODUCER], located at [PHYSICAL ADDRESS] ("Producer"), and [NAME OF PUBLISHER], located at [PHYSICAL ADDRESS] ("Publisher"), concerning the rights to a musical composition entitled "_____" written by _____ ("Composition"). The following terms and conditions shall apply:

1.   The motion picture ("Picture") covered by this license is: _____.

> *Comment:* Include other identifying details in addition to the title.

2.   The type and number of uses of the Composition to be recorded are: _____.

> *Comment:* Be very specific and complete in describing how the music is going to be used in your film. Be sure to include the maximum length you want to use.

3.   The "Territory" covered hereby is: _____.

> *Hint:* You want to acquire these rights throughout the universe.

4.   Provided the Composition is included in the Picture, Producer shall pay Publisher the sum of $_____ upon the earlier of thirty (30) days after the Producer enters a distribution agreement for the Picture or upon first commercial exploitation, Publisher hereby grants to Producer, its successors, and assigns the non-exclusive, irrevocable right, license, privilege, and authority to record, dub, and synchronize, throughout the Territory, the Composition in synchronization or in timed relation with the Picture and to make copies of such records and import said recordings and/or copies thereof throughout the Territory and exploit, market, and perform said Picture perpetually throughout the Territory in all media and by all devices, whether now known or hereafter invented, including, without limitation, theatrically, television, videocassettes, DVDs, Internet, and other audio-visual devices, all in accordance with and subject to the term and limitations hereinafter set forth.

> *Note:* Fees are negotiable. Most publishers will require payment with this agreement _before_ they countersign. What you get is a non-exclusive license. Other filmmakers can use the same music.
>
> *Comment:* This is also where the language should be inserted if you can't afford all of the above rights and are just obtaining a festival license. Language such as the following should suffice, although many publishers have their own version of a festival rights license that they prefer to use. Obviously, you will have to fill in the proper amount, but in your negotiations start with the $100 that I inserted in the form.

> *"For twelve (12) months from the date of this agreement, Producer may exhibit the Picture in the Territory at film festivals and private-invitation screenings for which the Producer receives no compensation for the purpose of promoting the Picture and/ or obtaining distribution for the Picture for a flat fee of $100, payable upon execution hereof."*

5.   Publisher hereby grants to Producer the non-exclusive, irrevocable right and license to publicly perform for profit or non-profit and authorize others so to perform the Composition in the exhibition of the Picture to audiences in motion picture theaters and other places of public entertainment where motion pictures are customarily exhibited throughout the Territory, including the right to download or stream the Picture, and to televise the Picture into such theaters and such other public places, with the understanding and upon the condition that the Picture shall not be exhibited in the U.S. by means of television for any other purpose whatsoever, except according to the next paragraph.

6.   The right to perform the Composition in the exhibition of the Picture in the U.S. in any and all media and by any means now known or hereafter devised, including, without limitation, all forms of theatrical and non-theatrical distribution and exhibition (including, without limitation, free broadcast, pay television, cable, subscription, pay-per-view, video on demand, DVD, and Internet) is and shall be available only under the following circumstances:

(a)   The public performance of the Picture may be made by means of television by networks, local stations or closed-circuit systems having valid performance licenses from the American Society of Composers, Authors and Publishers ("ASCAP") or Broadcast Music, Inc. ("BMI"), as the case may be.

(b)   The public performance of the Picture by means of television by networks, local stations, or closed-circuit systems not licensed for television by ASCAP or BMI is subject to clearance of the performing rights either from Publisher or ASCAP or BMI or from any other licenser acting for or on behalf of Publisher.

> **Note:** *This insures that the composer gets paid for U.S. television exhibition. Television networks in the U.S. generally pay blanket licenses for music. A blanket license is a license obtained by the periodic payment of a flat fee for the right to perform various pieces of copyrighted music. Logs of the music played during each quarter of the year are sent to the performing rights societies, where the fees are divided up among the various publishers.*

7.   It is understood that clearance by performance rights societies in such portion of the Territory as is outside of the U.S. will be in accordance with their customary practices and the payment of their customary fees.

8. Producer shall have the right to use the name and likeness of the writer of the Composition in connection with the Picture and the advertising and promotion thereof.

9. Publisher hereby further grants to Producer the non-exclusive right to cause or authorize the fixing of the Composition in and as part of the Picture on in any and all media and by any means now known or hereafter devised, including, without limitation, all forms of theatrical and non-theatrical distribution and exhibition (including, without limitation, free broadcast, pay television, cable, subscription, pay-per-view, video on demand, DVD, and Internet) and:

(a) To utilize such Videograms for any of the purposes, uses, and performances set forth herein; and

(b) To sell, lease, license, or otherwise make such Videograms available to the public as a device intended primarily for "home use" (as such term is commonly understood in the entertainment industry).

The foregoing rights granted in this Paragraph may be exercised by Producer without any additional fee or royalty to Publisher.

Producer shall accord the following end-roll credit on all prints of the Picture, together with a similar credit for other music used in the Picture, substantially as follows:

_____

_____

10. This license does not authorize or permit any use of the Composition not expressly set forth herein and does not include the right to alter the fundamental character of the music of the Composition, to use the title or subtitle of the Composition, as the title of a motion picture, to use the story of the Composition or to make any other use of the Composition not expressly authorized hereunder.

> **Note:** *This form is designed for producers. Expect the publisher to strike "the fundamental character of." Also, this paragraph specifically confirms that this synch license does not grant "film rights to the song's story" or to the title of the song as the title of your film.*

11. The recording and performing rights granted herein include such rights for screen, video, and television trailers for the advertising and exploitation of the Picture.

> **Note:** *Expect to pay extra—up to 25%—for this right. It is not always worth extra to independent filmmakers, but try the above language in your first draft.*

12. The recording and performing rights granted herein shall inure for the periods of all copyrights throughout the Territory in and to the Composition, and any and all renewals or extensions thereof.

13. Producer agrees to furnish Publisher a cue sheet of the Picture within thirty (30) days from the first public exhibition of the Picture at which admission is charged (except so-called "sneak previews").

14. No failure by Producer to perform any of its obligations hereunder shall constitute a breach hereof, unless Publisher gives Producer written notice of such non-performance and Producer fails to cure within sixty (60) days of receipt of such notice.

> **Note:** *Cure periods are good, but you'll be lucky to get 30 days to cure. Only an inattentive publisher will allow 60 days.*

15. Publisher's remedies under this Agreement shall be limited to an action or law for damages. In no event will Publisher have a right to enjoin or restrict the exploitation of the Picture.

> **Comment:** *This sounds harsh, but it is absolutely necessary in a studio deal. You should have this protection so that you have maximum flexibility on how and where to set up your film for financing and distribution, because no studio will take on a project without it.*

The parties agree to the above effective as of _____, 20__.

Publisher: _____ Producer: _____

_____   _____

_____   _____

(address)   (address)

> **Note:** *Go to Chapter 10 to finish up this document by adding the No Obligation to Produce, Representation and Warranty, Assignment, the Arbitration, and the Indemnification paragraph, and the Remedies paragraphs.*

You can download this form at www.clearanceandcopyright.com Use the code: ibotCC3

16.02   MOTION PICTURE MASTER-USE LICENSE

THIS AGREEMENT, effective _____, 20__, is made by and between [NAME OF PRODUCER] ("Producer") located at [PHYSICAL ADDRESS], and [NAME OF OWNER] ("Owner"), located at [PHYSICAL ADDRESS].

1.   The master ("Master") covered by this license is: _____ _____ and performed by: _____ ("Artist").

2.   The Master covered by this license is: _____

3.   The motion picture ("Picture") covered by this license is: _____.

> **Comment:** *Include other identifying details in addition to the title.*

4.   The type and number of uses of the Master to be used are: _____.

> **Comment:** *Be very specific and complete in describing how the music is going to be used in your film. Be sure to include the maximum length you want to use.*

5.   The "Territory" covered hereby is: _____.

> **Hint:** *You want to acquire these rights throughout the universe.*

6.   (a) Owner hereby grants Producer, Producer's successors and assigns, the non-exclusive worldwide right, license, and authority to use the Master solely in synchronization or in timed relation with the Picture in any and all media now known or hereafter devised and by all devices including, without limitation, all forms of theatrical and non-theatrical distribution and exhibition (including, without limitation, free broadcast, pay television, cable, subscription, pay-per-view, video-on-demand, DVD, and Internet). Owner reserves the rights not expressly granted to Producer hereunder.

> **Note:** *This grant does not allow you to use the music in the trailer or advertisements for the film. If you want that you will have to ask for it and pay for it.*

(b) In consideration of the rights granted to Producer hereunder, Producer shall pay to Owner the sum of $_____, payable upon execution of this license.

> **Note:** *You might want to do the step deal described in the Synch license. If so, be sure to set out the step payments for the festival license and then for the broader use required here. In that case, you will only have to pay a small fee to run the film at festivals and a larger fee only if you obtain distributors.*

7.   Producer shall accord Owner and Artist appropriate credit on all prints of the Picture, together with similar credit for other recordings used in the Picture, substantially as follows: _____

_____.

8.   Owner shall provide Producer with all the necessary information to enable Producer to pay all reuse fees that may be required by the applicable unions, in accordance with said unions' contracts and regulations. Producer hereby agrees to pay all such reuse fees and any and all pension and/or welfare payments required with respect to Producer's use of the Master as provided herein. Producer hereby agrees to defend, indemnify, and hold Owner harmless from and against any and all claims, demands, or actions with respect to such fees and payments.

> **Note:** *Be sure to figure this out ahead of time. This is extra money you may have to pay to performers who are members of the American Federation of Musicians.*

9.   Producer shall be solely responsible for obtaining the appropriate synchronization and performance license from the copyright owner or controller of the musical composition embodied in the Master and for paying all fees with respect thereto. Producer hereby agrees to defend, indemnify, and hold Owner harmless from and against any and all claims, demands, or actions with respect to such fees and payments.

10. The term of this Agreement is for the periods of all copyrights throughout the Territory in and to the Master, and any and all renewals or extensions.

11. Owner shall furnish Producer with a duplicate master tape of the Master satisfactory for the uses contemplated hereunder. If Owner does not furnish Producer with such master tape and Producer is required to make one, then, upon presentation of invoices, Licensor shall reimburse Producer for the actual cost of creating said duplicate master tape and for shipping charges to and from designated destination, or Producer shall deduct and offset such amount from any monies becoming payable to Owner hereunder.

12. Licensor warrants, represents, and agrees that:

(a) Licensor owns or controls all the rights herein granted and no third-party consents are required and Licensor is under no disability, restriction, or prohibition, whether contractual or otherwise, with respect to Licensor' right to execute this Agreement, to grant the rights herein granted and to perform each and every term and provision hereof;

(b) The Masters, nor any part or parts thereof, violate or infringe or will violate or infringe upon any common law statutory or other right of any person, firm, corporation, or labor organization, including, without limitation, contractual rights, property rights, copyrights, and rights of privacy or unfair competition; and

(c) Licensor's agreements with all third parties who render services in connection with the Masters shall provide that third parties will look solely to Licensor for any payment in connection with the use of the Masters in the Picture, (except all so-called "re-use" and "new-use" fees and "conversion costs") and that Producer shall have no responsibility whatsoever with respect thereof.

13. No failure by Producer to perform any of its obligations hereunder shall constitute a breach hereof, unless Owner gives Producer written notice of such non-performance and Producer fails to cure within sixty (60) days of receipt of such notice.

14. Owner's remedies under this Agreement shall be limited to an action or law for damages. In no event will Owner have a right to enjoin or restrict the exploitation of the Picture.

Owner: _____   Producer: _____

_____   _____

_____   _____

(address)   (address)

> **Note:** *Go to Chapter 10 to finish up this document by adding the No Obligation to Produce, Assignment, and the Arbitration paragraphs.*

*You can download this form at www.clearanceandcopyright.com
Use the code: ibotCC3*

CHAPTER 17

HIRING A COMPOSER TO WRITE ORIGINAL MUSIC

Given the hassle and expense involved in clearing pre-existing music, it is no wonder that so many independent filmmakers decide to use nothing but original music in their films. Add to this the fact that you will undoubtedly hire a composer anyway to write some underscore for your film, and hiring a composer to write original music for the entire film may be just too good to pass up.

WHEN TO START

One of the most important aspects of a film—the music—is frequently neglected during most of the filmmaking process. The specifics of music are too often addressed at the very last moment. Money, time, and creative energy are assigned to it on an "as available" basis. My strong recommendation is that music be considered carefully, very early in the process.

The kind of music and whether it is original or pre-existing music are both very important questions. Many financial and legal considerations flow from those basic creative decisions.

Personnel issues must also be decided. You must decide whom to hire to do what with respect to the music in the film. If you make this decision during pre-production, your music supervisor can go through the script with you and perhaps enrich the script with musical references once clearance is verified.

A Worthwhile Search

Finding the right composer is not a simple task. Listen to lots of music. If the composer has scored other films, look at them and listen carefully. Talk to other producers and some directors with whom the composer has worked to find out as much as you can about costs, work methods, and compatibility. (Silman-James Press has an excellent book on the subject—*Getting the Best Score for Your Film* by David Bell.)

There are also a few talent agencies in Hollywood that specialize in representing composers for film and television. Here are two:

Gorfaine-Schwartz Agency
(818) 260-8500
www..gsamusic.com

The Carol Faith Agency
(310) 274-0776
carolatcfa@aol.com

As your list of potential composers gets shorter and shorter, it is common to have the candidates screen the film and discuss their musical concepts for the film. Your basic concern is whether the composer is going to write that perfect score that will help move the story along. Don't get caught up in soundtrack album fantasies at this initial stage.

Negotiating the Deal

HIRING
A COMPOSER
TO WRITE
ORIGINAL
MUSIC

319

Generally speaking, you will be able to choose from a wide range of composers based on their style, talent, and experience. As an independent producer, you will not be able to pay what the studios pay up front, so you may have to share the publishing rights to the score and revenues from soundtrack albums. (In the old days, the studios hired composers on long-term contracts to compose and to conduct orchestras that were also made up of employees of the studios.)

The entire music budget can range from 2% to 5% of the film's total budget for studio pictures. Often, independent producers are running out of money at this point and have to appeal to composers on non-financial terms and back-end terms to get the one they want on their film. What follows is just enough information to make you dangerous, but at least you will know the primary areas of potential back-end income for the composer, so you can at least "talk the talk."

Here are the main income sources for the composer. The first three categories listed are called performance royalties and are the composer's main source of back-end income.

1. Theatrical exhibition. When your film plays in a theater, the music is being "performed." Normally, a performance royalty would have to be paid. Because of an old court case, no royalties are paid for the music for theatrical play dates in the United States. However, in other parts of the world, royalties are paid to the performance royalty societies, who forward the money (less a handling fee) to their counterparts in America: ASCAP, BMI, and SESAC. The royalties range from about 2.5% to 5% of the ticket price, so they can be quite substantial. Half of that amount is called the writer's half and automatically goes to the composer; the other half is called the publishing half. Most producers try for all the publishing. However, the publishing half typically is shared 50/50 between the

composer and producer for independent films, but you may have to give more to get the composer you want.

2. Videocassettes and discs. Most studios don't allow royalties to be paid to composers on these sales. You will probably have to split the income on these sales with your composer.

3. Cable, pay, and free television. When your film plays on television, the music is "performed" and performance royalties have to be paid. These royalties are paid by the television entity to the performance royalty societies (ASCAP, BMI, and SECSAC), which negotiate blanket royalties for all the music that is played on television. The performance royalty societies divide the money up according to the composers and publishers listed on the cue sheets for your film. That is why cue sheets are so important. Cue sheets are a listing of all music in a film, including where it appears and for how long, with identifying information about the composer and the society to which they belong. Historically, free network television has paid the highest royalties, but the differences among cable and pay television are diminishing every day as the audience for the various types of television shifts and changes. If your movie goes into syndication, the same kind of royalty arrangement exists with the local syndication station and the performance royalty societies.

4. Sheet music. Not a big source of income. The composer gets a negotiated rate.

5. Mechanicals royalties. This amounts to about seven cents per cut on what used to be a record and now includes the audio tapes and CDs.

It is easy to create an agreement based on the principle of work for hire so that you own all rights to the work from the beginning. Income flows to the music's copyright holder from performance royalties generated when the film is played on television, in theaters outside of the U.S., or when the music is played apart from the film on radio, for example. Half of such income always goes to the composer, if the composer is a member of ASCAP, BMI, or SESAC. The other half is called publishing income. To hold down your front-end costs, some or all of the publishing income may be retained by the composer. Among independent producers, it is common to split publishing income 50/50 between the composer and the producer. Publishing income can be as much as $50,000-$100,000 for a film with a limited theatrical release, plus some television play and foreign sales. It can be well into six figures for a major release. This money is paid directly to the holder of these rights by such organizations as ASCAP and BMI (discussed in the next chapter), which collect royalty fees from theaters outside the United States or television and radio anywhere in the world. Because the future income for the composer is tied to the number of times and places the film is screened, as opposed to the profits of the film, composers are often willing to write on spec (or near spec). They do not have to worry about the integrity or bookkeeping methods or financial strength of the producer or distributor. If the film plays in theaters outside the U.S. or on television anywhere in the world, checks are forthcoming to the composer. They do not flow through the producer or the distributor.

At the end of this chapter is a simple composer's agreement. Notice that it assumes that half the publishing income will go to the composer and that only a nominal fee is paid to the composer up-front. Again, this contract is generic. It only has the deal terms for the composer.

The Package Deal

You can take the notion of putting all your musical eggs in one creative basket one step further. Often, if you are sure that you have the composer you want, you negotiate a so-called package deal. The composer in this package agreement composes all the music, hires the musicians, records the music, and delivers all the fully recorded music to the producer for a fixed fee. This is the way most independent films are scored.

Basically, you are contracting out all the music in your film to one person. You had better be sure that this is the right person. If you have found the right person, there is nothing cleaner and neater than the package approach to film scoring. If you miss, it's a big miss because all your musical eggs are in one basket—and some of your legal eggs are there also, because the package is responsible for acquiring rights from all the musicians.

17.01 COMPOSER AGREEMENT

HIRING
A COMPOSER
TO WRITE
ORIGINAL
MUSIC

323

This Agreement, effective as of _____, 20___, is made by and between [NAME OF PRODUCER] ("Producer"), located at [PHYSICAL ADDRESS], and [NAME OF COMPOSER] ("Composer"), located at [PHYSICAL ADDRESS]. The following terms and conditions shall apply:

1. **Engagement:**

    1.1 Producer hereby engages Composer to furnish Composer's services as a work for hire to compose and arrange the complete musical score ("Score") for use in the soundtrack of the motion picture currently entitled _____ ("Picture"), and Composer hereby accepts such engagement, upon the terms, covenants, and conditions set forth herein on the following schedule.

    1.1.1 Start Date: _____

    1.1.2 Completed Score: _____

    1.2 Composer's services hereunder shall include the "spotting" of the Picture for the placement of music, and consulting on an ongoing basis with Producer and/or persons designated by Producer. Composer shall render all services on an exclusive basis. Composer shall deliver the Score to Producer per Producer's reasonable technical requirements.

    > **Comment:** Spotting is picking the points in the film where music will be heard. The producer, director, and music team typically do this together.

2. **Compensation:**

    2.1 Producer agrees to pay Composer the sum of $_____, payable as follows:

    2.1.1 $_____ upon commencement of services

    2.1.2 $_____ upon delivery of full orchestra score satisfactory to Producer.

    2.2 With respect to the exercise of publishing rights in the music, Composer shall be entitled to fifty percent (50%) ownership of the "Publisher's share."

    > **Hint:** 50/50 of Publishing is a common split if you are getting an experienced composer and you want to keep the initial fee down. Studios often keep 100% of Publishing. You may have to give up more than 50% to get an experienced composer if you have limited funds to pay up front. Once the split is determined, the issue arises of whose publishing company will administer the publishing rights. Usually the Composer already has a publishing company. Not many independent film producers do, but sometimes you may want to set up your own publishing company.

2.3 In the event Producer exploits a recording of the soundtrack containing the Score, Composer shall receive a performer's royalty of ___% and a producer's royalty of ___% of the suggested retail price of such recording with respect to music sold through normal retail channels of music distribution worldwide.

3.   Rights: Composer hereby grants Producer rights to synchronize the Score provided to the Picture and thereafter to exploit the Picture, in any and all media and by any means now known or hereafter devised, including, without limitation, all forms of theatrical and non-theatrical distribution and exhibition (including, without limitation, free broadcast, pay television, cable, subscription, pay-per-view, video-on-demand, DVD, and Internet).

> **Hint:** *This language is the core of your agreement. Accept no less!!*

4.   Credit: Provided the Music is used in Picture, screen credit shall be accorded Composer substantially in the following form:

Music composed by: _____

which credit shall appear in the main titles on a separate card or frame, or its equivalent in the event of a roll. Composer shall be accorded this credit in all paid advertising, including posters, DVD jackets, and all other media, except congratulatory and team ads.

> **Hint:** *The extent of credits is always negotiable.*

> *Go to Chapter 10, Provisions Common to Most Agreements, to finish up this contract. The Indemnification paragraph is so important to the Composer Agreement that generally you cannot obtain E&O insurance if you do not include it. Use the signature block, changing "Owner" to "Composer," and the following paragraphs:*
>
> *Representations and Warranties (except Subparagraph C unless the composer is also a lyricist)*
>
> *Indemnification*
>
> *No Obligation to Exploit*
>
> *Notice*
>
> *Cure*
>
> *Remedies*
>
> *Arbitration*

You can download this form at www.clearanceandcopyright.com
Use the code: ibotCC3

HIRING
A COMPOSER
TO WRITE
ORIGINAL
MUSIC

325

17.02   MUSIC PACKAGE AGREEMENT

This Agreement, effective as of _____, 20___, is made by and between [NAME OF PRODUCER] ("Producer"), located at [PHYSICAL ADDRESS], and [NAME OF COMPOSER] ("Composer"), located at [PHYSICAL ADDRESS]. The following terms and conditions shall apply:

1.   Engagement:

1.1 Producer hereby engages Composer to furnish Composer's services as a work for hire to compose, arrange, and record the complete musical score ("Score") for use in the soundtrack of the motion picture currently entitled _____ ("Picture"), and Composer hereby accepts such engagement, upon the terms, covenants, and conditions set forth herein on the following schedule.

1.1.1 Start Date: _____

1.1.2 Completed Score: _____

1.1.3 Completed Recording of Score: _____

1.2 Composer's services hereunder shall include the "spotting" of the picture for the placement of music, and consulting on an ongoing basis with Producer and/or persons designated by Producer. Composer shall render all services on an exclusive basis. Composer shall deliver the Music to Producer per Producer's reasonable technical requirements.

1.3 The fee set forth in Paragraph 2.1 below shall be inclusive of all costs related exclusively to the production of the music soundtrack. These costs do not include transferring ¼-inch audio tape or DAT masters to 35mm magnetic film or any other media. It is understood that Composer shall [pick one of the following] hire an orchestra or ensemble of any size or will not be requested to hire an orchestra or ensemble, but will create the music by synthesis or by any method Composer deems appropriate or will hire at least ___ musicians to record the music.

> **Comment:** Select the language in the last sentence that best describes your agreement with the composer. Four different choices are offered for the three most common situations.

2.   Compensation:

2.1 Producer agrees to pay Composer the sum of $_____, payable as follows:

2.1.1 $_____ upon commencement of services.

2.1.2 $_____ upon delivery of music master recording satisfactory to Producer.

2.2 With respect to the exercise of publishing rights in the Score, Composer shall be entitled to fifty percent (50%) ownership of the "Publisher's share."

2.3 In the event Producer exploits a recording of the sound-track containing the Score, Composer shall receive a performer's royalty of ___% and a producer's royalty of ___% of the suggested retail price of such recordings with respect to music sold through normal retail channels of music distribution worldwide.

3.   Rights: Composer hereby grants Producer rights to synchronize the Score provided to the Picture and thereafter to exploit the Picture in all media whether now known or hereafter created in perpetuity throughout the universe.

4.   Credit: Provided the Music is used in the Picture, screen credit shall be accorded Composer substantially in the following form:

Music by: _____

which credit shall appear in the main titles on a separate card or frame, or its equivalent in the event of a roll. Composer shall be accorded this credit in all paid advertising, including posters, DVD jackets, and all other media, except congratulatory and team ads.

> **Hint:** *The extent of credits is always negotiable.*

> *Go to Chapter 10, Provisions Common to Most Agreements, to finish up this contract. The Indemnification paragraph is so important to the Composer Agreement that generally you cannot obtain E&O insurance if you do not include it. Use the signature block, changing "Owner" to "Composer," and the following paragraphs:*
>
> *Representations and Warranties (except Subparagraph C unless the composer is also a lyricist)*
>
> *Indemnification*
>
> *No Obligation to Exploit*
>
> *Notice*
>
> *Cure*
>
> *Remedies*
>
> *Arbitration*

You can download this form at www.clearanceandcopyright.com
Use the code: ibotCC3

CHAPTER 18

CLEARING FILM CLIPS

The same family of myths swirls around film clips as swirls around the use of music in films. Many filmmakers believe that there is some magic length of film that can be used without having to clear the clip. "Two minutes?" they ask hopefully. "It is two minutes, isn't it? I can use up to two minutes of a film clip without getting permission, can't I? It's called fair use." The simple answer to that question is, "NO!" There is no such rule. If you are planning to use a clip under fair use, study Chapter 2 carefully and hire a lawyer the insurance companies trust. This chapter is a how-to guide to clearing film clips.

CLEARING CLIPS WITHOUT ACTORS
OR MUSIC—STOCK FOOTAGE

Many independent filmmakers have saved a bundle on a chase scene or an explosion or a sunrise or crashing waves or a running deer by using stock footage. Stock footage is pre-existing film that you can license for use in your film. It is usually obtained from a stock footage house, a business that owns the rights to license clips. The various stock footage houses have collections that are small to very large, a broad selection to highly specialized, and collections that are difficult to sift through or very well-curated and organized. Most stock footage houses have their own written forms, which are quite adequate but give you no protection.

However, if anything goes wrong, the fact that you "thought" that you had cleared all the rights is of little help. Such good intentions can protect you from punitive damages in the event of litigation, but you still have to pay for your mistakes. The solution: When you license a film clip, be sure to establish the ownership of rights held by the person you are getting the film clip from. That person or business entity cannot grant you any more rights than they possess. If they don't hold all the rights you need, either go elsewhere for your clip or do your own investigation to locate and license the rights you need.

The film-clip release at the end of this chapter adequately covers all the points you need. Remember that these releases only cover the exact clip you described, for the exact length you requested, and only in the film you described. Any different or more extensive use has to be cleared. You might want to wait to finalize your contract until you are sure of the exact use you are going to make of the clip.

Usually, if you have the opportunity to use stock footage, you want to check out the resources of a stock footage house. They have remarkable choices available to you. The following is a sampling of some of the reputable stock footage houses:

Penn State Media Sales–Stock Footage
(800) 770-2111
www.mediasales.psu.edu
wpsu@psu.edu
Penn State has an extensive collection of footage dating back to 1932. Categories include agriculture, anthropology, education, health, science, wildlife, classic psychology, and primates.

Silverman Stock Footage
(917) 470-9104
www.silvermanstockfootage.com
donald@silvermanproductions.com
Specializes in aerial time-lapse scenes plus "wild and wacky glimpses" of Americana.

Producers Library Service, Inc.

(818) 752-9097

(800) 944-2135

www.filmfootage.com

research@producerslibrary.com

More than 10 million feet of film and an extensive collection of B&W and color photographs covering motion picture subjects, vaudeville, radio and television, and Hollywood history. Founded in 1957. One of the country's oldest and largest independent stock footage houses providing 16mm and 35mm stock footage and photographs.

UCLA Film and Television Archive

(323) 466-8559

www.cinema.ucla.edu/footage

footage@ucla.edu

Internationally renowned for its pioneering efforts to preserve and showcase not only classic but current and innovative film and television.

Footage Hollywood Stock Footage Library

(818) 760-1500

www.footagehollywood.com

info@footagehollywood.com

Specializes in hard-to-get film and television footage from the silent movie era up to the present day.

Historic Films Stock Footage Library

(800) 249-1940

(631) 477-9700

www.historicfilms.com

research@historicfilms.com

Owns or represents more than 45,000 hours of 1895-1990 vintage television programs, musical performances, feature films, newsreels, industrial films, silent films, educational films, sales films, TV commercials, celebrity interviews, TV news, home movies, and travel films.

Air Power Stock Library
(516) 869-3082
www.airpowerstock.com
forflying@aol.com

Extensive collection of military, civilian, and archival footage. Features fighter planes, bombers, attack helicopters, aircraft carriers, tanks, troops, artillery, missiles, and ground support equipment and personnel. Non-military footage includes: explosions, plane crashes, special effects, firefighting, and police operations. All footage is edited and catalogued for your convenience.

BBC Library Sales
New York: (212) 705-9399
motiongallery.ny@bbc.com
Los Angeles: (818) 299-9720
motiongallery.la@bbc.com
Toronto: (416) 362-3223
motiongallery.toronto@bbc.com
www.bbcfootage.com

A division of BBC Worldwide. Offers comprehensive footage and sound library for film and television production, commercials, and interactive media. Includes more than 500 million feet of film, 300,000 hours of video, and 500,000 sound recordings.

F.I.L.M. Archives
(212) 696-2616
www.fastimages.com
info@filmarchievesonline.com

Contemporary and vintage images. Includes more than 100 years of film images, nearly two decades of news video (1986 to present) from News 12 Long Island, and exclusive representation of the British government film library.

NBC News Archives
New York: (212) 664-3797
Burbank: (818) 840-4249
www.nbcnewsarchives.com
footage@nbc.com

Since introducing the first radio network and the first television network, NBC has been capturing the sights and sounds of our times for more than 70 years.

Jazz on Film–The Chertok Archives

(845) 639-4238

jazzfilm@mail.com

Specializes in music and also covers the entertainment industry in general, including vintage television. An important source of African American images.

Action Sports–Scott Dittrich Films

(212) 681-6565

(310) 459-2526

www.sdfilms.com

Action sports footage produced by Scott Dittrich Films since 1972, plus nearly every sport and many of the world's top cinematographers.

All Stock

(310) 317-9996

www.all-stock.com

info@all-stock.com

A sister company to Action Sports/Scott Dittrich Films for an ever-expanding list of subjects.

Archive Films by Getty Images

(800) 462-4379

www.gettyimages.com/motion

sales@gettyimages.com

More than 15,000 hours of archival black & white and color footage.

Kesser Stock Library

(305) 663-4443

(800) STK-FTGE

www.kesser.com

Founded in 1984. Contains extensive archival, sun and fun, aerials, travel, underwater, sports, animal footage, and more.

Streamline Stock Footage
New York: (212) 925-2547
www.streamlinefilms.com
decroix@streamlinefilms.com

National Geographic Film Library
Washington, D.C.: (877) 730-2022
Los Angeles: (310) 734-5300
London: (44) 0207-7751-7730
www.ngdigitalmotion.com
Outstanding programming since 1968.

Institut National de l'Audiovisuel Media Pro
Paris, France: (33) 4423 -1220
www.inamediapro.com
inamediapro-tv@ina.fr

Absolutely Archives
Riverdale, MD (703) 967-3070
www.absolutelyarchives.com
info@absolutelyarchives.com

When you license stock footage, be sure that you understand what you are getting. If you rely on the stock footage houses for more than the visual images on the film stock, make sure that you obtain specific representations and warranties. When you license a piece of stock footage, there is usually no sound or effects on the film—a film-clip license does not usually grant any rights to music that may be on the film.

WRITERS AND DIRECTORS

Both the Writers Guild of America and the Directors Guild of America have specific agreements covering the "reuse" of material. Reuse under the union agreements refers to taking footage shot for one film and using it in another film. Clips from films produced under the Minimum Basic Agreement for either of these unions may require additional payments to the union members

who helped create the film from which you want to use a clip.
The theory for these provisions is that if you were not using the clip, you would have to create your own footage, and for that you would employ a writer and director. To the unions, it is a jobs issue. Even though the payment would be the obligation of the person who sold you the clip and not your specific obligation, you need to check this out, because if the unions do not get paid, they go after everybody— including you.

CLIPS WITH ACTORS

It is common, even in fictional films, to have scenes in which a television set is on. If the screen is visible and playing a program, you have two choices: You can create your own video and play it on the television set, or you can clear an existing clip. Such a clip usually has actors in it.

This process can be confusing to a filmmaker who licenses a clip from a television show or another feature. The owner of the copyright of the film or television program can grant you the right to use the actual film, but usually cannot grant you permission to use an actor who appears in the film clip.

If the person appearing on the screen is a member of either of the actors' unions (SAG or AFTRA), there are specific provisions in the Basic Agreement for each of the unions that cover reuse. In the case of reuse, the actor is due a payment, which must be negotiated separately from the agreement under which the actor originally rendered services and must be at least equal to one day's minimum wages under the union contract.

WHEN THERE IS NO UNION AGREEMENT

The situation is different when the creator of the original film is not a signatory to any of the union agreements or the footage being used was news or candid footage, so that the persons appearing are not union members. The argument that the use of this footage throws another actor out of work no longer applies. Your use of the film might well be lending reality to the film you are making as opposed to ripping someone off.

For example, legendary singer James Brown sued 20th Century Fox because the film *The Commitments* used 27 seconds of Brown's performance on a 1965 television show without his permission. Defendant's summary judgment motion was granted. The 27 seconds consisted of seven different cuts from *The T.A.M.I. Show* where James Brown is performing on a television set. Brown's name is not mentioned at all during this brief scene. Later in the film, Brown's name is simply mentioned in a laudatory fashion. In this case, pursuant to their agreement with the rights holders of the television clip, the producers did in fact secure the rights to use the lyrics and the musical composition from the music publishing company holding the copyright in those works.

Why did the court find for the defendant? Because the use was perceived by the court as building reality. It was much like a verbal reference to any living public figure. They did not use Brown's face to sell or promote the film. It was just there in the background. Because of the age of the film, no union agreement protected Brown.

Do not rely on the logic of the above case without checking with an experienced lawyer. Not all courts would agree with that case. California courts tend to be particularly protective of the value of celebrityhood. Even if you are right, you do not want to be sued. Remember the golden rule of filmmaking: When in Doubt, Clear. There is a letter at the end of this chapter that you can use to obtain permission to use a name and likeness in most situations.

CLIPS WITH MUSIC

By this time, it should be no surprise to you that you have the responsibility to clear the music playing at any time in your film, including the clips you use from other films. You either have to replace the music in a clip with new, cleared music or go through the music clearance procedure for the music that is already there. This is true even for the theme music in television programs. In that case, the music may well be owned by the studio that owns the program itself, but established composers can reserve rights in their music as part of the negotiation of their employment contracts. One of the more commonly reserved rights is the right to authorize producers other than the studio to use the music in connection with new motion pictures. These rights are held by the publishers of the music. See Chapter 16 for the details about music clearance. Because this music was often created especially for filmed entertainment, you may also have to make payments under the AFM agreement. The AFM is the American Federation of Musicians. Almost all studio musicians belong to it. The AFM's contracts—like those of the other unions discussed above—have special provisions to cover the reuse of music.

On a related topic, beware of the music video. For some reason, independent filmmakers are sometimes lulled into a belief that receiving a music video from a performer or a public relations company who wants you to use the video in your film serves to clear the music for your film. It is not the same. You receive the video to whet your appetite. If you want to use it in your film, you must go through all the steps that were outlined in Chapter 16 to clear music, even if the video comes to you from the record company.

How to Find the Copyright Owner of a Film

Once you have the name of the owner and general locale, you can check the phone directory. Today you have to check several directories in an area as some people are listed in one directory, but not in another. You can also Google the names of the entities and all individuals associated with the film and see what you come up with. If you are not successful, you need to do a more intensive search.

The really hard part is finding the name of the rightful owner if you don't have a flare for it. It requires a lot of experienced and some specialized knowledge. That leaves most of us standing in the corner when it comes to finding out who the owner of a property is when the owner's identification is not pretty obvious.

To answer this question, I interviewed Los Angeles-based Barbara Gregson, since finding owners is what she does for a living. It turns out that the search can be more extensive than I ever dreamed.

After spending an hour and half with Barbara, I felt a little overwhelmed. I also felt grateful for her and others like her who dedicate their careers to doing this type of research. They are usually credited in the end roll of a film as "Researcher." "Detective par excellence" would be more accurate. Here are the resources Barbara uses to find the copyright owners of a film. These resources are more or less in descending order of use, although every case is different.

1. Broadcast Information Bureau (BIB). This resource lists the current distributors of feature films, movies made for television, and television series, primarily in the United States. It does not list much foreign television or feature material. Access to the resource costs about $799.00 per year. Most professional researchers subscribe to it.

2. Internet Movie Data Base (IMDb). This listing of features and television shows is free to the public and lists the

production company and distributor of a production. Contact information for talent and other industry professionals are available here for a fee, but the essential information for this purpose is free.

3. The Copyright Office files are available at the website www.copyright.gov. These records will give you the names and contact information for the film's original applicant. The older the film, the less useful this information. Even studios change their names, merge, and sell their libraries. However, formal transfers of ownership are frequently recorded with the Copyright Office, and you should be able to locate those documents here also. The transfers usually give the name of the new owner, but no contact information unless you order up the transfer document itself. That will usually have a lot of contact information. Eric Kulberg of Universal Media in Washington, D.C., (202) 234-7292 will perform this service for a reasonable fee. Thomson and Thomson tend to be a little more expensive, starting around $600 for 10-day delivery, but every insurance company has confidence in the extent of their search, which includes media files and other off-line proprietary sources.

4. Studio System is a subscription Internet resource with box-office information and contact information for completed films and projects in development. The contact information is quite current, but is not very good for things more than 10 years old.

5. The Lincoln Center in New York City houses a library that is a very good resource when researching the history of various motion pictures.

6. The Radio and Television Museums in Chicago, New York, and Los Angeles are excellent sources for information about radio and television shows.

7. Trade shows publish books of attendees. These have detailed contact information as of the time of the show.

The most useful are National Association of Television Producers and Executives (NATPE), which takes place every January in Las Vegas, and MIP and MIPCOM, both of which take place in Cannes, France, for buyers and sellers of television programs.

8. Special issues of the trade magazines—*Variety* and *The Hollywood Reporter*—also publish information and contacts on attendees to events (NATPE, Cannes, American Film Market, and the European Film Market in Berlin).

If you have exhausted these resources and still can't find the owner of the copyright, you have to really start digging. Check out the credits on the film. An individual producer or the director or the writer or one of the actors might know something of the history of the film. The video distributor rarely has the right to license clips, but they might be able to give you a tip as to who does have that right. Also, collectors and people who write about film often have a lot of esoteric information about the history of films. Archivists, such as those employed by UCLA Film and Television Archives in Los Angeles, are also a wealth of information, even if they don't have copies of the materials themselves.

Many small collections exist around the world that have a specialized focus. Some examples are Jeff Joseph at Sabucat, who has a lot of movie trailers. Showcase Video has a lot of old television shows. J. Fred McDonald in the Chicago area has industrials, commercials, and television shows. Reeling in the Years is a company that specializes in rock-and-roll-related materials. Often these places do not have the rights, but they will allow you to copy their materials for your personal use if you pay an access fee.

The Association of Moving Image Archives (AMIA) has an online place to post a search if you are having trouble finding something. You can post a job for free to hire one of their members to work on your project. FOCAL International in the U.K. is a resource for both archival footage and international researchers. The best of the professional clearance community are the appointed members of CLEAR in Los Angeles. You can go online at www.clearinc.org and post a job search. You can also ask other filmmakers who have made films with similar things to clear as you are using in your film. Find out how good the person was at finding things for you and how good a negotiator they are. Many clearance professionals will save you more than their fee through their relationships and negotiating skills.

And don't forget to keep very accurate records of everyplace that you check. Most pros keep this information on a spreadsheet on their computer. Otherwise, you will go crazy trying to remember who has called you back and who hasn't and what information you received from whom. Eventually, the licensor's name will go into your "clearance log," and then you will have to track what documents you send out and what signatures you get back.

And this is what conscientious researchers do all day long. It is detailed. It requires patience. It requires perseverance. And that is why most filmmakers hire a professional researcher or clearance professional to do this work.

18.01   FILM CLIP RELEASE

THIS Agreement, effective as of _____, 20__, is made by and between [NAME OF OWNER], located at [PHYSICAL ADDRESS] ("Owner"), and [NAME OF PRODUCER], located at [PHYSICAL ADDRESS] ("Producer"), with regard to the use of a film clip owned by Owner to be used in a film being produced by Producer entitled "_____" ("Motion Picture"). The following terms and conditions shall apply:

1.   The Film Clip to be used by Producer is as follows:

Name of Source Film: _____

Maximum length of clip to be used: _____

Description of Motion Picture: _____

Approximate time of Motion Picture: _____

Description of how the clip fits into the Motion Picture: _____

_____

Black and white: _____   Color: _____

Fiction: _____   Non-fiction: _____

Describe the intended distribution: _____

Are distribution contracts in place? Yes _____ No _____

If so, with whom? _____

> **Note:** Be very specific and accurate and as complete as possible so that the permission you obtain covers your needs.

2.   Producer may use the above-referenced clip in perpetuity, throughout the universe ("Territory").

3.   Producer shall pay Owner the sum of _____ ($___), to be paid upon execution of this Agreement. Owner hereby grants Producer a non-exclusive, irrevocable license to include the specified Film Clip in the specified way and to advertise or exhibit such Motion Picture in every country of the world, to make copies of the Motion Picture, and to otherwise exploit such Motion Picture in any and all media and by any means now known or hereafter devised, including, without limitation, all forms of theatrical and non-theatrical distribution and exhibition (including, without limitation, free broadcast, pay television, cable, subscription, pay-per-view, video-on-demand, DVD, and Internet).

4.   This license does not authorize or permit any use of the Clip not expressly set forth herein and does not include the right to alter the fundamental character of the music of the Clip, to use

the title or subtitle of the Clip as the title of a motion picture, to use the story of the Clip, or to make any other use of the Clip not expressly authorized hereunder.

5.   The rights granted herein include such rights for screen, video, television, and Internet trailers for the advertising and exploitation of the Motion Picture.

> **Hint:** *Owners sometimes want extra money if you use their clips in advertising. If so, you have to decide if it is worth it. Generally, it isn't, in which case you would eliminate this paragraph.*

6.   This Agreement grants the use of the Clip as described herein and does not authorize or guarantee the right to use the name or likeness of anybody appearing in the Clip or to use any music in the Clip, the clearance of which is the sole and separate responsibility of Producer. Producer also has the sole and separate responsibility of complying with any obligations by any applicable union, included, but not limited to, the Writers Guild of America, the Directors Guild of America, the Screen Actors Guild, and the Association of the American Federation of Television and Recording Artists.

> *Go to Chapter 10, Provisions Common to Most Agreements, to finish up this contract. Use the signature block and the following paragraphs:*
>
> *Representations and Warranties*
>
> *(use B and D only; omit A and C)*
>
> *Indemnification*
>
> *No Obligation to Produce*
>
> *Remedies*
>
> *Arbitration*

**You can download this form at www.clearanceandcopyright.com
Use the code: ibotCC3**

18.02   ACTOR'S RELEASE FOR FILM CLIP USE

[date]

To: [your name]
   [your address]

This letter shall confirm that the undersigned person ("Actor"), for good and valuable consideration, the receipt and sufficiency of which is hereby acknowledged, has granted permission to _____ ("Producer") and its successors, assignees, and licensees to use Actor's name and/or likeness as such name and/or likeness appears in _____ ("Name of Clip Source") in the motion picture tentatively entitled _____ ("Picture") and in connection with advertising, publicizing, exhibiting, and exploiting the Picture and other motion pictures, in whole or in part, by any and all means, media, devices, processes, and technology now or hereafter known or devised, in perpetuity throughout the universe. Actor hereby acknowledges that Producer shall have no obligation to utilize Actor's Name or Likeness in the Picture or in any other motion picture.

> **Comment:** *Most actors will not authorize the use of their likeness in your advertising without substantial extra payment. It is generally not worth it, so you may have to take out that permission.*
>
> **Hint:** *If the Actor is a member of SAG or AFTRA, you will need to pay the Actor a reuse fee as discussed above.*

Producer's exercise of such rights shall not violate or infringe any rights of any third party. Actor understands that Producer has been induced to proceed with the production, distribution, and exploitation of the Picture in reliance upon this agreement.

Actor hereby releases Producer, its successors, assignees, and licensees from any and all claims and demands arising out of or in connection with such use, including, without limitation, any and all claims for invasion of privacy, infringement of Actor's right of publicity, defamation (including libel and slander), false light, and any other personal and/or property rights.

Very Truly Yours,

[Actor's signature]
[Actor's name]
[Actor's address]
[Actor's Social Security number]

> **Note:** *You need the actor's social security number so that you can fill out a W-2 tax form.*

*You can download this form at www.clearanceandcopyright.com
Use the code: ibotCC3*

PART IV

POST PRODUCTION

You're not finished just because your project is finished. There are still a lot of clearance and copyright issues that could, should, or might come up. This part covers all the clean up stuff that you can usually put off until production is complete and a few more general topics such as international law and copyright on the Internet.

CHAPTER 19 — **TITLE CLEARANCE**

CHAPTER 20 — **E&O INSURANCE**

CHAPTER 21 — **CHAIN OF TITLE**

CHAPTER 22 — **REGISTERING COPYRIGHT FOR YOUR COMPLETED FILM**

CHAPTER 23 — **COPYRIGHT INFRINGEMENT**

CHAPTER 24 — **COPYRIGHT ON THE INTERNET**

CHAPTER 25 — **INTERNATIONAL COPYRIGHT ISSUES**

CHAPTER 26 — **LEGAL REFERRAL SERVICES**

CHAPTER 19

TITLE CLEARANCE

Hey, what a great title! It is the best title for a film that anyone has ever heard of. But can you use it? Can you prevent others from using it? The *title* to your script or film is not protected under the law of copyright. It's not long enough. Copyright protects the *work* you create, not the title you give to it. It is a natural instinct to think that the first few words you put at the top of the first page will be protected by copyright in the same way that all the words that follow are protected. Not so. Many filmmakers find this out—for the first time—when the distributor asks for a formal legal opinion stating that you have the right to use the title you've selected.

HOW TITLES ARE PROTECTED

Commonly, people tend to be very protective of a title they have used, especially a title that has been successful. Plenty of lazy folks out there would love to sell a few extra tickets on opening weekend by trading on the good will built up in the title of someone else's film. Many a filmmaker has been scared away by a "lawyer letter" telling them to "cease and desist" use of a particular title.

My favorite response to one of those letters explained the legalities of title selection so well that I thought I would reprint a big chunk of it here with only a few deletions for space. The Marx Brothers made the film *A Night in Casablanca* in 1946, not too long after Warner Bros. had experienced great success with *Casablanca*. Here is the letter that Groucho Marx wrote to Warner Bros. after he received a warning not to use a title with the word "Casablanca" in it.

> . . . up to the time that we contemplated making a picture, I had no idea that the city of Casablanca belonged to Warner Brothers.
>
> However, it was only a few days after our announcement appeared that we received a long, ominous legal document warning us not to use the name 'Casablanca.'. . .
>
> I just can't understand your attitude. Even if they plan on re-releasing the picture, I am sure that the average movie fan could learn to distinguish between Ingrid Bergman and Harpo. I don't know whether I could, but I certainly would like to try.
>
> You claim you own Casablanca and that no one else can use that name without your permission. What about Warner Brothers— do you own that, too? You probably have the right to use the name Warner, but what about Brothers? Professionally, we were brothers long before you were.
>
> Even before us, there had been other brothers—the Smith Brothers, the Brothers Karamazov; Dan Brouthers, an outfielder with Detroit, and 'Brother, can you spare a dime?' This was originally 'Brothers, can you spare a dime,' but this was spreading a dime pretty thin. . . .
>
> . . . I have a hunch that this attempt to prevent us from using the title is the scheme of some ferret-faced shyster serving an apprenticeship in their legal department. I know the type—hot out of law school, hungry for success, and too ambitious to follow the natural laws of promotion, this bar sinister probably needled Warners' attorneys, most of whom are fine fellows with curly black hair, double-breasted suits, etc., in attempting to enjoin us.
>
> Well, he won't get away with it! We'll fight him to the highest court! No pasty-faced legal adventurer is going to cause bad blood between the Warners and the Marxes. We are all brothers under the skin and we'll remain friends till the last reel of *A Night in Casablanca* goes tumbling over the spool.

Not only is that letter clever, it correctly implies the governing rule of law: The test of the availability of a title is whether its use by a second person would mislead or confuse the public. Groucho argued that no one, but no one, would confuse the Marx

And he did it long before the courts had clearly enunciated that rule of law in a case involving another small town a half a world away.

Amityville: One Small Town, Six Horror Movies, Three Production Companies

In 1974, Butch DeFeo murdered his entire family—his father and mother and two sisters and two brothers—at the family home in a small and obscure town, Amityville, New York. His defense? The devil made him do it.

A year later, the home was purchased and occupied by George and Kathleen Lutz. Twenty-eight days after moving in, the Lutzes and their three children fled in fear of their lives. The house was haunted. They and Jay Anson wrote about their experiences in a book entitled *The Amityville Horror*. It became a major best-seller. The authors sold the film rights, retaining the right to publish literary sequels to the book and to exploit motion-picture sequels after a holdback period of five years. American International Pictures (AIP) produced and released the film *The Amityville Horror*. It also was a major hit.

In 1981, the book *The Amityville Horror II* was published using the Lutz's rights to do so. It also became a best-seller. Preparations were undertaken to film a motion picture based on the book. Screenplays were written. Budgets were prepared. In the meantime, Dino de Laurentiis produced a motion picture about a fictional family who lived in the Lutz house in Amityville prior to the Lutzes. Orion Pictures obtained whatever rights AIP had and released the film, which they said was based on a book about the real murder trial. Orion released it under the title *Amityville II: The Possession*. That film was so successful that Orion released another film in 1983 entitled *Amityville 3-D*.

Obviously, the Lutzes sued. You might think that this was a no-brainer for the Lutzes to grab a quick injunction. Actually, the defendants won at trial on a **judgment on the pleadings**, no less. A **judgment on the pleadings** is the worst—it means that the plaintiff (in this case, the Lutzes) could not even state their case clearly enough to require the defendants to file an answer! Not good. But the court of appeals said, "Not so fast." The court of appeals agreed that the lawyers had not stated a good cause of action, but said that all the various theories stated in the complaint would be merged into a cause of action for unfair competition. The court of appeals went on to say that, as a matter of law, the unfair competition claim could not be dismissed so early because "the status of secondary meaning can only be determined after an inquiry into the facts." The court found that: "Reduced to fundamentals, **secondary meaning** is a shorthand phrase that describes the existence of a condition from which public confusion will flow if the defendant is permitted to pursue his deceptive scheme."

The court confirmed that unfair competition must be based upon public confusion and/or deception. Anyone may use a title so long as the title is "not used in such manner as to induce the public to believe that the work to which it is applied is identical with the thing which it originally designated."

So, here is what it takes to get into court on a title claim. You must allege all three of the following elements:

1. that you have created a secondary meaning in all or part of your title, so that a substantial segment of the purchasing public associates the title with a particular person or film or source, even if they can't identify the source. For the Lutzes, they would have to allege that the word "Amityville" equaled their film.

2. that the public was misled into believing that the film was the anticipated sequel to the first movie.

3. that the defendant had intentionally traded on and appropriated for themselves the valuable secondary meaning created by the plaintiffs' efforts and expense.

It is interesting to note the involvement of the public in this process. Titles are not property in the sense that copyright and patents can be property of an owner. Only the public develops the secondary meaning in its collective brain and then is misled to purchase tickets, which trigger the unjust enrichment of the defendant. The court focuses entirely on public confusion, not disclaimers, not technicalities, not the plaintiff's efforts to build up and protect a title. The only thing that matters is the public's reaction to all of this.

Mounting a lawsuit based on public confusion is expensive because of all the polling that is needed to find out if the public is confused. But it is expensive to defend such suits also, and you cannot get rid of them on the pleadings or summary judgment motion. If the parties don't settle, they have to go to trial.

That is why insurance companies remain real sticklers on title reports, which are discussed later in this chapter. Insurance companies are not in the business of going to trial. If they are called on to finance a defense at all, they want to get out of the suit as early as possible.

Why Copyright Doesn't Help Here

Titles are too short to be protected by copyright. No short phrase is subject to copyright protection. When you copyright a script or film as a whole, the copyright does not cover the title. The title is considered the label for the script or the film rather than an integral part of the script or film. Distribution companies frequently change a title after the film is completed and copyrighted. Rarely are titles translated literally in every country in the world. This practice confirms the real-world truth of the legal theory.

Nevertheless, the fact that a title is not covered by the same copyright that protects the film often surprises people. It is not unlike obtaining a patent for an invention. The invention is marketed under a certain name. The name of the product is not protected by the patent. Similarly, the title of a script or film is not protected by the film's copyright. In that way, a title is like a product name.

The name of a product can be covered by a trademark. Unfortunately, the title of your film generally cannot be protected by a trademark. The reason is that the purpose of the trademark is to identify the source of a product. If you buy a soap and like it and want to buy another bar of soap just like it, all you have to do is to go to the store—any store—and find a bar of soap with the same trademark on it. The trademark (e.g., Dove) identifies the source of the soap. A studio trademarks its name, so the trademark *Disney* identifies films from a certain source. Individual film names are generally not able to be trademarked because they stand alone. At least that is what virtually all lawyers think. They think that because courts have said so again and again (for about 50 years to be exact) and because the trademark office had said clearly and publicly that the title of a single, creative work is not registrable on the Principal Register or the Supplemental Register. You can read it for yourself online in section 1202.08 of the Trademark Manual of Examining Procedures. It says a series title can be registered; a single title work cannot be registered. For example, the line of business books known as "_____ *for Dummies*" may be registered. An individual book title within that series, such as *Negotiating for Dummies* (another book with my name on the cover), is not given its own trademark. Only the general title is trademarked. The trademark for the series protects the titles within the series.

But wait! Aren't clever lawyers supposed to figure out ways around such pronouncements? A search of the registered trademarks indicates that a few titles have gained trademark status. *The Blair Witch Project, Reservoir Dogs*, and *Judge Dredd* have all been registered as trademarks, even though they are titles of single films, not a series of films. So it can be done. A look at the original documents shows that they were correctly identified as trademarks for films, but the fact that it was a single film was not noted on the application. Presumably the examiner didn't realize what was going on. Whether these marks would survive a legal challenge is unknown, but, in the meantime, there you have three exceptions. I'm not sure they disprove the rule, but they do demonstrate that every rule has its spotty enforcement.

You can also register your mark with the various states. State trademark law is not pock-marked with the prohibition against registering a mark for a single title. If you registered in California, New York, and Illinois, you would be covering the three largest cities in America and therefore pick up some protection for your title similar to federal registration. Your title would show up on any title search and give someone pause before they tried to use the same title.

There is also the possibility of filing in Canada. Most distributors view the U.S. and Canada in combination for marketing purposes and would not want to have to market the picture under two different titles. So, if you really want to trademark the title of your film, it is possible, although most lawyers will tell you that it is not.

TITLE PROTECTION

The most effective way to protect the rights to a film's title is by using that title in the marketplace. Generally speaking, there is no basis for protection of a title other than the body of law involving unfair competition, which is enshrined in the federal law called the Lanham Act. The **Lanham Act** covers a number of business practices. The two themes throughout the Act are the twin principles of fairness as between businesses and protection of the public from being misled. If titles are confusingly similar, the public may believe that a film is connected to a property to which it has no relation. The courts say that you are passing off a film under false pretenses.

Even when you have a good lawsuit, you may decide that you can live with the competing title in the marketplace. For years, I represented Michael Landon. When the pilot of his last series, *Highway to Heaven*, was about to air, he discovered that a book by the same title was being released almost simultaneously with the airing of his pilot. Both sides decided that they could live with the competing titles in the marketplace. When both projects are films, the decision is tougher. But some people are still willing to put up with the confusion rather than finance a legal fight.

MPAA TITLE REGISTRATION

Litigation is expensive, and it can consume your time and energy. The Motion Picture Association of America, Inc. (MPAA), has established a title registration system. As an independent film-maker, you need to read this entire section before registering your title with the MPAA.

The MPAA title registration service was set up to avoid litigation over identical or similar film titles intended for the theatrical marketplace here in the United States. Independent filmmakers may subscribe to the MPAA registration service by voluntarily signing one of their subscription agreements. Subscribers agree to abide by the rules and regulations of the title registration agreement. If there should be a conflict over title usage, the parties negotiate. If the title cannot be negotiated directly between the two parties, the MPAA provides arbitration to settle the conflict.

According to the MPAA Title Registration Bureau, there are about 3,400 new titles registered with their office each year, and roughly 20,000 objections to title usage filed each year. However, the amount of arbitrations to resolve disputes has dramatically decreased over recent years. There were only two MPAA title-use arbitrations in 2006. The MPAA attributes this small number of arbitrations to successful negotiations directly between the parties to resolve conflicts. For the MPAA to resolve a dispute over title usage, both parties must be subscribers.

Whether or not a company protests the use of a specific title is completely up to the companies who are subscribers to the title service. The protection that the MPAA can give to subscribers of their service only extends to other registered subscribers to their service. The MPAA does not have jurisdiction over people who do not subscribe to this service. There are about 400 subscribers to the MPAA service, and they encompass all the major producers and distributors of United States theatrical product.

Consider the following example of a title conflict reviewed by the MPAA. Two different films, *Forget Paris* starring Billy Crystal and *Paris Match* starring Meg Ryan, were scheduled to be theatrically released around the same time. The issue of title use went to arbitration because the similarity of titles. The arbitrator denied the producers of Meg Ryan's film the right to use the title *Paris Match* and the film was retitled *French Kiss* to avoid confusion. The MPAA does not make written opinions available to the public, so we will never know exactly why this result occurred.

Alternatively, Universal was convinced to allow Columbia to go forward with the title *Bram Stoker's Dracula*. Universal had the title *Dracula* in their 1930's film, but the studios concluded that the 1990's *Bram Stoker's Dracula* had a very different look, and so the public wouldn't be confused.

MGM was similarly convinced to allow New Line to use the film title *Austin Powers in Goldmember* after MGM initially objected that it was too similar to the title of its film, *Goldfinger*. However, such convincing reportedly included an unconventional compromise that included New Line offering the services of Mike Meyers to promote an ABC telecast of the original *Goldfinger*.

The reason an independent filmmaker should think twice before entering the MPAA system is because you are agreeing to be bound by the arbitration system that decides who has what rights. The "independent" arbitration panel is made up of a designee from each of three of the MPAA's member companies. These member companies—the major studios—fund the MPAA. These studios sign a "Member Title Registration Agreement." All the other independent producers and distributors that subscribe to the MPAA service sign a "Non-Member Title Registration Agreement."

If the arbitration is between an independent filmmaker and a studio, the three arbitrators who, by definition, are from major studios may have a bit of bias. Further, the factors they consider are strangely foreign to the legal principles of protecting the public from being confused. The governing rules have guidelines for the presentation of evidence, which include factors that have been of primary concern to arbitrators in the past. For unreleased films they look at: production plans; status of scripts and who the authors are; attached cast; producer and director; start date of principal photography; when film will be released and by whom; budget and amount spent to date; synopsis of the film; advertising budget; and estimation of popularity. For released films, the arbitrators consider: date of commercial release; name of author; extent of release; who were the stars; amount grossed; and plans for a remake or reissue. You can see that these factors are in large part economic and heavily weighted toward the studio over the independent filmmaker. A studio can have a film in development for a relatively short period of time and spend more money than your entire production budget.

TITLE REPORT

A **title report** lists all the films, books, songs, and plays that bear the same or similar titles, together with press mentions of those titles. Before anyone distributes your film, whether through a theatrical release or television or videocassette sale, you must have cleared your title. It is a relatively easy process.

You merely send your title along with the appropriate fee to one of the following names. Either one of them will prepare a report on the title you want to use and similar titles that have been used in the past for films, plays, songs, books, and other works. The cost ranges from $500 to $1,500, depending on how quickly you need the report and whether or not you also want a legal opinion with your report.

• Dennis Angel (New York), (914) 472-0820
www.dangelesq.com
requests@dangelesq.com
A firm that specializes in providing copyright information to the entertainment industry.

• Thomson CompuMark (Washington, D.C.), (800) 356-8630
(Boston, MA), (617) 479-1600

www.thomson-thomson.com

Thomson CompuMark is the leader in trademark and copyright services.

Experienced lawyers can issue opinion letters based on these reports as to whether any given title is available for use as the title of your film. Our firm routinely issues opinion letters for our clients and insurance companies. A sample report and a sample opinion letter can be found at the end of this chapter.

NAMING PEOPLE AND PRODUCTS IN YOUR TITLE

Some of you for various reasons may want to use the name of a famous person or trademark in the title of your film. Freedom of expression, right? Well, yes and no. There have been plenty of cases where celebrities have claimed that the use of their name in the title of a film has violated their rights of publicity or infringed their trademark. Real persons (or their estates) can sue for misuse of their name because they possess an economic interest in their identities similar to that of a trademark holder. A celebrity need not register his name for trademark protection, he only needs to show that a consumer is likely to be confused as to his association with the product. Even though courts generally recognize the public's right not to be confused as well as a celebrity's right to control the commercial use of his name and likeness, courts have also widely recognized a filmmaker's right to artistic expression.

Take for example a film by Italian filmmaker Federico Fellini. He made a movie based on the lives of a pair of fictional cabaret performers, who made a living by imitating Ginger Rogers and Fred Astaire. Fellini titled his film *Ginger and Fred*. Appropriate, right? Well Ginger didn't think so. She claimed that the title falsely implied she was associated with the film.

The court sided with the filmmaker and set forth the framework that most courts use today to determine whether an author or filmmaker can incorporate a famous name or trademark into the title of his or her work.

The court noted that titles are of a hybrid nature, combining artistic expression and commercial promotion. The court wanted to strike a balance between the public interest in avoiding consumer confusion and its interest in free expression. Thus, in determining whether the title of a work constituted trademark infringement under the Lanham Act, the court asked (1) whether the title was artistically relevant to the underlying work and, (2) if the title was artistically relevant, did it explicitly mislead as to the source or content of the work? The court said that the title *Ginger and Fred* was artistically relevant to the underlying work as it was genuinely related to story told in the film and the central characters who were nicknamed "Ginger" and "Fred." The court also answered the second question in favor of the filmmaker, reasoning that the title contained no "explicit" indication that Ginger Rogers had endorsed the film. The court conceded that some people could incorrectly assume that she had some involvement in the film, but that the risk of such misunderstanding was outweighed by the filmmaker's interest in artistic expression.

But beware! There are cases where such a misunderstanding could lead to your downfall. If you are making a film about a certain celebrity or other public figure, do not include in your title phrases such as "an authorized biography," or "the true story of" unless that is actually the case. The courts say it would be *explicitly* misleading otherwise. You should use a tagline such as "The Unauthorized Biography."

So back to Ginger Rogers. She also claimed that the title of the film violated her rights of publicity. But the court said not so. The court said Fellini was fine to use Ginger's name in the title of his film so long as it was not "wholly unrelated" to the movie or was "simply a disguised commercial advertisement for the sale of goods or services." For the same reasons the court decided that

Fellini did not infringe any trademarks by using Ginger's name in the title, it also ruled that the title did not violate her rights of publicity. It was very easy for the court to decide that the title was not "wholly unrelated" to the content in the film.

Ginger may not have been very lucky with her claims, but Rosa Parks was when she took on the popular hip-hop group OutKast.

OutKast relied on its rights to artistic expression when it titled one of its songs *Rosa Parks*. The song repeatedly states "move to the back of the bus." But this wasn't convincing enough for Rosa. She argued that the title was misleading. "Isn't it artistically relevant?" you might ask. Not in the court's eyes. The court examined the contents of the lyrics and determined that they had nothing to do with Rosa Parks or the civil rights movement. And it didn't help OutKast's cause when one of its members admitted that they didn't have Rosa Parks or the civil rights movement in mind when they were actually writing the lyrics of the song.

As for Rosa's claim that the title violated her rights of publicity, the court sided with her on that one as well.

The court had already decided that the title was not "artistically relevant" to the lyrics in the song when it analyzed her claim of trademark infringement. Thus, it was quite obvious to the court that OutKast had also violated her rights of publicity, ruling that the title was also "wholly unrelated" to the content of the song. The court noted that the title *Rosa Parks* could be viewed as a "disguised commercial advertisement."

Another court found an opposite result in the case of the song *Barbie Girl*. No, Barbie is not a name of a celebrity, but it sure is a famous trademark—and Mattel fought to protect it.

Mattel sued.

Mattel lost.

In applying the same test they used in the case involving Ginger Rogers, the court found that the title *Barbie Girl* was clearly relevant to the lyrics in the song. The song repeatedly makes fun of Barbie and Barbie's values in her plastic world.

As these cases make clear, if you want to use a famous trademark or name in the title of your work, there needs to be a strong connection between the title and the content of the work in order for it to fall within the realm of First Amendment protection. The strongest cases for protection will be those like the *Barbie Girl* case where the song or film is about the famous person or character or the values they represent. The weakest cases will be those where the content of the work is not about the person or trademark named in the title and where it appears that the title was chosen merely to capitalize on the increased marketing power of a work bearing the name or a famous person or trademark. The lesson is as follows: You have a constitutional right to create a biography or a work involving a famous person as a character or point of the story. The key thing for you to do is make sure that you do not imply an endorsement where none exists, an association that is fabricated, or a link to the real person or product that is more to sell your film or book than it is to describe the content of your work. The classic example of a safe, safe, safe use of someone's name in a title would be *The Unauthorized Biography of Hillary Clinton.* The relevance of the title to the content is obvious. The lack of approval or endorsement by the subject is equally obvious. The author is home free.

LAW OFFICES OF

DONALDSON & HART

MICHAEL C. DONALDSON
JOSEPH F. HART
LISA A. CALLIF

9220 SUNSET BOULEVARD
SUITE 224
LOS ANGELES, CALIFORNIA 90069-3501

CORRESPONDENT FIRM
COWAN, DEBAETS, ABRAHAMS
& SHEPPARD LLP

OF COUNSEL
R. LANCE BELSOME

TELEPHONE: (310) 273-8394
FACSIMILE: (310) 273-5370
WRITER'S E-MAIL: MCD@DONALDSONHART.COM

41 MADISON AVENUE, 34TH FLOOR
NEW YORK, NY 10010
TEL: (212) 974-7474

[DATE]

VIA E-MAIL AND U.S. MAIL

[NAME]
[ADDRESS]

RE: **TITLE OPINION**

Dear [NAME]:

You have forwarded to our firm for an opinion a title report prepared by Thomson CompuMark dated April 23, 2007 on **[NAME OF PROJECT]** for use in connection with a documentary film. The Thomson CompuMark report included a search of the Copyright Office, Thomson CompuMark's proprietary databases, and other entertainment databases and sources.

In forming my opinion, I received and reviewed the following items:

1. Thomson CompuMark Title Research Report dated April 23, 2007;
2. Thomson CompuMark Analyst Review – USPTO Report dated April 23, 2007;
3. Thomson CompuMark Analyst Review – Internet Domain Name Report dated April 23, 2007; and
4. Thomson CompuMark Reported Owner Index dated April 23, 2007.

Based upon my review and analysis of the April 23, 2007 Thomson CompuMark report, I am of the opinion that **[NAME OF PROJECT]** is available for use as the title of your documentary film.

Very truly yours,

MICHAEL C. DONALDSON

MCD/ kae

You can download this form at www.clearanceandcopyright.com
Use the code: ibotCC3

19.02   TITLE REPORT – CROSSINGS

We have conducted a search of the records of the Copyright Office, Thomson CompuMark's proprietary databases, and other entertainment databases and sources with regard to the proposed use of the title **CROSSINGS** for a documentary film.

This title was searched using the following strategy:

CROSSIN(')(G)(S)

The following references were found:

Motion Pictures

CROSSINGS: **Hong Kong and U.S. motion picture** in 102 minutes running time, produced by Riverdrive Productions in 1994, directed by Evans Chan, starring Anita Yuen, Lidzay Chan, and Simon Yam, registered for copyright in the name of Riverdrive Productions, Ltd., as published May 7, 1994, and described as a drama. Currently listed as **available** in a variety of video formats through Facets Multimedia, Inc.

CROSSINGS: **Motion picture short** in approximately 10 minutes running time, produced by Lee Bridgers/Musiak between 1988-90, in the series entitled "Variations on a Theme," and described as a film about a deer that has been killed by a car and which lies on asphalt as cars zoom past. *We do not find that this work is currently being distributed to television, nor is it available in video format under this title.*

Television

CROSSINGS: **Miniseries** consisting of three episodes in a total of 360 minutes running time, a.k.a. DANIELLE STEELE'S CROSSINGS, produced by Aaron Spelling Productions in 1986, directed by Karen Arthur, starring Jane Seymour, Lee Horsley, and Cheryl Ladd, registered for copyright in the name of Spelling Ventures Organization by Aaron Spelling Productions, Inc., a successor & [sic] interest to Spelling Ventures Organization, as published September 23, 1986, and described as a story set during WWII of an affair between a steel magnate and the wife of a French ambassador, based on a novel by Danielle Steel. This miniseries premiered over ABC on February 23, 1986. Currently listed as **available** for television distribution worldwide with exclusions through Warner Bros. International Television, Inc.

CROSSINGS: **Episode** in the series entitled *Alias*, registered for copyright in the name of Touchstone Television, an a.d.o. Disney Enterprises, Inc., as published January 8, 2004.

Games/Multi-Media

No references found.

Radio

No references found.

Books (Fiction and Non-Fiction)

CROSSINGS: At least 60 books have been published under this title from at least 1967, including at least 24 books currently listed as **in print**, and/or **available** in a audio formats.

CROSSINGS: A SERIES FOR YOUNG ADULTS: Book series consisting of at least four variously authored books published in Denver by Living the Good News, Inc. in 1998. Currently listed as **in print** in the U.S.

CROSSINGS: Book series consisting of at least 8 variously authored books published by Bordighera, Inc., from at least 1998 to 2001. Currently listed as **in print** in the U.S. CROSSING: At least 70 books have been published under this title from at least 1942, including at least 19 books currently listed as **in print**, and/or **available** in a audio formats.

CROSSING: Series consisting of at least one book by Isabella Morra entitled *Canzoniere. A Bilingual Edition,* published by Bordighera, Inc., in 1998. Currently listed as **in print** in the U.S.

Serial Publications

CROSSINGS: Serial, published irregularly in Dublin, Ireland, by University of Dublin, no commencing date listed, and currently listed as **active**.

Stories and Articles

CROSSINGS: At least five stories/articles have been published and/or registered for copyright under this title.

CROSSING: At least 7 stories/articles have been published and/or registered for copyright under this title.

Dramatic Works

CROSSINGS: Play by Barbara Schneider, published by Dramatists Play Service in 1983.

Sound Recordings

CROSSINGS: At least 13 sound recordings have been published and/or registered for copyright under this title, including at least 6 currently listed as **available**.

CROSSING: At least 18 sound recordings have been published and/or registered for copyright under this title, including at least 9 currently listed as **available**.

Trademark Search

We have conducted a search of federal and state trademark registrations in entertainment-related classes for the exact mark and closely related similars. Please see the attached trademark report containing: an analyst review including search strategy, class identifications, and date coverage; full references for selected USPTO and/or State marks; and analyst comments if applicable.

Domain Name Search
We have attached a computerized search of Thomson Compu-Mark's database of Internet Domain Names and related owner information.

Copyright Office Preregistration Records

The following preregistration applications have been filed for unpublished works intended for commercial distribution: No references found.

Newspaper and Trade Notices

Filmtracker.com reported on January 29, 2007, that the film entitled **THE CROSSING**, produced by Screen Gems and Pink Slip Pictures, and described as an action film, was **in development**. This film was previously in development with New Line Cinema.

You can download this form at www.clearanceandcopyright.com
Use the code: ibotCC3

CHAPTER 20

E&O INSURANCE

E&O insurance is the shorthand name for "errors and omissions insurance." **Errors and omissions insurance** is similar to that purchased by doctors, lawyers, and accountants to compensate others for damage caused by negligent mistakes. If you accidentally infringe a copyright, slander a trademark, invade someone's privacy, violate someone's right of publicity, or otherwise stub your toe on any of the many obstacles discussed in this book, E&O is the insurance policy that applies. Happily, you can now extend E&O coverage to fair use.

WHEN TO BUY E&O INSURANCE

You must purchase E&O insurance prior to any release of your film in any medium. Practices vary in foreign territories, so plan for it early. Because independent films are often made without distribution in place, independent filmmakers commonly put off purchasing E&O insurance until the last possible minute. Studios routinely have this insurance in place well before the commencement of principal photography. Cash flow does not always permit this luxury in the U.S. to guerrilla filmmakers.

Studios secure E&O insurance prior to the first big wave of publicity on a film because that wave of publicity often brings out the first claim. "That's my idea," someone hollers in pain. If the cry is first heard after the insurance is in place, the resulting claim is covered. If it is heard before the insurance is in place, the claim must be disclosed to the insurance company on the application—and may very well be excluded from coverage. You should always disclose known problem areas.

E&O insurance can be expensive. Typical premiums for independent films with no obvious legal problems are currently $7,000-$12,000 for a standard three-year policy with limits of $1,000,000 per claim and $3,000,000 total for all claims filed. The deductible amount for independently produced films is usually $10,000. However, be prepared to pay higher premiums as some distributors are now requiring higher-limit combinations of $3,000,000 or $5,000,000 per claim and $5,000,000 total for all claims filed with a $25,000 deductible. Additionally, legal problem areas that are identified to the insurance company may trigger changes to the typical premiums as discussed below.

WHERE TO BUY E&O INSURANCE

Here is a list of a few of the brokers who regularly sell E&O insurance and, therefore, are familiar with terms, rates, and the filmmaker's needs:

New York
C&S International Insurance Brokers, Debra Kozee (212) 406-4499
D.R. Reiff & Associates, Dennis Reiff   (212) 603-0231

California
DeWitt Stern Group, Inc., Winnie Wong   (818) 623-5400
Truman Van Dyke Company, Kent Hamilton   (323) 883-0012

Interestingly, all brokers who sell E&O insurance deal with the same small group of insurance companies that actually issue the policies. Media/Professional and Chubb probably write about 80%-90% of the E&O policies for filmmakers. Fireman's Fund is not as active as they were, but it is the granddaddy firm. It is the one that has stayed in the field over the years and will probably continue to stay in the field. Other insurance companies enter the field for a few years and then stop writing such insurance because of the difficulty of predicting the losses. Unlike auto insurance or life insurance, it is hard to figure the actual likelihood of a suit being filed on any given film. This is of no real concern to the filmmaker. As long as the insurance company is strong, it honors claims under your E&O policy, even if it is no longer in the business of writing E&O insurance.

INSURANCE AND FAIR USE

Working on behalf of the International Documentary Association and Film Independent, I was able to successfully negotiate a fair-use policy endorsement by Media/Professional Insurance that was announced in March of 2007. It was the first time an insurance company explicitly allowed filmmakers to rely on fair use without jeopardizing coverage. Within days, Chubb —a leading insurance company that has been offering E&O insurance for over 40 years—followed their lead. Other insurers tackle the issue more quietly on a case by case basis. Now filmmakers who use copyrighted materials pursuant to the doctrine of fair use are able to obtain insurance coverage for any copyright infringement claims that may arise from their use of the materials, provided that they obtain an opinion letter from an approved clearance attorney. Filmmakers who are interested in obtaining such coverage generally need to submit along with their E&O insurance application a copy of their film, a detailed clearance log, and a letter from an approved clearance attorney.

Media/Pro announced an indemnity-only policy that would be available to filmmakers who have a letter from the Stanford Fair Use Project stating that the use of the unlicensed material meets the criteria for fair use as set forth in the *Documentary Filmmakers' Statement of Best Practices in Fair Use* and that the Stanford Fair Use Project would defend the filmmaker on a pro bono basis if a claim was made.

Below is a list of the approved clearance attorneys issued by the two insurance providers who provide fair use coverage:

Media/Professional Insurance List of Approved Clearance Attorneys:

Michael Donaldson
Donaldson & Callif
400 S. Beverly Dr., Suite 400
Beverly Hills, CA 90212
(310) 277-8394

Lincoln Bandlow
Fox Spillane Shaeffer
1880 Century Park East
Suite 1004
Los Angeles, CA 90067
(310) 229-9300

Steve Contopulos or Brad Ellis
Sidley Austin
555 West Fifth Street
Los Angeles, CA 90013
(213) 896-6000

Anthony Falzone
Fair Use Project
Stanford Law School
559 Nathan Abbott Way
Stanford, CA 94305
(650) 736-9050

Karen Shatzkin
Shatzkin & Mayer, P.C.
1776 Broadway
21st Floor
New York, NY 10019
(212) 684-3000

F. Robert Stein
Pryor Cashman LLP
410 Park Ave.
New York, NY 10022
(212) 326-0830

J. Stephen Sheppard
Cowan, DeBaets, Abrahams
& Sheppard
41 Madison Ave.
34th Floor
New York, NY 10010
(212) 974-7474

Thea J. Kerman
Beigelman, Feldman &
Associates
100 Wall St.
23rd Floor
New York, NY 10005
(212) 213-6116

Laverne Berry
Law Office of
Laverne Berry
382 Warren St.
Brooklyn, NY 11201
(718) 852-1076

Robert Penchina
Levine Sullivan Koch &
Shultz, LLP
321 W. 44th St.
Suite 510
New York, NY 10036
(212) 850-6109

Dan Satorious
Lommen Adbo
IDS Center
80 S. Eighth St.
Suite 2000
Minneapolis, MN 55402
(613) 336-9332

Chubb Group of Insurance Companies List of Approved Clearance Attorneys:

Mark Bailen
Baker & Hostetler, LLP
Washington Square, Suite 1100
1050 Connecticut Ave., N.W.
Washington, DC 20036
(202) 861-1715

Michael Donaldson
Donaldson & Callif
400 S. Beverly Dr., Suite 400
Beverly Hills, CA 90212
(310) 277-8394

Leopold, Petrich & Smith
2049 Century Park East,
Suite 3110
Los Angeles, CA 90067
(310) 277-3333

Matt Murphy
Gordon & Rees
2100 Ross Ave.
Suite 2650
Dallas, TX 75201
(214) 231-4660

Robert Penchina
Levine Sullivan Koch &
Shultz, LLP
321 W. 44th St.
Suite 510
New York, NY 10036
(212) 850-6109

John Williams
Lord, Bissell & Brook LLP
111 S. Wacker Dr.
Chicago, IL 60606
(312) 443-0371

AIG will also provide a fair-use endorsement for its policies.

How to Buy E&O Insurance

The procedure for obtaining a policy is not unlike buying health insurance. You select your insurance agent and call for an application, which you fill out and return as discussed below. (You must include your lawyer's name on this application.) The application is forwarded to the insurance company underwriters. **Underwriters** are the people who assess risk and decide whether to issue a policy and what it should cost. If there are any identifiable risks disclosed on your application—such as the depiction of a living person, the inclusion of written material that was not purchased, reliance on public domain material, or any other "flag"—the application is sent to a law firm that advises the underwriters. Usually it is Leopold, Petrich & Smith or Ted Gerdes, both of which are located in Los Angeles, California.

The reviewing attorney contacts you or your attorney with any questions. Based on the answers that are given to the reviewing attorney, a recommendation is made to the insurance company's underwriters, who, in turn, quote the price and terms very quickly thereafter. Because of the consequences of this relatively brief conversation, you want to have an experienced attorney listed on your insurance application. There is an element of negotiation for any adjustment to the norm that applies to a problem area, such as the price or exclusions or deductions to the policy. Let your lawyer handle these areas since they almost always involve nuances of law. It is the threat and cost of litigation and the merits of your position that will be discussed. It can be quite technical. The review process is very fast—this all occurs within two or three days, unless the circumstances are more complicated.

Generally, attorneys for the underwriters try to assess the likelihood that a suit will be filed, and, if filed, the likelihood of getting you out of the case on a motion for summary judgment. A **summary judgment motion** is heard by a judge, who determines whether there are issues of fact that should be tried by a jury. If a case cannot be resolved at this level, it is going to be expensive. Only areas of settled law can be considered in deciding if a motion for summary judgment is likely to be successful. **Settled**, as used as an adjective for the law, means that the law is not likely to change because of the number of courts that have issued decisions in the area over a long period of time.

Even if the underwriter's lawyers agree with your position, they may not recommend taking the risk to their client (the insurance company) if there is not a clear case that decides the legal point in your favor. Insurance companies do not want to be on the cutting edge of the law. They look for the protection of settled law or they do not issue the policy.

TIPS ON FILLING OUT YOUR E&O APPLICATION

Filling out the application form is not difficult, although its length is occasionally daunting to some filmmakers. You will find a reprint of a typical form at the end of this section. Your application may be slightly different, based on the company you are using as your agent, but the enclosed form should be close enough to be a very helpful guide. There are some common questions that many filmmakers have when filling out this form. The answers for the more commonly asked questions are addressed below.

The following notes apply to the example application at the end of this chapter.

Sections I, III, and IV: Each of these sections calls for straightforward factual information. Answer each question precisely.

Section II: Most independent filmmakers purchase insurance after they have an agreement to exploit the film and a contract that sets out coverage requirements. If you don't have this, go with the standard $1,000,000 and $3,000,000 in coverage and $10,000 in deductible when you answer these questions.

Section V: Questions 1-3 and 5-8 are straightforward. Answer each of these precisely.

4. Give the underwriter an honest feel for your project, but never, ever use more than the space allotted. It is simply not necessary.

9. Insurance companies generally ask you if you want coverage for merchandising activities. This is additional, special coverage for which there is an additional charge. Documentary filmmakers never need this. Independent fictional filmmakers rarely need this coverage. If you know that your film is going to spawn a major merchandising effort beyond T-shirts and caps, you might want to inquire about this coverage.

Section VI: Questions 4 and 13 ask for factual responses. Again, answer these precisely.

1. This is important, because the insurance company's attorney routinely calls this person. The attorney you choose should be completely knowledgeable on the law of copyright and clearance. She or he must also have sufficient knowledge about your project to dispose of any questions in a brief telephone conversation. This may take a couple hours of preparation.

2-3. You almost always have to answer these questions "yes" to have your application approved.

5-8. These are very specific questions regarding clearance that must be answered accurately. If you have made an affirmative decision not to obtain one or more licenses for some reason, your attorney needs all of the details so that the insurance company can be persuaded to provide coverage without the license. Under some circumstances, you may want to provide a pithy explanation right on the application.

9. The answer to this question is a simple factual report. However, refer to Chapter 19 for details on title reports. Generally speaking, your policy will not cover your title without a title report.

10. Again, this is a factual response. You will need a copyright report sooner or later to establish for sure that you have the right to make your film.

11. This question was put in the forms after the U.S. Supreme Court decided the *Rear Window* case, which was discussed in Chapter 6. For the reasons you learned in Chapter 6, you have to make a deal with the heirs of the author if you check the "yes" box, indicating that the music or underlying work was written in the time period that raises the renewal issues of *Rear Window*. You also have to give detailed answers as to exactly what material falls into this category.

12. This question is a short checklist for your clip-clearance procedure set out in Chapter 18.

14-15. These questions reveal the care you took in your music clearance as discussed in depth in Chapter 16. Sometimes you fill out your application before you actually perform these steps. If so, just say so and follow proper procedures when you do clear your music.

16. This question must be answered with brutal honesty. Please be as precise and accurate as possible.

Section VII. Like the question above, the question in this section asks for your personal representation. The notice following the question underscores the importance of this final question. If anything is written in the space provided, a question is raised. Of course, if you have or expect a claim, you are required to disclose it in the space provided. Specific claims known to the producer are the subject of specific negotiations between the production attorney and the insurance company. The following sections discuss these negotiations. Being less than honest is not a good option.

Consequences of a Failure to Disclose

Beware of friends who fudged on their insurance application and tell you, "We got our insurance. Everything was okay." They were telling you the truth, but before you follow their lead, stop and think. The reason that "everything was okay" is that no claims came in on the area where they fudged. Occasionally, someone fudges and a claim comes in and the insurance company does not catch it, but that is very, very rare. One of the first things an insurance company does when a claim comes in is to review the policy carefully. If there is any question about the non-disclosure of prior claims, they like to investigate further. That may result in a denial of coverage, or worse. Hmmmmmmmmmmmm. Not a pleasant thought. All those adjustors hunched over the fine language of the insurance contract you did not even read, but they know very well . . . and their sole purpose is to figure out if they should or should not pay a claim—and their salaries are paid by the insurance company. Scary!

There are three possible responses of an insurance company when an applicant has been less than forthcoming about a potential claim, and the claim that was only potential at the time of the application becomes a reality. The most draconian option is rescission of the policy, meaning the policy is void from inception. It never existed! This will invalidate the entire insurance agreement. That would only happen in an extreme case. The two more common responses to untruthful or incomplete responses to the last questions on the application are still draconian if you are on the receiving end of a claim. Here are the other two concepts:

1. There is no coverage for this particular claim at all (no defense and no indemnity);

2. A reservation of rights to recover the costs of defense and indemnity from you, the insured.

You will not have this problem because you have read this chapter and you know to fill out your application completely and honestly. If you must err, err on the side of full disclosure.

Basically, if the insurance company says that the policy does not cover a particular risk because the insured knew about it and did not disclose it, then the insurance company will not pay to defend or settle the claim. Somewhere deep in the fine print of the application or the policy it says that you are covered for a variety of copyright claims and claims of personal injury (invasion of privacy, slander, libel, misrepresentation, false light, and such things as are covered in Chapter 13) AS LONG AS you have fully disclosed all the facts known to you about the potential risk. The notice at the top of the application makes this crystal clear—at least, as crystal clear as anything that you are ever likely to receive from an insurance company. And, the law implies a duty on you, the applicant, of good faith and full disclosure.

The "Reservation of Rights" is a variation on the same theme. Basically, the insurance company says, "The applicant fudged on the facts here. Normally, the policy would cover this claim, but the insured wasn't honest with us, so we may not have a duty to defend [or pay] the claim." The insurance will provide the legal defense you need under a reservation of rights to recoup the money paid to the lawyers from you, the insured. That means that after the case is over, the insurance company may come after you for the costs of defense and any indemnity or settlement paid to the claimant. Given the high cost of litigation, legal talent, and the fact that you have little or no control over those bills, this can be a very expensive result indeed.

When Full Disclosure Reveals a Potential Claim

When filmmakers fudge on their applications, it is usually out of fear that they will be denied an insurance policy. Oops! You have already signed a distribution agreement that requires you to supply an E&O insurance policy. You can't possibly risk not being able to buy one. But wait, the insurance company is in the business of selling policies. They don't want to take on any unknown risks. Surely, this is a situation ripe for compromise.

So here are the alternatives you can negotiate—in descending order of attractiveness to you—in order to avoid the dreaded and unacceptable "no E&O insurance policy available."

1. Have your lawyer convince the insurance company that the risk is quite low.

2. Make some creatively acceptable modifications to your film.

3. Obtain an appropriate release or other clearance.

4. Allow a higher deductible with regard to that risk only.

5. Agree to a sub-limit for that risk only.

6. Pay a higher premium.

7. Exclude that particular risk from coverage.

Let's discuss each one of these alternatives and how you might go about negotiating them to your advantage. I put numbers next to the explanations that match the list above.

1. Obviously, you want to try to convince the insurance company that the risk is acceptable. In this regard, the standing of your attorney and the facts themselves are of considerable importance. Your lawyer will act as an educator to the insurance company lawyer. You should arm your lawyer with a fully annotated script and all of the facts. Your lawyer will try to convince the insurance company that you have enough independent sources for the material in your script that there should be no serious threat of suit and even less of a threat of losing.

Remember that insurance companies don't like lawsuits, even if they think that they can win them. Therefore, you not only want sources, but you want sources that are likely to have been seen by the objecting party. The argument then is that this very same material has been published before and no one complained, so there should not be any complaints when it shows up in your film. When independent filmmaker David Jacobson was writing *Dahmer*, based on the life of serial killer Jeffrey Dahmer, he imagined the potential claims and carefully double-sourced everything in order to convince the insurance company that this horrific story would pass legal muster in spite of the fact that the adults who most influenced Dahmer were all still alive and that the families of the victims were still around, as were the police officers who visited Dahmer, even with corpses in his apartment and a new victim pleading for help. The trick was to locate true double sources as opposed to the same source quoted in two different newspapers. Court records helped a lot. In fact, court testimony—preceded as it is with solemn oaths, enforced by perjury laws, and verified by cross-examination—is always a source of particularly high value.

2. The mention of making creative changes always runs counter to the basic instincts of independent filmmakers. If you liked taking notes from studio execs, you wouldn't be fighting the fierce battles to make a film independently. And then to take notes from lawyers in order to satisfy insurance coverage, well, that is just too much. You would be surprised at the number of times that minor changes of no consequence to the creative team

have saved a project from the prospect. Perhaps a few stories will help put your mind at ease. By way of example of how this works, let's stay with the Dahmer story of the above paragraph. The one area where our double sourcing did not persuade the lawyer for the insurance company was the police officers. The reason was that insurance companies want to avoid litigation rather than win litigation. The police officers had already fought the charges against them. The officers had been called out to Dahmer's place, and one of his victims tried to get the police to step in. Neighbors tried to get the police to step in. They allegedly left with the victim "in the care of" Dahmer. Needless to say, they are sensitive about any allegations surrounding these events. The screenwriter, who was also to be the director, was comfortable in toning down this scene. Overall dramatic effect of this elimination: zero. We would not have agreed to make a change if the overall impact weakened the storytelling. Use your creative talent to avoid future problems.

3. Obtaining releases after the fact is not always possible, but always worth exploring. When you are at the point in the process that insurance is being obtained, your picture is a reality. Sometimes people would rather be left in a picture than cut out, even if they are not all that happy with the depiction. You might think seriously about this one. There are many creative approaches. How you make the approach is important because you do not want to invite a claim where none might have been otherwise made. Better yet, get all your releases in advance.

4. Deductibles for a specific risk can be raised, sometimes as high as $50,000, in order to obtain coverage. Again, this is a negotiation. You don't want the deductible to go up at all, but if there must be an increase, your attorney negotiates for the smallest possible amount based on how early a motion for summary judgment can be filed and an appropriate sharing between insurer and insured of the increased risk. This is a highly technical negotiation. Also, a higher deductible overall may mean more money out of your pocket in the event of a claim, but could also lower your premium. It's all a negotiation.

5. A sub-limit for the problem risk means that the insurance company has a cap on what it will have to pay for that potential claim. That makes it more attractive to insure. The lower the risk to the insurance company, the more likely they will agree to provide some coverage. Of course, once your sub-limit is exhausted, the rest of the costs are on you. You probably have agreed to such policy limits in your auto insurance. This is all part of the negotiation.

6. Paying a higher premium is also a highly technical discussion involving risk-assessment and exposure. Exposure in this case refers to the potential costs that could be incurred. You don't want to go down this road unless you absolutely have to.

7. Excluding the risk entirely is generally unacceptable, although it is your ace in the hole if the insurance company wants to raise your premium too high. You can eliminate the premium problem by agreeing to exclude the particular risk that is troubling them. Unfortunately, it is the risk that the insurance company is most worried about that is usually the risk that you are most worried about . . . and probably every distributor and broadcaster. Some E&O insurance coverage is invariably a requirement of any broadcaster or distributor. No exceptions. So excluding the risk rarely solves all your problems.

Chubb Group of Insurance Companies
15 Mountain View Rd.
Warren, NJ 07059

MULTIMEDIA LIABILITY
Application for
Video/Film Producers

BY COMPLETING THIS APPLICATION THE APPLICANT IS APPLYING
FOR COVERAGE WITH EXECUTIVE RISK INDEMNITY INC. ("Insurer")

NOTICE: THE LIMIT OF LIABILITY TO PAY DAMAGES OR SETTLEMENTS WILL BE REDUCED AND MAY BE EXHAUSTED BY "DEFENSE EXPENSES," AND "DEFENSE EXPENSES" WILL BE APPLIED AGAINST THE RETENTION AMOUNT. IN NO EVENT WILL THE INSURER BE LIABLE FOR "DEFENSE COSTS" OR THE AMOUNT OF ANY JUDGMENT OR SETTLEMENT IN EXCESS OF THE APPLICABLE LIMIT OF LIABILITY. THE COVERAGE AFFORDED UNDER THIS POLICY DIFFERS IN SOME RESPECTS FROM THAT AFFORDED UNDER OTHER POLICIES. READ THE ENTIRE APPLICATION CAREFULLY BEFORE SIGNING.

APPLICATION INSTRUCTIONS:

1.   Whenever used in this Application, the term "**Applicant**" shall mean the Company and its subsidiaries.

2.   Provide a complete response to all questions and attach additional pages as needed.

I.   APPLICATION INFORMATION:

1.   Please attach a copy of the following for every **Applicant** seeking coverage:
   • Experience resume of its Producer and Executive Producer for each production (if less than three years experience);
   • Standard contract with authors, distributors, etc.;
   • Video/DVD copy of production or copy of script if production is not complete;
   • Financial statement or budget for production(s);
   • Title Search and Report; and
   • Any general information that would be helpful in evaluating the **Applicant**.

2.   Name of **Applicant**: _____

   Address: _____

   City: _____ State: _____ ZIP: _____

   Telephone: _____ Fax: _____

   Web site address: _____

II.   COVERAGE DESIRED:

1.   Limits of Liability desired:

   Each Claim or Related Claims: $_____ Aggregate for all Claims: $_____
   Desired term of policy: ○ 1 year   ○ 2 year   ○ 3 year

2.   Retention desired for each Claim or Related Claims:
   ○ $10,000   ○ $25,000   ○ $50,000   ○ $100,000   ○ Other: $_____

C33900 (1/2005 ed.)   Page 1 of 9   Catalog No.14-03-0706

377

Chubb Group of Insurance Companies
15 Mountain View Rd.
Warren, NJ 07059

MULTIMEDIA LIABILITY
**Application for
Video/Film Producers**

III.   GENERAL INFORMATION:

1.   The **Applicant** is:

- ◯ Individual
- ◯ Corporation
- ◯ Partnership
- ◯ Other: _____

- ◯ Non-profit
- ◯ Privately Held
- ◯ Publicly Traded

2.   Year established: _____

IV.   OTHER INSURANCE INFORMATION:

1.   Has **Applicant** had prior liability insurance on this particular production or a related production, including but not limited to media liability insurance or producers E&O insurance (e.g., a pilot episode, prequel, or an earlier cycle of the series)?   ◯Yes ◯No

   If Yes, attach a copy of prior policy and written history of any claims or threatened claims.

2.   **MISSOURI APPLICANTS/AGENTS - DO NOT ANSWER THIS QUESTION.**
   Has any liability insurance for the **Applicant** or this particular production(s) ever been declined or canceled?   ◯Yes ◯No

   If Yes, please attach an explanation.

3.   **Applicant's** estimated total gross revenues and production costs/budget for the production:
   Production Costs/Budget _____   Estimated Gross Revenues _____

V.   PRODUCTION DETAILS:

1.   Title of production to be insured: _____

2.   Estimated dates for first release or air date: _____

3.   Type of production:
- ◯ Motion Picture for Theatrical Release
   List distributor: _____
- ◯ T.V. Series
   Number of episodes: _____
- ◯ T.V Pilot
   Number of episodes: _____
- ◯ Radio Program
   Number of episodes: _____
- ◯ Other (e.g. theatrical stage presentation) Describe: _____

- ◯ Motion Picture for Television Release
   List network or cable outlet: _____
- ◯ T.V. Special
   Program Running Time: _____

- ◯ Direct to Video/DVD
   Program Running Time: _____

4.   Summary of plot, including time frame and setting: _____
_____
_____
_____
_____

5.   Names of authors and writers of: a) underlying works: _____

C33900 (1/2005 ed.)   Page 2 of 9   Catalog No.14-03-0706

378

Chubb Group of Insurance
Companies
15 Mountain View Rd.
CHUBB Warren, NJ 07059

MULTIMEDIA LIABILITY
Application for
Video/Film Producers

b) screenplays, etc.: _____

6. Production is:
    ○   Entirely fictional
    ○   Entirely fictional but inspired by real events or occurrences
    ○   True portrayal of real events or occurrences
    ○   True portrayal of real events or occurrences but includes some fictionalization
    ○   Based on another work
        Name of other work: _____
        Have the necessary agreements from the owners of the other work been obtained? ○ Yes ○ No
    ○   Other (Please explain) _____

7. Production is:
    ○ Drama   ○ Comedy   ○ Children's Show   ○ Documentary
    ○ Reality   ○ Variety   ○ Game or Quiz   ○ Musical
    ○ Investigative   ○ Animated   ○ Educational   ○ "How To"
    ○ Commentary or Forum ○ Sports
    ○ Previously released film
    ○ Other (Please explain) _____

8. **Applicant's** projected distribution:

    ○ International   ○ National   ○ Regional   ○ Local

9. Will any merchandise (such as toys, dolls, clothing, etc.) be created from the production? ○ Yes ○ No
    (a) If Yes, please describe all such merchandise: _____
         _____

    (b) Have all necessary consents and licenses been obtained from performers, authors,
         artists, etc., to produce and distribute this merchandise?   ○ Yes ○ No

    (c) Will appropriate trademark or other searches be made before merchandising
         characters or other matter that might be subject to trademark, unfair competition or
         other similar claims?   ○ Yes ○ No

    (d) Is the merchandise being designed and/or produced by licensees of the Applicant? ○ Yes ○ No

         If Yes, are the licensees providing warranties and indemnities that their contributions
         to the design, marketing and production of the merchandise and packaging will not
         infringe upon the rights of others?   ○ Yes ○ No

VI.   RISK MANAGEMENT PROCEDURES:

1. **Applicant's** attorney (individual's name): _____

    Firm name and address: _____

    Phone: _____ Fax: _____ Email: _____

2. Has the **Applicant's** attorney read the Clearance Procedures attached to this Application? ○ Yes ○ No

C33900 (1/2005 ed.)   Page 3 of 9   Catalog No.14-03-0706

379

Chubb Group of Insurance Companies
15 Mountain View Rd.
Warren, NJ 07059

MULTIMEDIA LIABILITY
Application for
Video/Film Producers

3.   Has the **Applicant's** attorney approved as adequate the clearance procedures used by the **Applicant** in connection with the production?   ⭘ Yes ⭘ No

If No, have the producer and attorney arranged that the producer will give the attorney adequate information and materials to approve clearance procedures prior to the completion of the production?   ⭘ Yes ⭘ No

If No to any part of this question, please describe all clearance procedures that the attorney has not yet approved (such as chain of title, script clearance, or review of contracts):_____
_____

4.   Does the **Applicant** have a process for processing unsolicited submissions?   ⭘ Yes ⭘ No

If Yes, please provide a copy of this process.

5.   Is the name or likeness of any living person used or is any living person portrayed (with or without use of name or likeness) in the productions?   ⭘ Yes ⭘ No

If Yes, have clearances been obtained in all cases?   ⭘ Yes ⭘ No
If clearances have not been obtained, please explain: _____
_____

6.   Is the name or likeness of any deceased person used or is any deceased person portrayed (with or without name or likeness) in the production?   ⭘ Yes ⭘ No

If Yes, have clearances been obtained in all cases from personal representatives, heirs or other owners of such rights?   ⭘ Yes ⭘ No
If clearances have not been obtained, please explain: _____
_____

7.   Is there any reasonable expectation that a living person could claim to be identifiable in the production, whether or not the person's name or likeness is used or the production purports to be fictional?   ⭘ Yes ⭘ No

If Yes, has a release been obtained from such person?   ⭘ Yes ⭘ No
If a release has not been obtained from such person, please explain: _____
_____

8.   Has the **Applicant** or any of its agents or predecessors failed to obtain an agreement or release after bargaining for:
     (a)   any rights in literary, musical or other material; or   ⭘ Yes ⭘ No

     (b)   releases from any persons in connection with the production?   ⭘ Yes ⭘ No

9.   Has a title report been obtained from any title clearance service?   ⭘ Yes ⭘ No

If Yes, please attach copy of the title report.

10. Has a copyright report been obtained?   ⭘ Yes ⭘ No

If Yes, are there any ambiguities or gaps in the line of copyright ownership ("chain of title")? _____
_____

If No, please explain why not: _____

Chubb Group of Insurance Companies
15 Mountain View Rd.
CHUBB Warren, NJ 07059

MULTIMEDIA LIABILITY
**Application for
Video/Film Producers**

11. Is there any literary or other material in the production that was copyrighted in the United States before January 1, 1978?   ○Yes ○No
    If Yes, please explain:_____

12. Are any clips (film or video excerpts from other sources) or photographs used in this production?   ○Yes ○No

    If Yes, have all licenses and consents for the clips been obtained?   ○Yes ○No

    If No, please explain: _____

13. Has a script research report been obtained (to clear character and business names, etc.)?   ○Yes ○No

    If Yes, have suggested changes been made and suggested permissions obtained?   ○Yes ○No

    If No to either question, please explain: _____

14. Have musical rights been cleared?   ○Yes ○No
    (a)   Recording and synchronization rights?   ○Yes ○No
    (b)   Performing rights?   ○Yes ○No
    (c)   Right to distribute for all forms contemplated (home video/DVD, etc.)?   ○Yes ○No
    (d)   If any part is answered **No**, will these rights be obtained prior to release?   ○Yes ○No

15. If original music was commissioned, have a warranty of originality and an indemnity against third party claims been obtained from the composer?   ○Yes ○No

16. In the past ten (10) years, has any **Applicant** or person or entity proposed for coverage been the subject of a claim or been sued or threatened with suit for any act, error, or omission relating to the gathering or communicating of information, including but not limited to libel, slander, any form of invasion of privacy or appropriation of name or likeness, infringement of copyright or trademark, infliction of emotional distress, false arrest, wrongful entry or trespass?   ○Yes ○No

    If Yes, please describe in detail the circumstances of each suit or threat of suit, including the identity of the claimant; the factual and legal basis for the claim; and the disposition, including the dollar amount of any defense expenses, settlements and judgments.

    _____

    _____

    _____

VII.   REPRESENTATION: PRIOR KNOWLEDGE OF ACTS/CIRCUMSTANCES/SITUATIONS:

1. No person or entity proposed for coverage is aware of any fact, circumstance or situation which he or she has reason to suppose might give rise to a future claim that would fall within the scope of any of the proposed liability coverages for which the **Applicant** does not currently maintain insurance, or within any of the larger limits of liability sought by the **Applicant**, except: None ○ or _____

C33900 (1/2005 ed.)   Page 5 of 9   Catalog No.14-03-0706

381

Chubb Group of Insurance Companies
15 Mountain View Rd.
Warren, NJ 07059

MULTIMEDIA LIABILITY
**Application for
Video/Film Producers**

Without prejudice to any other rights and remedies of the Insurer, the **Applicant** understands and agrees that if any such fact, circumstance, or situation exists, whether or not disclosed above, any claim or action arising from any such fact, circumstance, or situation is excluded from coverage under the proposed policy, if issued by the Insurer.

IX. MATERIAL CHANGE:

If there is any material change in the answers to the questions in this Application before the policy inception date, the **Applicant** must immediately notify the Insurer in writing, and any outstanding quotation may be modified or withdrawn.

X. DECLARATIONS, FRAUD WARNINGS AND SIGNATURES:

The **Applicant's** submission of this Application does not obligate the Insurer to issue, or the **Applicant** to purchase, a policy. The **Applicant** will be advised if the Application for coverage is accepted. The **Applicant** hereby authorizes the Insurer to make any inquiry in connection with this Application.

The undersigned authorized agents of the person(s) and entity(ies) proposed for this insurance declare that to the best of their knowledge and belief, after reasonable inquiry, the statements made in this Application and in any attachments or other documents submitted with this Application are true and complete. The undersigned agree that this Application and such attachments and other documents shall be the basis of the insurance policy should a policy providing the requested coverage be issued; that all such materials shall be deemed to be attached to and shall form a part of any such policy; and that the Insurer will have relied on all such materials in issuing any such policy.

The information requested in this Application is for underwriting purposes only and does not constitute notice to the Insurer under any policy of a Claim or potential Claim.

Notice to Arkansas, Louisiana, Maryland, Minnesota, New Mexico and Ohio Applicants: Any person who, with intent to defraud or knowing that he/she is facilitating a fraud against an insurer, submits an application or files a claim containing a false, fraudulent or deceptive statement is, or may be found to be, guilty of insurance fraud, which is a crime, and may be subject to civil fines and criminal penalties.

Notice to Colorado Applicants: It is unlawful to knowingly provide false, incomplete or misleading facts or information to an insurance company for the purpose of defrauding or attempting to defraud the company. Penalties may include imprisonment, fines, denial of insurance, and civil damages. Any insurance company or agent of an insurance company who knowingly provides false, incomplete, or misleading facts or information to a policy holder or claimant for the purpose of defrauding or attempting to defraud the policy holder or claimant with regard to a settlement or award payable from insurance proceeds shall be reported to the Colorado Division of Insurance within the Department of Regulatory agencies.

Notice to District of Columbia, Maine, Tennessee and Virginia Applicants: It is a crime to knowingly provide false, incomplete or misleading information to an insurance company for the purpose of defrauding the company. Penalties may include imprisonment, fines or a denial of insurance benefits.

Notice to Florida and Oklahoma Applicants: Any person who, knowingly and with intent to injure, defraud or deceive any employer or employee, insurance company, or self-insured program, files a statement of claim containing any false or misleading information is guilty of: a felony (in Oklahoma) or a felony of the third degree (in Florida).

Notice to Kentucky Applicants: Any person who, knowingly and with intent to defraud any insurance company or other person files an application for insurance containing any false information, or conceals for the purpose of misleading, information concerning any material fact thereto, commits a fraudulent insurance act which is a crime.

Notice to New Jersey Applicants: Any person who includes any false or misleading information on an application for an

Chubb Group of Insurance Companies
15 Mountain View Rd.
CHUBB Warren, NJ 07059

MULTIMEDIA LIABILITY
**Application for
Video/Film Producers**

insurance policy is subject to criminal and civil penalties.

Notice to Oregon and Texas Applicants: Any person who makes an intentional misstatement that is material to the risk may be found guilty of insurance fraud by a court of law.

Notice to New York and Pennsylvania Applicants: Any person who knowingly and with intent to defraud any insurance company or other person files an application for insurance or statement of claim containing any materially false information, or conceals for the purpose of misleading, information concerning any fact material thereto, commits a fraudulent insurance act, which is a crime and shall also be subject to: a civil penalty not to exceed five thousand dollars and the stated value of the claim for each such violation (in New York) or criminal and civil penalties (in Pennsylvania).

Date	Signature*	Title
_____	_____	Chief Executive Officer
_____	_____	Chief Financial Officer

*This Application must be signed by the chief executive officer and chief financial officer of the **Applicant** acting as the authorized representatives of the person(s) and entity(ies) proposed for this insurance.

Produced By: Agent:_____ Agency: DeWitt Stern Group, Inc._____

Agency Taxpayer ID or SS No.:_____ Agent License No.: _____

Address (Street, City, State, Zip): _____

Submitted By: Agency: DeWitt Stern Group, Inc._____

Agency Taxpayer ID or SS No.:_____ Agent License No.: 0C28262_____

Address (Street, City, State, Zip): _____

C33900 (1/2005 ed.)   Page 7 of 9   Catalog No.14-03-0706

383

Chubb Group of Insurance
Companies
15 Mountain View Rd.
CHUBB   Warren, NJ 07059

MULTIMEDIA LIABILITY
Application for
Video/Film Producers

Clearance Procedures

The Clearance Procedures below should not be construed as exhaustive and they do not cover all situations that may arise in any particular circumstance or any particular Production.

1.   **Applicant** and its counsel should monitor the Production at all stages, from inception through final cut, with a view to eliminating material that could give rise to a claim.

Consideration should be given to the likelihood of any claim or litigation. Is there a potential claimant portrayed in the Production who has sued before or is likely to sue again? Is there a close copyright or other legal issue? Is the subject matter of the Production such as to require difficult and extensive discovery in the event of necessity to defend? Are sources reliable? The above factors should be considered during all clearance procedures.

2.   The Producer and the lawyer need to read the script prior to commencement of Production to eliminate matter that is defamatory, invades privacy or is otherwise potentially actionable.

3.   A script research report should also be prepared *before* filming to alert the Producer to potential problems. Such problems may include: names of fictional characters that are coincidentally similar to real people; script references to real products, businesses or people if not cleared; or uses of copyrighted or other protected materials, etc. Fictional character names should be checked in relevant telephone directories, professional directories or other sources to minimize the risk of accidental identification of real people. Similar checks should be done for the names of businesses, organizations and products used in the Production. Special care should be taken to check names of person, businesses, etc., that are negatively portrayed. The Producer also must be alert to elements that do not appear in the script (such as art works used on the set) but that may need clearances.

4.   If the Production is a documentary and there is no script, the Producer should provide its counsel with a detailed synopsis of the project in advance of production. (If it is a documentary series, the lawyer should receive a detailed synopsis of each episode.) If the Production will involve negative statements about people or businesses, the Producer should provide counsel with full details about the allegations and their merit. Problem statements can then be identified and thus avoided while filming. During filming, the Producer should be careful to avoid (or consult with counsel about) possible problem areas. (Examples include: filming identifiable copyrighted items or performances, trademarks, persons who have not specifically consented to be filmed, or minors.) Relevant laws differ from place to place: some jurisdictions have very restrictive rules about filming persons, signs, buildings, public art, etc. Also, be careful to avoid narration or editing that accidentally implies negative things about pictured people, products and businesses.

5.   A copyright report on the underlying script, book or other work must be obtained, unless the work is an unpublished original, not based on any other work, and it is certain that it was not optioned or licensed to others prior to the **Applicant's** acquisition of rights. Both domestic and foreign copyrights and renewal rights should be checked. If a completed film is being acquired, a similar review should be made of copyright and renewals on any copyrighted underlying property.

6.   The origins of the work should be ascertained — basic idea, sequence of events and characters. Have submissions of any similar properties been received by the **Applicant** or someone closely involved with the Production? If so, the circumstances as to why the submitting party may not claim theft or infringement should be described in detail.

7.   Prior to final title selection, a title report must be obtained. TITLE COVERAGE WILL NOT BE OFFERED UNLESS A RECENT TITLE REPORT HAS BEEN SUBMITTED TO AND APPROVED BY THE INSURER.

Chubb Group of Insurance Companies
15 Mountain View Rd.
CHUBB Warren, NJ 07059

MULTIMEDIA LIABILITY
Application for
Video/Film Producers

8. Whether the Production is fictional or factual, the names, faces and likenesses of any recognizable living persons should not be used unless written releases have been obtained. A release is unnecessary if person is part of a crowd scene or shown in a fleeting background. Releases can only be dispensed with if the **Applicant** provides the Insurer with specific reasons, in writing, as to why such releases are unnecessary and such reasons are accepted by the Insurer. The term "living persons" includes thinly disguised versions of living persons or living persons who are readily identifiable because of identity of other characters or because of the factual, historical or geographic setting.

9. All releases must give the **Applicant** the rights to edit, modify, add to and/or delete material, juxtapose any part of the film with any other film, change the sequence of events or of any questions posed and/or answers given, fictionalize persons or events, and make any other changes in the film that the **Applicant** deems appropriate. If a minor, consent has to be legally binding.

10. If music (pre-existing or original) is used, the **Applicant** must obtain all necessary synchronization and performance licenses from copyright proprietors. All necessary licenses must also be obtained for recordings of such music.

11. Written agreements must exist between the **Applicant** and all creators, authors, writers, performers and any other persons providing material (including quotations from copyrighted works) or on-screen services.

12. If distinctive locations, buildings, businesses, personal property or products are filmed, written releases must be secured. This is not necessary if such real property is seen only as non-distinctive background.

13. If the Production involves actual events, it should be ascertained that the author's major sources are independent and primary (contemporaneous newspaper reports, court transcripts, interviews with witnesses, etc.) and not secondary (another author's copyrighted work, autobiographies, etc.).

14. Shooting script and rough-cuts should be checked to assure compliance with all of the above. During photography, persons might be photographed on location, dialogue added or other matter included that was not originally contemplated.

15. If the Intent is to use the Production or its elements on videocassettes, web sites, multimedia formats or other technology, rights to manufacture, distribute and release the Production must include the above rights and must be obtained from all writers, directors, actors, musicians, composers and others necessary therefor, including proprietors of underlying materials.

16. Film/video clips are dangerous unless licenses and authorizations for the second use are obtained from the owner of the clip, as well as licenses from all persons rendering services in or supplying material contained in the clip; e.g., owners of underlying literary rights, writers, directors, actors, music owners or musicians. Special attention should be paid to music rights as music owners often take the position that new synchronization and performance licenses are required.

17. Living persons and even the deceased (through their personal representatives or heirs) may have a "right of publicity." Clearances must be obtained where necessary. Where the work is fictional in whole or in part, the names of all characters must be fictional. If for some special reason particular names need not be fictional, full details must be provided to the Insurer in an attachment to the Application.

You can download this form at www.clearanceandcopyright.com
Use the code: ibotCC3

385

CHAPTER 21

CHAIN OF TITLE

Sooner or later, everybody with a completed film has to deliver a good "chain of title." **Chain of title** refers to the contracts and other documents that show any change in ownership of a film project from its inception. The documents are a trail of transfers from the original author of a work through the final film (or whatever stage the project is at at the time).

What is chain of title?

In some instances, the process is simple. The writer of an original screenplay based on his or her own original idea signs a Certificate of Authorship, which declares in no uncertain terms that 1) the writer wrote the script, 2) it was an original work, and 3) that no rights in the script have been previously granted. This one-page document is required of every writer who writes anything for a studio. It establishes ownership of the script and the right to sell it.

By the time you are an adult, the principle of ownership is well known. You cannot sell anything that you do not own. You cannot loan it, use it, or keep it without the owner's permission. When you own something, you are said to have good title to it. For most tangible things, the fact that you have possession is strong proof of ownership. You stop by a garage sale and look at all the articles the seller owns. You buy whatever *thing* attracts you and then you own it—you have good title to that *thing*. However, if there are 100 stereos for sale priced at $1.00 each, you might question whether the seller has legal ownership. If the stereos were stolen, then the "seller" does not have good title—the seller does not own them. If the seller does not own the stereos, you might get possession of a stereo for $1.00, but you will not own it, you will not have good title. If you ask how the "seller" came by so many stereos at such a good price, you would be questioning title.

For some things, more is required to prove good title than mere possession, free of suspicious circumstances. For instance, to sell an automobile, you must have the registration certificate. You must show that you own the automobile and then actually sign a form, supplied by your state, to transfer title of the automobile to another person. This is a simple process, but necessary to transfer ownership of the automobile to another person.

When you sell a piece of real estate, you have to do even more than sign a piece of paper in order for the transaction to be binding. You also have to show that you in fact own the interest that you are selling. This is accomplished through a title search. A **title search** traces the ownership records from an initial land grant—usually from the King of England on the East Coast or a Spanish Land Grant on the West Coast—through transfers from owner to owner by way of sale, death, subdivisions, marriages, divorces, and on and on, up to your ownership. This is the chain of title for a piece of real estate.

When you sell a script or try to enter into a distribution deal for a finished film, you have to show that you own the script (or film) that you are selling. The usual language is that the obligations (including payment) of the buyer, producer, or distributor with whom you are dealing is "subject to satisfactory proof of Chain of Title."

By proving your chain of title, you establish the fact that you have good title to a property. **Good title** means that you own that which you claim to own, free and clear of any encumbrances or liens. You must prove this at some point before your film is released. The bigger the producer you join up with, the earlier you have to prove your chain of title.

For example, let us assume that you wrote, directed, and produced your own film. Assume that a distributor asks you to prove your chain of title. This is straightforward, but still requires several documents. You need the following:

1. Certificate of Authorship, signed by you as the screen-writer

2. Copyright certificate for the script registered in your name

3. Copyright certificate for the film registered in your name

Often, even in this simple scenario, the film is actually produced by a partnership or some other entity other than the individual screenwriter. Let us assume that it was a partnership. The chain of title would look like this:

1. Certificate of Authorship, signed by you as the screen-writer

2. Copyright certificate for the script registered in your name

3. Assignment, sale, or other transfer of the right to make a film based on the script from you to the partnership

4. Copyright certificate for the film registered in the name of the partnership

Some lawyers would accept the four documents listed. Others would want a copy of the partnership agreement showing that the partnership is a real entity, who its members are, and what their respective rights are. The larger the studio or law firm where the lawyer works, the more likely you are to be asked for additional documents.

Let's consider a slightly more complicated example, but not an unrealistic or uncommon example, even in the community of independent filmmakers. In this example, you are asked to prove chain of title on a script you co-wrote based on a published novel. Suppose you contacted the author directly. He or she told you that the book was under option to a producer who had just delivered a script that everyone hated. You get on well with the author. You wait patiently for the option to lapse. As a precaution, you carefully avoid reading or even talking in great detail about the previous script.

As soon as the other producer's option lapses, you option the film rights to the book. You write two drafts but you are still not happy, even though you received significant help from a friend on the second of the two drafts you wrote. You finally do what you have been resisting, because you did not want to lose control of the project. You option your script to a studio with a piece of paper that guarantees that you will be attached as a producer.

The deal isn't everything you wanted, but you sign the agreement and wait for the initial, paltry check. However, the whole deal is subject to approval of the chain of title. That means that having signed the agreement and therefore having tied up the film rights, you have to submit a mountain of paper to be reviewed by a lawyer whom you never met and who does not work for you. Makes you wish you had taken care of this before signing the agreement! If requested, this material is generally reviewed before the deal is signed so that the project is not tied up while you jump over hurdles to obtain more and more documents. Also, you can generally negotiate an outside date by which this approval has to be given, or the deal is null and void. About 60 days is a standard length of time for this approval process.

Here is a drawing that shows what the above chain of title would look like:

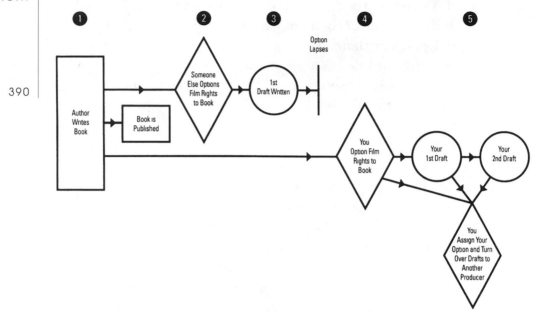

Here are the minimum documents you have to supply the distributor to establish the chain of title. The numbers refer to the numbers in the diagram above.

1. Certificate of Copyright on the book registered in the name of "Owner"

2. First Option Agreement that lapsed

3. The Writer's Agreement under which the first draft was created

4. Your Option Agreement

5. Your Agreement with Your Joint Author on your second draft

Here is another drawing of what this chain of title looks like:

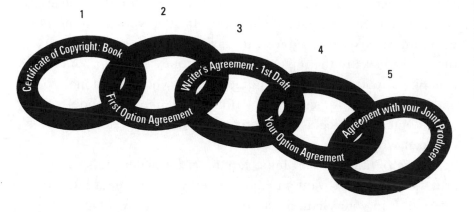

Here is the rub:

Many lawyers would agree that the list of documents set out above, assuming that they are internally correct, would establish a good chain of title. However, many lawyers would want more documents or might find your documents wanting. For instance, the reviewing lawyer might want to see the contract between the author of the book and the publishing company. This request would insure that the author did not grant the right to the publishing company to negotiate and/or sell the film rights in question. The lawyer also may require a Publisher's Release to be signed. Additionally, the reviewing attorney may require that the producing entity have the right to buy that first draft that neither you nor your friend ever saw. The purpose of such a request would be to reduce the risk of lawsuits.

The above example is about as simple as it gets. For instance, if the novel were based on a real person, most lawyers would want to see the release or agreement with that person on whom the author based the book.

Our office helped review all the documentation to prove chain of title for every film in a large library of films being considered for purchase by 20th Century Fox. The films included the *Rambo* series, *Cliffhanger*, and *The Doors*. About 40 documents were required to prove the basic chain of title on most of the films. More documents were reviewed for the music. Security Agreements, which could cut off title, were even more voluminous. A **security agreement** is issued by a film's lender or financier to secure the repayment of its money by the producer. It is like a mortgage on your home. Banks who loan money to make a film can foreclose on a film much like the lender on your home can foreclose on your home if you do not pay off the loan when it is due.

Chain of title is a very important area. Ultimately, this is one area for which you want an experienced entertainment lawyer. Every link in your chain must be strong and tightly attached to the next link.

RECORDING CHAIN OF TITLE DOCUMENTS

If you are registering a script written by someone other than yourself or have transferred any rights, there should be some written agreement that shows how that happened. You need to register these contractual documents with the Copyright Office.

To record any document transferring ownership in a copyright, use the form called Document Cover Sheet. You may copy the example at the end of this chapter, or you may create your own. Unlike the various forms used to register copyright in a script or film, this form does not have to be exactly like the one from the Copyright Office as long as the necessary information is there.

The person(s) submitting a document with a cover sheet are solely responsible for verifying the correctness of the cover sheet and the sufficiency of the document that is being registered. When the Copyright Office records a document submitted to it, it does not ascertain the document's validity or the effect of that document. The Copyright Office just records the document and Document Cover Sheet that comes with it. Only a court of law may determine the legal impact of the document you registered. However, this recording process gives notice to the world of how you came to have the right(s) that you claim to have in the copyright.

DOCUMENT COVER SHEET

Here is a simple guide to what to fill in on each of this form's blanks.

1. List the first three names of the parties who appear on the document you are recording exactly as they are written on the document. This information is only used to connect the Document Cover Sheet and the document if they become separated. It does not establish ownership.

2. List the title that first appears on the document you are recording. Again, this information is only used to connect the Document Cover Sheet and the document if they become separated and does not establish ownership.

3. Count the number of different titles mentioned in the document you are recording. The number of titles that are mentioned in the document determines the fee that you pay to the Copyright Office. The Copyright Office verifies your title count, so be accurate on your application or its processing time will be extended.

4. Calculate the fee from the information given in Space 3. The fee for a document of any length containing one title is, at the time of this writing, $95. No matter how long the document is that you are recording, you pay $25 for each group of 10 or fewer additional titles mentioned in the document you are recording.

5. Check whether you will be paying by check or money order. The Copyright Office only accepts U.S. checks and money orders. The box regarding the Copyright Office deposit account

should only be checked if you have a deposit account. The Copyright Office maintains a system of deposit accounts for people or companies that frequently use its services. The individual or company makes an advance deposit, a minimum of $450, and the Copyright Office charges copyright fees against the balance in the account.

6. Any document you record should be complete. If a document is not complete, it is referred to as an "as is" document. **"As is" documents** are always open to question. However, so-called Section 205 documents must be complete by their own terms in order to be recordable. **Section 205 documents** include almost all of the documents you will record as a filmmaker. Examples of Section 205 documents include transfers of copyright ownerships and other documents pertaining to a copyright, such as exclusive and non-exclusive licenses, contracts, mortgages, powers of attorney, certificates of change of corporate name or title, wills, and decrees of distribution. Section 205 refers to that specific section of the Federal Copyright Law that provides for the recording of these important documents. As a practical matter, there is almost nothing you will be able to record as a filmmaker on an "as is" basis.

7. Many people (including me) prefer to keep the document with the original signature if there is only one such document. You may, therefore, photocopy the entire original document and record the copy. In that case, you complete this section only if you are submitting a document that does not bear an actual signature on the document being recorded. That is, if the document contains only a photocopied signature, fill in this space. If the document you are sending to the Copyright Office bears an original signature (even if the document itself was photocopied before it was signed), do not fill in this space.

This certification is necessary because copyright law provides that any transfer of copyright ownership or other document pertaining to a copyright (a Section 205 document) may be recorded in the Copyright Office if the document bears the actual signature of the person or persons who executed (signed) the documents. If a photocopy of the original signed document is submitted, it must be accompanied by a sworn or official certification. A sworn certification signed by at least one of the parties to the document or their authorized representative (who is identified as such) at Space 7 satisfies that statutory requirement. It follows, therefore, that copies of documents that are taken from the files in a federal, state, or local government office must be accompanied by an official certification.

8. Fill in the name and address of the person to whom you want the recorded document returned. Fill in all of this information in case the Copyright Office needs to contact you.

21.01 DOCUMENT COVER SHEET

Copyright Office fees are subject to change. For current fees, check the Copyright Office website at www.copyright.gov, write the Copyright Office, or call (202) 707-3000.

DOCUMENT COVER SHEET
For Recordation of Documents
UNITED STATES COPYRIGHT OFFICE

DATE OF RECORDATION
(Assigned by Copyright Office)

Month   Day   Year

Volume _____ Page _____

Volume _____ Page _____

FUNDS RECEIVED _____

Do not write above this line.

To the Register of Copyrights:

Please record the accompanying original document or copy thereof.

FOR OFFICE USE ONLY

1 Name of the party or parties to the document spelled as they appear in the document (List up to the first three)

_____
_____
_____

2 Date of execution and/or effective date of the accompanying document

(month)   (day)   (year)

3 Completeness of document
❏ Document is complete by its own terms.
❏ Document is not complete. Record "as is."

4 Description of document
❏ Transfer of Copyright
❏ Security Interest
❏ Change of Name of Owner
❏ Termination of Transfer(s) [Section 304]
❏ Shareware
❏ Life, Identity, Death Statement [Section 302]
❏ Transfer of Mask Works
❏ Other _____
_____

5 Title of first work as given in the document _____

6 Total number of titles in document _____

7 Amount of fee calculated
$ _____

8 Fee enclosed
❏ Check
❏ Money Order

❏ Fee authorized to be charged to :
Copyright Office
Deposit Account number _____

Account name _____

9 **Affirmation*:** I hereby affirm to the Copyright Office that the information given on this form is a true and correct representation of the accompanying document. This affirmation will not suffice as a certification of a photocopy signature on the document.
(Affirmation *must* be signed even if you are also signing Space 10.)

Signature _____

Date _____

Phone Number _____   Fax Number _____

10 **Certification*:** Complete this certification in addition to the Affirmation if a photocopy of the original signed document is substituted for a document bearing the actual signature.
NOTE: This space *may not* be used for an official certification.
I certify under penalty of perjury under the laws of the United States of America that the accompanying document is a true copy of the original document.

Signature _____

Duly Authorized Agent of: _____

Date _____

Recordation will be mailed in window envelope to this address:

Name▼ _____

Number/Street/Apt▼ _____

City/State/ZIP▼ _____

YOU MUST:
• Complete all necessary spaces
• Sign your Cover Sheet in Space 9
SEND ALL 3 ELEMENTS TOGETHER:
1. Two copies of the Document Cover Sheet
2. Check/money order payable to *Register of Copyrights*
3. Document
MAIL TO:
Library of Congress, Copyright Office
Documents Recordation Section, LM-462
101 Independence Avenue, S.E.
Washington, D.C. 20559-6000

Fees are subject to change. For current fees, check the Copyright Office website at www.copyright.gov, write the Copyright Office, or call (202) 707-3000.

*Knowingly and willfully falsifying material facts on this form may result in criminal liability. 18 U.S.C.§1001.

Rev: June 2002—20,000   Web Rev: June 2002   ♻ Printed on recycled paper   U.S. Government Printing Office: 2000-461-113/20,021

You can download this form at www.copyright.gov

FORM 21.02 SAMPLE COVER LETTER FOR RECORD AGREEMENTS

Register of Copyrights
Library of Congress
Washington, D.C. 20559-6000

Dear Sir:

Enclosed please find the following:

1.   Document to be recorded entitled _____ _____ .

2.   Check in the amount of $_____ for Recording the Cover Sheet
for Document Recording

3.   Completed Cover Sheet; and

4.   Return Post Card

Please record the cover sheet.

We understand that the stamped original Cover Sheet will be returned to this office.

Thank you.

Very truly yours,

_____   _____

Enclosures

You should type this letter on your letterhead.

You can download this form at www.copyright.gov

FORM 21.03.   RETURN POSCARD FOR RECORDING DOCUMENTS

The copyright office will date stamp and sign and return to you a self-addressed, stamped postcard (not a letter, a postcard). If you fill it out properly, this postcard—worded for recording documents to show chain of title—can act as your proof of receipt. Use the following language on the back part of the postcard and you will have your proof.

BACK

This postcard shall act as a receipt for the following items:

Document Recordation Cover Sheet to record the following document:

_____

The Parties to the Document are: _____ and _____

A total of ____ titles are mentioned in this document.

Our check in the amount of $ _____.

FRONT

Your Name
Address

Your Name
Address

You can download this form at www.copyright.gov

CHAPTER 22

REGISTERING COPYRIGHT FOR YOUR COMPLETED FILM

Copyright in a motion picture is automatically secured when the work is created and "fixed" on film or video. Each element is absorbed into the final film and covered by one copyright. The script, music, photography, effects, design, and performances all merge into the film except, of course, items that are licensed from third parties. Some elements such as the script and music, standing alone, may also carry their own copyright. For numerous legal and industry reasons, you still must register the completed film with the copyright office.

WHEN TO REGISTER COPYRIGHT IN YOUR FILM

You should register the copyright in your film as soon as your film is locked. Locked means that the film is in its final form and ready to have prints struck. The most practical reason for registering the copyright in your film at the earliest possible time is that you have to lodge two copies of your film in the "best format" with the Library of Congress. If you do it immediately, you can usually get away with supplying a tape as opposed to a print, so early registration can save you money. See more on the deposit requirement later in this chapter.

IN WHOSE NAME DO YOU REGISTER THE FILM?

The author of the film and the copyright claimant are the same in almost all studio-film circumstances when it comes to a completed film. Both the author and the claimant are the production company that produced the film. Everyone who worked on the film should have signed work-for-hire agreements, making the production company the author of the film. The various contracts in this book (and every other book on filmmaking) provide work-for-hire language to insure that there is no confusion on this point.

FORM OF NOTICE FOR MOTION PICTURES

The use of a copyright notice is even more important for a finished film than for your script. It informs the public that your work is protected by copyright, identifies the copyright owner, and shows the first year of completion. It also should indicate the country of origin.

Today, use of the copyright notice on new films is optional under U.S. law, though it is still highly recommended. People are so used to seeing the notice that its absence might cause someone to jump to a wrong conclusion. Below is a notice that meets the copyright laws of every country in the world, including the small nation that still requires, as of this writing, "All Rights Reserved." (The notice usually is the last item in the credits.)

Copyright 2009, _____ [copyright owner's name]. All Rights Reserved.

The United States is considered the country of origin for purposes of the Berne Convention.

APPLYING FOR REGISTRATION OF
YOUR COMPLETED FILM

REGISTERING
COPYRIGHT
FOR YOUR
COMPLETED
FILM

401

To register a motion picture, send the following to the Copyright Office:

1. A SIGNED APPLICATION on Form PA. See Chapter 11 on how to obtain forms from the Copyright Office.

2. ONE COMPLETE COPY of the motion picture being registered.

3. A SEPARATE WRITTEN DESCRIPTION of the contents of the motion picture.

4. A NON-REFUNDABLE FILING FEE (which, at the time of this writing, is $45) in the form of a check, money order, or bank draft payable to: Register of Copyrights. Do not send cash.

Send the application, copy, description, and fee in the same package, along with a cover letter (like the one at the end of this chapter) describing all of the enclosed elements to:

Library of Congress
Copyright Office
101 Independence Avenue SE
Washington, DC 20559-6000

It is not absolutely necessary, but our office always takes two additional steps to create a record of sending. We send these letters by certified mail, return receipt requested. It is a little more trouble, but it provides a positive record for your files. We back this up with a postcard that the Copyright Office will date-stamp and return very quickly showing that they have received your packet and its contents. A sample of the postcard is at the end of the chapter with the cover letter.

FILLING OUT FORM PA FOR YOUR COMPLETED FILM

The following comments supplement the information provided in Chapter 11. (Check out Chapter 11 to be sure that you don't miss anything, especially where you are referred to Chapter 11 in the text below.)

SPACE 1: Nature of This Work

"Motion picture" is generally the appropriate term. It covers documentary and fictional films, feature-length and shorts, and color and black-and-white. There is no need to elaborate. If the motion picture is part of a multimedia kit or other larger work and you are claiming copyright in the entire work, you should indicate that in this space. For example, you could state "multimedia kit, including motion picture and workbook," if applicable.

SPACE 2: Name of Author, "Work Made for Hire," and "Nature of Authorship"

Ordinarily, a number of individuals contribute authorship to a motion picture, including the writer, the director, the producer, the camera operator, the editor, and others. In America, these individuals are hardly ever considered "authors," however, because a motion picture is almost always a "work made for hire." Chapter 7 explains why you should use the work-for-hire approach for your film. In the case of a work made for hire, the employer—not the individuals who actually created the work—is considered the author for copyright purposes. Without work-for-hire agreements, most of the above-the-line talent have a potential claim on your film.

1. If the entire work was made for hire, name the employer as author and answer "yes" to the work made for hire question. The employer can be you or you and your investor(s), but would generally be a single-picture production company that you create. Under "Nature of Authorship," state "entire motion picture." You should always be sure that everyone working on a film has signed a work-for-hire agreement.

REGISTERING
COPYRIGHT
FOR YOUR
COMPLETED
FILM

403

If the music in the film was composed specifically for the film, stating "entire motion picture" here will include all such music.

2. If no part of the work was made for hire, name all of the individuals who made the motion picture as authors and answer "no" to the work-made-for-hire questions. Under "Nature of Authorship," briefly describe what each person did: for example, "director," "producer," or "writer." This is not a good idea, but some people buy this book after things have begun to unravel with cast and crew and it is difficult to obtain signatures.

3. If part of the work was made for hire and part was not, separate the parts of the work that were made for hire from those parts that were not and fill in each section accordingly.

SPACE 3a: Year in Which Creation of This Work Was Completed
Give the year in which the final cut of the motion picture was completed. If the motion picture is a new version of an older film, give the year of completion of the version being registered.

SPACE 3b: What Is Publication?
Publication of a motion picture is one of the most confusing areas of copyright law. To avoid a mistake in this murky area, you should register your film as soon as possible after it is completed.

Publication of a motion picture takes place when one or more copies are distributed to the public by sale, rental, lease, or lending, or when an offering is made to distribute copies to a group of persons (wholesalers, retailers, broadcasters, motion picture distributors, and the like) for purposes of further distribution or public performance. Offering to distribute a copy of a motion picture for exhibition during a film festival may be considered a publication of that work. For such an offering to constitute a publication, copies must be made and be ready for distribution. Bear in mind that whether a film is old or new is not the relevant question. The issue is whether your film has been published in a legal sense. Sending a limited number of copies of the film to a select group of individuals to see if they want to distribute it does not publish the film for copyright purposes. Publication occurs when your film is shown to the public at large or prints are made for a public release, even a small release.

Publication of a motion picture publishes all of the components embodied in it, including the music, the script, and the sounds. Thus, if a motion picture made from a screenplay is published, the screenplay is published to the extent that it is contained in the published film.

Date of First Publication
If the work is published, give a complete date (month, day, year) and nation of first publication. You should register your film as soon as it is completed before publication, to reduce the deposit requirements. If the work is not published at the time the application is submitted, leave the publication lines blank.

SPACE 4: Copyright Claimant(s)
This should be a single-film production company that you created for this film alone.

SPACE 5: Previous Registration
This is rarely necessary with a motion picture. However, if the motion picture is based on a screenplay or book that has been registered, check "yes" for option C and give the registration number and year of registration of the underlying work.

SPACE 6: Derivative Work or Compilation
A motion picture is a derivative work of the screenplay. Therefore, at (a) state, "The movie was based on the script by the same name written by _____ and _____." At (b) state, "All cinematic elements."

SPACE 7: Deposit Account
Leave blank. You will pay by check.

SPACE 8: Certification

See Chapter 12 for a detailed explanation of this space.

SPACE 9: Address for Return of Certificate
Complete legibly. This will show through the window envelope used by the Copyright Office to mail back your completed form.

REGISTERING
COPYRIGHT
FOR YOUR
COMPLETED
FILM

405

DEPOSITING ONE COMPLETED COPY OF YOUR FILM WITH THE COPYRIGHT OFFICE

To register a completed motion picture, you will be required to deposit both a written copy of the contents of the motion picture and a copy of the film or video or DVD itself.

In addition to the separate, written description of the motion picture, the Copyright Office also requires, for an unpublished work, deposit of one complete copy of the motion picture, containing all of the visual and aural elements that the registration covers. This can be on tape or on film. Publication of the film makes the process potentially more expensive.

For a published motion picture, the Copyright Office requires deposit of one complete copy of the "best" edition of the work. For motion pictures first published abroad, deposit one complete copy of the film as it was first published abroad.

For motion pictures published in the United States, you have a legal obligation to deposit the "best" edition of the work within three months of publication.

The following is a list, in descending order, of the Library's current preference for what constitutes the "best edition":

1. Film rather than another medium:
   - Preprint material, by special arrangement
   - 70mm positive print, if original production negative is greater than 35mm
   - 35mm positive prints
   - 16mm positive prints
2. Videotape formats:

- Betacam SP
- Digital Beta (Digibeta)
- DVD
- VHS Cassette

To be complete, the deposit copy of the motion picture should be clean, undamaged, undeteriorated, and free from any defects that would interfere with showing the film or that would cause mechanical, visual, or audible defects or distortions.

The Examining Division of the Copyright Office does not have equipment to view motion pictures in certain formats, including 1-inch open-reel videotapes; and HDCAM, D-2, and 8mm videocassettes. Therefore, these are highly disfavored, and you must receive special permission to deposit one of these instead of a more accessible print or video.

Exceptions to the Normal Deposit Requirement For Film

Where it is unusually difficult or impossible to comply with the deposit requirement for a particular motion picture (usually because of the expense of striking an extra print of a published film), you may submit a written request for special relief from the normal requirement. The request should be addressed to the Chief of the Examining Division, U.S. Copyright Office, Library of Congress, Washington, DC 20559. It must state why you cannot provide the required copy and describe the nature of the substitute copy being deposited. This letter should be included with the registration material. Always put it on your own letterhead as opposed to your attorney's. The Copyright Office has the attitude that if you can afford a lawyer, you can afford to give them a pristine print.

The Copyright Office may or may not grant special relief in a particular case. They consider the difficulty of providing a required copy, the acquisitions policies and archival considerations of the Library of Congress, and the examining requirements for registration.

If relief is granted, you are usually required to sign a Motion Picture Agreement provided to you by the Copyright Office. Its terms are non-negotiable. The Motion Picture Agreement establishes several alternative deposit procedures for published motion pictures. If the Copyright Office grants relief, it still requires that you send a print after you are through using it.

All activities related to the Motion Picture Agreement are under the Motion Picture, Broadcasting, and Recorded Sound Division of the Library of Congress. For a copy of the Agreement, call the Motion Picture, Broadcasting, and Recorded Sound Division (MBRS) at (202) 707-5610, or write to:

Library of Congress
MBRS
ATTN: Reference Assistant
101 Independence Avenue SE
Washington, DC 20540-4805

In general, whether the motion picture is published or unpublished, the deposited material should present a full, complete, and detailed description of the work, including its running time. It may be a detailed synopsis or continuity. A continuity is the actual dialogue script annotated with timing code taken from a tape or work print of the feature film. I recommend a continuity because you have to prepare one anyway for sale to non English-speaking territories, and it provides you with a more complete and accurate description of your film than a synopsis.

MAILING

Everything for a single registration must go in the same envelope or box. Be sure that your application is signed, your check or money order is in the correct amount, and that you have enclosed either one or two deposits of the work you are registering. You should list all of this in a cover letter.

Mail the entire package to:

Library of Congress
Copyright Office
101 Independence Avenue SE
Washington, DC 20559-6000

SPEEDING UP THINGS AT THE COPYRIGHT OFFICE

There is little you can do or need to do to speed up the copyright process. Remember that having the registration certificate in hand does not change any of your ownership rights. Copyright attaches to your work the moment you fix your creation in some permanent form for the first time. Your registration is effective as of the date your completed application is received by the Copyright Office. That's why the forms in this book give you proof of receipt.

However, there are some circumstances for which you just have to have that little piece of paper quickly. Here are the most common circumstances:

1. You are going to sue for infringement of copyright, and you have to have the copyright registration number. Therefore, you need expedited service from the Copyright Office, since you only know the copyright registration number when your registration form is returned to you.

2. You have signed a distribution contract requiring that you have the actual registration certificate in hand. You can usually negotiate that a copy of the completed Form PA is sufficient if you can also show proof of receipt by the Copyright Office. You then promise to supply the certificate as soon as you receive it. If you cannot negotiate around this requirement, you may need expedited service from the Copyright Office.

3. You have asked customs to confiscate bootleg films coming into the country. They will not do this without a

copyright certificate. Proof of receipt of Form PA by the Copyright Office is not enough because of the disruptive, if not draconian, consequences of confiscation.

REGISTERING
COPYRIGHT
FOR YOUR
COMPLETED
FILM

409

These are about the only reasons recognized by the Copyright Office to expedite an application. To expedite an application, you must submit a Request for Special Handling in person or by mail. If you go in person, the Copyright Office will provide you with a form to fill out explaining your circumstances. If done by mail, you must submit a letter that explains your need for expedited service; this should be as detailed as possible. The request must also include a signed statement certifying that the information contained in the request is accurate to the best of your knowledge. Whether you request special handling in person or by mail, your request must be accompanied by your application form for registration, the required deposit copies, a nonrefundable filing fee, and a special handling fee. Even with requesting expedited service, it still takes at least a week and usually longer to receive the Form PA back with your registration number. There are certain services located in Washington, DC, that "walk through" applications for speedy handling. Some claim that they can obtain one-day results. This is not always the case. If you want to try this approach, Thomson CompuMark in Washington, D.C., (800) 356-0630, is one very reliable, well-established company that offers this service.

**22.01   SAMPLE COVER LETTER FOR MOTION PICTURE
REGISTRATION**

Date: _____

Certified
Return Receipt Requested
Library of Congress
Copyright Office
101 Independence Avenue SE
Washington, DC 20559-6000

Dear Register:

Enclosed please find the following:

1.   Check in the amount of forty-five dollars ($45.00) for the
Copyright Registration

2.   Completed Form PA

3.   Continuity

4.   Videocassette of film

5.   Return postcard

Please register the above film immediately.

We understand that the stamped original Form PA will be
returned to this office.

Thank you.

Very truly yours,

_____

Enclosures: as listed

You should type this letter on your letterhead.

***You can download this form at www.clearanceandcopyright.com
Use the code: ibotCC3***

22.02. RETURN POSCARD FOR MOTION PICTURE REGISTRATION

REGISTERING
COPYRIGHT
FOR YOUR
COMPLETED
FILM

411

The copyright office will date-stamp and sign and return to you a self-addressed, stamped postcard (not a letter, a postcard). That is your proof of receipt. Use the following language on the back part of the postcard and you will have your proof.

BACK

This postcard shall act as a receipt for the following items:

Form PA to register the motion picture entitled:

_____

Together with a check in amount of $45.00 and a copy of the Continuity of the motion picture and the motion picture itself for Registration of Copyright.

FRONT

Your Name
Address

Your Name
Address

You can download this form at www.clearanceandcopyright.com
Use the code: ibotCC3

CHAPTER 23

COPYRIGHT INFRINGEMENT

Oh happy day! Your film is opening in a week. You have overcome all the obstacles. All your troubles are behind you. All you have to do is go to the premiere, travel the talk-show circuit, and pick out an outfit for the Oscars. Oops! Think again.

WHAT IS INFRINGEMENT?

All too often, you will receive a letter claiming copyright infringement. Copyright infringement occurs when your film was based in whole or in part on the copyrighted work of another to such an extent that the court will say, "You took too much." These claims arise when somebody thinks they were ripped off.

These claims are very, very common. As the court said in denying a claim by a playwright against the creators of the film *E.T.*, there is an "obsessive conviction, so common among authors and composers, that all similarities between their works and any others that appear later must inevitably be ascribed to plagiarism." Plagiarism is the lay term for taking someone else's writing and calling it your own.

The frustration and pressure in getting a project off the ground are so great that when one sees a film that generally resembles a script or a treatment or even an idea that one was not able to get made, one immediately feels ripped off. The hurt, anger, and frustration send that person on a diligent search for a lawyer. Due to the over-population of lawyers in America, it is not difficult to find attorneys to take a case, even when they don't know that area of law particularly well.

You, of course, have protected yourself from such a frustrated reaction with E&O insurance, as discussed in Chapter 20. You want to give maximum help to the attorney whom your insurance company assigns to defend you. The following is a general discussion of the area of law known as copyright infringement. It is very hard to prove that a film infringes a previous work, whether the claimant is the copyright holder of a script, a treatment, or a book.

When reading the actual language in the cases, one gets the impression that this kind of lawsuit is disfavored by the courts. There is a strong public interest in promoting creativity among authors. There is also the inherent difficulty of assessing infringement claims.

The process of establishing copyright infringement involves four steps. The first two steps seldom involve serious problems, but nevertheless must be proved. The court will not just assume them to be true.

1. The person making the claim must own the copyright to the work being infringed.

2. The work must have been "copied."

3. The defendant must have had access to the pre-existing work.

4. There must be substantial similarity between the two works.

Ownership is generally proved by copyright registration, but even that is subject to attack if work-for-hire agreements have not been signed with the various people who helped to create your film. See the crew deal memo in Chapter 7 for a discussion of work for hire.

"Copied" carries a special meaning in the law of copyright. Being photographed in a film is not a copyright infringement for many copyrighted items because the form is so different. The item has not been "copied" in the sense that that word is used in copyright law. Making a movie from a script, book, or another film is exactly the kind of copying that the copyright law protects.

Access has a very special meaning in copyright infringement. The courts have defined and refined it through case law over the years. Access means the reasonable opportunity to review the copyrighted work. It is not necessary for the plaintiff to prove that the defendant actually read the copyrighted work, only that they had the reasonable opportunity to do so. Therefore, submission of a script to a studio could establish access for virtually everyone who was working in acquisitions at the studio at the time. In a case involving *Peter Pan*, the fame and frequency of the productions of this play was enough to establish access by the general public to that work. The court basically said, "C'mon, everybody knows the story of Peter Pan."

The courts rarely say so, but practitioners in the field know that the stronger the similarities, the less access needs to be shown. There is a seesaw relationship between access and substantial similarity. If you were to find a scene lifted in its entirety, word-for-word, from another script, that would itself be proof of access.

Substantial similarity is the courts' phrase to describe the situation in which two works are so similar that a jury could determine that the second work was copied from the first. If there is no substantial similarity, the case is dismissed. When one considers the plain-English meaning of the words "substantial similarity," one might think that plaintiffs would win most of these summary judgment motions. Surely, if the plaintiff and plaintiff's lawyer (and the plaintiff's circle of friends) all see substantial similarity, then the judge would at least let the case go to the jury.

Wrong!

Remember that substantial similarity, as a concept, has a legal meaning that has nothing to do with how you or I might define that term if it were up to us. Substantial similarity has been very narrowly defined by many courts over the years. It is very difficult to establish.

The first problem is that the law, as it has developed, is not really set up to deal with copyright infringement by films of a book or story. The early infringement cases dealt with one written work compared with another written work. Judges began the comparisons of written work to film with woefully inadequate case guidelines. You are stuck (as a plaintiff seeking redress) or benefited (as a defendant filmmaker fighting off a claim) by the state of law as it is today. Typically, copyright ownership and access to the work are conceded for the purpose of the summary judgment motion. The court just considers the issue of substantial similarity where they look at the different ways a given idea or theme can be expressed. The fewer ways to express an idea, the greater the similarities must be to amount to infringement. There are four steps in determining substantial similarity:

1. The plaintiff gets to dissect the work into its component parts to show the court all the areas that the plaintiff believes are substantially similar.

2. The court then decides which of the elements are protected by copyright law and which are not protected because they are facts or ideas or are otherwise in the public domain. As the cases discussed below show, this process often leaves very little to compare.

3. The court compares the protected elements in both works.

4. The court decides if there is substantial similarity between the protected elements as a result of the defendant's alleged copying of the plaintiff's work. If the substantial similarity came from the copying of unprotected material (e.g., public domain material), there is no infringement.

Some elements may be copied exactly and not be protected under copyright law. In such cases, there would be no copyright infringement. Three cases help illustrate the hurdles that have to be overcome to establish substantial similarity as it is used by the courts.

E.T. filmmaker Steven Spielberg was sued by a playwright who had submitted her play *Lokey from Maldemar* to Spielberg with the hope that a motion picture would be made out of her work. The court held that the two works were not substantially similar, even though both stories dealt with aliens from other worlds who are stranded on Earth. The court stated that the plaintiff cannot simply rely on a list of similarities. Such lists are inherently unreliable and should be approached with caution. Anyone can make a list of similarities between two films. Try it yourself as a game. List the comparisons between *Pocahontas* and *Gone With the Wind*. The court felt that no lay observer would recognize *E.T.* as *Lokey*, and that any similarity existed only at the most general level. The opening scenes with an alien coming to Earth may be similar. In fact, the court said that these scenes were more similar than stock scenes, but this did not constitute substantial similarity. The reason is that the events that flow from this general idea—an alien landing on Earth—are limited in the way that they could proceed. In fact, there are only three obvious possibilities: The aliens could be warmly welcomed, the aliens could be feared, or the aliens could arrive unnoticed. Each of these three possibilities carries its own set of subpossibilities, but there are finite choices. The courts call these scenes a faire. **Scenes a faire** is a fancy legal term that means that the scenes flow naturally from the general premise, so they are not protected by the law of copyright and copyright infringement.

Scenes a faire contain certain elements that come with the territory, so to speak. They are removed from the plot (at Step 2 above) before the court commences the substantial-similarity analysis. Scenes a faire are not protectable because they necessarily result from the choice of setting or situation. The film has copyright protection. The scenes a faire within the film are not protected, just as any facts contained in the film because facts are in the public domain and therefore cannot be protected. Both scenes a faire and public domain material can be used as elements of other films.

So, in the *E.T.* case, the plaintiffs lost. The same reasoning failed the plaintiffs in the next case, which was based on fact instead of fiction.

It is even harder to establish substantial similarity when the works are based on true events. The author of the book *Fort Apache* brought a suit alleging copyright infringement against the producers and screenwriter of the motion picture *Fort Apache: The Bronx*. Both stories take place in the early 1970s at the 41st Precinct, in the borough of the Bronx, New York City. Nicknamed "Fort Apache" by officers who worked there, the 41st Precinct had a reputation for a high incidence of violent crime since the late 1960s, and had attracted the attention of the press and other news media. The book's author was a New York City police officer who worked in the 41st Precinct in 1971 and 1972 and based his 1976 book on his experiences on the job.

Both the book and the movie begin with a prostitute shooting two police officers in their squad car with a handgun at close range; both depict cockfights, drunks, stripped cars, prostitutes, and rats; both feature, as central characters, third- or fourth-generation Irish policemen who live in Queens and frequently drink; both show disgruntled, demoralized police officers and unsuccessful foot chases of fleeing criminals.

However, the court felt that these similarities relate to uncopyrightable material. The killing of the two police officers actually occurred and was reported in the news media, which placed the historical fact of the murders in the public domain and beyond the scope of copyright protection. The court held that the filmmakers, who had also reviewed the newspaper articles, had not infringed on the book's story. Foot chases, prostitutes, shoot-outs, and the vermin associated with a story based on factual events in an urban police situation are scenes a faire that are not protected by copyright.

The author of *Fort Apache* had a separate story in each chapter so that, as a whole, the work was disconnected. In contrast, the movie *Fort Apache: The Bronx* linked many of the incidents together. For example, a prostitute who has murdered some police officers earlier in the film returns later to encounter other police officers, who kill her. A fact-based movie can still be protected by copyright because those facts are put in a particular order and arranged and depicted in a certain way. The facts, however, remain in the public domain.

Let's now examine a case in which the plaintiff won. The case is unusual because it is one of the rare cases that involves a comparison of film against film. The defendant filmmakers seemed to go out of their way to underscore the links between their film and the film that was being ripped off.

It concerned Universal's legendary movie *Jaws*. In an attempt to ride *Jaws'* wave of success, a low-budget movie production called *Great White* surfaced to catch some of the financial spillover. Both *Jaws* (released June, 1975) and *Great White* (released March, 1982) are fictional stories about a great white shark that terrorizes inhabitants of a town on the Atlantic seaboard.

The court stopped the release of *Great White* and dismissed the defendant's motion for summary judgment. This case shows that when a person uses many of the specific details of someone else's film, this is copyright infringement. The extent of similarity was overwhelming. The plot, the main characters, the development of major story points, and the sequence of incidents were so substantial that a copying of the work obviously had taken place.

- Both movies opened with teenagers playing on the beach and underwater shots of a swimmer (*Jaws*) or a windsurfer (*Great White*) that are accompanied by bass tones that build up tension to indicate the shark approaching its first victim.

- Both movies end with the skipper being eaten by the shark and the police chief (*Jaws*) or shark expert (*Great White*) killing the shark, which swallows an explosive device.

- For each major character in *Jaws*, there is a similar character in *Great White*, including skippers with English accents, a shark, a shark expert, and a politician.

- The action and theme of both films are similar: The shark expert and skipper, with motives of financial gain, try to kill the shark and characters try to bait the shark with raw meat at the end of a pier, but part of the pier breaks off and they fall in the water. The political figure attempts to downplay the shark attacks.

The court pointed out that *Great White*'s main character was Peter Benton, and the name of the author of *Jaws* was Peter Benchley. Even though titles are not protected by copyright, the opinion considered that *Great White* was made from a screenplay originally titled *The Last Jaws*. Neither of these two facts have anything to do with substantial similarity, but it is just this kind of brazen attitude that causes defendants to lose their lawsuits. Here, the defendant's film was enjoined from further exhibition. It was ordered off the market. It has no more economic value.

WHAT IF THE COPYRIGHT TO YOUR
FILM IS INFRINGED?

As an independent filmmaker, you might find yourself on the plaintiff's side of such a contest. You might be hard at work on a project or you may have a fully developed script that you have been shopping around Hollywood for years. Suddenly you begin receiving congratulatory calls from friends who saw in the trades that a film that sounds like your movie is being made or saw a trailer for what they were sure was your film.

The first thing you feel is a stab to your heart. The upset and disappointment are hard to describe. You check it out. It is true. Your dreams are dashed by a bad imitation of what you were going to make. Then, you spring into action. You sue.

On whichever side you land, be sure to obtain an expert litigator familiar with this particular area of the law. Your lawyer must be conversant with the cases and principles discussed above. Before you ever go in to see the attorney, make a list of similarities between the two works. Analyze them based on character, theme, setting, point of view (who's telling the story), plot, mood/tone, and type (drama, comedy, mystery). If you find dialogue similarities, be sure to note them. Matters that are identical are particularly important. However, as noted above, the courts do not look with a great deal of favor on lists of random similarities when they make the threshold decision of substantial similarity.

As you make this list, be mindful of which similarities are your creations and which flow naturally from the situation. Remember that when an alien comes to Earth, there are only three language choices: It learns the language quickly and easily, it never learns the language, or something in between.

Write a separate memo on access. Exactly why do you think that the filmmaker had a chance to view your work? Add in any other little tidbits concerning the possibility of access, such as an executive moving from one studio to another. Often, it is an internal studio memo that provides the smoking gun.

Finally, and perhaps most importantly, make a list of the differences. Eventually, this bridge must be crossed. A lawyer is more likely to take your case if you are being realistic and helpful. No one likes surprises, especially in a litigation situation. So look at the differences as thoroughly (if not as passionately) as you look at the similarities.

Substantial similarity is a very difficult concept to sell to a judge. Judges tend to lean toward finding works to be not substantially similar, even when experts are brought in to crystallize the similarities. Be aware that you will have to spend time and money to file the case and fight the defendant's motion for summary judgment. Studios and their insurance companies have an army of lawyers to fight off such attacks, a stack of summary judgment motions to be filed, and they do not quickly offer settlements.

CHAPTER 24

COPYRIGHT ON THE INTERNET

For the second edition, my editor wanted a chapter about copyright on the Internet. "It's the big, new thing," he said. "It's the cutting edge," he said. "Sure, sure," I said, but what I meant was, "Nobody knows anything. The landscape is changing so fast that all I can do is point out a few issues." But it probably was a good idea to include such a chapter, so that no one thinks that they now know everything there is to know about copyright. In this third edition I will fix the things that I got wrong, cover a few new things that I now know, and try to explain why this is all still so unpredictable.

THE INTERNET: THE STRONG, NEW FORCE IN THE ENTERTAINMENT INDUSTRY

When we say Internet, we mean that collection of rights for digitally transmitted materials that include broadband, private secure networks, cell phones, PDAs, iPods, and the "traditional Internet." To distribute a work on the Internet requires separate and specific authority to do so, in the same way that separate and specific authority is needed to distribute your film on television or through videocassettes.

This may seem so basic and obvious that it doesn't need to be said, but a lot of people have forgotten a fundamental fact: The Internet is a relatively new and separately licensed medium. Some thought they could throw your movie on the Internet, just because they had some sort of distribution rights.

Don't feel bad if you were among the folks gazing into a picture of the Internet future without stopping to think of this fundamental truth. Even *The New York Times*, which hires many freelance writers, became seduced by this vision. In its old freelance agreement, *The New York Times* had the right to print an article in the newspaper, but the author retained the copyright and the right to any exploitation of the material other than the newspaper. When *The New York Times* launched an Internet edition of its newspaper, it reprinted the entire newspaper on the Internet without asking freelance authors for permission, without paying those authors, and without remorse. *The Times* never looked back.

Great for readers addicted to the Internet. The freelance writers who worked laboriously on their articles were not so happy. They owned the copyrights, so they felt entitled to extra compensation or at least the right to say "yea" or "nay" to the Internet idea.

The writers sued.

The writers won . . . in court.

The New York Times got the last laugh, however. They said, "Fine, give us a free license for the additional Internet use of your material or you won't ever write for this newspaper again. We'll strip your articles off the Internet, apologize for that oversight, and not print another word of yours until you come around to our way of looking at things." Pretty powerful stuff. As near as I can tell, pretty effective, also.

YOUR LESSON: When you acquire the right to any element of your film, including all materials, performances, effects, clips, pieces of music, and underlying property, you want to be sure to acquire the right to retain the clip, music, or underlying property no matter how it is exploited, even if it is exploited over the Internet. The forms in this book accomplish that purpose. Many old contracts cover this exploitation possibility of a film with a fairly common phrase that has brought a smile to many a non-lawyer. The phrase is "by any means, whether now known or hereafter created." Somebody was thinking ahead.

YOUR OTHER LESSON: When you license your film to others, you can retain or grant Internet rights. Internet rights don't automatically flow to a distributor of your films. Read on to learn how these rights or some piece of them might be much more valuable to you if you retain and exploit them yourself.

THE INTERNET IS FREE, NOT THE STUFF THAT IS ON IT

Many folks believe they can just take anything off the Internet and use it any way they feel like. It is on the Internet. That means that it is free for the taking ... and the using ... and whatever ... without having to pay anything to anyone.

Wrong.

You still need the same old licenses that you always needed from the copyright holder in order to incorporate what you saw or heard into your film. You can't use something in your film just because it is on the Internet. The old copyright laws still apply.

When I say this to my clients, the two most common responses are: "It's all over the Internet. It must be in the public domain." Or, "Well, how does so-and-so get away with using it?" There are five possibilities, and only the last two possibilities are sure to present no problem if you use something without permission:

1. So-and-so is using it with permission. You really can't tell by looking at a program whether the proper permissions were obtained.

2. So-and-so doesn't have permission; so-and-so has a big headache because he or she just got one of those threatening

letters from a lawyer representing the material's copyright owner. Yikes!

3. So-and-so doesn't have permission, but the owner—who has other things to do—doesn't know. Just wait until he or she finds out.

4. So-and-so doesn't have permission and the copyright owner knows, but just doesn't care.

5. So-and-so is using it and it is really in the public domain.

If you spend time and are able to provide clear evidence that possibility #4 is true or that there are a lot of high-visibility users who have used the item over a fairly long period of time and have not received so much as a letter, you might be able to get insurance coverage because the risk of the copyright owner coming after you is so small.

The big problem with items you find on the Internet is that identifying their copyright owners can be very difficult. This means the item might be an orphan work. Right now, that is no help to you in your efforts to create something new and different using the item you think is an orphan work. But, to find out legislative relief that might be coming along fairly quickly, check out the section on orphan works in Chapter 4, Public Domain.

In a nutshell, you can only take things off the Internet for your own personal use, including research for your film, viewing on your big screen, or listening in the comfort of your home or car. If you have any doubt about this, consider the $3,740,000 award Playboy won against a San Diego-based company for distributing over the Internet almost 7,500 photographs owned by Playboy. Some of the photos were obtained from other Internet user groups that traded the digital photographs. The judge arrived at the figure by valuing each photograph at $500. That should make you think twice before entering into such a scheme.

Napster, eBay, TiVo, YouTube, and Others that Provide Cool Things Through the Internet

Many people wonder why the file-swapping services of Napster put the company out of business, while eBay prospers even though copyrights and personal rights are sometimes violated by the sale of stuff over the eBay system. These high-visibility cases cast a confusing shadow over the one question that consumers are most concerned with: "What can I do on the Internet and with the stuff I find there?"

In truth, your life is not much affected by the ongoing legal battles between the large companies that facilitate what you do and that create the software and the hardware that you use to do what you do. Because those cases are so in the news, I will spend enough time on them to show you why they don't affect you.

The Digital Millennium Copyright Act provides a safe harbor for the likes of eBay because eBay has a system in place for investigating and knocking off vendors once eBay receives notice of problems with the products being sold. Such a notice must be in writing from the legitimate owner of the violated rights. Then the vendor is given a limited time to respond. This system allows eBay to stay in business even though some of its vendors are occasionally shut down.

Napster, on the other hand, refused to recognize the rights of copyright holders, held copyrighted songs on its master server, and, therefore, was found to be actively aiding in the unauthorized swapping of copyrighted songs among its subscribers. The court said that was a "no-no." So Napster shut down under the burden of a $200,000,000-plus judgment against it. Almost immediately, other services grew up that facilitated the same result without storing the songs on a master server and without even knowing who was giving what to whom. It is the law of the technological jungle that as soon as one perceived dragon is slain, one or two other dragons will pop up that do just about the same thing. Innovation happens.

TiVo and SONICblue let viewers record programs without knowing anything more than the name of the program. The devices capture programs whenever they air, extend the recording time if a program runs over, and tells you about similar programs, just in case you are interested. SONICblue was in litigation with all the major studios and the networks because it added features that automatically skip over the commercials and allow its customers to send programs to other customers over the internet. TiVo wisely sat back and let the fireworks occur. In the meantime, the expense of the litigation contributed to SONICblue having to file protection with the bankruptcy court. The parties settled, so these questions were not answered, but TiVO and other DVRs haven't implemented the content-sharing function that made SONICblue so cool.

Telephone companies and folks who inadvertently help people get to a site where they can obtain infringing materials have avoided liability under the copyright laws because of rules protecting common carriers and the requirement for substantial participation in infringement before one is liable. This situation probably will not change, because the accused parties are essentially innocent participants in a process that only leads to infringing activity in a tiny percentage of the traffic on their systems.

WHEN YOUR FILM SLIPS INTO INTERNET LAND

If you discover infringing copies of your movie on the Internet, the Independent Film and Television Alliance® (IFTA®) has some good suggestions. The *IFTA® Practical Guide to Copyright Protection* states (and I agree) that you should take the following steps.

1. Identify the Internet Service Provider (ISP) of the unauthorized user so you know who to contact to remove or block the infringing material and potentially establish liability for the infringement. Identifying the end infringer may be too difficult in a peer-to-peer system due to the

possibility of multiple end infringers whose identities may be difficult to discover. A notice to the ISP is usually the most cost-effective solution.

2. Determine the law(s) and remedies available in the country where the infringing website is located.

- Depending on the national copyright law of the country where the website is located, a website proprietor may be legally obligated to provide the identity and contact information of the end infringer. In any case, you should demand such information, and a proprietor may provide it even without any legal obligation.

- Determine whether the local law provides for ISP liability or for safe harbors for the ISP when infringing copies are posted on their site by an unrelated third party. Also determine if the applicable law(s) provide for notice and takedown procedures with which the ISP must comply.

- Determine whether the website provides a "Term of Use" or some similar type link that lists available procedures in the event of an infringement on the site. Most websites outline procedures to block or remove offending material.

- YouTube has an automatic video monitoring service called "Claim Your Content," which will automatically identify copyrighted material and remove it from its site.

3. If the website or network provides any contact information for the proprietors of the website, contact them in writing to notify them of the offending content and demand that such content be removed or blocked. Also include a demand of the identity and contact information of the end infringer.

4. If no contact information is provided on the website: Use online tracking resources such as www.dnsstuff.com to find information, such as the domain name proprietor(s), the domain name registrar or registering agency, if any, and the

website ISP. The search result will often vary depending on the information contained in the search database. An infringing website may register the domain name through a registering agency (e.g., Domains by Proxy) commonly used to intentionally conceal the domain name proprietor's identity and contact information. However, the tracking tools provide a solid basis to begin the search.

5. Send a Notice of Infringement letter similar to Form 24-01. Although the letter contains copyright infringement notification requirements of the DMCA, you may also use the letter as a template for copyright infringement notification worldwide.

INTERNET RESOURCES FOR THE FILMMAKER

The Internet can help your film in four primary ways: Research, Licensing, Communicating with the Copyright Office, and Advertising.

Research on Your Film's Subject and Potential Cast and Crew

For this purpose, you can think of the Internet as the biggest library in the world. If you know how to do it, you can browse to your heart's content. As with any other research tool, you can use all of the facts you gather to create your own original work. Remember to make a note of your sources. You may need them for the script annotation that is required by many studios for fact-based films, and you may need to know the sources of your facts in your discussions with the insurance company.

Several resources are available for seeking out information about film-industry types. The best source for credits is IMDb .com (Internet Movie Database). This is an advertiser-supported service that is incredibly complete, though occasionally inaccurate.

You can type in almost anyone's name and find out the films they were in and the credits they received. Beware of someone who says that they really produced a picture, but their credit was as an associate producer. A whole lot of people didn't earn the producer credit that they were awarded. Few receive a credit that is less than what they actually did on the picture.

Another fine resource is iFilm.com. It offers information similar to IMDb but not as broad a range or as complete.

Licensing Artwork and Film Clips

Almost every business in the country has a website today. Even lawyers have websites. Most, if not all, of the various services from which you can license photos, artwork, and film clips have websites. On most of those websites you can view materials and then, usually, order and pay for the materials over the Internet. I have tried to include e-mail addresses for many of these resources in this book. You can find them in the chapters dealing with the kind of item you want to obtain. Use them.

Interfacing with the Copyright Office

This process is fully explained in the chapter on registering your script with the Copyright Office. Once you use it, you may never go back to the old way of ordering the forms through the mail or—worse yet—running to the post office to pick up the forms you need. You can go to www.copyright.gov/forms to pull up all the forms that you need. For more general information, go to www.loc.gov/copyright. It has an enormous amount of helpful information about the copyright law and about the Copyright Office and its procedures.

You can also use the website of the Copyright Office to find out who owns what. You can very quickly find out who owns a property if it is a matter of public record. This process is a big boon to strapped and time-pressed filmmakers. Nonetheless, their electronic database is not complete as it does not contain every item registered with the Copyright Office before 1978. Chapter 20 refers you to Thomson and Thomson CompuMark. This company still has a big role to play in tracking such rights because it has a huge library of information and can determine the copyright owner of older properties. Its library even includes a lot of newspaper and magazine references because people with an interest in a property often will issue a press release before they file anything with the Copyright Office.

Advertising and Marketing Your Film Project

No savvy filmmaker overlooks the Internet as an effective medium for promoting a film. The classic example of this is *The Blair Witch Project*. The long lead-up and the mystique that were built on the Internet were phenomenal. When the filmmakers came to me, I wasn't very Internet savvy. I took a look at their project and made an old-fashioned judgment to pass on it because it looked like a mess to me. Well, maybe it was a mess, but the film, produced for a few hundred thousand dollars, grossed over $150,000,000 in worldwide box office receipts. Those numbers make *Blair Witch* the best return on investment of any film ever made. And it is all because of the filmmakers' promotional efforts on the Internet.

When you set up your website and select a domain name, make your selection based on a legitimate connection to your project—usually the title of your movie. The law surrounding domain names is still developing, but it is clear that you cannot trade off someone else's name for commercial gain. You cannot mislead or confuse the public. The good thing is that in order to resolve disputes, registrants must use speedy and relatively inexpensive arbitration procedures that have been set up through the World Intellectual Property Organization Arbitration and Mediation Center. This arbitration is binding unless you fail to file a court case to confirm the award within 10 days of receiving your decision from the arbitrator.

BE CAREFUL ABOUT GRANTING
INTERNET DISTRIBUTION RIGHTS

Because of the pervasiveness of the Internet, most distributors are pushing hard for the right to include Internet distribution along with all the rights they want to acquire. There are a lot of reasons for this, but the main reason is that there has got to be money in them thar hills. Even if not a buck is made today, there surely will be many bucks to be made sometime in the future. The promise of video-on-demand (VOD) is already being fulfilled by a variety of suppliers.

Video-on-demand is a phrase that covers several different technological developments that will make it possible for you and I to select our motion pictures for the evening from hundreds of thousands of titles and order them and receive them instantly in the comfort of our homes. MGM, Paramount, Sony, Universal, Disney, Miramax Lions Gate, and Warner Bros. have formed a joint venture called Movielink to offer an almost unlimited selection of films over the Internet. Other enterprises will pop up either over the traditional Internet or satellite broadcast or private, secure systems, or something that has not yet been created.

In selling your film to a distributor, you will often split the foreign and domestic rights. You can split television rights between a foreign sales agent and a domestic distributor because the territories are different. The Internet crosses all these political boundaries. That is part of the beauty of it. For you, it makes it imperative that you give the Internet distribution rights to only one entity. Today, every distributor wants to grab these rights from you at the earliest possible time.

In reaching for Internet rights, many distributors will tell you truthfully that they send trailers and sometimes the entire film to potential buyers around the world using secure Internet lines. This is true. This, however, does not require that you give them Internet distribution rights. It only requires that you give them permission, in writing (as part of the contract), to send the entire film, the trailer, or selected clips to their clients around the world through the Internet for the limited purpose of selling those clients the rights to further distribute the film in their territories. That permission is a lot narrower than the unfettered right to distribute your film on the Internet.

USING THE INTERNET TO SELL YOUR DVDS

And here is the big news for filmmakers. Today it is quite possible to distribute your film over the Internet without anybody in the middle. When you consider how few filmmakers are happy with their distributors, you might consider this approach. My clients who have tried it think that they earned more money with less aggravation than going through conventional DVD distributors. They all used the services of Peter Broderick, a consultant to independent filmmakers. Peter's company, Paradigm Consulting, is located in Santa Monica, California.

Filmmakers have turned to Peter for four very specific reasons.

1. Loss of control. After enjoying 100% control over the creation of a film (if you are truly an independent film-maker), you have 0% control when you turn your film over to a distributor. After a tough negotiation, you may get some pretty decent consultation rights, but that is a far cry from control.

2. Even if you are lucky enough to get a theatrical distribu-tion guarantee, you will find it very difficult to enforce if the first weekend's box office does not go well. Those promised additional weeks simply won't happen.

3. If you give all the DVD rights to your distributor, the DVDs will usually be distributed by their own subsidiary or by a company with whom they have an output deal, which may not necessarily be the best company for your picture and not necessarily run by folks who are passionate about

your film. Your picture may be just another product to fill a pipeline.

4. And then there is Hollywood accounting. Do I really need to take up space in this book to tell you about Hollywood accounting?

The best way to hang on to the right to sell DVDs of your film over the Internet is to ask to be able to sell videos on your website. Most video distributors will say "yes." They figure that it will never amount to a hill of beans, and those will be sales that they don't get anyway. Some distributors know that their retail sales might even increase if you effectively promote your film online to core audiences. Everybody wins when the pie gets bigger. Then the big issue in the negotiation will be what you have to pay them for the DVDs that you buy to sell from your website. Try to get them down to $4 or less. I have gotten this price as low as $2.50 fully packaged, but that was unusual. Some distributors have sold them to filmmakers at cost, which should be under a dollar.

Now do a little math. Most self-distributed DVDs go for about $24.95 or $29.95. Every time you sell 10,000 copies, it is going to produce over $200,000 after the cost of goods sold. I can tick off a number of titles that I represented and Peter consulted on that sold several tens of thousands. They were all independent films, mostly documentaries, and you probably haven't heard of one of them.

A great example is *Faster*, Mark Neale's documentary on motorcycle racing. While *Faster* was in theatres, the filmmakers started selling a "preview edition" DVD (the entire film with no extras) from their website. They sold over 13,000 DVDs at $24.95 plus shipping and handling. Then they made a deal with New Video to distribute the "ultimate collector's edition" (a two-disc set with 2½ hours of additional materials) to stores, Amazon and other online retailers, and Netflix. The filmmakers also started selling this edition from their website (offering a free T-shirt to anyone who had previously purchased the preview edition).

The filmmakers sold more than 7,000 copies of this edition from their website, and New Video (thanks in part to the promotional efforts of the filmmakers online) sold more than 50,000 DVDs. Mark Neale then made a second film about motorcycle racing, *The Doctor, The Tornado, and The Kentucky Kid*, and again used the strategy of first selling the film directly from the website and then in retail.

If you want to go this route, consulting with Peter or other experts in the field can be very helpful and is well worth the money. He can help you design and implement a distribution strategy customized to your film and your core audience(s). John Sloss has set up a new sales company in New York called Cinetic Rights Management that will focus exclusively on the Internet and all the new media outlets. Without-a-Box in Los Angeles is also trying to help independent filmmakers to exploit their films in ways that do not involve a theatrical distribution deal.

The earlier you have a sophisticated distribution strategy, the better. It may be crucial to getting your film financed. Investors will be impressed if they believe you can sell 50,000 DVDs (netting over $1 million) from your website, no matter what happens with traditional distributors. You can read all about it in an article entitled *Maximizing Distribution*, available on Peter's website (www.peterbroderick.com). He is also writing a book to empower filmmakers to maximize revenues, audience, and impact for their films. You have to identify your core audience and figure out how to reach them. The rewards can be very satisfying. And you won't have to join the chorus of complainers singing the blues about the fact that no one saw their movie.

USING THE INTERNET TO SELL DOWNLOADS OF YOUR FILM

Taking all of the above one step further, consider the possibility of selling downloads of your films over the Internet in addition to selling DVDs. Netfilx and other companies are already in this business. The studios are all tiptoeing into this distribution channel, too. Why shouldn't you? It is not particularly difficult if you delegate all the technical setup stuff to your web host. If you visit my website, you can find a downloadable book that is a companion to the negotiating DVD that is available there.

If you think you might want to do this one day, make your reservation of right a bit broader than DVDs. Talk about the sale of DVDs to the distributor, but make the language broader so that it covers downloading also. You don't want to alarm the distributor. But, you must also be careful not to mislead either. This is a delicate dance, but the rewards could be significant in the future, especially when DVDs go the way of videotapes.

THE NEW COPYRIGHT LAWS RESPONSIVE TO THE INTERNET

Of course, no self-respecting legislative body can sit by while the people develop a widget without passing widget laws. So that is just what Congress did. They passed the Digital Millennium Copyright Act. That is a mouthful, so in this section I am going to refer to it as DMCA, like most everybody else does. It was so long and complicated and counter-intuitive that when I first sat down to read it, I gave up. Quit! I couldn't understand it, didn't believe what I thought I understood, and generally felt inadequate. If I couldn't understand the text of this important piece of legislation, how could I call myself a copyright expert?

I reviewed that legislation more carefully for the last edition of the book and for a scholarly article. I was right the first time. The DMCA is too long. It is internally inconsistent. It is counter-intuitive. It is the product of the powerful forces that have grown up around the multi-billion-dollar businesses that control copyright in creative works, such as movie studios and large record labels. Congress listens carefully to advocates of copyright holders. If you think traditional copyright holders are going to yield anything to the new playground called the Internet, you are in for a major surprise.

The movie studios are just starting to get comfortable playing in this field, but there are still a lot of things about it that scare them. Ordinary citizens can make perfect copies of their movies. Ordinary citizens can send these copies far and wide for very little money. Ordinary citizens can edit their movies using readily available, low-cost programs and devices. All of this is very scary to these behemoth corporations that are behemoths because they own and control a myriad of copyright-protected properties.

The chief purpose of the DMCA is to protect copyrights on the Internet any way the copyright holders want, including making properties inaccessible even for legitimate fair use purposes, such as writing a critique or to educate. DMCA then goes on to make illegal anything you try to do to get around the copyright protection, even if your purpose in getting around the protection is to exercise one of your fair use rights, such as criticism or private viewing, or simply to copy something in the public domain. Under this law, asking your sister for her password in order to enter a file could be considered a criminal act. Obviously, the law will not be enforced so vigorously against individual citizens, but the law is on the books, and it is—at this writing—a mess, in my opinion.

Oops. I had no sooner written those words than the record industry began filing thousands of lawsuits against its best potential group of customers who were using peer-to-peer programs to obtain free music. Many of us thought they were looking for a test case. A test case means that the case's main purpose is to obtain a judicial ruling. In fact, they settled all but one of the thousands of cases they filed for a reasonable amount and a promise not to do it again. One defendant refused to settle and lost her lawsuit to the tune of $240,000.

At the time of this writing, the recording industry is still pursuing this oddest of all strategies. Will the movie studios follow that same course? All indicators are that they will if they feel that they have to, but they are trying to work out Internet distribution themselves. They call it video-on-demand or VOD (often listed as a separate right). Watch out for those VOD rights. They are uniformly part of overall distribution deals at the present time. Retain those rights or share them, if you can.

So I scratched around some more and discovered that, indeed, the criminal provisions of the DMCA were being used. So far, the criminal provisions have only been used against folks who made a lot of bootlegged copies of videotapes, which is a totally appropriate use of the criminal law system. A California man was the first to be convicted in that state in the Spring of 2002. The U.S. Attorney in Nebraska had already obtained a conviction earlier that year. But there are those who fear the DMCA noose will tighten to include less egregious cases.

The far-reaching right to try to control access to copyright-protected materials, as opposed to controlling the copying of protected works, is new and mind-boggling to those among us who enjoy dabbling around with copyright-protected materials on their own for their own use. The major studios have gone a step further and tried to control efforts to circumvent fair use protections for even the most legitimate reasons, such as education, critiques, and comment. The good news is that the DMCA has a provision that allows anyone to apply for an exception to the draconian lock-breaking provisions of the DMCA. The Register of Copyright has hearings every three years. The next ones are set for the fall of 2009 and then the fall of 2012. As of this writing, only six exceptions have been granted. The first five grants were to circumvent on certain very narrowly defined programs. But the last round included an exception for professors of cinema who want to compile clips from films in their school's library to use in their classroom lectures. The MPAA fought hard against this "opening of the flood gates" to no avail. The next round of hearings will undoubtedly bring forth other groups seeking exemptions.

Most of the big court cases involve the rights of those big companies that manage traffic on the Internet and what they have to do when they receive take-down notices and such. As an individual player in this drama, a filmmaker can only keep current and interested, but there is not much you can do about it.

FUTURE TRENDS IN COPYRIGHT LAW
FOR THE INTERNET

It's helpful to understand how copyright law grows and changes. With copyright law, the process has become a negotiation among interested businesses (with their many lobbyists) and Congress. The public has not had much in the way of input or even the opportunity for input. It is the copyright lawyers for the studios and publishers and related businesses who work out the legislation. No wonder the law is so convoluted and often counter-intuitive. The unions wanted a mandatory royalty on recording devices to make up for lost revenue. The manufacturers resisted. They negotiated a 3% royalty on every blank tape, and Congress passed their joint solution. In this case it was a $1.00-$8.00 royalty on every tape machine, no matter how you or I are going to make use of these items.

However, a feeling is spreading that the recent amendments to the copyright law are not fair, not workable, and are not right. It is quite possible that individual citizens, who have never participated in the process before, may very well find a place at the bargaining table where legislation is crafted. Whether this will produce better legislation or just protracted wrangling is not foreseeable at this point.

Whether copyright protections will be strengthened and whether the new copyright law modification will make it clear that individual downloading and copying for the purpose of private viewing is acceptable is uncertain at this writing. It seems clear to me that criminalizing individual conduct, which most people think is a birthright, will never work. Like prohibition, such laws won't be obeyed in spite of strong efforts to enforce them. So some loosening of the DMCA restrictions on circumventing copy protection devices is sure to be sought by consumer groups.

The lobbying strength of the studios is not what it used to be. In the old days the studios made movies. When television came along, they also made television programs. When they went to Washington, they had a very high success rate in getting what they wanted from the United States Congress. In fact, Congress generally limited its work to being sure that all the studios agreed.

Today the studios are part of international conglomerates. Their interests are not always so clearly aligned. Occasionally, they are on opposite sides of a legislative issue. For instance, the most recent copyright battle was embodied in a piece of legislation introduced by Senator Ernest Hollings (Democrat of South Carolina), the Chairman of the powerful Senate Commerce Committee. His legislation would help block the unauthorized downloading of movies and music. Great for Warner Bros. studio, bad for AOL. Both companies are part of the same international conglomerate, which also is one of the country's largest print media and cable operators.

With Internet legislation, the public begins to experience copyright law first-hand and for the first time, and the public is forming opinions about what should and should not be in the copyright law. That is why this area is so vulnerable to change in the future.

There are stirrings in the land that this esoteric area of the law is no longer the exclusive domain of the copyright experts employed by large corporations. The intense press interest in the Supreme Court hearings about the copyright extension bear this out. The editor of the American Bar Association's *Entertainment and Sports Lawyer* newsletter recently wrote: "A protection racket is defined as money extorted by racketeers posing as a protective association. A racketeer obtains money by an illegal enterprise usually involving intimidation. With the advent of digital file sharing over the Internet, hard-hitting tactics by copyright owners and their lawyers are beginning to look a lot like intimidation." Pretty heavy stuff!

The prospect of readers of this book and other individuals rising up and expressing their personal views on the copyright law is exciting to me. It will create a balance in the law that has not been there in the past (and has not been sought in the past). Good luck to you in all your copyright encounters. We will be keeping general updates on the website for the book.

FORM 24-01   COPYRIGHT INFRINGEMENT NOTIFICATION

Print this on your letterhead.

Infringement Complaints under the DCMA [or other applicable law]
[Website]
[Address]
Facsimile: [Fax Number]

Re: Notification of Claimed Infringement

Dear _____:

I am writing with regard to ongoing acts of copyright infringement on the website located at [Website Address] operated by [Website] (the "Website"). In accordance with the Digital Millennium Copyright Act (or applicable law of another jurisdiction), you are provided with the following notification of claimed infringement:

Overview of Claimed Infringement:

I am the owner of the copyright in the audiovisual work entitled "_____" (the "Picture"). The Picture has been registered in the United States Copyright Office on _____ with registration no. _____.

[Website] is engaged in ongoing acts of direct and contributory copyright infringement by allowing third parties to post unauthorized copies the Picture on the Website and then making such copies available for public access without authorization from me. Specifically, on _____, 200_, I examined the Website and found that [Website] has posted or continued to post unauthorized copies of the Picture on the Website.

[Set forth any additional infringing acts.]

I have not authorized any person to post any copy of the Picture on the Website. Moreover, I have not authorized [Website] to make any copy of the Picture available on the website.

I demand that the Picture identified above be removed immediately from the Website. I note that the Picture was posted on the Website on a regular basis. I have not authorized and have no intention of authorizing any party to post the Picture on the Website. Moreover, you now know that I own the copyright in the Picture. Therefore, conducting such a search using the search feature on the Website on a routine basis provides you with information reasonably sufficient to permit you to locate material that infringes my copyright. As such, I request and expect that you will adopt ongoing procedures to ensure that such infringing material, if again posted on the Website, is timely identified and removed from the Website.

If you have any questions or comments regarding the contents of this notification, you may contact Owner or me at the following locations;

<u>Contact for Owner</u>:
[Name]
[Address]
Facsimile: [Fax Number]

<u>Contact for Legal Counsel</u>:
[Name]
[Address]
Facsimile: [Fax Number]

This letter is not necessarily a full statement of my rights or remedies in the matter, all of which rights and remedies are expressly reserved.

Very truly yours,

Owner

You can download this form at www.clearanceandcopyright.com Use the code: ibotCC3

CHAPTER 25

INTERNATIONAL COPYRIGHT

I meet with clients all the time who are befuddled about the possibility of problems with their film in foreign territories. Given the fact that each country has its own different set of copyright laws, international copyright can be a very confusing topic. However, a basic understanding of a few simple concepts will help prepare you for talking to a lawyer about your specific international copyright problem.

THE BIG PICTURE

Keep in mind that copyright law is a western concept, which falls under the umbrella of "Intellectual property law," distinct from the law that protects tangible objects.

The international copyright legal system really has two parts—the treaties that link different countries together (and provide for some minimum standards) and national laws that provide the substances of the protection. The good thing about national laws is that you will be treated the same way under those national laws as a citizen of the country is treated. This is called "national treatment." There's a complication here that probably needs to be acknowledged: Although "**national treatment**" is the general rule, it doesn't always apply, especially with respect to issues of ownership, which usually are controlled by the law of the country of origin. **Country of origin** means the country where the work was created. Even if a screenwriter travels around while writing, one country must be selected as the country of origin. In the screenwriter example, it is usually the legal residence of the writer.

Historically, there was separation between the copyright regimes of France (and other countries in Continental Europe) and Great Britain (and those that followed her approach)—a separation that was wider than the English Channel. These varied copyright systems initially sprung from two different legal traditions—mainly the common law for the English and the civil law for the Continent. Generally, the Anglo-American concept was of an instrument of commerce to help proliferate intellectual-property works in the market, whereas the Continental concept champions authors' rights and emphasizes the need for authors to have continuing control over their works. Lately, these two very different systems are morphing so that Continental Europe seems to be headed toward a more pragmatic version of the Anglo-American model, one that increasingly translates into greater use of copyright protection, more infringement claims, and tougher penal sanctions for both legal systems. The copyright laws of the Anglos addressed the needs of the author through protection, but the primary financial benefits seem to drift to larger and larger corporations in these property-driven, profit-driven economies.

To thrive in either copyright regime, one must be a "rights-holder." Without this claim to "property," copyright is futile. Currently, we witness harsher international and national laws, and more severe judicial pronouncements against infringers, matched with greater penal sanctions. I try to avoid judging these trends, partly because they have spawned a broader interest in the subject matter covered by *Clearance and Copyright* than I ever imagined possible when I wrote the first edition of the book in the early '90s.

In both systems, it is the expression of ideas that merit that protection, and in both systems, the work must be created by an author. The bar for obtaining copyright protection is higher in Continental Europe than in the United States as to what qualifies as a creative effort. And speaking of honoring true creativity, the Continental European system does not recognize the possibility of original works coming from sources other than the individual author, whereas we here in the United States have the work-for-hire provisions that artificially put a corporation (employer) at the keyboard of your computer.

Additionally, in contrast to the Anglo-American tradition, the Continental European system celebrates moral rights and does not allow them to be waived. More on that later in this chapter.

START WITH WHAT YOU KNOW

Let's start with an example completely outside the film or publishing industries. Suppose you are a citizen of the United States and you live in Chicago. You go to London and rent a German car to see the sights. You have some problems remembering to drive on the left side of the road, but all in all you do pretty well. Unfortunately, not everyone makes the conversion as well as you, and a Frenchman rear-ends you. You sue the driver since the accident was his fault.

Here comes the $10,000 question (or about £5000 at the time of this writing, since we are, hypothetically, in England): Where do you bring your lawsuit? Since you are American, do you have to go back to the U.S. or France or Germany and sue the driver in one of those countries?

Most people get this question right: since the accident happened in England, the lawsuit also belongs in England. Now here comes the bonus question: Does American law or British law govern the case?

This one is a little tougher, but you will probably guess correctly on this one also. Here's the answer: British law applies on British soil. Since your accident happened on British soil, British law applies. So your lawsuit happens in England, with British law providing the framework for you to sue.

Now you should be able to transfer that to intellectual property. Keep asking, "Where did the accident happen?" It's not a perfect analogy, but it will help to keep you focused in a variety of circumstances. If a French filmmaker copies your film in England without your permission, you will probably want to prevent them from doing that, and the best way to do it is through the courts. Since the infringement happened on English soil, you would have to bring suit in the English courts, and English copyright law would apply . . . just like the auto accident example. It does not matter that your film was created in the United States. What matters is where the infringing act in question happened . . . where the accident happened. Since copying was the act of infringement and that act took place on English territory, the lawsuit must be brought in England under English law. Get it? Good.

The same analysis applies when you use a clip of a foreign film in your own film. If your American film is being distributed and exhibited in the U.S., American law applies. If the foreign filmmaker thinks you are illegally using a clip from their film, they would have to sue in the U.S. under American law. If your film or television show gained distribution in a foreign country, the filmmaker could sue in that country under that country's law—but only for the specific acts performed in that country. In this example, the act would be the distribution and exhibition of your film, so that is the act that could be stopped in that country. Remember, what matters is *where the alleged activity was conducted*, not where the work was created, or where the creators reside.

The implications for licensing can be deeply troubling if you're a stickler because you need to be in compliance with the laws of various countries where your film may be distributed. That would be quite a burden. Most filmmakers (in my experience) don't worry about it because, in most cases, copyright damages are much more under control than in the U.S. They know that the worst that can happen if they make a mistake is that they will be required to pay a reasonable licensing fee.

VIVE LES DIFFERENCES

Now you know that copyright law is different in each country. Something that is against the law here might be legal elsewhere, and vice versa. The *really* confusing part of international copyright comes at the point where the law between two countries differs substantially.

To prevent situations like this from happening, nations from around the world got together and signed a **treaty**. A **treaty** is simply a contract between one or more nations. Each nation that signs the treaty is called a member nation.

The treaties say that the member nations would standardize certain basic tenets of their copyright laws. In essence, it set minimum requirements that each member country had to have. These requirements mostly have to do with what kind of works receive copyright protection, when copyright first applies to a work, and the length of the copyright term—the building blocks of any copyright law. This treaty was deemed the **Berne Convention** in honor of the city in which the meetings first began (Berne, Switzerland). The first meeting of the Berne Convention concluded in 1886, but the United States did not become a member for more than 100 years—1989 to be exact. (Some slight differences in requiring notice prevented us from doing so; these were brought into compliance in 1989, and the U.S. became a member nation.) There are other treaties that establish minimum copyright protection between countries. The Universal Copyright Convention (UCC) and The Agreement on Trade Related Aspects of Intellectual Property Rights (TRIPS) are the most important treaties behind the Berne Convention.

TRIPS is an international agreement administered by the World Trade Organization (WTO) that sets down minimum standards for many forms of intellectual property regulation. The TRIPS agreement introduced intellectual property law into the international trading system for the first time, and remains the most comprehensive international agreement on intellectual property to date. TRIPS has all the substantive provisions of Berne, except those on moral rights. Several countries that are not members of the Berne Convention are signatories to the UCC (which has lesser standards than Berne), in addition to a number of nations who are Berne signatories.

The Berne Convention said that each member would recognize copyrighted works from other member nations as soon as the country in which the work was created recognized it as copyrighted. We know from Chapter 1 that your work is protected in the United States as soon as you fix it in a tangible medium of expression. Because the United States is a member of the Berne Convention, that means that once your work is fixed in a tangible form, you gain copyright protection in all of the member nations of the Berne Convention at the same time. That's more than 130 countries! Pretty cool, huh? What's more, many European countries (and those that derive their laws from Europe) don't have such a fixation requirement. Therefore, unfixed U.S. works would technically be protected in those countries, even though they don't enjoy copyright here. That's even cooler, although I personally think that such protection in unfixed works is of slim value because of the difficulty in proving what was created if it never was fixed.

Even Russia has become a party to the Berne Convention and a member of the World Trade Organization (and, thus, a party to TRIPS). So U.S. works still enjoy protection in Russia because of these treaties, although the rampant piracy in Russia shows that the Russians still have a lot to figure out in the copyright enforcement department. You actually have to reach pretty deep in the barrel to find a country that isn't bound by the basic provisions of Berne and TRIPS (my usual example is North Korea).

There are many other international copyright conventions, agreements, and treaties that have been signed by various nations. They include the bilateral copyright arrangements between just two countries and other trade agreements that include copyright obligations.

The United States is obligated in one form or other, under all of these treaties and agreements, to provide protection for works of foreign nationals in the United States under the basic principle of **national treatment**. In return, the United States receives protection for U.S. works and sound recordings abroad because of the obligation of other countries to these treaties. **National treatment** means that a country that has signed a treaty must provide—at a minimum—the same level of copyright protection for foreign nationals as it provides for its own nationals under domestic law. So, an American author is provided the full panoply of protection under French copyright law and in the same manner, as is provided for French authors and under French law. This is because France is a member of the Berne Convention, and even has a bilateral copyright agreement with the United States since 1891.

The Berne Convention standardized many aspects of copyright law around the globe. But there are still differences, some of which are important enough to mention. The Berne Convention did not harmonize the term of copyright. That's why Canadian works (for example) don't get life plus 70 years in the EU.

Also, there are scattered idiosyncrasies across nations. For instance, the character Peter Pan is in the public domain in the United States due to its age. However, the Parliament of Great Britain has given *Peter Pan* special status so that it has permanent copyright protection within Britain. Steven Spielberg had to make peace with the Great Ormond Street Children's Hospital in London before he could distribute the film *Hook* (which is clearly a derivative of *Peter Pan*) in Great Britain. It owns the copyright to the story *Peter Pan* and all the characters in it. Special circumstances sometimes apply to certain works or in certain countries, so it is best to have an experienced copyright attorney involved if you think you are dealing with something like this.

For me, one of the most interesting differences is how each country defines the author of a work if there is no specific written document. Because there is such a wide variation, there is almost always a written contract among everybody assigning rights to a company so that one person or entity is in control of the copyright. This can be important when you are trying to figure out who is the holder of the moral rights because moral rights are held by authors personally.

In all countries in Europe, the director is always one of the authors of a motion picture. And then it becomes a real random mix. One or more of the cinematographers, the screenwriter, and the composer are often included. There's another wrinkle, too: In most of these countries the producer is treated as the person entitled, in the absence of a contrary agreement, to exploit all the "economic" rights in the film.

The problem of authorship expands when there are two or more people working on a script, a song, or a book. What constitutes a joint author and what that means to the individuals involved are wildly different from one country to another. The U.S. rules are outlined in Chapter 8, but those rules are for the U.S. only.

For Americans considering (or fearing) litigation on foreign soil, the biggest single difference between the U.S. and anywhere else in the world is the size of the damages and the cost of litigation. Both are substantially higher in the U.S. than anywhere else in the world.

MORAL RIGHTS

The most glaring difference between international copyright laws concerns something the French call *droit moral*, or moral rights. **Moral rights** are concerned with protecting the personality and reputation of authors. These are to be distinguished from the economic rights in a work, which are involved in most other copyright provisions. The main moral rights are "right of attribution" and "integrity right."

For example, suppose I make a film that contains a substantial amount of violence to make the point that violence is the wrong answer to any situation. Then another filmmaker uses a clip of my film in their own film, in a scene in which the two main characters watch my film and it inspires them to go on a killing spree—essentially transforming my work into something that creates violence rather than discourages it. The filmmaker does not pay me for that use. The economic right is my exclusive right to copy—I should be compensated every time my film is used by someone else, since I created it. This right was infringed when I was not paid for the other filmmaker's use of my film. The moral right would be my right to protect my reputation—I do not want to be associated with causing violent behavior (which is why I made a film discouraging it), and I should be able to prevent someone else using my work to do so.

Moral rights only exist in the United States in very narrow circumstances. In fact, they are so limited that in most situations they essentially do not exist. It is a different story across the European Union. Perhaps that is why one of the the best definitions of moral rights comes from the United Kingdom Patent Office website www.intellectual-property.gov.uk/faq/copyright/moral_rights.htm]:

Moral rights are granted to the authors of literary, dramatic, musical, and artistic works and to film directors.

- to be identified as the author of the work or director of the film in certain circumstances, e.g., when copies are issued to the public

- to object to derogatory treatment of the work or film that amounts to a distortion or mutilation or is otherwise prejudicial to the honor or reputation of the author or director

The UK definition certainly is clear in its wording, but its (and some other national laws) focus on the issue of the author's reputation is not universal. In France, for example, the question isn't whether the unauthorized use would do reputational harm but simply whether it is one of which the author approves or (if he/she is dead) would have approved. That can generate different results.

For example, John Huston's 1950 black-and-white film *Asphalt Jungle* was one of the greatest crime films of all time. Sterling Hayden and a near-perfect cast created one of the real gems in the MGM library. When Turner Broadcasting acquired the MGM films, the package included this Huston classic.

Shortly thereafter, Turner colorized the film. By then John Huston had died, but Huston's estate wanted to prevent the colorization. Suing in the United States wouldn't do any good because the U.S. doesn't recognize moral rights. So the estate sued in French courts to prevent the exhibition of the film in France under moral rights, which French law says cannot be waived by an artist. Even if the artist signs a contract saying that they waive their moral rights, the rights are not given up or waived (although this is not necessarily the rule in other European countries). The Huston estate won, and the colorized *Asphalt Jungle* cannot be exhibited or sold in France.

Don't get too excited. In French law, there are many examples of implied waiver. **Implied waiver** occurs if you (or your agent) authorize a particular economic exploitation (say a movie adaptation of a novel). The French courts typically will not allow you to complain about the reasonably foreseeable changes that are made in the process. A good example is a case about the movie *Shine*, brought by the Rachmaninoff heirs, who didn't like the way several of the composers' pieces were sliced and diced in the film. Boosey & Hawkes, the agents of the composers, had given a synch license to the filmmakers. The court said that the heirs had nothing to complain about. This is an implied waiver rather than an express waiver, but it has a pretty powerful reach.

As a producer, you want to be sure that the contract with

your director has language to minimize the impact of droit moral. Even though they cannot be waived in France, they can be waived in several other countries that recognize them (e.g., Great Britain). You also want the contract to affirmatively grant to you all the rights that you need. A paragraph like this should do the job nicely:

> **Grant of Rights:** All of the results and proceeds of Director's services shall constitute a "work made for hire" for Producer. Accordingly, Producer shall be deemed the author and the exclusive owner thereof and shall have the right to exploit any or all of the foregoing in all media, whether now known or hereafter devised, throughout the universe, in all versions, in perpetuity, as Producer determines at Producer's sole discretion. Director waives any so-called moral rights.

Note how the waiver of moral rights is at the end of the paragraph. Some producers like to have a separate paragraph so that there is no question about the waiver. Remember that under the law of many countries, the author of a work of art cannot waive moral rights.

There is a substantial movement in this country, led by the Directors Guild of America and The Artists Rights Foundation, to lobby Congress for some movement toward the European model concerning artists' rights. Interestingly, Dreamworks SKG, which was founded by Steven Spielberg, Jeff Katzenberg, and David Geffen, announced at its formation that it would not require artists to waive moral rights. However, Dreamworks—like everybody else—uses work-for-hire language, so the concession may not be of much value to the individual artists until the U.S. law is changed. It does make for good public relations, however.

IS FAIR USE "FAIR" AROUND THE WORLD?

So moral rights in the United States are basically a non-issue. However, using copyrighted works pursuant to the doctrine of fair use is a growing trend. Does fair use hold up when your film is being shown in another country?

The answer to that question is, "More often than you might think, but not always." As we have now learned, copyright is a national issue, which means that every copyrighted work is given protection governed by the country in which protection is claimed. Copyrights from Berne Convention member nations are also given any additional protections that are provided in the Convention.

The Berne Convention itself addresses the fair use issue. It contains a provision which provides, among other things, that an author can "make quotations from a work which has already been lawfully made available to the public, provided that their making is compatible with fair practice, and their extent does not exceed that justified purpose . . ." This wording has generally been recognized to be more liberal than the U.S. concept of fair use. Since it is outlined in the Convention, that means it is a right recognized in all member nations, regardless of national law. However, the regulations issued by the individual countries as they implement the Berne Convention have many European lawyers scratching their collective heads. National law will still be an issue as to how stringent the fair-use equivalent standards are in any particular country. In countries like France, the scope actually is pretty narrow. On the other hand, in some countries (UK, Canada, Australia) there are some helpful specific exceptions for "incidental" use that actually may go beyond U.S. fair use.

To help clarify the situation, your intrepid author trekked to the Rome International Film Festival in 2007 to meet with producers and lawyers from across Europe. After a day of discussions, they began work on a resolution with the aim and intent of coming up with guidelines similar to those contained in the *Documentary Filmmakers' Statement of Best Practices in Fair Use*. That document is summarized in Chapter 2 on Fair Use. By early in 2008, the resolution was officially approved and unveiled in various publications and at the Berlin International Film Festival. Here is an edited version of the European resolution so that you can understand its starting point. The full text can be found on the website for this book.

RESOLUTION

ON FREEDOM OF EXPRESSION AND INFORMATION
IN DOCUMENTARIES

We, Documentary Filmmakers of Europe, having met in Rome
on October 19th, 2007, under the auspices of Doc IT (Italian
Documentaries Association) and IDA (International Documentary
Association) in order to discuss the proposal for a "European Best
Practice on Fair Use in Documentaries,"

1. *Considering* that freedom of expression and information are
   fundamental principles of a democratic society, . . .

2. *Considering* that audiovisual works, and film documentaries
   in particular, are essential today for the effective realization of
   freedom of expression, . . .

3. *Considering* that the ability of film documentaries, as creative
   treatments of actuality, to perform such critical functions
   depends on their ability to quote or otherwise use third-party
   copyrighted works (i) as the object of criticism or review, or
   (ii) to illustrate an argument or point, or (iii) when they are
   captured in the process of filming something else, or (iv) to tell
   a historical sequence (this, and other similar uses of third-party
   works, being hereinafter referred to as "Fair Use," and the right
   to adopt them regardless of the copyright owner's consent as
   "Fair Use in Documentaries");

4. *Considering* that national laws on Fair Use differ from each other,
   being based on different legal concepts such as "fair practice,"
   "good practice," fair dealings," . . .

5. . . . .

6. *Noting* that the development in the United States of the *Docu-
   mentary Filmmakers' Statement of Best Practices in Fair Use*
   ("U.S. Best Practices") generated positive effects in the United
   States, . . .

7. *Believing* that, in any event, there is a need in today's market
   to address to what extent the U.S. Best Practices could find an
   application in Europe in order to facilitate global exploitation
   of audiovisual works;

8. . . . .

9. *Noting* that, while evaluating the actions to be taken to address
   the above-mentioned issues, careful considerations should be
   given to both the economical and moral rights of all the parties
   involved;

10. . . .

Now, therefore, we agree to make our best efforts to fulfill the following goals:

- To conduct a European Study on the increasing costs and legal uncertainty associated with rights clearance and the application of Fair Use in Documentaries;

- To promote a European and global debate on Fair Use in Documentaries, seeking collaboration of all the independent producers' associations, major film festivals and institutions, public and private archives, multimedia and film institutions, and all the collecting society involved in dealing with copyrights issues.

- To obtain financial support from national institutions or private sponsors in our own countries to help this initiative.

CHAPTER 26

LEGAL REFERRAL SERVICES

Certainly, you will have many legal questions down the road. Your concerns may be personal to your situation and fall beyond the scope of this book. The following list of Bar Association's and nonprofit referral services can help point you toward a lawyer in your area. The role of the referral services is simply to refer you to a lawyer competent to assist you, not to give out legal advice. They usually charge a small fee for that service. Generally, the initial consultation with the lawyer will be free or at a highly reduced rate.

Bear in mind that the time you have to speak to the attorney to whom you are referred may be limited. It is in the best interests of both parties for you to realize that this is a preliminary stage of consultation. Therefore, a good approach is to think, develop, and write down your questions ahead of time. Perhaps you will be able to answer them yourself, especially after referring to this book. In the event that new questions arise in your conversation, there will be time for the attorney to address them, provided that you have prepared well prior to the conversation.

Your thorough preparation insures the most valuable communication between you and your attorney in the shortest time.

By knowing what you want to ask, you are more likely to gain credibility and respect from any lawyer you contact through a referral service.

Los Angeles is the entertainment center of the world. As a result, there are more legitimate entertainment attorneys practicing there than in other major cities. When I co-chaired the entertainment section of the Beverly Hills Bar Association, we had more than 500 members. Therefore, you may want to call the Beverly Hills Bar Association's Lawyer Referral and Information Service at (310) 553-4022. In providing a referral, the Beverly Hills Bar Association reviews many attorneys who practice in the area of entertainment law. The Beverly Hills Bar Association requires a referral fee of $25, which entitles you to one referral and a half-hour consultation with an attorney. You are under no obligation to retain the attorney. (In fact, before doing so, you should question the attorney about his or her experiences with problems that are similar to yours.)

In addition to Los Angeles, several other cities have groups that provide helpful legal information to filmmakers. The executive directors of the various services listed below tell me that the clear majority of people who call these services do not need an attorney for their problem. Some of these organizations provide workshops on various topics of interest to the independent filmmaker. Be precise when you call such services. For instance, if you feel that your script has been ripped off, ask for a plaintiff's attorney for a copyright-infringement case. If you are being sued, ask for a defense attorney. For any contract preparation or interpretation, ask for a transactional lawyer. Always, always employ a lawyer to look over contracts as complicated as film distribution and sales agreements.

AMERICAN BAR ASSOCIATION (312) 988-5000
(HQ in Chicago)
www.abanet.org
service@abanet.org

The ABA does not have a referral service, although its website has a direct link to Martindale-Hubbell. The Martindale-Hubbell website provides a referral service of attorneys for each state. Visit www.martindale.com for more information.

California

Beverly Hills Bar Association (310) 553-4022
www.bhba.org
submit@bhba.org

Los Angeles County Bar Association (213) 243-1525
www.lacba.org
webmaster@lacba.org

California Bar Association (213) 765-1000
www.calbar.ca.gov
barrcomm@calbar.ca.gov

California Lawyers for the Arts (310) 998-5590
(Los Angeles)
www.calawyersforthearts.org
userCLA@aol.com

California Lawyers for the Arts (415) 775-7200, ext. 107
(San Francisco)
www.calawyersforthearts.org
cla@calawyersforthearts.org
A nonprofit, tax-exempt service organization founded in 1974 that provides both lawyer referrals and dispute resolution services.

Colorado

Colorado Lawyers for the Arts   (303) 722-7994

www.lawyersforthearts.org

cola@lawyersforthearts.org

The organization provides pro bono legal services, mediation, and legal education. Pro bono is Latin, meaning "for free." I guess the only way lawyers can give it away is to say it in Latin. Be sure to always verify the fee arrangement before you start your meeting.

Florida

Florida Bar Lawyer Referral Service   (800) 342-8011

www.floridabar.org

Georgia

Georgia Volunteer Lawyers for the Arts   (404) 837-3911
(Atlanta)

www.glarts.org

gla@glarts.org

Illinois

Lawyers for the Creative Arts   (312) 649-4111

www.law-arts.org

wrattner@law-arts.org

This not-for-profit, tax-exempt organization provides pro bono legal services to qualifying individuals.

Louisiana

New Orleans Film, Video Society   (504) 309-6633

www.neworleansfilmfest.com

admin@neworleansfilmfest.com

Arts Council of New Orleans   (504) 523-1465

www.ArtsCouncilOfNewOrleans.org

mail@ArtsCouncilOfNewOrleans.org

Maryland

Maryland Lawyers for the Arts   (410) 752-1633

imani2@msn.com

Massachusetts

Volunteer Lawyers for the Arts of   (617) 350-7600
Massachusetts, Inc.
www.vlama.org
mail@vlama.org

Volunteer Lawyers for the Arts of Massachusetts, Inc. (VLA), is a non-profit organization established to meet the legal needs of the state's artistic community.

Minnesota

Resources and Counseling for the Arts (St. Paul)
www.rc4arts.org
Chris@rc4arts.org

Missouri

St. Louis Volunteer Lawyers & Accountants   (314) 863-6930
for the Arts
www.vlaa.org
vlaa@stlrac.org

They provide free legal and accounting assistance and sponsor a wide range of affordable educational programs.

New York

New York Bar Association   (518) 463-3200 x2700
www.nysba.org   (statewide)
foundation@nysba.org

The official statewide organization of the legal profession.

Volunteer Lawyers for the Arts   (212) 319-ARTS, ext. 1
www.vlany.org
vlany@busy.net
vlany@vlany.org

VLA provides pro bono legal services, education, and advocacy to the New York arts community.

Nevada

Lawyer Referral and Information   (702) 382-2200, ext. 404
Service
www.nvbar.org
lynne@nvbar.org

North Carolina
North Carolina Bar Association   (800) 662-7660
www.ncbar.org
ncba@ncbar.org

Ohio
Cleveland Bar Assoc. Volunteer Lawyers   (216) 696-3532
for the Arts
www.clevelandbar.org
lchenault@clevelandbar.org

Has legal education programs for both attorneys and the public and provide a lawyer referral service for those who need to find an attorney.

Oregon
Northwest Lawyers and Artists, Inc.
Artcop@aol.com

Pennsylvania
Philadelphia Volunteer Lawyers for the Arts   (215) 545-3385
www.libertynet.org/pvla
pvla@libertynet.org

Provides pro bono legal assistance and basic business counseling to area artists and cultural organizations.

Rhode Island
Ocean State Lawyers for the Arts   (401) 789-5686
www.artslaw.org
dspatt@artslaw.org

Dedicated to providing legal assistance regarding contracts, copyrights, trademarks, tax-exempt status, collection of accounts, and any other arts-related problems.

Texas

Texas Accountants and Lawyers   (713) 526-4876

for the Arts–Houston

(800) 526-TALA

www.talarts.org

info@talarts.org

Provides pro bono legal and accounting services to artists and arts organizations.

Washington

Washington State Lawyer Referral Service

www.wsbar.org

Refer to the website to find contact information on attorneys by county.

In step with the current legal trend for conflict resolution, referral services and volunteer lawyers for the arts organizations often offer mediation. Mediation is a formalized settlement meeting with all disputing parties and a trained professional who runs the meeting. The purpose is to reach a settlement, but you do not have to agree to anything unless you think that it is in your best interests to do so. You have nothing to lose by pursuing such mediation.

Mediation is never binding. It is designed to have the parties reach a voluntary settlement agreement. An Interstate Mediation Network has been established among several of the above organizations. Parties to a conflict often wish to settle disputes quickly and cost-effectively without the hassle of going through tedious litigation and the court system. A mediator acts as a neutral third party to help the disputing parties reach a settlement. Experienced mediators are usually successful in finding a remedy for your problem. Fees range from modest to very substantial, so be sure to shop. Some of the organizations listed above purport to arrange for pro bono mediators.

Before you close this book in amazement at the amount of space spent on selecting a lawyer, reflect on the cases in this book. They all grew out of oh-so-typical situations. There was

one exotic situation in the bunch. The cases involved prop-
or people of sufficient notoriety to make them interesting,
.ne real situations that gave rise to these lawsuits were very
.ommon. You may or may not find yourself in these situations.
These cases are expensive. All of the cases mentioned in this
book went through the trial courts. Most went on to the appellate
courts, and sometimes to the Supreme Court of the United States.
Choose your lawyer carefully. You are not searching for bravado.
You are searching for experience, integrity, and unflinching
honesty in all communications you have with your attorney.

Good luck! If you carry the lessons of this book with you,
you have significantly reduced your chances of being embroiled
in legal entanglements. If you back away from doing business
with those you don't trust, with whom you don't connect on a
human level, you have reduced the odds of unhappy encounters
even more. Choose your friends and your business associates
with uncompromising care. You won't have to spend so much
time with lawyers.

APPENDIX A

GLOSSARY

Abandonment. The act of leaving a work's rights unused and unattended for years. It requires some clear, unequivocal, affirmative act by the copyright owner.

Access. The reasonable opportunity to review a copyrighted work.

Adaptation rights. The right to change or add to the music or lyrics of a piece of music or literature.

Annotated script. A script that has references to the various sources the writer relied on when writing it. A script is annotated by placing handwritten numbers, which refer to factual sources, directly on its factual assertions.

Anonymous. An author whose name is not given on copies of a script.

"As is" document. An incomplete document.

Audiovisual rights. The same as film rights, but better anticipates the possible development and use of future technologies.

Bible. Primarily a television term for a detailed story, more detailed than the typical treatment.

nket license. A license obtained by the periodic payment of a flat fee for the right to perform various pieces of copyright-protected music.

Case citation. The exact book and page number where a case summary and the court's opinion may be found in a law library.

Ceiling. The maximum price to be paid, regardless of the budget.

Chain of title. A collection of the contracts and other documents that show any change in ownership of a film project from its inception. The documents are a trail of transfers from the original author of a work through the final film (or whatever stage the project is at at the time).

Cite. *See* "Case citation."

Clear. To obtain written permission from the proper individual or entity to use a certain item in your film.

Compilation. A work formed by the collection and assembling of pre-existing materials.

Consideration is legalese shorthand for whatever is of value that you give up for what you get. Money is the "consideration" that most people think of. Your promises can also be consideration.

Continuity. The actual dialogue script annotated with timing code taken from a tape or workprint of the feature film.

Copyright infringement. The situation in which a work is based in whole or in part on a copyrighted work to such an extent that a court will say, "It takes too much."

Copyright report. A detailed history of a work's copyright ownership and related registered items.

Country of origin. Country where the work was created.

Damages. The money a court awards the winning party at the end of a lawsuit.

Defined term. A term that is defined somewhere in a contract and has a special meaning throughout that contract.

de minimus. The injury is too trivial for the court to bother with.

Derivative work. Work that is a modified or altered from a pre-existing work.

Double source. To have two separate and independent sources for each factual assertion in a script.

Double vested. In control of two production or development entities, one of which is a signatory of a union agreement and the other of which is not.

Droit moral. *See* "Moral rights."

Enjoin. To restrain someone from a certain activity by means of a court order.

Errors and omissions (E&O) insurance. Insurance to compensate others for damage caused by negligent mistakes.

Express contract. A contract in which the parties have agreed to the terms in specific words, either orally or in writing.

Fair use. Recognizing that it simply is not fair to say that every copying is a violation of the law, and some copying of a copyrighted work is necessary to promote the creativity that the protection was designed to promote, "fair use" is a defense that can be used when one is sued for copyright infringement.

False light. Untrue statements that fall short of being defamatory yet cause some harm or embarrassment to the party they address.

Film rights. A film-industry term for a collection of different rights. Those rights include the right to make a film for initial exhibition on television or in theaters, the right to make sequels and remakes of that film, the right to distribute the film on videocassettes and other media, even those that aren't invented yet. Sometimes referred to as motion picture rights.

Floor. The minimum price to be paid, regardless of the budget.

Franchise. A character, concept, or title that is supposed to guarantee a good opening for a film. James Bond is the best example in film history.

Good title. Ownership of that which one claims to own, free and clear of any encumbrances or liens.

Grand performing right. Performance of a song or other piece of music as part of the story of a play or a film. *See* "Small performing right."

Holdback period. A period during which certain rights that are possessed are not used.

Implied contract. An agreement that arises without any party specifically stating the terms.

Independent contractor. An employee or independent business entity who controls the time, the place, and the manner in which their tasks are performed.

Injunction. The court says you can't do something. In our world, that usually means you can't distribute a film.

Joke. Something that is said or done to evoke laughter or amusement. It can be a one-liner or an amusing story with a long-awaited punch line.

Judgment on the Pleading. A court ruling that finds that the plaintiff could not state a good complaint, so the defendant wins without even filing an answer to the lawsuit.

Knock-off. A slang term for something that has been created especially to appear very similar to another, often notable, thing.

Laches. You sat on your rights too long before suing, so you lose.

Lanham Act. A Federal Law covering various business practices, which is the source of protection for the title of film or script.

Leading case. Refers to the first case to come out and clearly state a certain conclusion of law.

Library. A group of films whose copyright is owned by one entity.

Limited Liability Corporation. A hybrid business entity that provides the shared responsibilities of a partnership with the protection from personal liability of a corporation.

Master license. License to use a specific recording. This name refers to the fact that you are licensing the master recording of a song.

Mechanical rights. The rights to reproduce a piece of music on audio records, CDs, or tapes.

Mediation. A formalized settlement meeting with all disputing parties and a trained professional who runs the meeting.

Moral rights (droit moral). A group of rights that protect a work from being changed without permission of the person who, by the act of creating that work, holds moral rights.

Mortgage of copyright. A document that is signed in order for someone to acquire a security interest in your film['s copyright]. This mortgage allows someone to foreclose on the copyright in your film if you don't do what you say you are going to do.

Most favored nations. A term that describes the way a party wishes to be treated in an agreement in comparison to other parties.

Music clearance. Obtaining the permissions necessary to use specific pre-existing pieces of music in a film.

Music cue sheet. A document that lists each song or portion of a song used in a film, along with the composers, publishers, performing rights affiliations (ASCAP or BMI or SESAC), usage, and timing of each song. (Music cue sheets also list the composers, performing rights affiliations, usage, and timing of each underscore cue.)

Music publisher. An entity that manages a song and collects money for the writer from the royalties derived from its exploitation.

Music supervisor. The person who helps select music, supervise the clearing of music, hire a composer and supervise the recording of the score.

National treatment. Copyright agreement provision by which a signatory country grants to foreign nationals at least the same copyright protections that its domestic laws grant to its own citizens.

Negative pick-up. When a studio agrees to pay for your finished film in exchange for all the rights and the negative of your film.

Non-disclosure agreement. An agreement that states that a producer will not disclose to others a pitched idea unless he or she buys it.

Off air. A film or video copied directly off a television as the program is coming across the cable or over the airwaves.

Out of Context Rights. The right to use the music from your film in a trailer advertising the film.

Option. The exclusive right to purchase something in the future, on fixed terms and conditions.

Oral contract. A non-written contract.

Orphan works. Any work for which you can't find the legitimate owner after you have made a substantial search.

Package deal (music). An agreement between a composer and a producing entity that specifies that the composer composes all the music, hires the musicians, records the music, and delivers all the fully recorded music to the producer for a fixed fee.

Parody. A new, copyrightable work based on a previously copyrighted work to such an extent that the previous work is clearly recognizable, but not taking more from the copyrighted work than is necessary, and that makes a social commentary which is at least in part directed to the subject matter of the previous work, usually humorously, and that is not likely to hurt the value of the previous work.

Per diem. A specific amount paid to cover all expenses without any need to provide receipts or an accounting.

Performing rights society. An organization that monitors the performance of music and collects royalties due the songwriter from performances on radio and television, in restaurants, lounges, bars, hotels, and retail stores playing music on a radio, and workout/dance studios playing music for aerobics classes.

Prequel. Something of a slang term to describe a sequel that is set earlier in time than the original.

Product placement. The practice of receiving some consideration from the company that owns the trademark for a product that is clearly used or displayed in a film.

Pseudonymous. The author of a script identified by a fictitious name.

Public domain. Literally, "owned by the public." A property to which no individual or corporation owns the copyright.

Public performance rights. The right to perform a piece of music in public. Licensing this right allows you to recite, play, sing, dance, or act out a piece of music.

Publication. Distribution of copies of the script to the public by sale, or transfer of ownership, or by rental, lease, or lending.

Published. Copies of a work that are distributed to the public via sale, lease, or other ownership transfer.

Publishing company (music). The company that administers the various rights that flow from ownership of the copyright to a song or other piece of music.

Publishing income (music). The income flowing to the copyright holder of music, such as performance royalties when the film is played on TV or in theaters outside the U.S., or when the music is played apart from the film, on radio, for example.

Quote. The price that a writer received for past assignments.

Remake. A movie in which the script that formed the basis for another film is recast and reshot.

Reproduction rights. The rights to reproduce a piece of music (these include synchronization rights and mechanical rights).

Reuse. Taking a piece of film or video that was shot for one purpose and using it for another purpose.

Reuse fee. Payment that is required by union contracts when a piece of a film made after 1960 is taken and used in another work

Right coupled with an interest. A situation in which your representative also has an interest in the thing being represented. This makes it difficult to terminate the relationship.

Safe harbor. A provision that gives one protection as long as efforts were made to comply with the law.

Scenes a faire. A legal term that means that the scenes flow naturally from the general premise, so they are not protected by the law of copyright and copyright infringement. (Scenes a faire are not protectable because they necessarily result from the choice of setting or situation.)

Screen grab. A still shot of an image from a motion pictures or television program.

Script clearance. The process of identifying all the potential problems contained in a script and then obtaining either written permission from the proper person or a legal opinion that such permission is not necessary.

Secondary meaning. A shorthand phrase that describes the existence of a condition from which public confusion will flow if the defendant is permitted to pursue his/her deceptive scheme.

Section 205 documents. These include almost all of the documents you will record as a filmmaker. Examples of Section 205 documents include transfers of copyright ownerships and other documents pertaining to a copyright such as exclusive and non exclusive licenses, contracts, mortgages, powers of attorney, certificates of change of corporate name or title, wills, and decrees of distribution. (Section 205 refers to that specific section of the Federal Copyright Law that provides for the recording of these important documents.)

Security agreement. An agreement issued by a film's lender or financier to secure the repayment of their money by the producer.

Sequel. A story that uses some or all of the same characters in a different story, set in a different time.

Settled. As used as an adjective for legal matters, a law is not likely to change because of the number of courts that have issued decisions in the area over a long period of time.

Small performing right. The right to perform a song or other piece of music by itself, apart from a play or a film. *See* "Grand performing right."

Soundalike. One performer or group of performers legally recording a song in the manner and style of another performer or group of performers.

Spec script. A script written on speculation—the speculation that a producer will want to option and/or purchase the script and make it into a movie.

Spotting. Picking the points in a film where music will be heard. The company and director and music team do this together.

Statutory damages. Awards granted by a court when a copyright owner's work has been infringed but the owner cannot prove the actual losses or the losses are quite small.

Stock footage. Pre-existing film that can be licensed for use in another film.

Story characters. Characters based on or originating in works of literature, such as Frankenstein and James Bond. Dialogue, plot, and interaction with other characters define these characters.

Submission agreement. An agreement that provides that if a prospective producer reads a script, the script's writer will not bring a claim against the producer for copyright infringement if he or she produces a similar movie without the writer's participation.

Substantial similarity. The situation in which two works are so similar that a jury could determine that the second work was copied from the first.

Summary judgment motion. A motion heard by a judge who determines whether there are issues of fact that should be tried by a jury.

Synch rights. The rights to record music to be heard as part of a film.

Target defendant. Anyone who looks as though they have the capacity to pay big bucks to avoid being sued.

Title report. A list of all the titles of films, books, songs, and plays together with press mentions of these titles.

Trade libel. Falsely assigning a bad attribute to a trademark. One does not have the right to hold a product up to ridicule or do anything that harms the reputation of a product.

Trademark. The combination of words or symbols or both that identifies a product or service.

Transformative. Work that has added something new and different to the underlying work, when the underlying work is used for a new and different purpose, and when the underlying work is an ingredient in a new and different work.

Treatment. A script story in abbreviated form. It can be a few paragraphs, a few pages, or more than 20 pages.

Turnaround provision. A contractual provision that allows a screenwriter to purchase a script back from a production entity.

Underlying rights. The foundational rights that you must control to have the right to make and distribute a film based on a script that is based on an underlying property.

Underscore. Background music that accompanies (and often comments on what is happening in) a film.

Underwriters. The people who assess risk and decide whether to issue an insurance policy and what it should cost.

Visual character. A character based on a drawing. It is not so much a character as a copyrighted drawing, figure, or image.

Work for hire. Defined in U.S. Copyright Law as either (1) a work prepared by an employee within the scope of employment; or (2) a work specially ordered or commissioned for use as one of a very limited number of specified works.

APPENDIX B

TABLE OF FORMS

1.01   NON-DISCLOSURE AGREEMENT

2.01   TEMPLATE CLEARANCE LOG

6.01   OPTION AND PURCHASE AGREEMENT
        (for Underlying Rights)

7.01   WRITER AGREEMENT—WORK FOR HIRE
        Exhibit A: Credit Determination
        Exhibit B: Certificate of Authorship

8.01   COLLABORATION AGREEMENT

9.01   OPTION AND PURCHASE AGREEMENT (for Script)
        Exhibit A: Assignment (Short Form)

9.02   SUBMISSION AGREEMENT

10.01   BOILERPLATE PROVISIONS

11.01   FORM PA FOR A SCRIPT

11.02   CONTINUATION SHEET

11.03   SCRIPT REGISTRATION COVER LETTER

11.04   SCRIPT REGISTRATION POSTCARD

11.05   SAMPLE FORM TX

11.06   FORM CA

13.01   LIFE STORY RIGHTS AGREEMENT

13.02   INDIVIDUAL RELEASE

15.01   EXCERPTS FROM A SCRIPT CLEARANCE REPORT

15.02   LOCATION AGREEMENT

16.01   SYNCHRONIZATION AND PERFORMANCE-RIGHTS
         AGREEMENT
16.02   MOTION PICTURE MASTER-USE LICENSE
17.01   COMPOSER AGREEMENT
17.02   MUSIC PACKAGE AGREEMENT
18.01   FILM CLIP RELEASE
18.02   ACTOR'S RELEASE FOR FILM CLIP USE
19.01   OPINION LETTER
19.02   TITLE REPORT
20.01   E&O INSURANCE FORM
21.01   DOCUMENT COVER SHEET
21.02   COVER LETTER TO RECORD AGREEMENTS
21.03   RETURN POSTCARD FOR RECORDING DOCUMENTS
22.01   SAMPLE REGISTRATION COVER LETTER
22.02   SAMPLE REGISTRATION POSTCARD
24.01   COPYRIGHT INFRINGEMENT NOTIFICATION

APPENDIX C

TABLE OF CASES

PART I

Chapter 1—Copyright & Ideas: The Big Picture
- Desny v. Wilder, 46 Cal. 2d 715; 299 P.2d 257 (1956)
- Blaustein v. Burton, 9 Cal. App. 3d 161; 88 Cal. Rptr. 319 (1970)
- Mann v. Columbia Pictures, Inc., 128 Cal. App. 3d 628; 180 Cal. Rptr. 522 (1982)
- Grosso v. Miramax Film Corp., 383 F.3d 965 (9th Cir. 2003)

Chapter 2—Fair Use
- Folsom v. Marsh, 9 F. Cas. 342 (CCD Mass. 1841)
- Campbell v. Acuff-Rose Music, 510 U.S. 569 (1994)
- Harper & Row v. Nation Enterprises, 471 U.S. 539 (1985)
- Sony Corp. v. Universal City Studios, Inc., 464 U.S. 417 (1984)
- Hofheinz v. AMC Prods. Inc., 147 F. Supp. 2d 127 (E.D.N.Y. 2001)
- Hofheinz v. A&E TV Networks, 146 F. Supp. 2d 442 (S.D.N.Y. 2001)
- Hofheinz v. Discovery Communs., Inc., 2001 U.S. Dist. LEXIS 14752 (S.D.N.Y. 2001)
- Los Angeles News Serv. v. KCAL-TV Channel 9, 108 F.3d 1119 (9th Cir. 1997)
- L.A. News Serv. v. Reuters TV Int'l., 149 F.3d 987 (9th Cir. 1998)

- Richard Feiner & Co. v. H.R.I. Indus., 10 F. Supp. 2d 310, 312 (S.D.N.Y. 1998)
- Video-Cinema Films v. CNN, Inc., 2001 U.S. Dist. LEXIS 25687 (S.D.N.Y. 2001)
- Roy Export Co. Establishment etc. v. Columbia Broadcasting System, Inc., 503 F. Supp. 1137 (S.D.N.Y. 1980)
- Bill Graham Archives v. Dorling Kindersley Ltd., 448 F.3d 605 (S.D.N.Y. 2006)
- Wade Williams Distrib., Inc. v. ABC, 2005 U.S. Dist. LEXIS 5730 (S.D.N.Y. 2005)
- L.A. News Serv. v. CBS Broad., Inc., 305 F.3d 924 (9th Cir. 2002)
- Midway Mfg. Co. v. Publications Int'l., 1994 U.S. Dist. LEXIS 6264 (N.D. Ill. 1994)
- Elvis Presley Enters. v. Passport Video, 357 F.3d 896 (9th Cir 2003)
- Italian Book Corp. v. American Broadcasting Cos., 458 F. Supp. 65 (S.D.N.Y. 1978)
- Higgins v. Detroit Educ. TV Found., 4 F. Supp. 2d 701, 703 (D. Mich. 1998)
- Grand Upright Music, Ltd. v. Warner Bros. Records, Inc., 780 F. Supp. 182 (D.N.Y. 1991)
- Newton v. Diamond, 388 F.3d 1189 (9th Cir. 2003)
- Lennon v. Premise Media, 2008 WL 2262631 (only Westlaw citation currently available) (S.D.N.Y. 2008)

Chapter 3—Parody, Satire, and Jokes

- Loew's, Inc. v. Columbia Broadcasting System, Inc., 131 F. Supp. 165 (S.D. Cal. 1955), aff'd sub nom.
- Campbell v. Acuff-Rose Music, 510 U.S. 569 (1994)
- Dr. Seuss Enters., L.P. v. Penguin Books USA, Inc., 109 F.3d 1394 (9th Cir. 1997)
- Columbia Pictures Indus. v Miramax Films Corp., 11 F Supp. 2d 1179 (C.D. Cal. 1998)
- Kane v. Comedy Partners, 68 U.S.P.Q.2D (BNA) 1748 (S.D.N.Y. 2003)
- SunTrust Bank v. Houghton Mifflin Co., 268 F.3d 1257 (11th Cir. 2001)
- Winter v. DC Comics, 30 Cal. 4th 881 (Cal. 2003)
- Mattel, Inc. v. MCA Records, 296 F.3d 894 (9th Cir. 2002)
- Dallas Cowboys Cheerleaders, Inc. v. Pussycat Cinema, Ltd., 604 F.2d 200 (2nd Cir. 1979)

- Meta-Film Associates, Inc. v. MCA, Inc., 586 F. Supp. 1346 (C.D. Cal. 1984)
- Blanch v. Koons, 467 F.3d 244 (2nd Cir. 2006)
- Rogers v. Koons, 960 F.2d 301 (2nd Cir. 1992)
- Foxworthy v. Custom Tees, 879 F. Supp. 1200 (N.D. Ga. 1995)

Chapter 4—Public Domain

- Houts v. Universal City Studios, 603 F.Supp. 26 (C.D. Cal. 1984)
- Marshall v. Yates, 1983 WL 1148 (C.D. Cal. 1983)
- International News Service v. Associated Press, 248 U.S. 215 (1918)
- National Basketball Ass'n. v. Motorola, Inc., 105 F.3d 841 (2d Cir. 1997)
- Maljack Productions v. UAV Corp., 964 F. Supp. 1416 (C.D. Cal. 1997)
- Comedy III Prods., Inc. v. New Line Cinema, 200 F.3d 593 (9th Cir. 2000)
- Wendt v. Host Int'l., 125 F.3d 806 (9th Cir. 1997)
- Frederick Warne & Co. v. Book Sales, Inc., 481 F. Supp. 1191 (D.N.Y. 1979)
- Comedy III Prods., Inc. v. Gary Saderup, Inc., 25 Cal. 4th 387 (2001)

Chapter 5—Characters and Costumes

- New Line Cinema Corp. v. Bertlesman Music Group, Inc., 693 F. Supp. 1517 (S.D.N.Y. 1988)
- Anderson v. Stallone, 1989 U.S. Dist. LEXIS 11109 (C.D. Cal. 1989)
- Rice v. Fox Broad. Co., 330 F.3d 1170 (9th Cir. 2003)
- Metro-Goldwyn-Mayer, Inc. v. American Honda Motor Co., 900 F. Supp. 1287 (C.D. Cal. 1995)
- Filmvideo Releasing Corp. v. Hastings, 509 F. Supp. 60 (S.D.N.Y. 1981)
- Detective Comics, Inc. v. Bruns Publications, Inc., et al., 111 F.2d 432 (2d Cir. 1940).
- Silverman v. CBS, Inc., 870 F.2d 40 (2d Cir. 1989)

PART II

Chapter 6—Acquiring the Rights to Someone Else's Property

- Stewart v. Abend, 495 US 207; 110 S.Ct. 1750 (1990)
- Konigsberg Int'l., Inc. v. Rice, 16 F.3d 355 (9th Cir. 1994)

Chapter 8—Writing With a Partner

- Danjag LLC v. Sony Corp., 263 F. 3d 942 (9th Cir. 2001)
- Aalmuhammed v. Lee, 202 F.3d 1227 (9th Cir. 2000)
- Thomson v. Larson, 147 F.3d 195 (2d Cir. 1998)
- Berman v. Johnson, 518 F. Supp. 2d 791 (E.D. Va. 2007)
- Mike Batt/John Cage case settled for an undisclosed six figure sum.

Chapter 12—Others Who May Have Rights in Your Film

- Huston v. la Cinq (France)
- Hi-Tech Video Prods. v. Capital Cities/ABC, 58 F.3d 1093 (6th Cir. 1995)
- King v. Innovation Books, 976 F.2d 824 (2d Cir. 1992)

Chapter 13—All Those Pesky People

- Gates v. Discovery Communications, Inc., 34 Cal. 4th 679 (2004)
- Cox Broadcasting Corp. v. Cohn, 420 U.S. 469 (1975); Okla. Publishing Co. v. District Court, 430 U.S. 308 (1975); Smith v. Daily Mail Publishing Co., 443 U.S. 97 (1979); The Florida Star v. B.J.F., 491 U.S. 524 (1989)
- Wiseman v. Massachusetts, 398 U.S. 960 (U.S. 1970)
- Wilkins v. National Broadcasting Company, 71 Cal. App. 4th 1066 (1999)
- DeGregorio v. CBS, Inc., 473 N.Y.S. 2d 922, 925 (1984)
- Food Lion Inc., v. Capital Cities/ABC, Inc., 194 F.3d 505 (1999)
- Waits v. Frito-Lay, Inc., 978 F.2d 1093 (9th Cir. 1992)
- Midler v. Ford Motor Co., 849 F.2d 460 (9th Cir. 1988)
- Eastwood v. Superior Court, 149 Cal. App. 3d 409 (Cal. Ct. App. 1983)

Chapter 14—Trademark, Logos, and Business Signage

- Dallas Cowboy Cheerleaders, Inc. v. Pussycat Cinema, Ltd., 467 F.Supp. 366 (S.D.N.Y. 1979); aff'd 604 F.2d 200 (2d Cir. 1979)
- Eastman Kodak Co. v. Rakow, 739 F. Supp. 116 (W.D.N.Y. 1989)
- Caterpillar Inc. v. Walt Disney Co., 287 F. Supp. 2d 913 (C.D. Ill. 2003)

- Wham-O, Inc. v. Paramount Pictures Corp., 286 F. Supp. 2d 1254 (N.D. Cal. 2003), appeal dismissed by WHAM-O, Inc. v. Paramount Pictures Corp., 101 Fed. Appx. 248 (9th Cir. 2004)
- Hormel Foods Corp. v. Jim Henson Prods., 36 U.S.P.Q.2D (BNA) 1812 (S.D.N.Y. 1995); aff'd. by Hormel Foods Corp. v. Jim Henson Prods., 73 F.3d 497 (2nd Cir. 1996)
- American Dairy Queen Corp. v. New Line Prods., 35 F. Supp. 2d 727 (D. Minn. 1998)

Chapter 15—Sets and Set Dressings
- Woods v. Universal City Studios, 920 F. Supp. 62 (D.N.Y. 1996)
- Leicester v. Warner Bros., 232 F.3d 1212 (9th Cir. 2000)
- Ringgold v. Black Entertainment TV, 126 F.3d 70 (2d Cir. 1997)
- Sandoval v. New Line Cinema Corp., 147 F.3d 215 (2d Cir. 1998)
- Amsinck v. Columbia Pictures Indus., 862 F. Supp. 1044 (D.N.Y. 1994)
- Jackson v. Warner Bros., 993 F. Supp. 585 (E.D. Mich. 1997)

Chapter 18—Clearing Film Clips
- Brown v. Twentieth Century Fox Film Corp., 799 F. Supp. 166 (D.D.C. 1992)

Chapter 19—Title Clearance
- Lutz v. De Laurentiis, 211 Cal. App. 3d 1317 (Cal. Ct. App. 1989)

Chapter 22—Registering Copyright for Your Completed Film
  (none)

Chapter 23—Copyright Infringement
- Litchfield v. Spielberg, 736 F.2d 1352 (9th Cir. 1984)
- Hospital for Sick Children v. Melody Fare Dinner Theatre, 516 F. Supp. 67 (E.D. Va. 1980)
- Walker v. Time Life Films, Inc., 784 F.2d 44 (2d Cir. 1986)
- Universal City Studios, Inc. v. Film Ventures International, Inc., 543 F. Supp. 1134 (C.D. Cal. 1982)

Chapter 24—Copyright On The Internet
- N.Y. Times Co. v. Tasini, 533 U.S. 483 (2001)
- Playboy Enters. v. Sanfilippo, 46 U.S.P.Q.2D (BNA) 1350 (S.D. Cal. 1998)
- A&M Records v. Napster, Inc., 284 F.3d 1091 (9th Cir. 2002)

Chapter 25—International Copyright Issues
- Huston v. la Cinq (France)

FILM AND TELEVISION SHOWS MENTIONED IN THIS BOOK

Chapter 1

Ace in the Hole   Idea protection case that found a writer (Desny) who shared his story idea with director Billy Wilder and had an implied oral contract.

Rounders   The case that involved this film took the idea-submission protection one step further and said that ideas in a film could be similar to ideas in a specific script that the studio saw but didn't purchase.

Shampoo   In a case similar to the one regarding the film *Ace in the Hole* (see above), a writer sued Warren Beatty, Columbia Pictures, and Robert Towne over the authorship of the idea for the film *Shampoo*. This case helped spell out the specific requirements for a writer to achieve idea protection.

Taming of the Shrew   The case that involved this film extended the protection for idea submissions to the producer who came up with the idea for this film and pitched it to Elizabeth Taylor and Richard Burton. Note that the film was based on Shakespeare's public domain play.

Chapter 2

FILMS
& TV SHOWS
MENTIONED
IN THIS
BOOK

485

*Aliens Invade
Hollywood*

This is a film that Ms. Hofheinz controlled. She lost her lawsuit for the use of clips from her film in a documentary about aliens because the court found the use to be a fair use.

Apollo 13

This film integrated actual historical film clips into its story.

The Definitive Elvis

This was a documentary that incorporated a lot of clips and performances without obtaining permission. The court found that there was no fair use because the producers used more than what was necessary to demonstrate their points. The court was more upset at the way they chose to advertise and promote the documentary.

Expelled

This was a documentary that incorporated a 10-second clip from John Lennon's song "Imagine" without first obtaining permission. The court found that there was fair use because the producers used no more than was necessary to demonstrate their point.

Forrest Gump

This film integrated actual historical film clips into its story.

*It Conquered
Hollywood! The
Story of American
International Pictures*

This documentary used clips from Ms Hofheinz's film without paying. The producers were sued and won on a fair use defense.

*Peter Graves: Mission
Accomplished*

This documentary also used clips from one of Ms. Hofheinz's films. She sued but the producers won on a fair use defense.

*Robot Monster, Plan
Nine from Outer
Space, Queen of Outer
Space*

These three films by Ed Wood were the source of clips used by *Good Morning America* to illustrate points about how aliens are depicted in movies. The court found fair use. You can view the clip from *GMA* by visiting the website for this book.

Smoke and Mirrors	Major use of clips of television commercials for cigarettes were used under the fair-use doctrine without obtaining permission from the tobacco companies because the documentary was about the history of cigarette advertising.
This Film is not Yet Rated	This film by Kirby Dick used 134 film clips, mostly from major motion pictures in order to demonstrate inconsistencies in the MPAA rating system. The film has become the poster child for fair use. It could not have been made without fair use because the studios don't license clips from their films if they are going to be used in a film that is critical of the industry in any way. You can rent this film from Netflix.
Wanderlust	This film used a large number of film clips, mostly from major studios, that fell within fair use. The filmmakers approached the studios, giving them a choice between a low license fee and having the clips used under fair use. Most of them chose the license. The filmmakers were able to complete their film because of a savings of over $300,000 in license fees (even after attorney fees.) You can read *The New York Times* article on this film by visiting the website for this book.

Chapter 3

Animal House	In an unrelated case, a court declared *Animal House* to be a satire on college fraternity life.
Daily Show, Sandy Kane Show	A clip from *The Sandy Kane Show* used by John Stewart on *The Daily Show* was found to be fair use, but the court went to some pains to explain why this use of the clip is not a parody of *The Sandy Kane Show*.
Debbie Does Dallas	This film was permanently enjoined because of slander to the trademark of the Dallas Cowboys Cheerleaders.

FILMS
& TV SHOWS
MENTIONED
IN THIS
BOOK

487

Gaslight	This film was parodied by Jack Benny. The Supreme Court decision was that the parody was not a fair use without issuing any comment of its own.

Chapter 4

Amy Fisher: My Story	This TV movie is mentioned with reference to purchasing life rights related to a public domain news story.
Asphalt Jungle	The estate of John Huston asserted his moral rights in France to enjoin exhibition of the colorized version of his famous black-and-white film.
Beyond Control: The Amy Fisher Story	This TV movie is mentioned with reference to purchasing life rights related to a public domain news story.
Casualties of Love: The Long Island Lolita Story	This TV movie is mentioned with reference to purchasing life rights related to a public domain news story.
Cheers	Some actors from this TV show sued the bars that licensed replicas of the show's set because these bars also included look-alike dolls of the actors, implying the actors' endorsement of the bar.
It's a Wonderful Life	A copyright-like protection for the re-release of this film, which had fallen into public domain, was achieved through the film's music, which carried separate and still-enforceable copyrights.
Long Kiss Goodnight	New Line did not have to pay the Three Stooges for use of their name and likeness in a clip from a public domain film.
McLintock!	Copyright-like protection for this film was achieved through its music.
The Positively True Adventures of the Alleged Texas Cheerleader-Murdering Mom	This TV movie is mentioned with regard to film stories based on public domain materials.

Chapter 5

Nightmare on Elm Street

The Fresh Prince and DJ Jazzy Jeff used their version of Freddy Krueger in a music video. The studio for the film sued and won because Freddy is a character protected under copyright.

Rocky

A court held that the character of Rocky is copyrighted when an author used the character in a script without obtaining permission.

Chapter 6

My Big Fat Greek Wedding

This film illustrates the need to obtain underlying rights.

Rear Window

This 1954 Hitchcock film was based on Cornell Woolrich's short story of the same name (published in 1944). For the film's 1962 re-release, Universal had to pay for the rights to the story again because of the unique copyright renewal provisions provided by the copyright laws of the time.

Sabrina

The 1995 film directed by Sidney Pollack is an example of a remake of the original film directed by Billy Wilder.

Chapter 8

Malcolm X

A contributor to this film's script sued Spike Lee and Warner Bros. for screenwriting credit and profit shares, but failed to win his suit.

Thunderball

Highlighting the importance of a good collaboration agreement, the co-author of the film *Thunderball* and other Bond films was in litigation for years with Ian Fleming and his successors after creating a cinematic James Bond that was quite different from the literary character in Fleming's novels.

FILMS
& TV SHOWS
MENTIONED
IN THIS
BOOK

489

Chapter 9

Shampoo

In a case similar to the one regarding the film *Ace in the Hole* (see above), a writer sued Warren Beatty, Columbia Pictures, and Robert Towne over the authorship of the idea for the film *Shampoo*. This case helped spell out the specific requirements for a writer to achieve idea protection.

Chapter 12

Asphalt Jungle

The estate of John Huston asserted his moral rights in France to enjoin exhibition of the colorized version of his famous black-and-white film.

Lawnmower Man

Stephen King won an injunction against the use of his name beyond that specifically allowed in the contract because the film was such a departure from his short story.

Switchblade Sisters

Quentin Tarantino's affection for this B-film by Jack Hill led him to organize its re-release, making the original independent filmmaker very happy because he still owned the copyright.

Chapter 13

Fahrenheit 9/11

In this film, note the interview with a soldier. He signed a release, but felt that the film portrayed him as more negative than he was at the time and—worse—he supported the war at the time of the film's release. He sued. Eventually, he lost, but the lawsuit was a big hassle and expense for Michael Moore.

Roger and Me

Filmmaker Michael Moore was sued by a man who felt this documentary portrayed him in a false light. The jury agreed with the plaintiff.

The Search for Signs of Intelligent Life In the Universe

Lilly Tomlin found out that a written release is not necessary if you agree to be filmed. The court said that since she agreed to be filmed without putting any conditions on it, she could not later enjoin the film because she didn't like the way she was portrayed in parts of it.

Chapter 14

Dickie Roberts:
Former Child Star

Watch as David Spade completely misuses a water slide for comedic effect. When Wham-O sued in the belief that their trademark was being tarnished, the court said that even a small child would understand that the product wasn't defective in any way, it was being misused. Therefore, there was no trademark tarnishment.

Drop Dead Gorgeous

The court found tarnishment of the Dairy Queen trademark by New Line's mockumentary originally titled *Dairy Queens*. The court felt that there was a good chance of the public believing that Dairy Queen was associated with the film.

Duckman

This film poked fun at Hormel's Spam by reeling off a fake list of ingredients. Hormel sued for trademark tarnishment, but the court said anyone watching this sequence would understand that it was a joke, not a serious reading of ingredients. Therefore, no tarnishment.

George of the Jungle 2

Caterpillar sued Disney because Caterpillar bulldozers wreaked havoc in this film. The court thought it was obvious that the havoc was caused by the maniacal operators of the bulldozers, not the bulldozers themselves. Therefore, there was no trademark tarnishment.

Goal! The Dream
Begins

This film is an example of extreme product placement. In fact, Addidas financed the film.

Muppet Treasure
Island

In this film, Jim Henson named a boar "Spa'am." Hormel feared trademark tarnishment and sued. They lost. The court actually analyzed the boar's character, noting that he was not unhygienic and that he eventually becomes a friend of the protagonist. Therefore, the court noted, Hormel's trademark was not tarnished by having a boar called Spa'am in this movie.

Chapter 15

FILMS
& TV SHOWS
MENTIONED
IN THIS
BOOK

491

12 Monkeys

The producers of this film were sued because one of its sets closely resembled a noted architect's drawing. The court issued a preliminary injunction and the parties ended up settling.

Batman Forever

The statue that formed the basis of this film's advertising campaign did not have to be cleared because it was an architectural element of the office building location used in the film, as opposed to a separate decorative sculpture.

Devil's Advocate

A sculpture based on an existing sculpture was prominently displayed and contextually altered in this film. Use of the existing sculpture should have been licensed. It was not, so the distribution of the film was enjoined and the film's video release required alterations.

Immediate Family

This film shows a particular mobile that hangs over a child's crib. Although the mobile was prominently displayed and copyright-protected, it did not have to be cleared because it was a fair use.

Made in America

This film shows a couple of artworks in the background. The artist sued but lost due to fair use.

Roc

Producers of this series were sued when an episode's set displayed a poster depicting a noted artwork. The court said that this was not a fair use.

It's a Wonderful Life

A copyright-like protection for the re-release of this film, which had fallen into public domain, was achieved through the film's music, which carried separate and still-enforceable copyrights.

| *Rear Window* | This 1954 Hitchcock film was based on Cornell Woolrich's short story of the same name (published in 1944). For the film's 1962 re-release, Universal had to pay for the rights to the story again because of the unique copyright renewal provisions provided by the copyright laws of the time. |

Chapter 18

| *The Commitments* | James Brown sued 20th Century Fox because of this film's use of 27 seconds of a Brown television performance from 1965. |

Chapter 19

Amityville Horror, Amityville II: The Possession, Amityville 3-D	Three of six movies using similar titles that were approved by the court on the theory that the public was not confused.
Casablanca, Night in Casablanca	Marx Brothers answered a lawyer's letter to cease and desist using a title containing the word "Casablanca."
Dracula	Universal Studios felt that, because of its very different look, the film *Bram Stoker's Dracula* would not be confused with Universal's classic *Dracula* film.
Forget Paris, Paris Match	This film's release was scheduled for around the same time as a film entitled *Paris Match*. Reviewing the possible competition and confusion of these films' titles, MPAA arbitrators denied the use of the title *Paris Match*, which was changed to *French Kiss*.
Goldfinger, Austin Powers in Goldmember	MGM allowed New Line to use the title *Austin Powers in Goldmember* after it had initially objected because it thought it was too similar to the title of its film *Goldfinger*. The studios came up with an unconventional compromise.

Chapter 20

| *Dahmer* | This film is discussed in relation to E&O insurance. |

FILLS
& TV SHOWS
MENTIONED
IN THIS
BOOK

493

Rear Window	This 1954 Hitchcock film was based on Cornell Woolrich's short story of the same name (published in 1944). For the film's 1962 re-release, Universal had to pay for the rights to the story again because of the unique copyright renewal provisions provided by the copyright laws of the time.

Chapter 21

Cliffhanger, The Doors, Rambo series	These three films are typical of the complexity of chain of title in older titles. There were 40 documents, including loan documents, transfers, and licensing. There were separate documents for the music. Many films contain more.

Chapter 23

E.T.	In the case involving this film, similarities to the plaintiff's work were found to be "scenes a faire," meaning they flowed naturally from a general story premise and therefore were not evidence of infringement.
Great White	This film was enjoined by the court from further distribution because it infringed the film *Jaws*.
Fort Apache: The Bronx	In a case involving this film, similarities to the plaintiff's work were found to be "scenes a faire," meaning they flowed naturally from a general story premise and therefore were not evidence of infringement.
Jaws	The producer of *Jaws* sued and won their copyright infringement case against the producer of *Great White*. (Comparing these two films will give you an excellent grasp of just what it takes to win an infringement action.)
Peter Pan	*Peter Pan*, the play and character created by J.M. Barrie, received special copyright protection in perpetuity in Great Britain only due to a special act of Parliament.

Chapter 24

The Blair Witch Project	Noted as the best Internet marketing campaign ever created.
The Doctor, The Tornado, and Kentucky Kid	This documentary produced great DVD sales from the producer's own website and then in retail.
Faster	The filmmakers were able to sell this motorcycle racing documentary to thousands on their own website. A retail distributor was also able to sell more than 50,000 copies of the DVD online.

Chapter 25

Asphalt Jungle	The estate of John Huston asserted his moral rights in France to enjoin exhibition of the colorized version of his famous black-and-white film.
Hook, Peter Pan	*Peter Pan*, the J.M. Barrie play on which *Hook* is based, is public domain in the United States, but an act of Parliament granted it a special copyright protection in perpetuity in Great Britain. *Hook*'s producers had to make special arrangement to show the film in the UK.

INDEX

Aalmuhammed, Jefri, 160
abandonment, 75, 463
ABC, 33, 42–43
Abend, Sheldon, 112–13
above-the-line personnel, 241, 402
Absolutely Archives, 332
access, pertaining to copyright infringement, 414, 420, 465
Ace in the Hole, 12, 484
Action Sports—Scott Dittrich Films, 331
Act One Script Clearance, Inc., 288
actors
    as employees, 139
    nonunion, 224
    residuals to, 230
    rights in film, 224
    union, 195
Actor's Release For Film Clip Use, 342
actual damages, 196, 197
adaptation rights, music, 302, 465
Adidas, 265
advertising
    fair use in, 45–48
    on the Internet, 428
    use of a name in, 241
A&E, 31
African American images, sources of, 331
AFTRA, 333
The Agreement on Trade Related Aspects of Intellectual Property Rights (TRIPS), 447–48
agreements, provisions common to most, 182–87
Air Power Stock Library, 330
Aliens Invade Hollywood, 32, 485
Aligo, James, 238
Alley, Kirstie, 263
All Stock, 331
Almo/Irving Music, 305
"Alone Again (Naturally)", 52
amateur performing rights, 123

American Bar Association *Entertainment and Sports Lawyer,* 439
    headquarters, 459
American Dairy Queen Corporation, 263–64
American Federation of Musicians (AFM), 315, 335
American Film Market, 240
American International Pictures (AIP), 347
    fair use cases, 30–32
American Movie Classics (AMC), 30–31
American Society of Journalists and Authors, 118
Amityville 3-D, 347, 492
The Amityville Horror, 347, 492
The Amityville Horror II, 347, 492
Amityville II: The Possession, 347, 492
Amos and Andy, 102
Amsinck, Carol, 279–80, 281
Amy Fisher: My Story (NBC), 78, 79, 487
Anderson, Timothy, 98, 99
Angel, Dennis, 352
Animal House, 69, 486
animators, 135
Anne, Queen, 4, 5
annotated script, 80–81, 420, 465
Annotation Guide for Scripts Based on Facts, 81, 94
anonymous authorship, 202, 465
Anson, Jay, 347
anticipatory default, 149
AOL, 439
Apollo 13, 30, 485
arbitration, 24, 167, 181, 352, 353, 430
arbitration clause, 187
architectural appointments, 272–73
architectural feature, vs. decorative artwork, 273

Archive Films by Getty Images, 331
Arkoff, Sam, 30
artists, moral rights of, 282
Artists Rights Foundation, 223
art work, created for public display, 277, 282
ASCAP, 297, 309, 319, 320, 321
"as is" document, 394, 465
Asphalt Jungle, 85, 222–23, 452, 487, 489, 494
assignment, 128, 138, 142, 170, 189, 190, 204, 285, 388
assignment (short form), 170, 175, 179
Associated Press, 82
Association of Moving Image Archives (AMIA), 338
Astaire, Fred, 355
attorney fees, 196, 197
Attribution Share Alike 3.0 license, 87–88
Attribution 3.0 U.S. license, 87
audio-visual rights, 465. *See also* film rights
Aufderheide, Pat, 36
Austin Powers in Goldmember, 353, 492

Authors Guild, 119
authorship
    anonymous, 202
    nature of, 203
    pseudonymous, 202
Author's League of America, 119
Azoff, Irving, 58

B. Z. Rights, 308
back-end income, 319
background music, 299
bankers' film rights, 229–30
Barbie doll, 65
Barbie Girl, 357
"Barbie Girl," 65
Barbour, Cassandra, 270
Bardsley, Elizabeth, 270
Barney, 107
Barrymore, Drew, 79

"based on" credit, 226
Basinger, Kim, 304
Batman Forever, 272–73, 491
Batt, Mike, 162
BBC Library Sales, 330
Beastie Boys, 53
Beatty, Warren, 15–16, 171
Bell, Book and Candle, 14
Bell, David, 318
below-the-line personnel, 241
Berman-Bogdan, Jessica, 270
Berne Convention, 447, 448, 449, 454
"best edition," 405–6
Beverly Hills Bar
    Association Lawyer
    Referral and Information
    Service, 458
*Beyond Control: The Amy
    Fisher Story* (ABC), 79, 80, 487
bible, 114–15, 465
The Big One, 61
Bill Graham Archives, 35
biopics, rights of
    individuals, 232
Biz Markie, 52
The Blair Witch Project, 350, 430, 494
Blanch, Andrea: "Silk
    Sandals by Gucci," 69–71
blanket license, 311, 466
blanket royalties, 320
Blaustein, Julian, 14–15
blue-screen projections, 30
BMI, 297, 309, 319, 320, 321
Bob Tur cases, 32–33, 34, 46, 197
boilerplate, 182, 186–93
Bond, James, 101–2, 104, 116, 156–58
Bond (string quartet), 162
bonus compensation, 130, 177
book covers, copyright
    protection, 47–48
books, copyright protection, 6, 7, 269
Boosey & Hawkes, 452
bootlegged films, 408–9
bootlegged videotapes, 437
Borat, 248
Boston Globe, 62
Bram Stoker's Dracula, 353
Branagh, Kenneth, 83
"Bread and Butter," 306–7
Broadcast Information
    Bureau (BIB), 336
Broderick, Peter, 432, 433, 434
Broken Arrow, 14
Brown, James, 334
Brown, Nicole, 228
building reality, 334

buildings, 272–73
Burns, Ken, 206
Burton, Richard, 14–15
Bush, George H. W., 67
Buttafuoco, Joey, 78–79, 121
Buttafuoco, Mary Jo, 78, 79, 121

cable, pay, and free
    television, composer's
    royalties, 320
Cable News Network, 62
Cage, John, 162
California Supreme Court, 234
Cannes Film Festival, 240
captions, 185
The Carol Faith Agency, 318
cartoon characters, 103
Carvey, Dana, 67
Casablanca, 346–47, 492
case citation, 466
case law
    AIP cases, 30–32, 34
    Hofheinz cases, 30–32
    Rear Window case, 112–13, 308, 370, 488, 492, 493
    table of, 478–83
    Tur cases, 32–33, 34, 46, 197
*Casualties of Love: The Long
    Island Lolita Story* (CBS), 79, 487
Caterpillar trademark, 261–62
The Cat In the Hat (Seuss), 60–61
The Cat Not In the Hat, 60–61
The Cat Not in the Hat, 71
CBS, 33
ceiling, 130, 145, 176, 466
celebrities, right of
    publicity, 239
Certificate of Authorship, 142, 154, 386, 388
Certificate of Copyright, 200
certification, copyright
    application, 207–8
chain of title, *390, 391*
    defined, 386–92, 466
    documents, 169, 198
    recording, 392–93
    return postcard
        for recording
        documents, 398
    sample cover letter for
        record agreements, 397
Chaplin, Charlie, 33
character delineation test, 105
character(s), 95–104
    cartoon, 103
    independently
        copyrightable
        creations, 116

not visually depicted, 102–3
protected, 105
story characters, 101–4, 103–4, 472
visual, 96–100, 473
Cheers, 92, 487
Chicago Tribune, 62
The Chicken, 107
"Choir" (Newton), 53
choreography, 225
Chubb Group of Insurance
    Companies, 364, 365
    list of approved
        clearance attorneys, 366
"Church Picnic Story Quilt," 277–78
cinematographer, 225
Cinetic Rights Management, 434
cite. *See* case citation
The Civil War, 206
Classical Graffiti, 162
CLEAR, 338
clear, 466
clearance
    film clips, 327–39
    props, 284–85
    script, 232, 286–89, 473
    titles, 345–51
    See also music clearance
clearance culture, 86
clearance log, 338
clearance log template, *55*
clearance professionals, 338
Cliffhanger, 392, 493
Clinton, Hillary, 63
clothing in a film, artwork
    appearing on, 106
CNN, 33
co-authorship, 160–61, 169, 203, 488
collaboration agreement, 156, 157, 163, 164–67, 169
collaborators, hiring, 162–63
Collins, Floyd, 12
colorized films, 85, 125
Columbia Pictures, 15–16, 61, 353
Comedy Central, 61–62
comic books, film rights, 120
The Commitments, 334, 492
compensation
    composer agreement, 323, 325
    contingent, 130, 131, 146, 177
    fixed, 144, 145
    life story rights
        agreement, 255
    music package
        agreement, 325
    work for hire
        agreement, 145

compilation, 206–7, 404, 466
compilation CDs, 305
composer, hiring to write original music, 317–27
negotiating the deal, 319–21
searching, 318
when to start, 317–18
composer agreement, 323–24
composers
main income sources for, 319–20
package deal, 321–22
rights of, 224
work for hire, 320–21
writing on spec, 321
conflict resolution, 463
consideration, 466
continuity, 407, 410, 411, 466
contracts
boilerplate, 186–93
captions, 185
defined terms, 185
identifiers, 184–85
international, 186
negotiation, 182–83
offers and counteroffers, 183
signatures, 185
structure of, 184–86
termination provisions, 185
written vs. oral, 184
copies, 7–8
copyright
history of, 3–5
vs. trademark, 258
Copyright Act, 91, 165
copyright application
beta tester for online registration service, 199
Certificate of Copyright, 200
continuation form (FORM RE/CON), 212
cover letter, 199, 213
deposit requirement, 208
fees, 208
FORM CA, 209, 217–18
FORM CO, 199
FORM PA, 199, 210–12, 402–405, 408
FORM TX, 209, 215–16
instructions for filling out, 199–209
address for return of certificate, 208
author, 201–3
certification, 207–8
copyright claimant(s), 204

creation and publication, 203–4
deposit account and correspondence, 207
derivative work, 205–7
previous registration, 204–5
title of work, 201
mistakes in, 209
postcard, 214
registering book, article, or story on which film is based, 208–9
copyright claimant(s), 204, 400, 404
The Copyright Clearing House, Ltd., 306
copyright infringement
access, 414, 420
defined, 412–19, 466
establishing, 413–14
scenes a faire, 416–17
steps to take, 419–20
substantial similarity, 414–16, 420
Copyright Infringement Notification, 441–42
copyright law
before 1978, 84
abandonment, 75
activities covered by, 7–9
coverage today, 6
definition of joint work, 159–61
fair use, 26–27
first U.S., 5
and ideas, 11
new laws responsive to the Internet, 435–37
Section 205 documents, 394
written contracts, 184
Copyright Music & Visuals, 308
copyright protection
length of, 9–10
ownership of, 10–11
when a works qualifies for, 7
copyright registration
applying for registration of completed film, 401
"best edition," 405–6
copyright registration number, 408, 409
depositing one completed copy of film to copyright office, 405–7
exceptions to normal deposit requirement for film, 406–7
filling out Form PA for completed film, 402–405

form of notice for motion pictures, 400
mailing, 407–8
request for special handling, 409
return postcard for motion picture registration, 411
sample cover letter for motion picture registration, 410
speeding things up, 408–9
when to register, 399–400
in whose name to register, 400
copyright reports, 76–77, 125, 466
costume copyright, 106–7
costume designer, 224
counteroffers, 183
country of origin, 444, 466
Court TV, promotion of Williams & Watson trial coverage on, 46–47
Cox Enterprises, 62
creative changes, 372
Creative Commons, 76, 86–89
credits, 44–45
artists, 281–82
co-authors, 159–61
composer agreement, 324
determination, work for hire agreement, 151–53
life story rights agreement, 255
music package agreement, 326
name and likeness, 226
option and purchase agreement, 132
writer, 176–78
crew deal memos, 225, 412
crew rights, 224–25
crimes, always reportable, 254
Crystal, Billy, 353
C&S International Insurance Brokers, 364
cue sheets, 320

Dahmer, 374, 492
Dahmer, Jeffrey, 374–75
The Daily Show, 61–62, 486
Dallas Cowboys Cheerleaders, Inc., 68–69
damages, 196, 467
Dateline, 236–37
The Day the Earth Stood Still, 14
Debbie Does Dallas, 68–69, 486
decorative arts, 276–82

deductibles, 375
defamation, 242, 244
    defenses to, 246–47
DeFeo, Butch, 347
defined terms, 185, 467
The Definitive Elvis, 49–50,
    485
de Laurentiis, Dino, 347
de minimus, 278, 467
Denny, Reginald, 32, 46, *47*
deposit account, 207
deposit copy, 405–6
deposit requirement, 208
    exceptions to, 405–6
derivative work, 83, 84, 85,
    87, 404, 467
    copyright application,
        205–7
    defined, 8
    knock-offs as, 285
designer's logos, 106
Desny, Victor, 12–14, 18
Desny case, 12–14, 15, 16,
    17, 19
Devil's Advocate, 286, 491
DeWitt Stern Group, Inc.,
    364
Diamond Time, Ltd., 308
Diane Prentice—Music
    Clearance, 308
Dick, Kirby, 39
*Dickie Roberts: Former Child
    Star,* 262, 490
Digital Audio Transmission,
    9
Digital Millennium
    Copyright Act (DMCA),
    88, 425, 435, 436, 437,
    438–39
digital-rights management
    system (DRM), 88
directors, rights of, 222–23
Directors Guild of America,
    43, 44, 223, 332–33
Disney, 103, 261, 350
    Snow White, 82–83
distribution, 8
distribution contract, 340,
    408
DJ Jazzy Jeff and the Fresh
    Prince, 97
*The Doctor, The Tornado,
    and The Kentucky Kid,*
    434, 494
documentaries
    danger of altering reality
        by requesting a
        clothing change, 106
    fees to archives for clips
        from public domain
        films, 92–93
    insurance coverage for
        fair use of music
        in, 295
    location interiors, 274
    on-camera verbal
        release, 247
    and right of privacy, 234

rights of individuals, 232
documentary filmmakers,
    and fair use, 36–40
*Documentary Filmmakers'
    Statement of Best
    Practices in Fair Use,*
    36–40, 365, 454–56
Document Cover Sheet, 392,
    393–94, 396
domain names, 430
Domains by Proxy, 428
domestic rights, 431
Donaldson Golden Rule
    of Filmmaking: Always
    get it in writing, 102,
    139–40
Donaldson test of parody,
    57, 58–59, 60–61, 62
The Doors, 390, 493
double sourcing, 244–45,
    467
double vested, 141, 467
Douglas, Kirk, 12
Dracula, 353, 492
Dramatic Publishing
    Company, 123
Dramatist Play Service, 123
Dramatists Guild, 122
drawn characters. *See* visual
    characters
Dreamworks, 223
droit attribution, 45
droit moral (moral rights),
    222–23, 450–53, 467
Drop Dead Gorgeous, 264,
    490
Duckman, 263, 490
Dunst, Kirsten, 263

Eastman Kodak, 261
Eastwood, Clint, 245
"Easyfun-Ethereal" (Koons),
    69–71
eBay, 425
The Ed Sullivan Show, 49
end-roll credit, 241
engagement, 143, 323, 325
English, language of
    international commerce,
    186
enjoining, 234–35, 467
*Entertainment and Sports
    Lawyer,* 439
equitable relief, 31, 190
errors and omissions (E&O)
    insurance, 51, 77, 90,
    413, 467
    application, 377–83
    clearance procedures,
        384–85
    consequences of failure
        to disclose, 371–73
    and fair use, 365–68
    how to buy, 367–68
    tips on filling out
        application, 369–76

when full disclosure
    reveals potential
    claim, 373–76
when to buy, 363–64
where to buy, 364–65
E.T., 96, 412, 416, 417, 493
European Film Market, 240
European Resolution on
    Freedom of Expression
    and Information in
    Documentaries, 455–56
European Union, moral
    rights, 451
Evan M. Greenspan, Inc.
    (EMG), 51, 308
"Ex Nihilo" (Hart), 286
Expelled, 54, 485
express contract, 12, 467
extension/exercise of
    option, 127–28, 174, 251

facts and events
    and annotated scripts,
        80–81
    hot news exception, 82
    in public domain, 74–75,
        79, 80
    underlying rights, 77–78
Fahrenheit 9/11, 248, 489
fair use, 27–29
    American International
        Pictures (AIP) cases,
        30–32, 34
    Bill Graham Archives
        case, 35
    Bob Tur cases, 32–33,
        34, 46
    crediting source
        material, 44–45
    defined, 465
    and documentary
        filmmakers, 36–40
    and film clips, 29–30
    "heart of" concept, 33
    history of, 25–27
    insurance rider, 50
    and international
        copyright, 453–54
    parody defense, 57–59
    reuse fees, 43–44
    safe harbor for, 41–42,
        54
    spectrum of, *41*
    transformative concept,
        34, 35, 46, 64, 70,
        107, 475
    whether to ask or not,
        42–43
fair use and music, 50–54
    fair use of composition
        vs. fair use of
        recording, 53
    sampling rights, 52–54
fair use in advertising,
    45–48
    Pac-Man books, 47–*48*
false light, 72, 78, 242,
    245–46, 467

defenses to, 246–47
Falwell, Jerry, 63–64
Farmer, Francis, 81
Faster, 433–34, 494
federal anti-trust legislation, 285
Federal Communications Commission (FCC), 266
fees
    to archives for clips from public domain films, 92–93
    copyright application, 208
    reuse fees, 43–44, 315, 342, 472
Fellini, Federico, 355–57
"Festival License," 299
fictional books and stories, film rights, 117–19
fictional films, and people in public places, 238
fictionalized biographies, 81–82
file sharing, 439
filing fee, 401, 409
F.I.L.M. Archives, 330
film clips
    The Definitive Elvis, 49–50
    and fair use, 29–30
    release, 328, 340–41
film clips, clearance
    clearing clips without actors or music— stock footage, 327–32
    clips when there is no union agreement, 333–34
    clips with actors, 333
    clips with music, 335
    how to find copyright owner of a film, 336–39
film festivals, 247, 403, 456
Film Independent, 365
film music
    parody, 67
    separate copyright and ownership, 92
film rights
    bankers, 229–30
    to comic books, 120
    defined, 467
    to fictional books and stories, 117–19
    investors, 227–28
    name and likeness, 226
    non-fiction books, magazine articles, and newspaper stories, 120–21
    old movies, 124–25
    plays, 122–24
    songs, 121–22
    what rights to acquire, 111–15

whom to contact, 116–25
film rights, others who may have, 221
    actors, 224
    composer, 224
    crew, 224–25
    directors, 222–23
    writers, 221–22
films
    bootlegged, 408–9
    colorized, 85, 125
    copyright certificate for, 388
    pan-and-scan, 85
    publication of, 403–4
    public domain, 84–85
Filmways, 83
final mix, 296
Fireman's Fund, 364
First Amendment, 233
first-draft screenplay, 143
first negotiation, right of, 104
first option agreement, 390
Fisher, Amy, 78–79, 121
fixed compensation, 144, 145
Fleming, Ian, 156–58
floor, 130, 145, 176, 468
FOCAL International, 338
Food Lion, 237
Footage Hollywood Stock Footage Library, 329
force majeure, 190
Ford Foundation, 39
Ford Motor Company, 243
foreign-sales agent, 186
foreign syndication, 303
Forget Paris, 353, 492
forms/agreement
    collaboration agreement, 156, 157, 163, 164–67, 169
    composer agreement, 323–24
    cover letter for copyright application, 199, 213
    cover letter for motion picture registration, 410
    cover letter for record agreements, 397
    document cover sheet, 392, 393–95
    first option agreement, 390
    life-story rights agreement, 249, 250–56
    location agreement, 272, 274–76
    music package agreement, 325–26
    non-disclosure/non-circumvention agreement 18, 23-24

option and purchase agreement, 142, 170, 173–79
option and purchase agreement, underlying rights, 126–34
partnership agreement, 388
return postcard for motion picture registration, 411
return postcard for recording documents, 398
security agreement, 392, 473
submission agreement, 17–18, 171–72, 180–81, 474
synchronization and performance rights agreement, 299, 300, 310–13
table of, 476–77
work for hire agreement, 140, 141–42, 143–54, 285, 400, 402–403
www.copyright.gov/ forms, 429
See also copyright application
Forrest Gump, 29–30, 485
Forsythe, Tom, 65
Fort Apache: The Bronx, 417–18, 493
"433," 162
Fox Broadcasting Company, 99–100
Fox Searchlight, 238
Foxworthy, Jeff, 72
franchise, 104, 468
franchised character, 104, 116
Francis, 81–82
Frankenstein (character), 101, 103
Frankenstein (Shelley), 82, 83
Frankenstein (Universal), 83
freelance agreement, 422
free press, 233
free speech, 233
French Kiss, 353
friend-of-the-court briefs, 63
full disclosure, 373–76

Gabor, Eva, 43
Gaslight, 57, 487
gatekeepers, 39
Geffen, David, 223
General Partner, 229
George of the Jungle 2, 261, 262, 490
Gerdes, Ted, 368
Gershwin, George, 298
"get it in writing," 113–15

Getting the Best Score for Your Film (Bell), 318
Giannoulas, Ted, 107
Ginger and Fred, 355–56
Goal! The Dream Begins, 265, 490
Godzilla, 33
Goldfinger, 353, 492
Gone With the Wind, 62
Good Morning America, 42
good title, 386–87, 388, 468
Good Unit Production Managers, 266
Google, 336
Gorfaine-Schwartz Agency, 318
Gotham Group, 17
government properties, 86
grand performing right, 468
grant of rights, 223, 453
"graphic novel," 120
Great Ormand Street Children's Hospital, London, 449
Great White, 418–19, 493
Gregson, Barbara, 269–70, 3364
Grimms' fairy tales, 82–83, 103
Grosso, Jeff, 16–17

handwritten signature, 207
"Happy Birthday," 122, 299
Harcourt, Nic, 309
Harper Valley P.T.A., 121, 122
Hart, Frederick E., 286
Hatch, Orrin, 89
Hayden, Sterling, 222
HBO, 277
hidden camera, 236–37, 238
Highway to Heaven, 351
Hill, Jack, 228
historical films, rights of individuals, 232
Historic Films Stock Footage Library, 329
Hitchcock, Alfred, 112
Hi Tech Video, 225
hoaxes, 237
Hofheinz, Susan Nicholson, 30–32
holdback period, 103–4, 468
Holland, 21
Hollings, Ernest, 439
Hollywood Product Placement, 266
The Hollywood Reporter, 33, 338
Hollywood Script Research, 288
Holmes, Sherlock, 103
"home use," 312
Honda, 101–2
Hook, 93, 449, 494
Hopalong Cassidy, 102
Hormel Foods, 262–63

"hot news" exception in public domain, 82
humor, as defense to defamation and false light, 246–47
Hunter, Holly, 80
Hustler magazine, 63–64
Huston, John, 222, 450

idea protection, 11, 12, 15, 16, 19–22
iFilm.com, 429
IFTA® Practical Guide to Copyright Protection, 426–28
"Imagine," 54
IMDb.com (Internet Movie Database), 428, 429
Immediate Family, 278–79, 491
implied contract, 12, 13, 15, 17, 468
implied waiver, 452
inadvertent noncompliance, 91
independent contractor, 139, 468
Independent Film and Television Alliance® (IFTA®), 426
Independent Film Channel (IFC), 39
individual release, 257
I Need a Haircut, 52
infringement cases, 172, 196, 197
injunction, 286, 468
innocent mind, 232
Institut National de l'Audiovisuel Media Pro, 332
insurance
    coverage requirements, 304
    fair use rider, 50
    See also errors and omissions (E&O) insurance
insurance policy, rescission of, 372
integrity right, 451
intellectual property law, 443
intent, and joint authorship, 159
interactive and multimedia rights, music, 303
interiors, shooting on location, 274
international contracts, 186
international copyright, 84, 443–50
    Anglo-American model, 444–45
    Continental concept, 444–45
    country of origin, 444
    and fair use, 453–54

moral rights, 450–531
national treatment, 443–44, 449
problem of authorship, 450
International Documentary Association, 365
International News Service, 82
International Promotions, 266
Internet
    and copyright infringement, 421–28
    distribution rights, 431–32
    future trends in copyright law for, 438–40
    new copyright laws responsive to, 435–38
Internet Movie Data Base (IMDb), 336
Internet resources for the filmmaker
    advertising and marketing a film project, 430
    interfacing with the Copyright Office, 429–30
    licensing artwork and film clips, 429
    research on film's subject and potential cast and crew, 428–29
    use of to sell downloads of a film, 434–35
    use of to sell DVDs, 432–34
investors' film rights, 227–28
It Conquered Hollywood! The Story of American International Pictures, 30–31, 485
It's A Wonderful Life, 92–93, 307, 487, 491

Jackson, Earl, 280–81
Jackson, Michael, 305
Jacobson, David, 374
Jaszi, Peter, 36
Jaws, 418–19, 493
Jazz on Film—The Chertok Archives, 331
Jim Henson Productions, 262–63
Joan Pearce Research, 288
joint work, 158–61
jokes
    and copyright law, 72
    defined, 71, 466
    and personal rights, 72–73

vs. parody and satire,
71–72
Jonah Hex, 64
Jones, Spike, 83
Joseph, Jeff, 338
Judge Dredd, 350
judgment on the pleadings,
347–48, 468

Katzenberg, Jeff, 223
KCAL-TV, 32–33
Kesser Stock Library, 331
Kindersley, Dorling, 35
King, Rodney, 32
King, Stephen, 226
knock offs, 285–86, 469
Konigsberg, Frank, 113–15
Koons, Jeff, 69–71
Krueger, Freddy, 96, 97–98
K-tel album, 306
Kulberg, Eric, 337

laches, theory of, 158, 469
Landon, Michael, 351
Lanham Act, 226, 285, 351,
356, 469
Larson, Jonathan, 161
The Last Jaws, 419
*Laurel & Hardy's Laughing
20's,* 33
Lawnmower Man, 226
leading case, 277, 469
Leahy, Patrick, 89
Learning Channel, 32
Lee, Spike, 160
legal referral services,
457–64
Leicester, Andrew, 272–73
Lennon, John, 54
Leno, Jay, 71
Leopold, Petrich & Smith,
368
libel, 244
library, film, 125, 469
Library of Congress,
399–400
Motion Picture,
Broadcasting, and
Recorded Sound
Division, 407
life story rights, 77–79, 206
and sensational criminal
cases, 79–80
life story rights agreement,
120, 249, 250–56
Limited Liability
Corporation (LLC), 198,
229, 469
Limited Partnership (LP),
229
Lincoln Center, 337
location agreement, 272,
274–76, 292–94
locked, 399
Lokey from Maldemar, 416
The Long Kiss Goodnight,
91, 487
lookalikes, 243–44

Looney Tunes®, 264
Los Angeles riots of 1992,
32–33, 46
Los Angeles Times, 62
Lutz, George and Kathleen,
347, 348

MacArthur Foundation, 36
made for hire work,
copyright, 11. *See also*
work for hire; work for
hire agreement
made for television movie,
79, 80, 201
Made in America, 280–81,
491
magazine articles, film
rights, 120–21
magazines
as props, 283
as set dressing, 269,
276, 283
magazine shows, and right
of privacy, 234
Malcolm X, 160, 161, 488
Mann, Mrs., 16
manufacturer's logos, 106
Marshal Plumb Research,
288
Martindale-Hubbell website,
459
Marx, Groucho, 346–47
Marx Brothers, 346
Mary Shelley's Frankenstein,
83
master use license, 306, 469
master-use rights, 304
Mattel, 357–58
Maximizing Distribution,
434
MCA Records, 64
McCain, John, 63
McCarthy, J. Thomas, 239,
240
McClory, Kevin, 156–58
McDonald, J. Fred, 338
McLintock!, 85, 487
Mechanical-Copyright
Protection Society, 162
mechanical rights, 121, 299,
469
mechanical royalties, 320
Media/Professional
Insurance, 364
fair-use policy
endorsement, 365
insurance list of
approved clearance
attorneys, 366
mediation, 462, 469
Men in Black, 61
Merrie Melodies®, 264
Meyers, Mike, 353
MGM, 101–2, 353
Mickey Mouse, 10, 96
Midler, Bette, 243, 306
Milano, Alyssa, 79
military stock footage, 330

Minimum Basic Agreement
(MBA), Writers Guild of
America (WGA), 140–41
film clips produced
under, 332–33
MIP, 338
MIPCOM, 338
Miramax, 17, 61, 228
Mitchell, Margaret, 62
Mitchum, Robert, 33
mockumentary, 263
Moore, Michael, 61, 245–46
moral rights (droit moral),
222–23, 450–53, 467, 469
mortgage of copyright, 230,
469
Mosquito Productions, 288
most favored nations (MFN),
303–4, 470
Motion Picture Agreement,
407
Motion Picture Association
of America (MPAA), 7,
39, 437
arbitration, 352, 492
title registration, 352–54
Title Registration
Bureau, 352
Motion Picture Master-Use
License, 314–16
Motion Picture Registration.
See copyright
registration
motion picture rights. *See*
film rights
Motorola, 82
Movielink, 431
multimedia kit, 402
The Mummy, 114–15
Muppet Treasure Island,
262–63, 490
music, fair use, 50–54
The Music Bridge, LLC,
308, 309
music clearance, 335
adaptation rights, 302
clearing pre-existing
music, 294–304
clearing use of a
specific recording,
304–7
defined, 470
help with, 307–8
"in perpetuity," 302
interactive and
multimedia rights,
303
locating the rights
holder, 296–98
master use license, 306,
469
most favored nations
(MFN) clause, 303–4
negotiating the deal,
298–300
other deal points,
302–304

out-of-context rights, 301
public performance rights, 300
reproduction rights, 300–1
sending out or requesting the contract, 304
television rights for domestic and foreign syndication, cable, pay TV, and home video, 303
used as background music, 299
used as featured song, 299
music clearance houses, 298, 307–8
music cue sheet, 309, 470
Music Package Agreement, 325–26
music publishers, 121, 296, 297, 470
music supervisor, 309, 470
music video, 335
My Big Fat Greek Wedding, 112, 488
The Mystery Magician, 99–100

name and likeness, 226, 287
Napster, 425
National Association of Television Producers and Executives (NATPE), 338
National Basketball League, 82
National Cathedral, Washington D.C., 286
National Geographic Film Library, 332
national treatment, 443–44, 449, 470
National Writers Union, 119
NBC News Archives, 330
Neale, Mark, 433–34
negative pick-up, 198, 470
Negotiating for Dummies (author), 350
Netflix, 433, 435
Netscape Communications, 264
The New Beats, 306–7
New Line Cinema, 91, 97, 263, 264, 353
Newspaper Guild, 118
newspaper stories, film rights, 120–21
new technologies, 303
Newton, Isaac, 86
Newton, James W., 53
New Video, 431, 434
New York Artists' Authorship Rights Act, 282

The New York Times, 62, 422
Nicholson, James, 30
Nickerson, Susan, 270
A Night in Casablanca, 346–47, 492
Nightmare on Elm Street, 97, 488
A Nightmare on My Street, 97
Nike, 259
1968 Comeback Special, 49
9½ Weeks, 306
no defense/no indemnity, 372
non-disclosure/non-circumvention agreement 18,23–24
non-fiction books, film rights, 120–21
non-union actors, 141, 224
non-written contract, 12
notice of Infringement letter, 428
novelty, 14

Obama, Barak, 63
Ode to Billy Joe, 121
off air, 197, 470
"Oh, Pretty Woman," 50–51, 58–59
old movies, film rights, 124–25
old properties, rights, 82–83
on-camera verbal release, 247–48
Once, 238
"A One Minute Silence," 162
Ono, Yoko, 54
opinion, as defense to defamation and false light, 246
opinion letter, 359
option, 113–15
defined, 113, 470
termination, 171
option and purchase agreement, 142
sample, 170, 173–79
underlying rights, 126–34
oral contract, 12, 15, 184, 471
Orbinson, Roy, 51, 58
original music, hiring a composer to write, 317–27
Orion Pictures, 347
orphan works, 89–91, 424, 471
Orphan Works bill, 89–90
Orwell, George: 1984, 230
O'Sullivan, Gilbert, 52
OutKast, 357
out-of-context rights, music, 301, 470

Pacino, Al, 286

package deal, 321–22, 471
Pac-Man books, 47–48
pan-and-scan film, 85
paparazzi, 239
paper trail, 19–20
Paradigm Consulting, 432
Paris Match, 353, 492
Parks, Rosa, 357
parody
defense, 57–59
defined, 56–57, 471
in a film score, 67
"Oh, Pretty Woman, 50–51, 58–59
and personal rights, 63–64
and social commentary, 57, 59, 61, 62
trademark, 65–66
vs. ridicule, 62–63
what it is not, 66–67
partnership agreement, 388
"The Party's Over," 67
patent, 349
Penn State Media Sales—Stock Footage, 328
PEN (Poets, Essayists, and Novelists), 119
per diem, 188, 471
performance bonuses, 131, 177
performance rights, 121
performance royalties, 319
performing-rights societies, 296–97, 300, 309, 320, 471
permissions, 268, 275, 286, 287, 295, 423, 470
personal rights. See rights of people
Peter Graves: Mission Accomplished, 31, 485
Peter Pan, 93, 414, 449, 493, 494
Peter Rabbit books, 92
photographs, 6, 69, 226, 239, 277, 278, 424
plagiarism, 172, 412
The Planets, 162
Plan Nine from Outer Space, 43, 485
Playboy, 424
plays, film rights to, 122–24
playwright-in-residence, 122
polish, 144, 145, 170
political cartoons, 63
political figures, 244
Pollack, Sydney, 124
Porgy and Bess, 298
The Positively True Adventures of the Alleged Texas Cheerleader-Murdering Mom (HBO), 80, 487
posters, 35, 274, 277
post production, 343
Powell, David, 308, 309

pre-existing music, clearing, 294–304
preliminary injunction, 97–98, 271, 286, 491
prequel, 124, 206, 471
pre-sales, 240
Pretty Woman, 299
previous or alternative titles, 201
PrimeTime Live, 237
principal photography, 194, 198, 219
Principal Register, 350
privacy, right of, 72, 73, 78
Producers Library Service, Inc., 329
production company
  as author of film, 400
  as copyright claimant, 201, 204, 207, 400
  single-purpose, 198, 402, 404
product placement, 264–66, 267
prominence, 241, 278
propmaker, 224
props, 283–84
  clearance, 284–85
  creation of as work for hire, 285
protected character(s), 105
pseudonymous authorship, 202, 471
public
  confusion, 68, 348, 349, 473
  interest, 29, 52, 232, 233, 356, 413
  right to know, 233
public display, 8–9
public domain
  abandonment, 75
  and Amy Fisher story, 78–79
  and annotated scripts, 80–81
  Creative Commons, 86–89
  defined 74–77, 471
  government properties, 86
  "hot news" exception, 82
  old properties, 82–83
  orphan works, 89–91, 474, 471
  recapture, 91–93
  and sensational criminal stories, 79–80
  technical flaws, 84–85
  and underlying rights of facts and events, 77–78
  variations by country, 93
publicity, right of, 72–73, 78
public official, 232
public performance rights, music, 8, 300, 472

published work
  defined, 84, 472
  as digital transfer via the Internet, 84
publisher's share, 323, 326
publishing company, music, 121, 296, 297, 472
publishing half, 319–20
publishing income, 321, 472
publishing rights, 121
purchase agreement. *See* option and purchase agreement
Pussycat Cinema, 68–69

Queen of Outer Space, 43, 485
quilt, 277–78
Quincy, 81
quote, 145, 472

Radio and Television Museums, 337
Rakow, D. B., 261
Rambo series, 392, 493
reality, building, 334
Rear Window, 112–13, 308, 370, 488, 492, 493
recapture, 91–93
recording company, 305
Recording Industry Association of America (RIAA), 7
Reed, Donna, 92
Reeling in the Years, 338
releases
  Individual release, 257
  Life-Story Rights Agreement, 249, 250–56
  for people in public places, 238
  written, 248–49
remake rights, 124, 125
remakes, 206, 472
remedies, 89–90, 138, 139, 427
renewal term, 307, 308, 309
Rent, 160–61
reproduction rights, music, 300–1, 472
Republic Pictures, 307
reservation of rights, 372–73
reserved rights, 335
Reservoir Dogs, 350
residuals, 230
return postcard for motion picture registration, 411
return postcard for recording documents, 398
reuse, 332, 333, 472
reuse fees, 43–44, 315, 342, 472
Reuters News Service, 33
reversion, 113
Rice, Anne, 114–15
Rice, Robert, 99–100

Richards, Denise, 263
Ricketts, Debra, 270
ridicule, and parody, 62–63
rights
  actors, 224
  adaptation, 302, 465
  amateur performing, 123
  attribution, 282, 451
  bankers, 229–30
  composers, 224
  coupled with an interest, 165, 472
  crew, 224–25
  directors, 222–23
  domestic, 431
  droit moral (moral rights), 222–23, 450–53, 467
  of first negotiation, 104
  grand performing, 468
  grant of, 223, 453
  of individuals, 232
  integrity, 451
  interactive and multimedia, 303
  of last refusal, 104
  life story, 77–79, 206
  master-use, 305
  mechanical, 121, 301, 469
  old properties, 82–83
  out-of-context, 301
  of people, 72–73, 231–32
  of people in public places, 235–39
  performance, 121
  personal, and jokes, 72–73
  privacy, 72, 73, 78, 232–35, 242
  publicity, 72–73, 78, 232, 239–42, 244, 357
  public performance, 8, 300, 472
  public right to know, 233
  publishing, 121
  remake, 124, 125
  reproduction, 300, 301
  reservation of, 372–73
  reserved, 335
  sampling, 52–54
  services and, 225
  against slander, 72
  small performing, 300, 474
  to story characters, 103–4
  synchronization, 121, 301, 475
  underlying, 111–12, 126–34, 475
  writers, 221–22
rights-holder, 444
Ringgold, Faith, 277–78, 281, 282
Robot Monster, 43, 485
Roc, 277, 491

Rockefeller Foundation, 36
Rocky, 98–99, 488
Roger & Me, 245–46, 489
Rogers, Ginger, 355–56
Rolling Thunder, 228
Rosa Parks, 357
Rounders, 17, 484
royalties
    blanket, 320
    composer's, 319, 320
    mechanical, 320
    performance, 319
Rudner, Rita, 71
"Rudolph the Red-Nosed
    Reindeer," 76
Russia, 448
Ryan, Meg, 353

Sabrina, 124, 488
safe harbor for fair use,
    41–42, 54, 75, 425, 472
sampling rights, 52–54
Samuel French, Inc., 123
The Sandy Kane Show,
    61–62, 486
satire, 67–71
scenes a faire, 416–17, 473
Scheimer, Lou, 83
Screen Actors Guild (SAG),
    43, 44, 194, 222, 230,
    333
    actors, 224
    Basic Agreement, 224
screen grabs, 46, 473
screenwriter. *See*
    scriptwriter
script registration, 194–219
    copyright certificate
        for, 388
    legal benefits from
        registering, 195–97
    name in which script is
        registered, 198
scripts
    annotated, 80–81, 428,
        465
    buying, 168, 171–72
    clearance, 232, 286–89,
        473
    clearance reports, 234,
        288–89, 290–91
    spec, 16–17, 168, 171,
        474
    unsolicited, 171–72
scriptwriter
    always the author
        for purposes of
        copyright law, 138
    default, 150
    exclusivity, 144
    hiring, 135–36
    incapacity, 148–50
    independent contractor,
        139
    right to cure, 150
sculptures, 6, 7, 70, 272–73,
    277, 286, 491

*The Search for Signs of
    Intelligent Life in the
    Universe,* 247–48, 489
secondary meaning, 348,
    3487, 473
Section 205 documents,
    394, 473
security agreement, 392,
    473
security interest, 229
self-mailing, 21
sequels, 124, 125, 206, 473
services and rights, 225
SESAC, 297, 309, 319, 320,
    321
set and set dressing, 268–69
    buildings and their
        architectural
        appointments,
        272–73
    creating sets on a stage,
        271
    help with, 269–70
    knock offs, 285–86, 469
    location interiors, 274
    magazines, newspapers,
        books, and other
        works that are not
        decorative, 283
    paintings, posters, and
        other decorative
        items, 276–82
    shooting sets on
        location, 272
    signs and logos, 273
    state law protection
        of moral rights for
        artists, 282
set designer, 224
settled, 368, 473
Seven, 278
Sevier, Laura, 270
sex, 70, 233
Shampoo, 16, 171, 484, 489
Shapiro, Evan, 39
sheet music, composer's
    royalties, 320
Shelley, Mary: *Frankenstein,*
    82, 83
The Shell Game., 17
Sheppard, Steve, 36
Shine, 452
short-form assignment, 170
Showcase Video, 338
Siegel, Joel, 42–43
signs and logos, 273, 275
"Silk Sandals by Gucci"
    (Blanch), 69–71
Silverman Stock Footage,
    328
Simon & Schuster, 60
Simpson, O. J., 60, 71, 80,
    228
single-purpose production
    company, 198
slander, 244
slander, right not to be
    subjected to, 72

Slip 'N Slide, 262
Sloss, John, 434
small performing rights,
    300, 474
Smoke and Mirrors, 28–29,
    486
Snow White, 103
*Snow White and the Seven
    Dwarfs,* 82–83
social commentary, and
    parody, 57, 59, 61, 62
songs
    film rights to, 121–22
    in public domain, 122
SONICblue, 426
"Son of Sam" statute, 79
SONY Music Entertainment,
    Inc., 305
soundalikes, 243–44, 306,
    474
soundtrack, redone, 85
Spade, David, 262
Sparks, Mr., 25–26
spec scripts, 16–17, 168,
    171, 474
Spielberg, Steven, 93, 223,
    416, 449
spotting, 323, 325, 474
Stallone, Sylvester, 98
standard day-player
    contract, 224
standard weekly contract,
    224
Stanford Fair Use Project,
    365
The Star, 245
Statement of Best Practices,
    51
state trademark law, 351
Statute of Anne, 4, 5
statutory damages, 196,
    197, 474
Stein, Ben, 54
"step" deal, 303
The Steve Allen Show, 49
Stewart, Jimmy, 92
Stewart, Rosella, 12, 13–14
stock footage, clearing,
    327–32, 474
stock footage houses, 3275,
    328–32
story being told test, 105
story characters
    defined, 474
    obtaining rights to, 104
    tips for dealing with
        copyright, 103–4
The Story of G.I. Joe, 33
story quilt, 277–78
Streamline Stock Footage,
    332
"String of Puppies" (Koons),
    70–71
studio system, 337
sub-limit, 373, 376
submission agreement,
    17–18, 171–72, 180–81,
    474

substantial similarity, 414–16, 420, 474
summary judgment motion, 368, 474
Summit, 238
Sundance, 39
superintendence, 160, 161
Superman, 96, 103
Supplemental Register, 350
Suzy Vaughn Associates, Inc., 308
Switchblade Sisters, 228, 489
synchronization and performance rights agreement, 299, 300, 310–13
synchronization rights, 121, 301, 475
syndication, 383

Take Aim Research (888-TAKEAIM), 30
The T.A.M.I. Show, 334
Taming of the Shrew (Shakespeare), 14, 484
The Tampa Tribune, 62–63
Tarantino, Quentin, 228
target defendant, 269, 475
Taylor, Elizabeth, 14–15
technical flaws, 84–85
telephone numbers, 287
Temperton, Rod, 305
term writers, 136
test case, 65, 436
thank-you notes, 19, 20
20th Century Fox, 334, 391
theatrical exhibition, composer's royalties, 316
theatrical performance license, 300
theme music, 335
third party licenses, 305
This Film Is Not Yet Rated, 39, 486
Thomson, Lynn, 160–61
Thomson and Thomson, 337, 430
Thomson CompuMark, 355, 409, 430
Three Stooges, 91–92
"Thriller," 305
Thunderball, 156–58, 488
time, place, and manner, 139
Titicut Follies, 234–35
title report, 354–55
    defined, 475
    sample, 360–62
titles
    clearance, 345–51
    naming people and products in, 355–58
    not subject to trademark protection, 350
    previous or alternative, 201
    protection, 351–520
    search, 387

TiVo, 426
Tomlin, Lily, 247–48
Towne, Robert, 16
trade libel, 259–60, 475
trade magazines, 338
Trademark Manual of Examining Procedures, 350
trademarks
    defined, 258–59, 475
    dilution, 260
    infringement, 260
    parody, 65–66
    tarnishment, 260–61
    true parody, 260
    using someone else's in film, 259–61
    vs. copyright, 258
    vs. user, 261
trade shows, 337
trailers, 45, 301
transformative work, 34, 35, 46, 64, 70, 107, 475
treatment, defined, 20, 475
treaty, 447
"true" orphan work, 89–90
true parody, 260
truth, as defense to defamation and false light, 246
Tur, Bob, 32–33, 34, 46, 197
Tur, Marika, 32–33
turnaround provision, 475
Turner, Ted, 85, 125
Turner Broadcasting, 222, 452
12 Monkeys, 271, 491
The 2 Live Crew, 50–51, 58–59

UAV, 85
UCLA Film and Television Archives, 329, 338
underlying property rights, 111–12, 113
    defined, 475
    option and purchase agreement, 126–34
underscore, 317, 475
underscore cue, 309, 470
underwriters, 367–68, 475
unfair competition, 348, 351
United Kingdom Patent Office, 451–52
Unit Production Manager, 275
Universal Copyright Convention (UCC), 447, 448
Universal Media, 337
Universal Studios, 103, 112, 271, 353
unsolicited scripts, 171–72
Untold Stories (Aufderheide and Jaszi), 36
Upham, Charles W., 25–26
Urban, Jennifer, 88

Vanessa Mae, 162
Variety, 338
verbal releases, on film, 247–48
videocassettes and discs, composer's royalties, 320
video-on-demand (VOD), 431, 437
visual characters
    defined, 475
    not all protected by copyright, 99–100
    work-for-hire agreement for creation of, 96
vocal soundalike recordings, 306

Waites, Tom, 243, 306
waiver, 223, 249, 452–53
The Wall Street Journal, 62
Wanderlust, 39–40, 486
Warner Bros., 160, 272–73, 280, 286, 346–47
Washington, George, 25
Wayne, John, 85
WGA, 43, 44
Wham-O, 262
Where Death Delights, 81
Wilder, Billy, 12, 13, 18, 124
Williams, Wade, 42–43
Willis, Bruce, 271
The Wind Done Gone, 62–63
Winter brothers, 64
Wiseman, Frederick, 234, 235
Without-a-Box, 434
Wonderman, 103
Wood, Ed, 42
Woods, Lebbeus, 271
Woolrich, Cornell, 112–13
work for hire, 10–11, 120
    actors, 224
    crew, 225
    defined in U.S. Copyright Law, 136–38, 475
    set decoration, 285
work for hire agreement, 141–42, 285, 400, 402–403
    certificate of authorship, 154
    compensation, 145
    for creation of visual characters, 96
    credit determination, 151–53
    writer agreement, sample, 143–54
    written agreement, 140
World Intellectual Property Organization Arbitration and Mediation Center, 430
World Trade Organization (WHO), 448
writer. *See* scriptwriter

Writers Guild of America
(WGA), 172
agreements covering
"reuse" of materials,
332–33
East, 169
Minimum Basic
Agreement (MBA),
140–41
registering a character
with, 96
registration (www.
wgawregistry.org),
19, 20
rules about annotated
scripts, 80–81
West, 169
writer's half, 319
writer's rights, 221–22
writing partnership, 155–67
joint work, 158–61
and superintendence,
160, 161
written release, 248–49
www.copyright.gov/forms,
429

Yellow Submarine, 122
YouTube, 427

"Zanja Madre" (Leicester),
272–73
Zeffirelli, Franco, 15

ABOUT THE AUTHOR

Michael C. Donaldson is an entertainment attorney who has been fighting for independent filmmakers for more than 30 years. As President of the International Documentary Association, he negotiated with the cable networks to prevent the wholesale migration of credits from the screen to the Internet by organizing and leading the Documentary Credit Coalition. He served on the Advisory Committee for the *Documentary Filmmakers' Statement of Best Practices in Fair Use* and serves on the Advisory Committee of the Stanford Fair Use Project. He negotiated with Media Professional Insurance Company, Chubb Insurance Company, and other companies to offer fair use riders on the E&O insurance policies, which allowed many films to be made under the fair use doctrine. He helped draft and lobbied strenuously for Orphan Works legislation. Donaldson helped draft the *Rome Resolution* to harmonize Fair Use across the European Union. He lectures frequently at law schools and film schools in Europe and across the United States. In addition to representing writers, producers, and directors, he serves as General Counsel to Film Independent (home of the Independent Spirit Awards and the Los Angeles Film Festival) and the Writers Guild Foundation.

In addition to this book, he wrote *The E & Legal Guide to Trademarks & Copyrights, Negotiating for Dummies* (now in its second edition and translated into 10 languages), and *Fearless Negotiating*, published in hardback in 2007 by McGraw-Hill.

He is an avid skier, a world hiker, and an award-wining photographer. He won a gold medal at the 1998 Senior Olympics for Parallel Bars and a silver medal on the rings.

HOW TO CONTACT
Michael C. Donaldson
2118 Wilshire Blvd., Suite 500
Santa Monica, CA 90403-5784
Email: info@michaelcdonaldson.com

And for free downloads of various forms, go to clearanceandcopyright.com. Use this code: ibotCC3